Palgrave Studies in Economic History

Palgrave Studies in Economic History is designed to illuminate and enrich our understanding of economies and economic phenomena of the past. The series covers a vast range of topics including financial history, labour history, development economics, commercialisation, urbanisation, industrialisation, modernisation, globalisation, and changes in world economic orders.

More information about this series at
http://www.palgrave.com/gp/series/14632

Luca Clerici
Editor

Italian Victualling Systems in the Early Modern Age, 16th to 18th Century

palgrave
macmillan

Editor
Luca Clerici
Università degli Studi di Padova
Padua, Italy

ISSN 2662-6497 ISSN 2662-6500 (electronic)
Palgrave Studies in Economic History
ISBN 978-3-030-42063-5 ISBN 978-3-030-42064-2 (eBook)
https://doi.org/10.1007/978-3-030-42064-2

Cover illustration: PRISMA ARCHIVO/Alamy Stock Photo. Ambrogio Lorenzetti (attested 1319–1348), *Effects of good government in the city and in the countryside*, fresco, 1338–1339, detail: crafts and trades in the city. Siena, Palazzo Pubblico, Sala dei Nove.

This Palgrave Macmillan imprint is published by the registered company Springer Nature Switzerland AG.
The registered company address is: Gewerbestrasse 11, 6330 Cham, Switzerland

Acknowledgements

This book is the result of a research project stretching over the past seven years, and it benefited from the input and the advice of many colleagues. The editor and the authors would like to thank all of them: Stefano d'Atri, Claudio Bargelli, Paolo Calcagno, Fabien Faugeron, Giovanni Fort, Alberto Guenzi, Luca Lo Basso, Giuseppe Stefano Magni, Ivo Mattozzi, and Daniel Muñoz Navarro. The late Renzo Paolo Corritore was among the first promoters of the project. Unfortunately, he left us in 2015. This book is dedicated to his memory. Renzo, with the vast culture that characterised him, spent a lifetime of research on deeply investigating all issues related to victualling systems. His main work on Mantua, La *naturale "abbondanza" del Mantovano. Produzione, mercato e consumi granari a Mantova in età moderna* (Pavia 2000), is a cornerstone in this area of studies.

Contents

Notes on Contributors

Luca Andreoni is a Researcher in Economic History at the Polytechnic University of Marche, Ancona. He holds a PhD from the Higher School of Historical Studies of the University of San Marino, and he has been a Research Fellow at the Polytechnic University of Marche. His publications include the books *I conti del camerlengo. Finanza ed economia a San Marino fra Sette e Ottocento* (San Marino 2012) and *"Una nazione in commercio". Ebrei di Ancona, traffici adriatici e pratiche mercantili in età moderna* (Milan 2019).

Luca Clerici is a Fellow at the University of Padua and attached to the École Normale Supérieure of Paris. After his *Diplôme d'Études Approfondies* in History and Civilisations at the École des Hautes Études en Sciences Sociales of Paris, and his PhD in Economic and Social History at the Bocconi University of Milan, he obtained the qualification as *maître de conférences* in Early Modern and Modern History in France. He has taught Economic History at the Bocconi University and Early Modern History and Principles of Economics at the University of Padua. He has authored several publications in economic and social history and in the history of economic thought, among which the critical edition of the treatise *Delle virtù e de' premi*, of the Neapolitan philosopher of the Enlightenment Giacinto Dragonetti (Milan 2018).

Fabrizio Costantini is Adjunct Professor of Early Modern History at the University of Milan. He holds a PhD in Economic History from the University of Verona, and his researches focus on borders and frontiers in early modern Italy, more particularly those between the State of Milan and the Republic of Venice. His areas of interest include illicit economies and cereals, salt, olive oil, and silk smuggling. He is the author of *"In tutto differente dalle altre città". Mercato e contrabbando dei grani a Bergamo in età veneta* (Bergamo 2016), as well as several articles and essays.

Ida Fazio is Full Professor of Early Modern History at the University of Palermo, where she also teaches Economic and Social History. She is a founder of the Italian Society of Women Historians, and she is the Editor-in-Chief of *Genesis. Rivista della Società Italiana delle Storiche.* Her main fields of expertise are the economic and social history of seventeenth- to nineteenth-century Sicily, focusing on provisioning systems and the wheat trade; women's and gender history, exploring the transmission of property and informal trades carried out by women in early modern and modern Italy and Sicily; and illegal trades in southern Mediterranean during the Napoleonic period (corsairing and smuggling). She is the author of *La politica del grano. Annona e controllo del territorio in Sicilia nel Settecento* (Milan 1993) and *"Sterilissima di frumenti". L'annona della città di Messina in età moderna (secc. XV–XIX)* (Caltanissetta 2005).

Luciano Maffi is a Research Fellow in Economic History at the University of Genoa and teaches Economic History at the Catholic University of Milan. He was previously a Research Fellow at the University of Brescia, and he has collaborated with the Bocconi University of Milan. In 2014–2015 he was a Visiting Researcher at the Blackfriars Hall of the Oxford University. He is interested in economic and social history, with particular attention to the primary sector and the food production in the Early Modern and Modern Age. His studies also involve the history of tourism, especially in relation to demographic trends and to infrastructural and economic changes of the nineteenth and twentieth centuries.

Luca Mocarelli is Full Professor of Economic History at the University of Milan-Bicocca. He is the President of the International Association for Alpine History, the Vice President of the Italian Association of Urban History, and a member of the management committee of the Italian Society of Historical Demography. His researches focus on labour, environmental, and markets history. He is the author, together with Giulio Ongaro, of *Work in early modern Italy, 1500–1800* (Cham 2019), and he has edited *Quando manca il pane. Origini e cause della scarsità delle risorse alimentari in età moderna e contemporanea* (Bologna 2013).

Marco Moroni has been Associate Professor of Economic History at the Polytechnic University of Marche, Ancona. His publications include the books *L'economia di un grande santuario europeo. La Santa Casa di Loreto tra basso Medioevo e Novecento* (Milan 2000), *L'Italia delle colline. Uomini, terre e paesaggi nell'Italia centrale (secoli XV–XX)* (Ancona 2003), *Alle origini dello sviluppo locale. Le radici storiche della terza Italia* (Bologna 2008), *L'impero di San Biagio. Ragusa e i commerci balcanici dopo la conquista turca (1521–1620)* (Bologna 2011), *Nel Medio Adriatico. Risorse, traffici, città fra basso Medioevo ed Età moderna* (Naples 2012), and *Recanati in età medievale* (Fermo 2018).

Giulio Ongaro is a Researcher in Economic History at the University of Milan-Bicocca. He holds a PhD in Economic History from the University of Verona, and his thesis was on the construction of the Venetian military structure in the Mainland dominion and the effects on local public budgets. His current researches focus on the functioning of the cereals market in eighteenth-century Italy and Europe, especially in terms of market integration and behaviour of the economic players (merchants, producers, and public institutions). His interests also involve early modern rural history and labour history. He is the author, together with Luca Mocarelli, of *Work in early modern Italy, 1500–1800* (Cham 2019).

Donatella Strangio is a PhD and Full Professor of Economic History at the Sapienza University of Rome, where she is also the Director of the Master Programme in Business Management. She is the author of numerous books and articles on national and international journals, among which are *Crisi alimentari e politica annonaria a Roma nel Settecento* (Rome 1999) and *Italy in a European context: Research in business, economics, and the environment*, edited together with Giuseppe Sancetta (Basingstoke/New York 2016). Her more quoted works are on famines in pre-industrial age, migration, public finance, colonisation and decolonisation, institutions and long-run economic growth, and the history of tourism. She was a Research Fellow and a Visiting at the London School of Economics, the Maison des Sciences de l'Homme of Paris, the University of Adelaide, the University of Buenos Aires, and Columbia University of New York.

List of Figures

List of Tables

List of Maps

Maps are taken from *Atlante novissimo, illustrato ed accresciuto sulle osservazioni, e scoperte fatte dai più celebri e più recenti geografi. Tomo III.* 1785. Engravings by Giuliano Zuliani and Marco Alvise Pitteri. Venezia: Antonio Zatta.

Courtesy of Università degli Studi di Padova, Biblioteca di Geografia Scienze Economiche Emeroteca Ca' Borin, Sezione di Geografia (ATL.PRE.9.3):
https://phaidra.cab.unipd.it/o:328149
https://phaidra.cab.unipd.it/o:328178
https://phaidra.cab.unipd.it/o:328150
https://phaidra.cab.unipd.it/o:328158
https://phaidra.cab.unipd.it/o:328153
https://phaidra.cab.unipd.it/o:328167
https://phaidra.cab.unipd.it/o:328170
https://phaidra.cab.unipd.it/o:328166
https://phaidra.cab.unipd.it/o:328201

Map 1.1 Italy (1782)

CHAPTER 1

Italian Victualling Systems in the Early Modern Age: An Overview and a Critical Assessment

Luca Clerici

1.1 Historical Perspectives on Victualling Systems, the Market, and Society

This volume aims to illustrate the complexity and variety of the victualling systems established in Italian cities since the twelfth century and then substantially strengthened by mid-sixteenth. Seven relevant case studies are presented, exploiting the vast documentation preserved in the countless public and private archives existing in Italy, a heritage which constitutes a noteworthy peculiarity in the international landscape. This allows scholars to perform both in-depth investigations on delimited realities—by combining information from different sources—and long-term analyses on continuous and homogeneous archival series; similarly, it makes it possible to compare the patterns characterising different cities and regions, and the trajectories they followed over long periods. The term 'victualling system'

L. Clerici (✉)
Università degli Studi di Padova, Padua, Italy
e-mail: lclerici@unipd.it

L. Clerici (ed.), *Italian Victualling Systems in the Early Modern Age, 16th to 18th Century*, Palgrave Studies in Economic History,
https://doi.org/10.1007/978-3-030-42064-2_1

will be employed here to designate an organised set of public and private channels, evolved typically in urban contexts, for the procurement, storage, and distribution of goods essential for the daily life of common people ('victuals'—not necessarily only foodstuffs). According to this definition, specifically, a victualling system included also the market, as one of the different channels for the procurement, storage, and distribution of goods. In this sense, the term *sistema annonario* came into use in Italy from the second half of the eighteenth century.[1] However, for a long time, the historiography of urban provisioning systems in late medieval and early modern times featured a conceptual opposition between victualling administration and the market. On the one hand, markets were understood as a manifestation of private economic freedom, which some historians considered legitimate and others arbitrary, depending on their ideological approach. On the other hand, victualling offices and boards were understood as machineries arranged by public authorities in order to regulate and intervene in the economy, an action likewise considered harmful by some and providential by others.

This opposition between victualling administration and the market was a legacy of the eighteenth-century debate on the freedom of trade, especially concerning crops, and above all of the nineteenth-century radical economic liberalism of the Manchester School and of the Anti-Corn Law League.[2] As such, it paid the price for the attribution of the existence of victualling offices and boards to the (at best) anachronistic will to maintain administrative control over trade, if not to Adam Smith's implicit foundation of the market (while speaking of the division of labour) on "a certain propensity in human nature [...] to truck, barter, and exchange one thing for another" and his metaphor of the functioning of the market as if individual actors were "led by an invisible hand", and their subsequent absolutisations.[3] In the twentieth century, a historiographical distinction was introduced between a private or free market, animated by big merchants who were relatively autonomous in trading on long distances, and a public or regulated market, where small, local trade was carried out under the control of public authorities.[4] This distinction was sometimes combined with a further one, elaborated by anthropologists, between the rules relevant to the autonomous functioning of the market in industrial societies, and those relevant to the overall organisation of traditional societies, in which the exchange was embedded.[5] It is worth noting that this conceptual convergence was favoured by the fact that both historians and anthropologists shared the belief that the authentic nature of the market lay in the autonomy of its rules with respect to social ones.

In the last decades, the focus progressively shifted on four lines of analysis, some synergic and some opposing. The first approach analyses the market from a neo-institutional perspective, focusing on the role played by institutions in reducing uncertainty and in consequently lowering transaction costs, favouring contractual exchanges, and fostering economic growth.[6] The second approach, more quantitative in nature, sets aside the question of trade regulation and concentrates instead on the process of market integration and economic growth in the long run (where the former is preferentially inferred from the converging trends of some variables, chiefly prices).[7] The third approach, more historical in nature, analyses the spread of the market as an allocation system—the commercialisation—in late medieval and early modern societies, also in connection with changes occurring in consumption styles and living standards.[8] Finally, the fourth approach tackles the historical question of the market in the context of the wider design of civil life traced in European societies, starting from the late medieval urban rebirth.

The change of perspective introduced by the last approach entails a redefinition of the traditional subject of trade regulation and direct intervention by public authorities into what appears, instead, to be a real process of construction of the market as a part of an institutional system whose setting—notwithstanding the difficulties arising from the slow and progressive stratification of its component parts over time in an often empirical way, in response to specific and contingent needs—was coherent on the whole.[9] This general design was reflected, on the urbanistic plane, in the process of construction of the public space of the *forum*, i.e. the complex consisting of the city hall and the main square, which constituted at once the heart of the city from a political, administrative, judiciary, and economic point of view. In northern and central Italy, this process was substantially strengthened in the decades following the Peace of Constance (1183), with which the Empire recognised to a large extent the autonomy of communes.[10] At the same time, the foundations of the regulation of victuals circulation and trade were set for the following six centuries.[11]

In the context of European urban development from the eleventh century onwards, northern and central Italy were characterised by several distinctive features. Firstly, the convergence of civil and ecclesiastical functions, deriving both from the Roman legacy as *municipia* and from the institution of bishoprics. Secondly, the convergence of all social strata into cities, representing mercantile and artisanal interests as well as the agrarian, military, and ecclesiastical. Thirdly, the relatively small number of settlements having the rank of *civitas* (a few dozens in approximately 100,000 square kilometres) and, correspondingly, the relatively large extension of their rural districts (on average, 1,500–2,000 square kilometres). Fourthly, the substantial administrative and economic control exerted by cities on their rural districts. Fifthly, as previously mentioned, the early conquest of a high degree of autonomy with respect to superordinate authorities (chiefly, the Empire).[12]

With the formation of Italian regional states starting in the fourteenth century, the pattern of subjection of the rural district to the city was applied—in a somehow recursive way—by capital cities to their new dominions. Despite this, a balance between central and local powers was established, and formerly independent cities maintained their communal institutions and their control over their rural districts.[13] As urban communes acquired control over their surrounding territories—transforming them into their rural districts—market squares increased their importance as the victualling heart of cities.[14] The plurality of supply channels was then safeguarded by differentiating sellers on the basis of several criteria (enrolled—or not—in an urban craft guild; resellers or direct sellers; shopkeepers or hucksters; residing in the city, in its rural district, or elsewhere), and by allotting to each category exact limits concerning places (private shops and shop-houses; shops and stands on the public ground let by the municipality; market squares; streets open to itinerant trade), days (market days or not; weekdays or holydays), hours (before or after a certain hour), and the activity's scale (retail or wholesale trade).

After the century-long demographic stagnation which followed the 1348–1351 plague,[15] the spreading of Renaissance ideals of order and ornamentation determined a resumption of this process in the cities of northern and central Italy. From mid-fifteenth century, population and city growth were accompanied not only by the monumental transformation of public buildings, but also by the enlargement of public squares and the meticulous regulation of market areas.[16] At the same time, this growth required a reinforcement and, often, a transformation, of the old mechanisms of urban provisioning. The view of the public market was also changing, and people buying victuals on it were increasingly qualified as the 'poor' (*pauperes*).[17] Nevertheless, this transformation reflected the long-lasting influence of medieval doctrines, which prescribed helping the *pauperes*, a category which comprised not only the needy, but also—and more generally—all those who did not fall into the category of the 'powerful' (*potentes*): in practice, the majority of the population.[18] In fact, among the period's several definitions of the term *pauper*, those which referred to the necessity of working in order to earn one's living were widespread.[19] Furthermore, poverty was considered a reason for admitting and protecting sellers on public ground, not lastly in order to avert marginal people from the circuits of illegal exchange.[20] Therefore, the economic and social process underway was conveying the weakest subjects, both buyers and sellers, towards the public market, increasingly perceived, in its essence, as a market of the poor for the poor, thus acquiring a charitable undertone.

Attention to the legitimacy of economic behaviours was very sharp in the delicate subject of the transformation and sale of victuals. Systems devoted to supply cities with these goods were already established during Antiquity and had common features in the entire Mediterranean basin area.[21] When these, or some of their parts, were resumed in medieval Europe, they were connoted in a Christian sense—and endowed with a powerful language—in conjunction with the development of the ethico-theological doctrines on economy, society, and government. The design of civil life traced in these doctrines was centred on the concept of the 'common good' (*commune bonum*) or—using an alternative concept derived from Roman law[22]—'public utility' (*publica utilitas*). According to these principles—which also influenced urbanistic policies[23]—market exchanges could be compatible with the realisation of the common good only if they were regulated according to the fundamentals of the community in which they were effected.[24]

The more these concepts defied any attempt towards unambiguous definition, the greater was their evocative strength. It was only in a practical way that a specific definition could be achieved on each occasion, by adapting it to the specific circumstances encountered. Consequently, the institutional solutions deriving from the application of these principles were the result of a process of negotiation and mediation, certainly not without elements of conflict, between the needs and interests of the various social, economic, and political actors involved.[25] It is precisely the plurality of these actors, and the dynamics of their relations, which, together with the variety of cultural, social, economic, and geographic contexts, explains the great institutional variety characterising late medieval and early modern societies, especially in Italy, which at the time was among the most populous and urbanised areas in Europe.[26] And it is precisely these dynamics and this variety that emerge from the many studies devoted to Italian cities. As regards the Early Modern Age, in particular, the fact that victualling systems at the time were not relics of the age of communes is clearly demonstrated by their reinforcement during the mid-sixteenth-century food crisis.[27]

1.2 Victualling Systems in Late Medieval and Early Modern Italy

First of all, public authorities had to ensure the abundant and cheap supply requested by buyers and, in particular, by the consumer population. Whether it was a true support to the principles of good government, more or less inspired by religious beliefs, or a consideration of political opportunity, in order to legitimate themselves in front of the people and preserve social peace, rulers had to respect the ancient, non-written pact based on the assurance of subsistence for the ruled.[28] The most famous portrayal of this civic ideal is possibly the fresco *The effects of good government in the city and the countryside*, painted by Ambrogio Lorenzetti in the city hall of Siena between 1338 and 1339 (the front cover of this book is a detail from said fresco). Actually, when the conditions of production and marketing were favourable, plentiful goods and low prices were attained without public authorities being forced to adopt particular measures. Usually, direct intervention was not their preferential choice, but simply one of the available options, and public authorities had recourse to it or not in relation to circumstances. The urban scene was normally crowded by a variety of actors who—in different ways and to different extents—contributed to providing the population with victuals. Short-, medium-, and long-range supplies were involved, depending on place, time, and goods.

Guilds performed a fundamental function in maintaining the circuits of daily supply, and—as a matter of fact—they contributed to shape the victualling policy of the cities.[29] The presence of more or less direct sellers who did not belong to any guild, whether they resided in the city or came from its rural district or from other territories, contributed to multiply the supply channels (even if not always with the regularity ensured by guilds) and to moderate prices. More significant commercial flows were directed from the countryside to the city when production was more strongly market-oriented, through the circuits fed by tenants and rural merchants. Also large landowners, both laic and ecclesiastical, sold to some extent the products exceeding their needs in the city. Most importantly, they fed a non-negligible part of the urban population through self-consumption within families or institutions, gifts among peers, and charitable distributions to the needy. The experience of big merchants in long-distance commercial networks was precious in case of chronic or incidental shortage, when contracts with public administration could be stipulated for provisioning cities from far regions (but also when it was necessary to sell off public stocks, when they were no longer necessary, or when they needed to be renewed). Even the activity of smugglers was tacitly encouraged, or at least not contrasted, when they procured necessary goods. At the same time, the primacy of the cities' provisioning entailed a certain control over the circulation and trade of victuals also in the areas where production normally exceeded local needs.

It is in the light of this variety that it is worth reconsidering the subject of public involvement. Its quintessential field of intervention were the cases in which there was an imbalance between needs and resources. This was—for example in the well-known case of wheat, the basis of urban nutrition—contrasted either by establishing the obligation of transporting and sometimes also selling in the city a part of the surplus produced in the rural district, or by allocating contracts to merchants for supplying the necessary quantity, or by directly involving public bodies in the phases of procurement and distribution, or a combination of these measures, adding some forms of retail price policing if necessary. These measures, especially in times of crisis, had strong impact and evidence, also from the documentary point of view. Nevertheless, their importance must not be exaggerated, in comparison to the managing of normal situations, in order to gain an unbiased understanding of the functioning of urban victualling systems in late medieval and early modern times. Moreover, a given measure could be adopted with different purposes. The official setting of maximum selling prices, for instance, not only had the aim of protecting consumers from possible rises in the prices of currently used goods, whether in case of real shortage, or when their marketing was controlled by a limited number of persons. It also had the aim of allowing sellers to get reasonable earnings, so as to motivate them to guarantee a convenient level of supply. In this respect, the use of the assize of bread is also known as an instrument for supporting agricultural rents and production.

The situation was further complicated by the necessity of feeding public finances.[30] The development of indirect taxation, which in Italy took place during the fourteenth century, did not spare the goods which were currently consumed in the cities, even if the burden of such taxation did not mainly fall on this kind of goods and, in any case, it became lighter by the following century. Fiscal revenues were integrated by patrimonial revenues, coming from the rental of stands on public ground, shops, and other structures owned by public administration, as butcheries and covered markets. They were also integrated by a number of activities directly managed by public bodies, not necessarily in a monopolistic position, with the aim not only of controlling production and distribution in sectors which were considered strategic, but also of making some profits. Taxes, duties, and rents represented costs for craftsmen and traders: as a consequence, when public authorities set them—as well as the prices of the goods directly sold to consumers—they had to balance the opposite requirements of financing public coffers and moderating retail prices. With this latter aim, public authorities accompanied the setting of taxes, duties, and rents with that of official maximum prices and with controlled forms of selling.

It is important to notice that the requirement of profitability arose also in those cases in which public authorities directly marketed and sometimes produced specific goods—not only foodstuffs, but also raw materials and semi-finished products required by manufactures—by establishing some special bodies which, as a matter of fact, did not necessarily operate at a loss. The case of public monopolies on the production and sale of salt, which ensured both abundant fiscal revenues and operating incomes for the concerned bodies, was paradigmatic. Nevertheless, it was not uncommon for the same to occur also in the case of the other foodstuffs marketed by public administration. Sometimes, as in the case of the public granaries in which crops and flour were sold or lent, the control over the distribution to the needy, and the prices paid by them, could have priority over the profitability of the body during periods of particular shortage, and free distributions could also take place. Yet, in this case also, an exceptional situation must not be considered as a paragon for judging the normal functioning of a body which, after all, could benefit from the political support of patrician landowners, as long as it did not exert an excessive moderating effect on prices. Moreover, the distribution of foodstuffs to the needy was not a prerogative exclusive to the municipal or state administration, but was carried out also by religious congregations, charitable institutions, and confraternities, whose existence contributed to render the picture of urban provisioning more complex.

Lastly, it must be considered that the ruling classes constituted a group whose composition and interests were very diversified. Furthermore, the civic functions associated to the offices their members held, and the personal interests as receivers of agricultural rents and commercial or manufacturing profits, were often intertwined: it was thus difficult to separate the 'public' and the 'private' sphere. This is clearly demonstrated in the case of wheat: on the one hand, supplying the city could contrast with seeking more profitable destinations; on the other hand, managing the victualling administration could also prove a lucrative business. This was even more the case as long as, by the sixteenth century, population growth and foodstuff price rise made land an increasingly profitable investment. Moreover, public authorities did not constitute a homogeneous group from the administrative and political point of view. This depended not only on the different origin and entity of their political and economic fortunes, but also on the structure of public administration, especially after the shift from urban to territorial states had made it more complex and articulated. In these last cases, when the provisioning of the capital city came into conflict with that of subject cities, peripheral authorities, sent by the centre but endowed with responsibilities at the local level, were compelled to act as mediators between demands which often were not compatible. As a consequence, they did not necessarily always safeguard the interests of the capital city, but sometimes did their best in favour of those of subject cities. Therefore, the circumstantial examination of the action of the different administrative bodies brings a substantial contribution to understand the stratification of the parts forming the complex urban victualling systems in late medieval and early modern times.

What characterises the Italian case in the European context are both the earliness of these institutions, and the long-lasting political and economic fragmentation of the peninsula: these factors determined the great variety and complexity of the solutions adopted. In order to show these features, the analyses of the case studies presented here focus on four central issues. Firstly, systems and their configuration, which require to ascertain the relations between the victualling administration in the strict sense, and the many other ways in which the procurement and distribution of goods was organised (direct intervention by public, semi-public, or private institutions; conclusion of contracts and agreements between public institutions and private actors; control of the distribution chains by guilds; existence of more or less regulated marketplaces, and of more or less licensed itinerant traders). Secondly, institutional pragmatism and variety, which requires to examine the multiplicity of the solutions adopted in relation to circumstances and, therefore, those adopted in different places and periods, for different goods. Thirdly, the articulation of circuits, which requires to investigate the geographic ramifications and logistic organisation of the circuits along which the procurement and distribution of goods was carried out, from the phase of production to that of consumption. Fourthly, the plurality of actors, which requires to stress the plurality and heterogeneity of the groups of actors involved (the consumer population; guilds; other craftsmen and traders; farmers and landowners; central and local public authorities) and the complexity of the procedures for comparison and composition of their respective claims.

Consideration of demographic, productive, and consumption aspects—that is to say, examining the relationships between population dynamics, productive systems, consumption styles, living standards, and victualling systems—is of course a part of our analysis: it however does not constitute its core. In particular, although not neglecting the topic of famines—which was also recently the object of several studies, highlighting the response of victualling systems to situations of stress[31]—we do not devote special attention to it. We do not address the exceptional, but rather the normal functioning of these systems, even if, as it is well known, an exceptional situation often brings on the foreground that which is normal and, for this very reason, usually unexpressed.[32] This is true not only for famines, but also for epidemics and wars (which, besides, were often linked to each other[33]). On the other hand, the normal arrangement of a victualling system constituted the basis on which the response to exceptional situations was formulated.

1.3 Systems and Their Configuration, Institutional Pragmatism and Variety, Articulation of Circuits, and Plurality of Actors

The cases analysed here focus on the Early Modern Age—the period of maturity for Italian victualling systems—and cover a wide range of institutional arrangements, from the north to the south of the peninsula: the State of Milan, the Republic of Venice, the Papal States, and the Kingdom of Sicily. They include large-sized cities—such as Milan and Rome—medium-sized cities—such as Bergamo, Vicenza, and Ferrara—and entire regions—such as the March of Ancona, and Sicily—. This allows the reader to appreciate regional and local peculiarities in detail, following a route which is not only geographic and institutional, but also economic and social in nature. The great complexity of urban victualling systems from the economic, social, and political point of view, is well illustrated by the case of Milan, in Lombardy. Milan was one of Europe's largest and most populous cities, the capital of an independent Duchy until 1535, and subsequently subjected to Spain and, from 1706, to Austria. It was the centre of an economically dynamic and diversified territory, densely populated thanks to its advanced agricultural and livestock production. This combination of high food production and high population allowed the State of Milan to achieve cereal self-sufficiency only in years of abundance, and complicated the satisfaction of the capital city's consumption needs.

As a result, Milan had a very complex victualling administration, which was one of the main points of intersection of interests through which city and state life was organised. As a matter of fact, victualling administration—as well as the state bank, which gradually was entrusted with the financial administration of the most profitable municipal taxes and duties, including those on victuals—was managed by the city's patriciate. Nevertheless, the monitored cereals marketplace—where exchanges were mediated by public brokers—was just one of the channels through which Milan was provisioned, approximately covering only 50% of total consumption in the second half of the eighteenth century. Merchants' warehouses along the shores of the city's main canal, and the network of grocers' shops, were also important, as well as direct provisioning in rural markets, and especially in farms. The two important categories of flour sellers, and bakers who took the contract for managing the municipal bakeries (where white bread was baked and sold wholesale) got cereals through all these channels. Furthermore, several actors and institutions (large landowners, monasteries, charitable institutions, hospitals, orphanages, prisons) also operated—and often to a large extent—outside the market, directly feeding 15–20% of the city's population.

If the case of Milan shows the variety and interconnection of a city's public and private provisioning channels, in the presence of a well-structured but not invasive victualling administration, the case of Bergamo draws attention on the role played by illegal trade in border areas. Bergamo was a middle-sized city at the extreme western border of the Republic of Venice, gravitating towards the State of Milan from the economic point of view. Contrary to what one may expect according to the traditional view of victualling systems, the position and the barrenness of the province of

Bergamo did not lead to strict regulation of foodstuff circulation and trade. Instead, they led to the diffusion of smuggling—even tacitly encouraged by local authorities, in order to attract supplies—as in the noteworthy cases of wheat and olive oil. As regards wheat, contrary to what usually happened elsewhere (as, for instance, in the other main cities of the Venetian mainland), in normal times the circulation of crops was left free within the Bergamo province, no surveys of the crops harvested each year were performed, and no obligation to transport a part of the wheat surplus into the city was imposed.

Only in years of scarcity wheat provisioning was managed by the Municipality, which sent its emissaries in other parts of Italy and even north of the Alps. On the contrary, in years of abundance wheat was illegally imported from the State of Milan—which, according to the period's estimates, covered approximately 25–50% of the city's needs—thanks to the protection granted to smugglers, disguised in the form of specific immunities and privileges. The situation of Bergamo was peculiar also as regards olive oil provisioning, which was fundamental for the province's important wool industry. Because of its geographic position, Bergamo was authorised to procure olive oil in the Republic of Genoa and Tuscany—instead of Venice—in case of need or high prices; in any case, supplies had to pass through the capital city, for fiscal reasons. As a matter of fact, the length and costliness of these routes gave origin to significant illegal flows: during the second half of the seventeenth century and the first half of the eighteenth century, olive oil supplies coming from Venice constituted approximately only 30–40% of Bergamo's imports.

When a subjected city was closer to the capital city of the state than Bergamo was to Venice, the needs of the latter exercised stronger influence. This was due, for instance, to the presence of larger commercial flows directed towards the capital city, the greater economic penetration of its patriciate in the territory, and the stronger administrative control which could be exerted from the centre. This was the case of Vicenza, another middle-sized city belonging to the Republic of Venice, situated immediately beyond the capital city's first provisioning belt. As regards crops, Vicenza had no permanent body or office specifically in charge of provisioning, and the presence of public granaries distributing crops and flour on advantageous conditions—often opposed by patrician landowners—is discontinuously attested. On the contrary, the system of surveys of the crops harvested in the rural district and compulsory transportation of wheat surplus into the city, still exceptional at the beginning of the sixteenth century, became permanent by the middle of the century, on the impulse of the city's Venetian rectors.

On the local level, this gave rise to conflicts between the Vicentine patriciate and Venetian rectors. Nevertheless, on the state level, the municipality and rectors of Vicenza were often united in contrasting the ancient obligation, for Venetians receiving agricultural rents in any part of the Mainland, to transport their crops surplus into Venice. The importance of the interests on the table becomes clearly visible if one considers that, in the second half of the sixteenth century, crops supplies coming from the Mainland constituted approximately 60% of Venice's imports. Nevertheless, wheat was not the only good for which the needs of Mainland cities and Venice were opposed. Similar contrasts regarded meat in the first half of the sixteenth century, when problems with livestock imports from Eastern Europe obliged Venice to impose compulsory provisions from the Mainland, giving rise to a long and rather successful opposition.

Victualling systems dealt with abundance as well as with scarcity, as it is shown by the case of Ferrara, in eastern Emilia. Ferrara, like Milan, was initially the capital city of a Duchy, which in 1597 came under the direct rule of the pope. Ferrara found itself in the opposite situation compared with that of Bergamo, but not unlike Bergamo it is puzzling when approached with the traditional view of victualling systems. In fact, despite the high volume of the province's cereals production and the development of a rich export economy, Ferrara was characterised by a noteworthy victualling administration. Its activity in managing reserves and monitoring imports and exports was thickly tangled with that of landowners and merchants, making it thus difficult to distinguish between private and public interests. At the beginning of the seventeenth century, the wheat reserves that were to be stored by the victualling administration corresponded to the city's needs for approximately two months: a not insignificant amount in an area characterised by surplus (but not free from famines) like that of Ferrara, revealing a prudential policy by urban authorities.

The role of the city's prominent families was multifarious. On the one hand, landowners and merchants (the latter operating on both a regional and an international scale) sold cereals to the victualling administration preferably in times of scarcity, when prices were sufficiently high. On the other hand, when the victualling administration renewed its reserves, merchants bought large amounts of cereals at low prices and resold them in more profitable markets. Furthermore, the financial problems suffered by the victualling administration—originated by the difference between purchase and sale prices—constituted an investment opportunity for landowners and merchants, through the city's mount of piety, other public charitable financial institutions, and private banks. The interconnection between the interests of, on the one hand, the victualling administration, and, on the other hand, those of landowners and especially of merchant-bankers, is further demonstrated by the participation of members of these families in the managing of the former.

The multifaceted role played by cereals merchants also emerges from the case of another province of the Papal States: the March of Ancona, which stretched from the Apennines to the Adriatic Sea. It was a homogeneous territory, from both the economic and the institutional point of view, without large cities, characterised by strong permeability between cities and countryside. The victualling system of cities was centred around harvest surveys and compulsory supplies for the weekly market and bakers; public mills and bakeries, whose managing was let out on contract by the municipality; public and semi-public charitable institutions providing wheat to poor citizens and peasants through in-kind and interest-free loans, as well as—in particularly hard times—free distributions. As in the case of Ferrara, a cereals export economy had developed in this province thanks to the high volume of production. Each year, the March of Ancona had to provision Rome—the capital city of the Papal States—with large quantities of wheat. Despite this, cereals were also exported outside the State, both legally and illegally.

Smuggling was widespread at the border with the Kingdom of Naples, while legal exports were authorised each year by central authorities, mostly benefiting large landowners and privileged institutions (such as the Holy House of Loreto). The connection between local cereals production and the international market was ensured by specialised merchants and speculators, who went around the whole province and funnelled stocks—chiefly, but not only—to Ancona. From Ancona—the most important port of the province, especially after the introduction of customs allowance in 1732—cereals were traded in the entire Mediterranean basin area. Although accused of depleting the province and causing price increase, merchants proved useful to the community in times of scarcity, when they imported cereals from abroad. This is demonstrated, for instance, by the fact that Ancona's Jewish merchants—who occupied an important place in the city's economic landscape—were accepted (although unofficially) within the local patriciate, in the eighteenth century, exactly by virtue of their role in provisioning the city.

The complex relationship between urban provisioning and international trade appears under a different light if considered from the point of view of a capital city. The victualling administration of the Papal States directed the country's food policy with the primary aim of ensuring Rome's provisioning. As regards cereals, their circulation from one province to another, or towards other countries, was controlled through the granting of specific licences. The northern provinces of the country—such as the Legation of Ferrara and the March of Ancona—faraway from Rome and without cities of a similar size, enjoyed free domestic circulation and could obtain licences for exporting abroad. On the contrary, the produce of Rome's rural district and of the southern provinces of the country, nearest to the capital city, was primarily destined to satisfy its consumption needs. Only domestic licences could be granted in those areas, and officials residing there were charged with buying the local wheat surplus and sending it to Rome. Here, other officials recorded the arrivals, stored stocks, and distributed them to bakers or in the monitored marketplace, where small farmers too sold their surplus.

Bakers got wheat also in the warehouses of a particular group of merchant-tenants coming from the countryside, where they rented one or more estates, directly cultivating a part of the land and letting the remainder to small farmers. The city's bakeries depended on the victualling administration and were subdivided in various categories, according to different criteria: ownership (private or, most commonly, public bakeries, which were let out on contract and enjoyed a privileged relationship with the victualling administration, especially regarding wheat provisioning); the kind of activity (whether they simply baked the dough prepared by customers, or produced and sold bread to the public); the variety and quality of the bread sold. Rome's victualling administration suffered from specific financial problems. The prevalence of large estates in the countryside hampered the achievement of agricultural reforms, and the victualling administration was able to face production crises only when they occurred, by importing cereals. The need for financing the administration's operating losses, and granting loans to farmers, originated a peculiar system, based on loans by public banks and—above all—the issue of public debt bonds, both on a central and on a local level.

The plainest case in which a victualling system was shaped within the framework of a substantial export economy is that of Sicily. This island at the southern end of Italy—initially subjected to Spain and then independent from foreign rule, by 1735, as did the Kingdom of Naples—was one of the most important wheat exporting regions in the Mediterranean. Nevertheless, its territory was highly differentiated: wine, olive oil, oranges, and silk were produced in the green north-eastern area, whereas wheat was cultivated in the large feudal estates of the dry central-western area, from which it was exported to the rest of the island and abroad. As regards wheat, a system was thus designed with the threefold aim of provisioning cities—starting from the most important ones, Palermo and Messina—and deficit areas, allowing large landowners and tenants to realise the value of the wheat produced and ensuring the Crown adequate fiscal revenues from domestic and foreign trade.

Each year, exports were authorised or forbidden by central authorities, on the basis of population and harvest surveys. The contact point between the internal and international market was the network of public warehouses existing along the shores of the whole island, where wheat was stored waiting for loading boats, negotiations and speculations took place (in addition to those in Palermo), and taxes and duties were levied. As regards urban victualling administrations, in normal times they operated by letting out on contract each year the wheat provisioning of public bakeries, on the basis of the estimated harvest and needs. In the sixteenth and seventeenth centuries, these purchases covered approximately 20% of Palermo's and 40% of Messina's needs. In major cities, specific public institutions were entrusted with collecting and spending the necessary funds; in their absence, local administrations recurred to loans or delayed payments. Contracts for provisioning cities with other foodstuffs—such as olive oil, wine, meat, and cheese—were also allocated, even if their trade was usually free.

1.4 Further Perspectives

Italian victualling systems have been traditionally examined in depth by historians: by taking into account the peculiar configuration of these systems, their institutional pragmatism and variety, the articulation of circuits, and the plurality of actors, the aim of this book is to draw attention on their complexity. Other case studies could enrich this panorama in the future: an interesting subject to approach would be that of prices, combining the traditional quantitative analysis of available data—both on market prices and on officially set prices—with the analysis of the geographic, economic, social, and institutional context in which they were formed. The cases analysed in this book provide some suggestions also in this direction, showing how the extremely rich Italian sources can be employed. In Milan, for instance, the public brokers operating on the monitored cereals marketplace even had to keep four books, in which different kinds of information were recorded: not only the price, but also the quality and quantity of the cereals traded, and the name of sellers and buyers. In the first book, wholesale exchanges mediated by public brokers—whose prices were used for setting the official weight of the bread loaf—were recorded; the second book was devoted to the exchanges of low-quality cereals; the third, to retail exchanges; the fourth, to cereals introductions into the marketplace. In Bergamo, the marketplace chosen for monitoring the province's cereals trade changed over time, with the aim of collecting reliable data on quantities and prices: that in the upper city of Bergamo, that of Romano di Lombardia (a town very close to the border with the State of Milan and, in particular, with the province of Cremona, from which wheat was mainly imported), and that of the lower city of Bergamo (a more easily reachable location than the upper city, and thus a location expected to attract traders).

Collecting all possible information on the specific transaction in which a price was formed—in addition to that on the more general context—and comparing prices from different sources for the same good in a given place and moment, is particularly important. The identity of sellers and buyers, their economic and social status, the kind and frequency of the relationships between them, and their networks; the quality and quantity of goods, and the places and circuits of exchange; the moment in which goods were exchanged, and seasonal effects; the monies, weights, and measures used to express prices, and the practical methods of measurement of goods; the forms of payment, and the existence of long-term relationships based on credit: these, for instance, are all important pieces of information to be taken into account for shaping an in-depth history of prices.[34] This is true also when the account books of families or institutions, like hospitals and monasteries, are concerned: despite the large amount of information they contain, they have traditionally been used as a simple store of data on prices, often abstractly considered as 'market' prices, without investigating the nature of the exchanges.

Particular care must be employed when official series of prices, formed on the basis of current market prices, are available. Actually, the difference between recording, ratifying, and setting was slight and shaded, and most of the times they intersected. Firstly, the purpose for which prices were recorded, and thus the interests gravitating around this operation, must be considered: general market monitoring; assessing the monetary value of an in-kind capital, rent, debt, or interest—or the other way round—over time; setting the terms of exchange of goods—either the price for a given quantity or the quantity for a given price—in all or in particular categories of transactions. Secondly, from the technical point of view, the marketplace in which prices were recorded (more or less controlled), the frequency of recording (daily, weekly, monthly, yearly), the size of the considered exchanges (starting or not from a certain threshold), the kind of recorded prices (minimum, average, maximum prices), the method of calculation of averages and its constancy or variability over time (arithmetic or weighted average; based on the prices of all exchanges, or simply on the minimum and maximum price, or on the prices recorded in two specific and important moments of the year), must all be taken into account.[35]

Regarding officially set terms of exchange, the purpose of setting is fundamental to understand the method applied, and the relationship with market values. The best-known case is that of the assize of bread, whose mechanisms have been largely analysed by historians.[36] On this subject, the interests of consumers (abundant and cheap supply), bakers (good earnings), landowners (lucrative sale of the produce), and public authorities (social peace and good fiscal revenues) intersected. Usually, the minimum weight of the loaves to be sold for a given price was set on the basis of the current market price of wheat (or of the other cereals transformed into bread), adjusted for a smoothing of its variability (and increased by baking costs, taxes and duties, and bakers' earnings, assessed and fixed for long periods). Wheat price variations were smoothed with the twofold aim of defending the purchasing power of consumers in times of dearth and allowing bakers to recover the ensuing losses (as well as supporting agricultural rents) when prices diminished. This adjustment could be more (as, for instance, in Bologna) or less pronounced (as in Ferrara, where not only local prices, but also those current in Venice were considered, together with the weight of bread in force in this city). Moreover, bakers could be allowed to bake loaves at a lower weight, or explicitly asked to bake them at a higher weight than the official one, especially when, for various reasons, it was decided to leave this weight unchanged. The setting of the weight of bread could also be accompanied by additional measures, especially in times of dearth: in some cases (as, for instance, in Rome), the victualling administration sold its wheat stocks to bakers at lower prices than current market prices; in other cases (as in Milan), it granted direct compensations to bakers.

This method could evolve into a real intertemporal compensation system managed by the victualling administration, as in the case of Venice, where the 'credits' accumulated by bakers when the current price of wheat was high but the weight of bread was not correspondingly low (corresponding to 'debits' of the 'poor') were compensated with the 'debits' accumulated by bakers when the current price of wheat was low but the weight of bread was not correspondingly high (corresponding to 'credits' of the 'poor'). Furthermore, the setting of the weight of bread also influenced market dynamics. In some cases, the price of wheat considered for setting the weight of bread acquired the nature of a real officially set price, in force in certain categories of transactions (even if departures from this rule could occur, especially when, for various reasons, it was decided to leave this price unchanged). It was at this price, for instance, that the victualling administration and bakers bought wheat in Ferrara. It was again at this price that the victualling administration sold its stocks to bakers in Rome. In other cases, this did not happen: nevertheless, this price constituted a benchmark for market exchanges, since it was the price that balanced bakers' accounts. At the same time, other prices could go beyond the limits of the use for which they were originally intended, and became a benchmark for other transactions as well: this was the case of the price of wheat set for regulating agrarian contracts (as, for instance, agricultural loans for sowing, and crops purchases before the harvest, in Naples and Sicily).

If the case of wheat and bread was the more complex, due to the importance of these goods in the period's urban consumption, the cases of other victuals are equally important for understanding the mechanisms at the basis of the official setting of the terms of exchange of goods. As regards olive oil, for instance, in the Venetian mainland it was a matter of distributing the oil imported into Venice from abroad. Consequently, official maximum prices were set on the basis of current wholesale prices in Venice, increased by transportation costs, taxes and duties, and sellers' earnings. Nevertheless, in seventeenth-century Bergamo, the large extent to which olive oil did not come from Venice was the origin of a long dispute between merchants and wool manufacturers—as well as between local and central authorities—concerning both the method of official maximum price setting and the structure of taxes and duties on olive oil trade.

Officially set maximum prices can be an interesting subject even when they were kept constant for long periods, for consensus reasons. In fact, public authorities were aware that inadequate prices could produce short supply for the legal circuits and an expansion of the illegal market, damaging both consumers and public finances. Therefore, other measures were put in place at the same time. This is shown, for instance, by the case of meat price in Vicenza in the first half of the sixteenth century. Not only were official maximum prices set at a level that normally safeguarded both butchers' earnings and public revenues, but a certain margin of variability was also recovered by modifying each year other elements affecting the terms of exchange, in order to deal with changing circumstances. These elements regarded the classification of the animals, and the possibility to charge overprices in certain periods of the year, to sell certain less valuable parts of the animals in addition to muscle meat, to sell other parts and by-products of slaughtering at unregulated prices, and to sell the meat of usually forbidden animals. Significantly, when compulsory meat provisions from the Mainland to Venice were imposed, prices in the Mainland were centrally set at a lower level than in Venice, in order to attract supplies to the latter. Moreover, the other aforesaid elements were crystallised once for all, thus depriving Vicenza's authorities of the discretionary power they had used to attract supplies to Vicenza, even in competition with Venice.

As regards the mechanisms of price formation, in the last decades historians have paid a great attention to late medieval and early modern doctrines on the just price (*iustum praetium*) and the common estimation (*communis aestimatio*), i.e. the determination of the just price by means of a collective assessment performed in the bosom of the community, taking the threefold form of current prices, officially set prices, and the experts' estimations. A useful vantage point for understanding what prices represented at the time is offered by considering them in the light of the period's idea of measure and measurement. In fact, weights and measures had a concrete and not an abstract nature, that is to say, they were defined and shaped not for measuring universal dimensions in the abstract, but concrete things in their daily use. This connected weights and measures to the specific purposes for which things were used, and caused their extreme local variety.[37] The same was true when money and prices were concerned: i.e. the unit and means of measurement of value, and the result of the act of measuring the value of goods respectively. The debate on the just price and on justice in exchanges can thus be considered in the light of a notion of 'justice' connoted as 'justness', that is to say, exactness descending from conformity to norms and standards, from a technical, juridical, and ethical point of view, combining the dimensions of accuracy, lawfulness, and fairness.

Notes

1. See, for instance, Beccaria (1990, nn. 639–640, 26 March 1781, pp. 446–447; n. 648, 28 April 1781, pp. 456–483; n. 654, 25 May 1781, pp. 490–492; n. 688, 15 September 1781, pp. 546–567); (1993, n. 1277, 24 March 1786, pp. 601–614). On the polysemy of the term *annona* in late medieval and early modern times (referring, from case to case, to the norms regulating the distribution of victuals, the offices appointed to it, the spaces in which related activities took place, the set of obligations and taxes which ensured the procurement of victuals, public stocks, the goods involved, and their prices), see Corritore (2012, pp. 5–6).
2. In fact, it must be stressed that both physiocrats and classical economists recognised a far from irrelevant role for the state in the economy and that their claims to free trade were not absolute, but were adjusted to the specific circumstances encountered (see, for instance, Vaggi 1987, pp. 109–114; Besomi and Rampa 2000 [1998], pp. 36–70; O'Brien 2004 [1975], pp. 327–334).
3. Smith (1776, vol. I, book I, chap. II, p. 16; vol. II, book IV, chap. II, p. 35).
4. Pirenne (1939 [1910], pp. 196–199); (1963 [1933], pp. 132–145); Everitt (1967, pp. 490–563); Thompson (1971, pp. 83–85, 89–94); Braudel (1979, pp. 112–113, 193–196, 363–366).
5. Polanyi (1957a [1944], pp. 43–76); (1957b, pp. 257–263, 266–269); Neale (1957); Polanyi (1977, pp. 47–62, 81–96, 123–142); Kaplan (1984, pp. 23–40).
6. See, for instance, North and Thomas (1973); North (1981, 1990); Epstein (2000); Ogilvie (2011).
7. See, for instance, Persson (1999); Bateman (2012). For a review of the literature on this topic, still see Federico (2012).
8. See, for instance, Britnell (1993); Coquery (2000); Galloway (2000); Cavaciocchi (2001); Blondé et al. (2006); Britnell (2009); Dijkman (2011).
9. Among recent studies, presenting different stances, see Langholm (1992); Todeschini (1994); Randall and Charlesworth (1996); Ago (1998); Randall and Charlesworth (2000); Todeschini (2002, 2004); Martinat (2004); Fontaine (2008); Prodi (2009); Bohstedt (2010); Lecuppre-Desjardin and Van Bruaene (2010); Todeschini (2011); Davis (2012); Fontaine (2014); Middleton and Shaw (2018). Historians also stress the importance of reciprocity in medieval and early modern societies (see, for instance, Duby 1973; Zemon Davis 2000; Algazi et al. 2003; Krausman Ben-Amos 2008; Heal 2014; Bassnett 2016).
10. Guidoni (1980, pp. 99–112); (1981, pp. 118–126); Grohmann (2003, pp. 75–76); Prodi (2009, pp. 9–10).

11. Collodo (1999 [1990], p. 49). More generally, the process was underway in all Europe, with many common features (still see, for instance, Pirenne 1963 [1933], pp. 132–145).
12. Chittolini (1989, pp. 689–695). In view of these considerations, in this book, all settlements having the rank of *civitas* will be called 'cities', independently of their size.
13. Chittolini (1979, pp. vii–xl); (1989, pp. 698–703).
14. On market squares in late medieval and early modern cities, see Calabi (1993, 1997a); Grohmann (1994).
15. Pinto (1996, pp. 51–63).
16. Calabi (1997b, pp. 10–15, 20–27).
17. Collodo (1999 [1990], pp. 65–67); Faugeron (2014, pp. 728–730).
18. Todeschini (2005, p. 166).
19. Ago (1998, pp. 82–89); Groebner (1993, pp. 15–19).
20. Shaw (2002, pp. 400–401); Faugeron (2014, pp. 659, 673).
21. On the *Annona* in the ancient Rome, see, for instance, Tengström (1974); Pavis d'Escurac (1976); Rickman (1980); Garnsey and Whittaker (1983); Garnsey (1988); Herz (1988); Sirks (1991); Centre Jean Bérard and École Française de Rome (1994); Virlouvet (1995); Höbenreich (1997); École Française de Rome (1998); Erdkamp (2005); Sanz Palomera (2010); Soraci (2011); in a comparative perspective, see Marin and Virlouvet (2004, 2016).
22. Ullmann (1970 [1955], pp. 287–288, note 2; pp. 425–426, note 2); (1978 [1961], pp. 67–68, 83–85, 133–134, 186, 197–198, 284).
23. Crouzet-Pavan (2003, pp. 20–22, 29–31).
24. Todeschini (2005, pp. 187–191, 203–210); Prodi (2009, pp. 64–68).
25. Tucci (1975, pp. 155–156); Guenzi (1982, pp. 137–141); Giusberti (1985, pp. 567–569); Guenzi (1994, pp. 737–738, 741–742, 755); Prodi (2009, pp. 67–68); Faugeron (2014, pp. 285–292).
26. In early modern Europe, Italy had the greater number of cities and towns with at least 10,000 inhabitants, and the largest urban population (considered according the same criterium). Considering the ratio of the latter over total population, the rate of urbanisation of Italy was 14.9% around 1500, 16.8% around 1600, 14.7% around 1700, and 18.3% around 1800. Its population was approximately 9,000,000 people around 1500, 13,273,000 around 1600, 13,481,000 around 1700, and 18,092,000 around 1800, with an average density of—respectively—29.0, 42.8, 43.4, and 58.3 inhabitants per square kilometre (Malanima 1998, p. 97, tables 3–4; p. 98, table 6; p. 100, table 7).
27. Among the volumes devoted to this subject, beginning from the studies in which urban provisioning was considered in conjunction with the history of agriculture, the history of trade, and the history of prices, see Dal Pane

(1932); Parenti (1939, 1942); Petino (1946); Canaletti Gaudenti (1947); De Maddalena (1949); Lombardini (1963); Zanetti (1964); Aymard (1966); Basini (1970); Cancila (1972); De Maddalena (1974); Macry (1974); Romani (1975); Pinto (1978); Vecchiato (1979); Tangheroni and Giorgioni Mercuriali (1981); de la Roncière (1982); Guenzi (1982); Cancila (1983); Chiacchella and Tosti (1984); Rossini and Zalin (1985); Grab (1986); Balani (1987); La Marca (1988); Palermo (1990); Pult Quaglia (1990); Franco et al. (1991); Fazio (1993); Alifano (1996); Strangio (1999); Corritore (2000); Blando (2003); Martinat (2004); Fazio (2005); Parziale (2009); Vertecchi (2009); Bargelli (2013); Faugeron (2014); Costantini (2016); Cazzola (2020). On other European cities and countries, see, for instance, Romano (1956); Stouff (1970); Kaplan (1976, 1982, 1984); de Castro (1987); Roeck (1987); Gauthier and Ikni (1988); Meuvret (1988); Reinhardt (1991); Campbell et al. (1993); Groebner (1993); Wiedmer (1993); Kaplan (1996); Clément (1999); Abad (2002); Montenach (2009); Bohstedt (2010); Kaplan (2015); de Vries (2019). Many articles were also published on these subjects. It is not possible to mention all here, making an exception for some collective works and monographic issues of journals: Centre Culturel de l'Abbaye de Flaran (1985); Istituto Formazione Operatori Aziendali (1986); Guenzi et al. (1999 [1998]); *Mélanges de l'École Française de Rome* (2008); Arízaga Bolumburu and Solórzano Telechea (2009); *Storia Urbana* (2012); Le Mao and Meyzie (2015); Clemente and Russo (2019).

28. Thompson (1971, pp. 79–88); Kaplan (1976, vol. I, pp. 1–8); Martinat (2004, pp. 30–36, 94, 119); Margairaz and Minard (2008, pp. 58–62); Bohstedt (2010, pp. 48–54, 58–63).
29. Massa (1999 [1998], pp. 390–391); Stabel (2001, pp. 803–808); Montenach (2009, pp. 206–212); Ogilvie (2019, pp. 36–82).
30. For a general review on these subjects, see Ginatempo (2001).
31. See, for instance, Oliva Herrer and Benito i Monclús (2007); Ó Gráda (2009); Bourin et al. (2011); Benito i Monclús (2013); Alfani and Ó Gráda (2017); Collet and Schuh (2018); Palermo et al. (2018).
32. This is Edoardo Grendi's concept of 'exceptional-normal' (Grendi 1977, p. 512; 1994, p. 544).
33. On early modern Italy, see, for instance, Alfani (2010).
34. For a study in this perspective, considering the price of land in seventeenth-century Piedmont, see Levi (1985).
35. On the different criteria employed in recording current market prices, for instance in Udine, see Fornasin (2000 [1999]).
36. See the literature mentioned in note 27.
37. See Kula (1986 [1970]).

Published Sources

Beccaria, Cesare. 1990. *Edizione nazionale delle opere di Cesare Beccaria*, dir. by Luigi Firpo and Gianni Francioni. Vol. VII: Atti di governo (serie II: 1778–1783), ed. by Rosalba Canetta. Milano: Mediobanca.

———. 1993. *Edizione nazionale delle opere di Cesare Beccaria*, dir. by Luigi Firpo and Gianni Francioni. Vol. VIII: Atti di governo (serie III: 1784–1786), ed. by Rosalba Canetta. Milano: Mediobanca.

Smith, Adam. 1776. *An inquiry into the nature and causes of the wealth of nations*. London: William Strahan and Thomas Cadell.

References

Abad, Reynald. 2002. *Le grand marché. L'approvisionnement alimentaire de Paris sous l'Ancien Régime*. Paris: Fayard.

Ago, Renata. 1998. *Economia barocca. Mercato e istituzioni nella Roma del Seicento*. Roma: Donzelli.

Alfani, Guido. 2010. *Il Grand Tour dei Cavalieri dell'Apocalisse. L'Italia del 'lungo Cinquecento' (1494–1629)*. Venezia: Marsilio.

Alfani, Guido, and Cormac Ó Gráda, eds. 2017. *Famine in European history*. Cambridge: Cambridge University Press.

Algazi, Gadi, Valentin Groebner, and Bernhard Jussen, eds. 2003. *Negotiating the gift: Pre-modern figurations of exchange*. Göttingen: Vandenhoeck und Ruprecht.

Alifano, Enrica. 1996. *Il grano, il pane e la politica annonaria a Napoli nel Settecento*. Napoli: Edizioni Scientifiche Italiane.

Arízaga Bolumburu, Beatriz, and Jesús Ángel Solórzano Telechea. 2009. *Alimentar la ciudad en la Edad Media*. Logroño: Instituto de Estudios Riojanos.

Aymard, Maurice. 1966. *Venise, Raguse et le commerce du blé pendant la seconde moitié du XVIe siècle*. Paris: Sevpen.

Balani, Donatella. 1987. *Il vicario tra città e Stato. L'ordine pubblico e l'annona nella Torino del Settecento*. Torino: Deputazione Subalpina di Storia Patria.

Bargelli, Claudio. 2013. *Dal necessario al superfluo. Le arti alimentari parmensi tra medioevo ed età moderna*. Milano: Angeli.

Basini, Gianluigi. 1970. *L'uomo e il pane. Risorse, consumi e carenze alimentari della popolazione modenese nel Cinque e Seicento*. Milano: Giuffrè.

Bassnett, Madeline. 2016. *Women, food exchange, and governance in early modern England*. Cham: Palgrave Macmillan.

Bateman, Victoria N. 2012. *Markets and growth in early modern Europe*. London: Pickering and Chatto.

Benito i Monclús, Pere, ed. 2013. *Crisis alimentarias en la Edad Media. Modelos, explicaciones y representaciones*. Lleida: Milenio.

Besomi, Daniele, and Giorgio Rampa. 2000 [1998]. *Dal liberalismo al liberismo. Stato e mercato nella storia delle idee e nell'analisi degli economisti*. 2nd ed. Torino: Giappichelli.

Blando, Antonino. 2003. *Istituzioni e mercato nella Sicilia del grano*. Palermo: Puntografica.

Blondé, Bruno, Peter Stabel, Jon Stobart, and Ilya Van Damme, eds. 2006. *Buyers and sellers: Retail circuits and practices in medieval and early modern Europe*. Turnhout: Brepols.

Bohstedt, John. 2010. *The politics of provisions: Food riots, moral economy, and market transition in England, c. 1550–1850*. Farnham/Burlington: Ashgate.

Bourin, Monique, John Drendel, and François Menant, eds. 2011. *Les disettes dans la conjoncture de 1300 en Méditerranée occidentale*. Rome: École Française de Rome.

Braudel, Fernand. 1979. *Civilisation matérielle, économie et capitalisme, XVe–XVIIIe siècle*. Vol. II: Les jeux de l'échange. Paris: Colin.

Britnell, Richard Hugh. 1993. *The commercialisation of English society, 1000–1500*. Cambridge: Cambridge University Press.

———. 2009. *Markets, trade and economic development in England and Europe, 1050–1550*. Farnham/Burlington: Ashgate.

Calabi, Donatella. 1993. *Il mercato e la città. Piazze, strade, architetture d'Europa in età moderna*. Venezia: Marsilio.

———, ed. 1997a. *Fabbriche, piazze, mercati. La città italiana nel Rinascimento*. Roma: Officina.

———. 1997b. La "plathea magna": il disegno, il committente, l'architetto. In Calabi 1997a, 9–32.

Campbell, Bruce Mortimer Stanley, James A. Galloway, Derek Keene, and Margaret Murphy. 1993. *A medieval capital and its grain supply: Agrarian production and distribution in the London region*, c. *1300*. Lancaster: Institute of British Geographers, Historical Geography Research Group.

Canaletti Gaudenti, Alberto. 1947. *La politica agraria ed annonaria dello Stato Pontificio da Benedetto XIV a Pio VII*. Roma: Istituto di Studi Romani.

Cancila, Orazio. 1972. *Aspetti di un mercato siciliano. Trapani nei secoli XVII–XIX*. Caltanissetta/Roma: Sciascia.

———. 1983. *Baroni e popolo nella Sicilia del grano*. Palermo: Palumbo.

Cavaciocchi, Simonetta, ed. 2001. *Fiere e mercati nella integrazione delle economie europee. Secc. XIII–XVIII*. Firenze: Le Monnier.

Cazzola, Franco. 2020. *Amministrare la fame. Politica annonaria a Ferrara tra Ducato estense e Legazione pontificia (1570–1640)*. Ferrara: Deputazione Provinciale Ferrarese di Storia Patria.

Centre Culturel de l'Abbaye de Flaran, ed. 1985. *L'approvisionnement des villes de l'Europe occidentale au Moyen Âge et aux Temps Modernes.* Auch: Comité Départemental du Tourisme du Gers.

Centre Jean Bérard and École Française de Rome, eds. 1994. *Le ravitaillement en blé de Rome et des centres urbains des débuts de la République jusqu'au Haut Empire.* Naples: Centre Jean Bérard/Rome: École Française de Rome.

Chiacchella, Rita, and Mario Tosti. 1984. *Terra, proprietà e politica annonaria nel Perugino tra Sei e Settecento.* Rimini: Maggioli.

Chittolini, Giorgio. 1979. *La formazione dello Stato regionale e le istituzioni del contado. Secoli XIV e XV.* Torino: Einaudi.

———. 1989. Cities, 'city-states', and regional states in north-central Italy. *Theory and Society: Renewal and Critique in Social Theory* 18 (5): 689–706.

Clément, Alain. 1999. *Nourrir le peuple. Entre État et marché, XVI*e*–XIX*e *siècle. Contribution à l'histoire intellectuelle de l'approvisionnement alimentaire.* Paris/Montréal: l'Harmattan.

Clemente, Alida, and Saverio Russo, eds. 2019. *La* polizia de' grani. *Mercati, regole e crisi di sussistenza nelle economie di Antico Regime.* Soveria Mannelli: Rubbettino.

Collet, Dominik, and Maximilian Schuh, eds. 2018. *Famines during the 'little ice age' (1300–1800). Socionatural entanglements in premodern societies.* Cham: Springer.

Collodo, Silvana. 1999 [1990]. Il sistema annonario delle città venete: da pubblica utilità a servizio sociale (secoli XIII–XVI). New ed. In *Società e istituzioni in area veneta. Itinerari di ricerca (secoli XII–XV)*, by Silvana Collodo, 47–67. Fiesole: Nardini.

Coquery, Natacha, ed. 2000. *La boutique et la ville. Commerces, commerçants, espaces et clientèles, XVI*e*–XX*e *siècle.* Tours: Université François Rabelais, Centre d'Histoire de la Ville Moderne et Contemporaine.

Corritore, Renzo Paolo. 2000. *La naturale "abbondanza" del Mantovano. Produzione, mercato e consumi granari a Mantova in età moderna.* Pavia: Università di Pavia.

———. 2012. Un problema negletto. Per un riesame della questione annonaria nelle città di antico regime. *Storia Urbana* 36 (1/134): 5–9.

Costantini, Fabrizio. 2016. *"In tutto differente dalle altre città". Mercato e contrabbando dei grani a Bergamo in età veneta.* Bergamo: Centro Studi e Ricerche Archivio Bergamasco.

Crouzet-Pavan, Élisabeth. 2003. "Pour le bien commun"… À propos des politiques urbaines dans l'Italie communale. In *Pouvoir et édilité. Les grands chantiers dans l'Italie communale et seigneuriale*, ed. by Élisabeth Crouzet-Pavan, 11–40. Rome: École Française de Rome.

Dal Pane, Luigi. 1932. *La questione del commercio dei grani nel Settecento in Italia.* Vol. I: Parte generale-Toscana. Milano: Vita e Pensiero.

Davis, James. 2012. *Medieval market morality: Life, law and ethics in the English marketplace, 1200–1500*. Cambridge: Cambridge University Press.

de Castro, Concepción. 1987. *El pan de Madrid. El abasto de las ciudades españolas del Antiguo Régimen*. Madrid: Alianza Editorial.

de la Roncière, Charles-Marie. 1982. *Prix et salaires à Florence au XIVe siècle (1280–1380)*. Rome: École Française de Rome.

De Maddalena, Aldo. 1949. *Prezzi e aspetti di mercato in Milano durante il secolo XVII*. Milano: Malfasi.

———. 1974. *Prezzi e mercedi a Milano dal 1701 al 1860*. Milano: Banca Commerciale Italiana.

de Vries, Jan. 2019. *The price of bread: Regulating the market in the Dutch Republic*. Cambridge: Cambridge University Press.

Dijkman, Jessica. 2011. *Shaping medieval markets: The organisation of commodity markets in Holland, c. 1200–c. 1450*. Leiden/Boston: Brill.

Duby, Georges. 1973. *Guerriers et paysans, VIIe–XIIe siècle. Premier essor de l'économie européenne*. Paris: Gallimard.

École Française de Rome, ed. 1998. *La mémoire perdue. Recherches sur l'administration romaine*. Rome: École Française de Rome.

Epstein, Stephan R. 2000. *Freedom and growth: The rise of states and markets in Europe, 1300–1750*. London/New York: Routledge.

Erdkamp, Paul. 2005. *The grain market in the Roman Empire: A social, political and economic study*. Cambridge: Cambridge University Press.

Everitt, Alan M. 1967. The marketing of agricultural produce. In *The agrarian history of England and Wales*, ed. by Herbert Patrick Reginald Finberg. Vol. IV: 1500–1640, ed. by Joan Thirsk, 466–592. Cambridge: Cambridge University Press.

Faugeron, Fabien. 2014. *Nourrir la ville. Ravitaillement, marchés et métiers de l'alimentation à Venise dans les derniers siècles du Moyen Âge*. Rome: École Française de Rome.

Fazio, Ida. 1993. *La politica del grano. Annona e controllo del territorio in Sicilia nel Settecento*. Milano: Angeli.

———. 2005. *"Sterilissima di frumenti". L'annona della città di Messina in età moderna (XV–XIX secolo)*. Caltanissetta: Lussografica.

Federico, Giovanni. 2012. How much do we know about market integration in Europe? *The Economic History Review* 65 (2): 470–497.

Fontaine, Laurence. 2008. *L'économie morale. Pauvreté, crédit et confiance dans l'Europe préindustrielle*. Paris: Gallimard.

———. 2014. *Le marché. Histoire et usages d'une conquête sociale*. Paris: Gallimard.

Fornasin, Alessio. 2000 [1999]. Il mercato dei grani di Udine. Indagine per una storia dei prezzi in Friuli (secoli XVI–XVIII). New ed. In *La Patria del Friuli in età moderna. Saggi di storia economica*, by Alessio Fornasin, 33–60. Udine: Forum.

Franco, Vincenzo, Angela Lanconelli, and Maria Antonietta Quesada. 1991. *Pane e potere. Istituzioni e società in Italia dal Medioevo all'età moderna*. Roma: Ministero per i Beni Culturali e Ambientali, Ufficio Centrale per i Beni Archivistici.

Galloway, James A., ed. 2000. *Trade, urban hinterlands and market integration*, c. *1300–1600*. London: University of London, Institute of Historical Research, Centre for Metropolitan History.

Garnsey, Peter. 1988. *Famine and food supply in the Graeco-Roman world: Responses to risk and crisis*. Cambridge: Cambridge University Press.

Garnsey, Peter, and Charles R. Whittaker, eds. 1983. *Trade and famine in classical antiquity*. Cambridge: Cambridge Philological Society.

Gauthier, Florence, and Guy-Robert Ikni, eds. 1988. *La guerre du blé au XVIIIe siècle. La critique populaire contre le libéralisme économique au XVIIIe siècle*. Montreuil: la Passion.

Ginatempo, Maria Ausiliatrice. 2001. Spunti comparativi sulle trasformazioni della fiscalità nell'Italia post-comunale. In *Politiche finanziarie e fiscali nell'Italia settentrionale (secoli XIII–XV)*, ed. by Patrizia Mainoni, 125–220. Milano: Unicopli.

Giusberti, Fabio. 1985. Regole e comportamenti alla "Ruga delle pescherie" (Bologna, sec. XVIII). In *Popolazione ed economia dei territori bolognesi durante il Settecento*, ed. by the Istituto per la Storia di Bologna, 553–575. Bologna: Istituto per la Storia di Bologna.

Grab, Alexander I. 1986. *La politica del pane. Le riforme annonarie in Lombardia nell'età teresiana e giuseppina*. Milano: Angeli.

Grendi, Edoardo. 1977. Micro-analisi e storia sociale. *Quaderni Storici* 12 (2/35): 506–520.

———. 1994. Ripensare la microstoria? *Quaderni Storici*, new series 29 (2/86): 539–549.

Groebner, Valentin. 1993. *Ökonomie ohne Haus. Zum Wirtschaften armer Leute in Nürnberg am Ende des 15. Jahrhunderts*. Göttingen: Vandenhoeck und Ruprecht.

Grohmann, Alberto. 1994. Spazio urbano e organizzazione economica nell'Europa medievale. Introduzione e problemi di metodo. In *Spazio urbano e organizzazione economica nell'Europa medievale*, ed. by Alberto Grohmann, 7–35. Napoli: Edizioni Scientifiche Italiane.

———. 2003. *La città medievale*. Roma/Bari: Laterza.

Guenzi, Alberto. 1982. *Pane e fornai a Bologna in età moderna*. Venezia: Marsilio.

———. 1994. La tutela del consumatore nell'antico regime. I "vittuali di prima necessità" a Bologna. In *Disciplina dell'anima, disciplina del corpo e disciplina della società tra medioevo ed età moderna*, ed. by Paolo Prodi, in cooperation with Carla Penuti, 733–756. Bologna: il Mulino.

Guenzi, Alberto, Paola Massa, and Angelo Moioli, eds. 1999 [1998]. *Corporazioni e gruppi professionali nell'Italia moderna*. Italian ed. Milano: Angeli.

Guidoni, Enrico. 1980. L'urbanistica dei comuni italiani in età federiciana. In *Federico II e l'arte del Duecento italiano*, ed. by Angiola Maria Romanini. Vol. I, 99–120. Galatina: Congedo.

———. 1981. Appunti per una storia dell'urbanistica nella Lombardia tardo-medievale. In *Lombardia. Il territorio, l'ambiente, il paesaggio. Dalle incisioni rupestri alla sintesi leonardesca*, ed. by Carlo Pirovano, 109–162. Milano: Electa.

Heal, Felicity. 2014. *The power of gifts: Gift-exchange in early modern England*. Oxford: Oxford University Press.

Herz, Peter. 1988. *Studien zur römischen Wirtschaftsgesetzgebung. Die Lebensmittelversorgung*. Stuttgart: Steiner.

Höbenreich, Evelyn. 1997. Annona. *Juristische Aspekte der stadtrömischen Lebensmittelversorgung im Prinzipat*. Graz: Leykam.

Istituto Formazione Operatori Aziendali, ed. 1986. *Mercati e consumi: organizzazione e qualificazione del commercio in Italia dal XII al XX secolo*. Bologna: Analisi.

Kaplan, Steven Laurence. 1976. *Bread, politics and political economy in the reign of Louis XV*. The Hague: Nijhoff.

———. 1982. *The famine plot persuasion in eighteenth-century France*. Philadelphia: The American Philosophical Society.

———. 1984. *Provisioning Paris: Merchants and millers in the grain and flour trade during the eighteenth century*. Ithaca/London: Cornell University Press.

———. 1996. *The bakers of Paris and the bread question, 1700–1775*. Durham: Duke University Press.

———. 2015. *The stakes of regulation: Perspectives on* Bread, politics and political economy *forty years later*. London/New York: Anthem Press.

Krausman Ben-Amos, Ilana. 2008. *The culture of giving: Informal support and gift-exchange in early modern England*. Cambridge: Cambridge University Press.

Kula, Witold. 1986 [1970]. *Measures and men*. English translation. Princeton: Princeton University Press.

La Marca, Nicola. 1988. *L'abolizione del vincolismo annonario nello Stato della Chiesa*. Roma: Bulzoni.

Langholm, Odd Inge. 1992. *Economics in the medieval schools: Wealth, exchange, value, money and usury according to the Paris theological tradition, 1200–1350*. Leiden/New York/Köln: Brill.

Lecuppre-Desjardin, Élodie, and Anne-Laure Van Bruaene, eds. 2010. *De bono communi: The discourse and practice of the Common Good in the European city (13th–16th c.)/Discours et pratique du Bien Commun dans les villes d'Europe (XIIIe au XVIe siècle)*. Turnhout: Brepols.

Le Mao, Caroline, and Philippe Meyzie, eds. 2015. *L'approvisionnement des villes portuaires en Europe du XVIe siècle à nos jours*. Paris: Presses de l'Université Paris-Sorbonne.

Levi, Giovanni. 1985. *L'eredità immateriale. Carriera di un esorcista nel Piemonte del Seicento*. Torino: Einaudi.

Lombardini, Gabriele. 1963. *Pane e denaro a Bassano. Prezzi del grano e politica dell'approvvigionamento dei cereali tra il 1501 e il 1799*. Venezia: Pozza.

Macry, Paolo. 1974. *Mercato e società nel Regno di Napoli. Commercio del grano e politica economica nel Settecento*. Napoli: Guida.

Malanima, Paolo. 1998. Italian cities 1300–1800. A quantitative approach. *Rivista di Storia Economica*, new series 14 (2): 91–126.

Margairaz, Dominique, and Philippe Minard. 2008. Marché des subsistances et économie morale: ce que 'taxer' veut dire. *Annales Historiques de la Révolution Française* 101 (2/352): 53–99.

Marin, Brigitte, and Catherine Virlouvet, eds. 2004. *Nourrir les cités de Méditerranée. Antiquité-Temps modernes*. Paris: Maisonneuve et Larose/Aix-en-Provence: Maison Méditerranéenne des Sciences de l'Homme/Madrid: Universidad Nacional de Educación a Distancia.

———, eds. 2016. *Entrepôts et trafics annonaires en Méditerranée. Antiquité-Temps modernes*. Rome: École Française de Rome.

Martinat, Monica. 2004. *Le juste marché. Le système annonaire romain aux XVIe et XVIIe siècles*. Rome: École Française de Rome.

Massa, Paola. 1999 [1998]. Annona e corporazioni del settore alimentare a Genova: organizzazione e conflittualità (XVI–XVIII secolo). In Guenzi et al. 1999 [1998], 390–403.

Mélanges de l'École Française de Rome. Italie et Méditerranée. 2008. 120 (2): Entrepôts et trafics annonaires en Méditerranée, ed. by Brigitte Marin and Catherine Virlouvet.

Meuvret, Jean. 1988. *Le problème des subsistances à l'époque Louis XIV*. Vol. III: Le commerce des grains et la conjoncture. Paris: École des Hautes Études en Sciences Sociales.

Middleton, Simon, and James E. Shaw, eds. 2018. *Market ethics and practices, c. 1300–1850*. London/New York: Routledge.

Montenach, Anne. 2009. *Espaces et pratiques du commerce alimentaire à Lyon au XVIIe siècle. L'économie du quotidien*. Grenoble: Presses Universitaires de Grenoble.

Neale, Walter Castle. 1957. The market in theory and history. In Polanyi et al. 1957, 357–372.

North, Douglass Cecil. 1981. *Structure and change in economic history*. New York/London: Norton.

———. 1990. *Institutions, institutional change and economic performance*. Cambridge: Cambridge University Press.

North, Douglass Cecil, and Robert Paul Thomas. 1973. *The rise of the Western world: A new economic history*. Cambridge: Cambridge University Press.

O'Brien, Denis Patrick. 2004 [1975]. *The classical economists revisited*. New ed. Princeton/Oxford: Princeton University Press.

Ogilvie, Sheilagh Catheren. 2011. *Institutions and European trade: Merchant guilds, 1000–1800*. Cambridge: Cambridge University Press.

———. 2019. *The European guilds: An economic analysis*. Princeton/Oxford: Princeton University Press.

Ó Gráda, Cormac. 2009. *Famine: A short history*. Princeton/Oxford: Princeton University Press.

Oliva Herrer, Hipólito Rafael, and Pere Benito i Monclús, eds. 2007. *Crisis de subsistencia y crisis agrarias en la Edad Media*. Sevilla: Universidad de Sevilla, Secretariado de Publicaciones.

Palermo, Luciano. 1990. *Mercati del grano a Roma tra Medioevo e Rinascimento*. Vol. I: Il mercato distrettuale del grano in età comunale. Roma: Istituto Nazionale di Studi Romani.

Palermo, Luciano, Andrea Fara, and Pere Benito i Monclús, eds. 2018. *Políticas contra el hambre y la carestía en la Europa medieval*. Lleida: Milenio.

Parenti, Giuseppe. 1939. *Prime ricerche sulla rivoluzione dei prezzi in Firenze*. Firenze: Cya.

———. 1942. *Prezzi e mercato del grano a Siena (1546–1765)*. Firenze: Cya.

Parziale, Lavinia. 2009. *Nutrire la città. Produzione e commercio alimentare a Milano tra Cinque e Seicento*. Milano: Angeli.

Pavis d'Escurac, Henriette. 1976. *La préfecture de l'annone, service administratif impérial d'Auguste à Constantin*. Rome: École Française de Rome.

Persson, Karl Gunnar. 1999. *Grain markets in Europe, 1500–1900: Integration and deregulation*. Cambridge: Cambridge University Press.

Petino, Antonio. 1946. *La questione del commercio dei grani in Sicilia nel Settecento*. Catania: Azienda Poligrafica Editoriale.

Pinto, Giuliano. 1978. *Il libro del Biadaiolo. Carestie e annona a Firenze dalla metà del '200 al 1348*. Firenze: Olschki.

———. 1996. Dalla tarda antichità alla metà del XVI secolo. In *La popolazione italiana dal Medioevo a oggi*, by Lorenzo Del Panta, Massimo Livi Bacci, Giuliano Pinto, and Eugenio Sonnino, 15–71. Roma/Bari: Laterza.

Pirenne, Henri. 1939 [1910]. Les anciennes démocraties des Pays-Bas. New ed. In *Les villes et les institutions urbaines*, by Henri Pirenne. Vol. I, 143–301. Paris: Alcan/Bruxelles: Nouvelle Société d'Éditions.

———. 1963 [1933]. *Histoire économique et sociale du Moyen Âge*, ed. by Hans van Werveke. New ed. Paris: Presses Universitaires de France.

Polanyi, Karl. 1957a [1944]. *The great transformation: The political and economic origins of our time*. Boston: Beacon Press.

———. 1957b. The economy as instituted process. In Polanyi et al. 1957, 243–270.

———. 1977. *The livelihood of man*, ed. by Harry W. Pearson. New York/San Francisco/London: Academic Press.

Polanyi, Karl, Conrad Maynadier Arensberg, and Harry W. Pearson, eds. 1957. *Trade and market in the early empires: Economies in history and theory*. Glencoe/Indian Hills: The Free Press.

Prodi, Paolo. 2009. *Settimo non rubare. Furto e mercato nella storia dell'Occidente*. Bologna: il Mulino.

Pult Quaglia, Anna Maria. 1990. *"Per provvedere ai popoli". Il sistema annonario nella Toscana dei Medici*. Firenze: Olschki.

Randall, Adrian, and Andrew Charlesworth, eds. 1996. *Markets, market culture and popular protest in eighteenth-century Britain and Ireland*. Liverpool: Liverpool University Press.

———, eds. 2000. *Moral economy and popular protest: Crowds, conflict and authority*. Basingstoke/New York: Palgrave.

Reinhardt, Volker. 1991. *Überleben in der frühneuzeitlichen Stadt. Annona und Getreideversorgung in Rom, 1563–1797*. Tübingen: Niemeyer.

Rickman, Geoffrey. 1980. *The corn supply of ancient Rome*. Oxford: Clarendon Press.

Roeck, Bernd. 1987. *Bäcker, Brot und Getreide in Augsburg. Zur Geschichte des Bäckerhandwerks und zur Versorgungspolitik der Reichsstadt im Zeitalter des Dreißigjährigen Krieges*. Sigmaringen: Thorbecke.

Romani, Marzio Achille. 1975. *Nella spirale di una crisi. Popolazione, mercato e prezzi a Parma tra cinque e seicento*. Milano: Giuffrè.

Romano, Ruggiero. 1956. *Commerce et prix du blé à Marseille au XVIIIe siècle*. Paris: Colin.

Rossini, Egidio, and Giovanni Zalin. 1985. *Uomini, grani e contrabbandi sul Garda tra Quattrocento e Seicento*. Verona: Università degli Studi di Verona, Facoltà di Economia e Commercio, Istituto di Storia Economica e Sociale.

Sanz Palomera, Gustavo. 2010. *La Annona y la política agraria durante el Alto Imperio romano*. Oxford: Archaeopress.

Shaw, James E. 2002. Retail, monopoly, and privilege: The dissolution of the fishmongers' guild of Venice, 1599. *Journal of Early Modern History* 6 (4): 396–427.

Sirks, Boudewijn. 1991. *Food for Rome: The legal structure of the transportation and processing of supplies for the imperial distributions in Rome and Constantinople*. Amsterdam: Gieben.

Soraci, Cristina. 2011. *Sicilia frumentaria. Il grano siciliano e l'annona di Roma, V a.C.–V d.C.* Roma: 'L'Erma' di Bretschneider.

Stabel, Peter. 2001. Markets and retail in the cities of the late medieval Low Countries. Economic networks and socio-cultural display. In Cavaciocchi 2001, 797–817.

Storia Urbana. 2012. 36 (1/134): Annona e strutture urbane a Ragusa, Venezia, Genova, Lione, Valencia, Milano, ed. by Renzo Paolo Corritore.

Stouff, Louis. 1970. *Ravitaillement et alimentation en Provence aux XIVe et XVe siècles*. Paris/La Haye: Mouton.

Strangio, Donatella. 1999. *Crisi alimentari e politica annonaria a Roma nel Settecento*. Roma: Istituto Nazionale di Studi Romani.

Tangheroni, Marco, in cooperation with Claudia Giorgioni Mercuriali. 1981. *Aspetti del commercio dei cereali nei Paesi della Corona d'Aragona*. Vol. I: La Sardegna. Pisa: Pacini.

Tengström, Emin. 1974. *Bread for the people: Studies of the corn-supply of Rome during the late Empire*. Stockholm: Svenska Institutet i Rom.

Thompson, Edward Palmer. 1971. The moral economy of the English crowd in the eighteenth century. *Past and Present* 20 (1/50): 76–136.

Todeschini, Giacomo. 1994. *Il prezzo della salvezza. Lessici medievali del pensiero economico*. Roma: La Nuova Italia Scientifica.

———. 2002. *I mercanti e il tempio. La società cristiana e il circolo virtuoso della ricchezza fra Medioevo ed Età Moderna*. Bologna: il Mulino.

———. 2004. *Ricchezza francescana. Dalla povertà volontaria alla società di mercato*. Bologna: il Mulino.

———. 2005. La riflessione etica sulle attività economiche. In *Economie urbane ed etica economica nell'Italia medievale*, ed. by Roberto Greci, 151–228. Roma/Bari: Laterza.

———. 2011. *Come Giuda. La gente comune e i giochi dell'economia all'inizio dell'epoca moderna*. Bologna: il Mulino.

Tucci, Ugo. 1975. L'Ungheria e gli approvvigionamenti veneziani di bovini nel Cinquecento. In *Rapporti veneto-ungheresi all'epoca del Rinascimento*, ed. by Tibor Klaniczay, 153–171. Budapest: Akadémiai Kiadó.

Ullmann, Walter. 1970 [1955]. *The growth of papal government in the Middle Ages: A study in the ideological relation of clerical to lay power*. 3rd ed. London: Methuen.

———. 1978 [1961]. *Principles of government and politics in the Middle Ages*. 4th ed. London: Methuen.

Vaggi, Gianni. 1987. *The economics of Francois Quesnay*. Basingstoke/London: Macmillan.

Vecchiato, Francesco. 1979. *Pane e politica annonaria in Terraferma veneta tra secolo XV e secolo XVIII. (Il caso di Verona)*. Verona: Università degli Studi di Padova, Facoltà di Economia e Commercio in Verona, Istituto di Storia Economica e Sociale.

Vertecchi, Giulia. 2009. *Il "masser ai formenti in Terra Nova". Il ruolo delle scorte granarie a Venezia nel XVIII secolo*. Roma: Università degli Studi Roma Tre.

Virlouvet, Catherine. 1995. *Tessera frumentaria. Les procédures de distribution du blé public à Rome à la fin de la République et au début de l'Empire*. Rome: École Française de Rome.

Wiedmer, Laurence. 1993. *Pain quotidien et pain de disette. Meuniers, boulangers et État nourricier à Genève (XVIIe–XVIIIe siècles)*. Genève: Passé Présent.

Zanetti, Dante. 1964. *Problemi alimentari di una economia preindustriale. Cereali a Pavia dal 1398 al 1700*. Torino: Boringhieri.

Zemon Davis, Natalie. 2000. *The gift in sixteenth-century France*. Madison: University of Wisconsin Press.

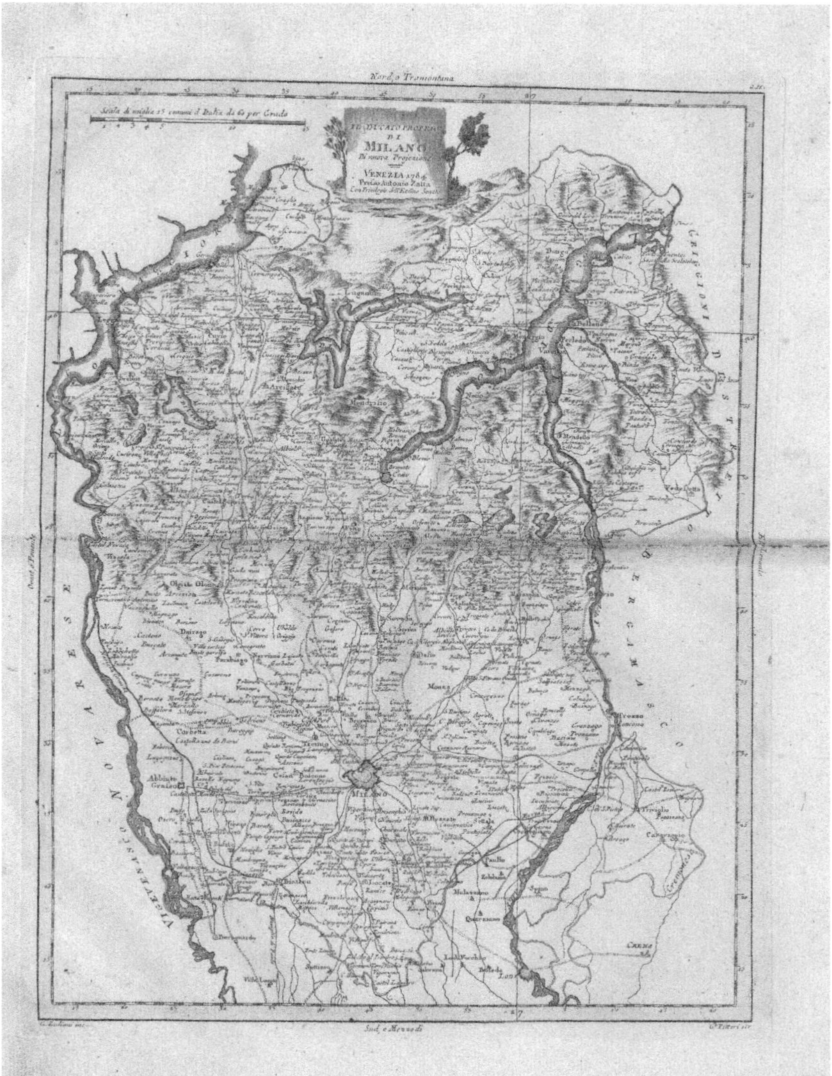

Map 2.1 The State of Milan (1784)

CHAPTER 2

Complexity and Efficiency: Milan in the Seventeenth and Eighteenth Centuries

Luciano Maffi and Luca Mocarelli

2.1 Introduction

The elaborate system of food supply in Old Regime societies is certainly something more complex than a set of laws and administrative and organisational structures. It represents one of the key mechanisms employed by authorities to organise city and state life. As stated by Renzo Paolo Corritore: "In the pre-industrial age, the *annona* is the complex of institutions (norms, activities, organisms) through which public authorities ensure subsistence for the population. It is however also a condition for the cities' existence. It allows the development of life and activities for

This chapter is the result of joint archival research and analysis of the data; however, Sects. 2.1, 2.2, 2.3, 2.4, and 2.5 were written by Luca Mocarelli, and Sects. 2.6, 2.7, 2.8, 2.9, and 2.10 were written by Luciano Maffi.

L. Maffi
Università Cattolica del Sacro Cuore, Milan, Italy

L. Mocarelli (✉)
Università degli Studi di Milano-Bicocca, Milan, Italy
e-mail: luca.mocarelli@unimib.it

L. Clerici (ed.), *Italian Victualling Systems in the Early Modern Age, 16th to 18th Century*, Palgrave Studies in Economic History,
https://doi.org/10.1007/978-3-030-42064-2_2

their inhabitants. In the form of infrastructures (quays, customs, market squares, accommodations, porches, public granaries, stores, cereals pits, public bakeries, etc.), the *annona* is a fixed social capital allowing the community to access resources that would otherwise be tiring and burdensome to procure. It also grants externality (the advantages of the division of labour outside of manufacture) to the work of individuals".[1]

Consequently, understanding the *annona*—that is to say the victualling system—requires an in-depth and broad-scope examination of urban society,[2] since the supply problem was inextricably linked to the city. This was an exceptional economic and social reality in Old Regime societies: the cities had to be fed in favourable harvest years, and this was even more necessary during years characterised by famines, epidemics, and wars. The victualling system arose as a result of the process of accumulation and maturation of a structured reality composed of a multitude of intermediate bodies: pre-industrial social, political, and economic realities. At that time, these were reflected in hierarchies, all of which were simultaneously involved, intersecting and overlapping each other. This vital aspect of urban societies was in the hands of the nobility, for they alone could get supplies outside of the victualling system. At the same time, a considerable part of the food entering the city came from the lands of the people who controlled the victualling administration, thus increasing the development and rate of return for those who managed it.[3]

Equally relevant are the correlations within the victualling system, specifically between the market and the guilds that dealt with the transformation and production of food products. In a society where food was cereal-based, the control of wheat, its trade and transformation, and the regulation of prices represented a fundamental aspect of social control and a crucial means to exercise political power. Precisely because different interests met and clashed on the subject of food supply, in order to delve productively into the victualling system, it is necessary to extend our scope beyond the city walls and, more specifically, to the often-opposing interests of cities and countryside, public administration and landowners, guilds and consumers. It is also necessary to do this taking into account two distinct situations: the years marred by productive and economic difficulties (when it was necessary to find a balance and to gauge the effectiveness of the victualling system[4]), and the years of more abundant harvest (when the problem was instead to ensure sufficiently high prices for producers[5]).

2.2 Milan and Its State: A Peculiar Case Study

The victualling system was very flexible and deeply embedded in society at that time. Consequently, to fully understand it, we cannot limit ourselves to an examination of the institutions responsible for the food supply and their policies: we must instead also consider their interaction with the complex context in which they existed. In other words, it is necessary to avoid easy generalisations and to instead deal with individual cases, since the victualling system was implemented in different ways depending not only on the institutional context, but also on the economic reality in which cities existed, as well as on their size. There is no doubt that, in this regard, Milan found itself in a very specific situation. The most important city of Lombardy was at the top of the European urban hierarchy for centuries, always remaining one of the fifteen most populous cities on the continent between 1400 and 1800 (see Table 2.1). At the same time, however, the presence of a large city such as Milan had not cannibalised the Lombard urban network, characterised throughout the Early Modern Age by the coexistence of several large cities (see Table 2.2).

In the seventeenth century, before the catastrophic 1630 plague, Lombardy was in fact one of the most urbanised regions of Europe: in addition to Milan, it had four cities with more than 20,000 inhabitants, and another four with more than 10,000.[6] Even later on, albeit losing its ranking in comparative terms to the regions of Northern Europe, Lombardy maintained respectable urbanisation rates. This is even more the case when the analysis is limited to the State of Milan.[7] After the considerable territorial reductions following the wars of the first half of the eighteenth century, the State of Milan had become a small but very densely populated political entity. In 1795, the approximately 7,900 square kilometres of the State hosted 1,177,488 inhabitants[8] with a very high urbanisation rate. In fact, urban cities and towns with over 7,000 inhabitants housed 20.9% of the overall population (246,659 people). The very high population density[9] of 149 inhabitants per square kilometre was above all an exceptional value. We must consider that in the year 1800, Holland and England had 51.0 and 60.8 inhabitants per square kilometre respectively. Furthermore, it must be considered that only 64% of the surface of the State of Milan was on a plain.[10]

Table 2.1 The fifteen largest European cities (excluding Russia) by population (1400–1800)

1400		1500		1600		1700		1800	
Paris	275,000	Paris	225,000	Paris	300,000	London	575,000	London	948,000
Bruges	125,000	Naples	125,000	Naples	275,000	Paris	500,000	Paris	550,000
Genoa	100,000	*Milan*	100,000	London	200,000	Naples	300,000	Naples	430,000
Venice	100,000	Venice	100,000	Venice	151,000	Amsterdam	200,000	Vienna	247,000
Granada	100,000	Granada	70,000	Seville	135,000	Lisbon	180,000	Amsterdam	217,000
Milan	90,000	Prague	70,000	Lisbon	130,000	Madrid	140,000	Dublin	200,000
Seville	75,000	Lisbon	65,000	*Milan*	120,000	Venice	138,000	Lisbon	195,000
Florence	55,000	Tours	60,000	Palermo	105,000	Rome	135,000	Berlin	172,000
Ghent	55,000	Genoa	58,000	Prague	100,000	*Milan*	125,000	Madrid	168,000
Lisbon	55,000	Florence	50,000	Rome	100,000	Vienna	114,000	Rome	153,000
Bologna	45,000	Ghent	55,000	Toledo	80,000	Palermo	100,000	Palermo	139,000
London	45,000	Palermo	55,000	Florence	76,000	Lyons	97,000	Venice	138,000
Naples	45,000	Rome	55,000	Rouen	70,000	Marseille	90,000	*Milan*	135,000
Toledo	45,000	Bologna	50,000	Granada	69,000	Brussels	80,000	Hamburg	130,000
Barcelona	40,000	London	50,000	Madrid	65,000	Seville	72,000	Lyons	109,000

Source: Bairoch et al. (1988, pp. 272–283)

Table 2.2 Population of the major Lombard cities and towns (1500–1800)

Cities and towns	1500	1600	1700	1800
Milan	100,000	120,000	109,000	124,000
Brescia	48,000	40,000	35,000	30,000
Cremona	40,000	40,000	22,000	25,000
Mantua	28,000	31,000	24,000	25,000
Pavia	16,000	25,000	23,000	25,000
Bergamo	15,000	18,000	20,000	36,000
Lodi	8,000	14,000	14,000	16,000
Como	10,000	12,000	9,000	15,000
Vigevano	10,000	8,000	9,000	12,000
Crema	9,000	11,000	7,000	9,000
Monza	–	9,000	6,000	10,000
Total	284,000	328,000	278,000	327,000

Source: Malanima (1998). Bergamo, Brescia, and Crema belonged to the Republic of Venice; Mantua was annexed to the State of Milan in 1708

In such a context, urban food supply was crucial and not always easy to manage, even considering the great agricultural and economic development of the State. This was a very dynamic area characterised by a high level of sectoral diversification. Particularly advanced agricultural practices in dairy production were established in the irrigated plains since the Middle Ages. In the dry plains and farther up the hills, great advances were made in the cultivation of mulberry bushes and in the raising of silkworms, to which the cultivation of maize was also soon added. Alongside this rich and diversified agricultural sector, a significant manufacturing sector also thrived. Transformation activities had carved out for themselves significant spaces not only in other cities of the State, such as Como, but also in the countryside and in smaller towns (the processing of cotton in the Olona Valley, metal drawing factories in Lecco, silk reeling and spinning in the entire State, etc.). Moreover, because of the boom in silk processing and yarn sales, Milan was strengthening its position as a leading commercial, banking, and financial centre.[11] Even in the presence of such an advanced economic development, feeding Milan remained a complex task. This was due both to the size of the city and to the very high density of the population in the State. Milan was self-sufficient when it came to cereals only during the years of good harvests.[12]

The *Annona* in Milan had been an institution since the Middle Ages, and it had maintained an important role throughout the Early Modern

Age, despite the presence of different dominations. As we shall see, the issue of supplying food to Milan involved different actors and diversified markets and exchange dimensions, that go far beyond the simple regulated market that took place every week at the *Broletto Nuovo*,[13] in which the *prestinari* (the bakers who took the contract for managing each of the thirteen—seventeen by 1771, and eighteen later on—*prestini* of the city, the municipal bakeries where white bread was baked and sold wholesale) and *farinari* (flour sellers) took part.

2.3 Supplying Food to Milan: The Urban Consumption of Cereals

To highlight this fact, a small calculation is sufficient, starting with the types and quantities of bread consumed by the Milanese population (a datum derived from contemporary estimates). For example, Baldassarre Scorza[14] for the year 1771 (when the city had 127,381 inhabitants) calculated a consumption of 157,500 Milanese *moggia*[15] of cereals of all kinds, and 10,000 *moggia* of paddy rice for a total of about 170,000 *moggia* (or 1.3 *moggia* per capita). Cesare Beccaria, starting from data coming from the milling tax, suggested a slightly higher figure: approximately 150,000 *moggia* of wheat and 54,000 of *mistura* (literally, 'mixture', that is to say, in this case, maize and rye), or 1.6 *moggia* per capita. Even larger (and perhaps a little excessive) are the estimates derived from the agreement between the *prestinari* and the *Regia Camera* ('Royal Chamber', that is to say the Treasury) in 1602 (about 2 *moggia* of bread per capita per year), and from a calculation made in 1748 by the *Magistrato delle Entrate Straordinarie* ('Magistracy of Extraordinary Revenues'), or simply *Magistrato Straordinario* ('Extraordinary Magistracy') (200,868 *moggia* of wheat and 62,335 of other cereals).[16] Per capita consumption was lower compared to consumption in the countryside, considered by all to be more than 2 *moggia* per capita per year. This depended on the exceptional nature of the Milanese case, where white bread eaters clearly prevailed. In this regard, contemporary observers had no doubt, and they estimated the consumption of wheat to be over 80% of the total. This fact provoked very strong complaints from Kaunitz. The exact opposite happened in the countryside, where consumption of maize almost exceeded three-quarters of the total.[17]

2.4 The *Broletto Nuovo*: An Insufficient Market for City Food Supply

It seems reasonable to estimate for Milan an annual consumption of cereals of at least 220–230,000 *moggia*, a much higher number than what is indicated by the data we have available for the transactions registered at the *Broletto* market and during two years without any particular harvest problems: 1769 and 1770. In 1769, for the forty-seven weeks for which we have the data regarding the quantities sold (the data for two weeks in February, two in August, and one in December are missing) we have transactions for 77,049 *moggia* of wheat, 12,358 of maize, and 2,054 of rye, for a total of just over 91,000 *moggia*. The following year (where the data for two weeks are missing) they sold 89,155, 13,113, and 2,420 *moggia* respectively, for a total of just under 105,000 *moggia*.[18] The remarkable fact is the substantial coincidence of the values for wheat sales with those for wheat used by the *prestini*, who consumed between 87,000 and 90,000 *moggia* each year.[19]

In truth, at least half of the cereals that came into the city and were baked in Milan did not go through the *Broletto* market. A further confirmation of this remarkable gap (hitherto curiously completely ignored) comes from data on wheat transported into Milan from July 1774 to March 1775. This amounts in fact to more than 107,000 *moggia*, a much greater number than what was sold in the *Broletto* market both in 1769 and in 1770.[20] If we consider that between April and June about 15–20% of the yearly wheat production was sold, in the agricultural year (July 1774–June 1775) one should register a transportation into Milan of over 130,000 more *moggia* of wheat. This represents at least 50% more than what was usually sold in the regulated market. And this is without counting illegal transportation, estimated at the time to be in the order of 10–15% of what entered the city according to the rules and regulations in force. There is therefore no doubt that in the Milanese case there was a consistent gap between the consumption of cereals and the quantities sold in the *Broletto* market. It is hence necessary to try to explain this discrepancy by focusing first and foremost on the supply routes: this brings attention to the presence of extra-urban markets, of different kinds of demand, and of many other protagonists.

2.5 Other Supply Routes, Alternative to the *Broletto* Market

One first aspect to stress is that a significant part of the cereals produced in the lower plains south of Milan was sold within large farms. These crops were the result of the most productive and advanced agricultural techniques at the time. Cereals brokers and other protagonists of the cereal-chain were those who went "to the tenant farmers' houses to negotiate and purchase any sort of crops".[21] They would then take the cereals to Milan, where they could sell them, often right outside the *Broletto* market, as well as "along the shore of this city's *Naviglio Maggiore*, where there are a good number of places called *sostre,* where cereals belonging to different merchants are stored to be sold to city's buyers, especially flour sellers and *prestinari*".[22] Many *prestinari* had begun to purchase large quantities of cereals directly from the producers, then asking for permission to transport them into the city.[23] This opportunity was originally granted only during critical harvest years, but it eventually became standard practice after 1602. As a result, in 1604 it was claimed that: "many merchants withdrew from that exercise, nor do they carry as abundant a quantity of cereals as they used to carry", precisely because many *prestinari* now "do by themselves or go through their own cereals agents".[24]

A difficult to quantify, but certainly not negligible part of the cereals produced, remained in the State's rural areas. This was due to significant self-consumption, but also to the presence of numerous authorised markets in the State of Milan. The number of markets increased further after the establishment of eleven new ones, which became operational in 1779.[25] Around Milan, there were about thirty markets serving approximately 950,000 inhabitants, and the criterion that guided their distribution was that of distance between one market and the other.[26] If we consider the entire State, there were a total of about forty markets, or one every 200 square kilometres. However, in actuality their concentration was much greater, because in the mountainous areas and within a radius of about 20 kilometres around Milan there were not any other cereals markets. It should also be noted that the exchange routes that supplied these markets did not interfere with the supply of Milan. This was because in the suburban markets, in areas where diet differed from that of the capital city, maize sales prevailed. In Milan the consumption of wheat accounted for more than 80% of the total. In Como, a much smaller city near the mountains, the consumption of wheat was in normal years just below 50% of the total. Maize made up the difference, particularly in bad harvest years.[27] In the State's mountainous and rural communities, it was normal to find places where 80–90% of cereals consumption was maize.[28]

However, if we analyse markets and exchanges, we cannot limit ourselves to wholesale sales such as those that occurred in the *Broletto* market. It is necessary to also consider the much more pervasive retail sales system. These were the prerogative of the grocers (*postari*), and their presence was very widespread inside and outside large cities.[29] Milan was no exception, considering that in 1795 there were 116 grocers. It is not surprising that, in a year of high prices such as 1773, the producers of mixed-cereals bread accused grocers of buying the cereals brought into the city only to store them and then resell them "second hand at ever increasing prices".[30] Grocers could however also resell products purchased from the *prestinari*. In an appeal dated 1791, grocers denounced the attempt "to return to the ancient jurisdiction of the *prestinari*, by not allowing them [grocers] to enjoy the freedom to profit from their talents and make purchases from the eighteen *prestinari*".[31]

2.6 A Fundamental Dimension: Actors and Institutions outside the Marketplace

This overview shows that there were different supply and market dimensions, each responding to different needs and concerned with different types of goods. A full reconstruction including them all would not however be complete without understanding the fundamental role played by those social groups and institutions that did not need to pass through the *Broletto* market: large landowners, monasteries, pious institutions, hospitals, etc. These individuals and organisations clearly represented a substantial share of the Milanese population, and they bought their supplies autonomously. If we compare the data available on transactions at the *Broletto* market with the data on city consumption, it is clear that the regulated marketplace supplied less than 60% of the city's inhabitants.[32] Even in the absence of specific studies on the subject, it is sufficient to consider some data in order to delineate the contours and the significance of this phenomenon. In the last decade of the eighteenth century over 1,500 nobles and rentiers lived in Milan (and therefore at least 7,000 people if we consider their families) with more than 5,000 servants, staff, lackeys, etc., while the clergy (despite the drastic downsizing imposed by Emperor

Joseph II), still amounted to approximately 3,500 individuals.[33] We are dealing with almost 20,000 individuals who depended on people being able to deliver their cereals directly to the *prestinari*, who would then supply the so-called *pane di fornitura*.[34] These same people could also afford to consume more bread than the vast majority of the population.

For example, the data available regarding food supply and nuns point to a level of wheat consumption close to 3 *moggia* per capita, almost twice the city's average. This is however also partly due to the fact that bread would be offered to visitors.[35] Moreover, in many convents there were more cereals available than those strictly necessary for the sustenance of the clergy. This fact is confirmed, as we know that during years of bad harvests convents were one of the first places officials sent by the *vicario di provvisione* (literally, 'provisions vicar') would go, in order to find stored cereals.[36] This was even more the case for nobles and rentiers. In particular, the Milanese aristocracy was forced to adopt expensive standards of living for social reasons. They would enjoy very high food consumption levels due to the great frequency of banquets, each with several dozen diners. Suffice it to say, for instance, that in 1520 the Trivulzio family alone purchased 1,061 *brente* of wine, equalling a consumption of over 200 litres a day, and almost 1,000 *moggia* of wheat, equivalent to three times the daily consumption of the entire city of Milan.[37]

There were also thousands of individuals receiving donations in-kind from the widespread welfare institutions of Milan, above all from the pious institutions. To understand the work of these institutions, it is important to note that in 1784 the owners of the *Luogo Pio della Misericordia*, the *Luogo Pio di Loreto*, and the *Luogo Pio delle Quattro Marie* also owned 4,395 hectares of land, and in several cases the tenants paid their rent in-kind. This allowed the institutions to help others with bread, wine, and other food supplies.[38] At the same time, pious institutions bought on the open market large quantities of cereals, which they would then bake, distributing the resulting bread to thousands of needy people. There were many people in terrible economic conditions. Their ranks would swell into the tens of thousands during times of crisis, such as during the 1576–1577 plague epidemic.[39] Even in the absence of comprehensive overall data, it is entirely plausible that pious institutions produced thousands of *moggia* of bread per year. We know that in a period without any serious economic problems such as 1763, the *Luogo Pio della Misericordia* alone distributed over 1,000 *moggia* of food: 367 *moggia* of white bread, 308 of mixed-cereals bread, and 390 of rice. During Christmas that same year they delivered white bread for 22,240 people.[40] Confirmation of this comes also from an estimate of the *Giunta d'Annona* ('*Annona* Board') reporting that in 1765, in order to satisfy the food demand of the clergy and the pious institutions, as many as 21,140 *moggia* of wheat per year[41] were necessary.

Similar considerations can be made regarding the *Ospedale Maggiore* ('Primary Hospital'), which in the 1930s was still the largest landowner in Lombardy. It owned over 9,000 hectares of land, 6,700 of which were farmed, and most of which were located in the irrigated plain.[42] The hospital, which housed and fed a very large number of individuals, was for centuries the largest in Europe and it represented an actual 'city within the city'. It also had flour mills for bread production. As early as the sixteenth century, this institution bought 5,600 *moggia* of cereals and 5,500 *brente* of wine, as well as meat, cheese, and eggs, to feed its patients.[43] These quantities grew even more as the institution was enlarged in the seventeenth and eighteenth centuries. The hospital hosted more than 2,000 people a day during the most crowded times in the twenty years between 1780 and 1799, with an average of over 23,000 patients hospitalised each year.[44] We cannot forget other welfare and support institutions within this very multifarious picture: hospitals, orphanages, mental hospitals (the *Senavra*), and prisons, all of which housed and fed several hundred people.[45] This great plurality of subjects and institutions operated outside the regulated *Broletto* market, using cereals coming from their extremely rich land properties or purchased directly in the places of production: they integrated the *Annona* and worked as a fundamental cog in the machinery of social and economic safety nets.

2.7 The Milanese *Annona* and Its Organisation

Indeed, while the regulated market fed approximately 60,000–70,000 people, the rest of the population depended, to a very large extent, on alternative distribution dimensions. These constituted a very effective, flexible, and dynamic victualling system. The Milanese administrative structure was made complex by the fact that, at the end of the Visconti-Sforza period, Lombardy found itself in a very difficult political position. It was divided into two parts and it ended up in a peripheral position when compared to the power centres that controlled it during the Early Modern Age: Venice in the eastern part; Madrid first, and Vienna later, in the western part. Milan was exceptional also because it continued to be one of the major European cities throughout the Early Modern Age, despite "it being located in the plains, its court being small, there being no sea nor river for trade, and it being the capital of a small state", as was pointed out by a keen seventeenth-century observer.[46] This had been possible because local leaders were able to protect and defend their own interests and autonomy in the face of loose political dependence. In other words, the wise strategy of the local elites granted the Lombard ruling class "its own sphere of civil, administrative, welfare, economic and class relations, removed from the occupier's non-mediated interference".[47]

Exemplary in this regard is the control exercised by the Milanese aristocracy on the most important political and economic areas of the State of Milan. This was successfully preserved until the period just before the French age, despite repeated attempts by the central power to be kept in the loop. The elites also had a hand in the choices in fiscal policy and in the management of public debt.[48] This ability to maintain control also included the victualling administration, a fundamental area where the demands of the central government and those of the city's offices often held overlapping jurisdictions.[49] Although the city's Senate had a regulatory function in this matter, it was rarely consulted in the definition of provisions. This left ample room for the action of the *Magistrato Straordinario*, who, after the closing of the *Magistrato delle Biade* ('Crops Magistracy') in the mid-sixteenth century, found itself at the top of the administrative structure of the *Annona*, with jurisdiction over the entire State. A dense network of administrative and judicial relations then linked the *Magistrato Straordinario* to the *vicario di provvisione*, to the *Tribunale di Provvisione* ('Provisions Tribunal'), and to the *giudice delle vettovaglie* ('victuals judge')—who all had the burden of guaranteeing the food supply for Milanese citizens—and to a whole series of lesser offices which managed the *Annona* machinery.[50] Milan was hence characterised by a clear duality between city and state victualling bodies, which generated a constant duplication and overlapping of competencies, resulting in strong conflict.

With the 1563 decree by Philip II of Spain, the *Magistrato Straordinario* had been commissioned to supervise and adjudicate the "preservation of public abundance", and it dealt in particular with regulating the transportation of crops into the city.[51] Twenty officials were part of this office, from the treasurer to the four porters. Eventually numerous commissioners and counter-writers were added, as appointed by the *Magistrato Straordinario*. The *capitani dello sfroso* ('contraband captains') and their officers resided in the various provinces. In smaller towns, local officials were in charge of the victualling administration: podestas, *sindaci*, and consuls, according to local custom.[52] The importance of the *Magistrato Straordinario* increased over the course of the seventeenth century, to the detriment of the city's *Tribunale di Provvisione*, which had become merely a consultation and execution body.[53] The latter, composed of the *vicario di provvisione* and twelve officials (the *dodici di provvisione*, 'the provisioning twelve'), was a stronghold of the Milanese aristocracy and had responsibilities that were not limited to the city, but extended to the surrounding countryside.[54] In addition to administrative tasks, the *vicario di provvisione* also had the power to issue edicts, proclamations (*grida*), and ordinances, which along with the city's statutes constituted the regulatory framework of the Milanese *Annona*.[55]

The *vicario* and the *dodici di provvisione* entrusted the material execution of their decisions to the *giudice delle vettovaglie*, who was elected for a one-year term and was supported by the *ufficiali alle cobbie* (literally, 'officials for barges', meaning the barges by which wares were transported on the city's canals). The *giudice di provvisione* had both administrative and judicial tasks. These were: following the harvest's progress, searching houses to verify the presence of illegal wheat stores, watching over the export of provisions from the city, inspecting *prestini*, and stamping out fraud during production. But, above all, the *giudice delle vettovaglie* had to be watchful of the prices of cereals charged by the *prestinari* during the week, find out from every *prestinaro* the exact price of the cereals they would buy per day and the quantity they would have, and then be present at the *Camera delli Malossari de' Grani* (literally, 'Chamber of the Cereals Brokers') every Saturday.[56] The *vicario di provvisione*, the *dodici di provvisione*, and the *giudice delle vettovaglie* sat at the helm of the *Camera del Broletto Nuovo* ('Chamber of the New *Broletto*'). This office set the *meta* (literally, 'limit') of bread and flour, that is to say, the minimum weight of the loaves to be sold for a fixed price and the maximum price of flour. For this purpose, they made use of the surveys made by the *malossari*, the public brokers. The *malossari* supervised wheat trades in the *Broletto* market and would then report each signed contract to the *Camera del Broletto Nuovo*.

Starting from the mid-seventeenth century, this highly fractured scenario changed even further due to the growing importance of the *Giunta d'Annona*. This institution was created during the dramatic 1628 crisis: it began by meeting every week with the participation of the heads of the central administration and the city's administration. This was "a collegial body, composed of the governor (or the grand chancellor on his behalf), the president and one or two members of the Senate, the president of the *Magistrato Ordinario* and that of the *Magistrato Straordinario*, the *vicario di provvisione*, the royal lieutenant, and the *giudice delle vettovaglie* of Milan".[57] Later on, during the Austrian domination, numerous intellectuals, including Gian Rinaldo Carli, Pietro Verri, and Cesare Beccaria, addressed the issue of the reorganisation of the *Annona*. In 1749, the *Magistrato Camerale* (literally, 'Chamber Magistracy') took the place of the *Magistrato Ordinario* and *Straordinario*, receiving from Vienna even greater supervisory authority over the administration of the victualling system and over law-breach prevention. This authority came with increased intervention by the governor and the State plenipotentiary in all matters regarding victualling, confirming the political importance of this subject.[58] The *Magistrato Camerale* moreover often found itself in disagreement with the *Tribunale di Provvisione*, as the *Magistrato* was the bearer of requests for liberalisation coming from Vienna, while the *Tribunale* maintained a much more conservative position.

2.8 A Key Point: Price Fixing

Faced with such an articulated and complex institutional framework, and a peculiar economic and social reality, it is important to investigate what relationships existed between the victualling administration and the processes of circulation of goods, including the market. To do this, however, it is necessary to forget a static description, adopting instead a dynamic perspective that takes into account cyclical variables and that considers what happened in the years of scarcity as well as how abundance was managed. An excellent litmus test in this regard is the meeting point between victualling policies, and the market as represented by the fixing of the *mete* of cereals prices.[59] Indeed one of the most controversial issues in the literature concerning the victualling policies is whether the *mete* were set *a priori* (in an attempt to reconcile the two opposite poles of the maximisation of land revenue versus the maximisation of bread weight), or if instead they reflected market trends.[60]

In Milan but also in many other Italian and European cities, the majority of wheat was publicly traded. This took place in one single central place: the *Broletto Nuovo* market, where sellers from the surrounding countryside arrived with their loads of wheat.[61] The wheat transported into the *Broletto* enclosure could not be withdrawn until the sale of the sacks was completed. These sacks consisted only of commercial wheat conforming to precise hygienic and qualitative standards. According to the *Statuta victualium Civitatis et Ducatis Mediolani* ('Victuals statutes of the City and Duchy of Milan') of the Visconti age, still in force in the Spanish and Austrian periods, only large-grain cereals (wheat, rye, millet) were allowed in the *Broletto* market. Starting from 1717 maize was added. As for flour, it was forbidden to bring pre-mixed flours into the market. The *malossari* played a central role in the negotiations. They had to deposit in escrow "a bail of 1,000 *scudi*, renewable every two years".[62] They would be present at the *Broletto* market from morning until nightfall, receiving samples from sellers in order to show them to potential buyers. Once the price was agreed upon, the *malossaro* witnessed the weighing of the sacks and recorded the names of the parties, the prices paid, and the quantities and the quality of the cereals sold. This information was reported every single day in order to set the *mete* of flours and of the various types of bread.[63] To allow the authorities to monitor their activities, the *malossari* were required to fill out four different reports.[64]

Aldo De Maddalena stated that "in the State of Milan, the victualling regulation was implemented with protectionist and socio-political purposes. This, however, did not prevent the bodies in charge of the victualling administration from adapting the norms to the objective conditions of the market, so that the *mete* were set only once the prices paid had become clear".[65] It appears however that the historian did not fully appreciate the significance of the important change occurring in 1602, when the *prestinari* were suddenly allowed to "buy from anywhere [and therefore also outside the *Broletto* market] any quantity of wheat to supply their *prestini*".[66] This development favoured merchants, *prestinari*, and landowners. The former two made their purchases in the places of production at low prices and then registered in the *Broletto* market the highest prices, while landowners could sell their cereals at very profitable prices. This was a widespread practice. For instance, in 1629, someone wrote to the *Magistrato Straordinario* the following report: "if we do not limit the opportunity for the *prestinari* to buy wheat, they will end up making the prices". And they indeed had the power to do so: "if a gentleman wants to sell his wheat at a higher price than the current, [the *prestinaro* can] come to an understanding with him; when the *prestinaro* goes and buys wheat at the market, he will pay for one or two *moggia* of wheat at that agreed upon price and everyone else will follow".[67]

One may wonder if this state of affairs (allowing advantages for merchants, *prestinari*, and landowners) was the real reason why it had always proved impossible to build an important public wheat warehouse in Milan, which would have moderated market prices. In this regard, the words of the *vicario di provvisione* are very important. In 1679 he opposed the government's attempt to impose upon owners the obligation to store their wheat in a public warehouse. The reasoning was that this would have meant "depriving the owner of his free will to sell, consume in his own home, pay for or consume, that wheat in his own way". Such a measure would have been detrimental not only to the owners' freedom but also "prejudicial to the masses, because they do not have ways of making money, and they cannot therefore afford to shop. The masses are fed in this manner, and if they stop working and trading, bread would run out altogether, and greater disorder would ensue".[68] The great ability of the Milanese elite in resisting external interventions became again apparent a century later, when Kaunitz and Firmian agreed on the advantages in the establishment of a large public wheat warehouse in Milan, considering it the ideal tool to moderate prices and fight famines. They found no one in the city willing to engage in the enterprise.[69]

2.9 Crisis Management

There was always the problem of how to protect the low-income segment of the population, particularly wage earners, who were the largest buyers of the *pane da numero*, when prices became high. Even then, however, price increases were managed in such a manner that it did not create any downsides for those who controlled the *Annona* and the city's supply. It has already been pointed out that during the most serious crises the intervention of pious institutions intensified. These institutions were firmly in the hands of the Milanese elite, who could thus extend their own networks and control on the city. On the other hand, the obligation to sell bread at a lower price did not create any disadvantage for the *prestinari*, because they knew that they would then be reimbursed by the Treasury. It is also significant to note that, even in this case, the Milanese elite managed to charge the Treasury for the cost of this project. The justification being that "it is the Government that keeps the price of bread low in order to keep the people happy. Therefore, it was up to the Treasury to reimburse the loss incurred by the *prestinari* and by the City".[70]

Taking this public intervention into due account is of particular importance, especially if we want to dwell on living standards. If we believe that living conditions are fundamental, it is not the wholesale prices of cereals that matters, but rather the cost of bread.[71] It is a well-known fact that dealing with Europe in the Early Modern Age, it is almost impossible to automatically convert the price of cereals into the cost of bread, precisely because of the existence of victualling systems.[72] This is especially true when market values rose, because it was precisely in those situations that the authorities intervened with price control. In the years 1773–1774 bad harvests caused a large increase in the prices of wheat and maize in Milan: they almost doubled in price compared to 1772.[73] In May 1775 the city of Milan intervened to mend the situation, pending the outcome of the new harvest. It paid the *prestinari* to continue selling wheat flour for 6 *lire correnti* and 4 *soldi* per *staio*, even though the price had risen to 6 *lire* and 14 *soldi*. At the same time, it allocated 35,000 *lire* to be paid to the *prestinari* to maintain a stable weight of 3.5 *once* for each *soldo* of bread, while on the basis of market prices it should have been 3 *once*.[74] The Milanese case was not exceptional. Turin, for example, also had to face the bad harvests of the early 1770s. In 1773 the city bought up 44,537 Turinese *sacchi* of cereals, selling them to the public at much lower market prices, losing 220,000 Piedmont *lire*. Later, it bought another 40,000 *sacchi* and distributed them to bakers at the fixed price of 4 *lire* and 3 *soldi* per *emina*, with a further loss of 250,000 *lire*. Furthermore, they allocated 39,000 *lire* to be repaid to the *prestinari* for the block enforced on low-quality bread.[75]

2.10 Conclusions

The great influence exercised by the elites, and their control over the *Tribunale di Provvisione*, put Milan in a very special position: this is clearly evident from a collection of printed documents related to deeds (drawn up between 10 October 1725 and 28 August 1727, but referring to a period that began in 1629), entitled *Alcuni papeli concernenti la materia delle vittovaglie, massime del pane venale* ('Certain papers concerning the subject of victuals, and especially of bread for sale').[76] The *Tribunale di Provvisione* found itself in a clear conflict of interest. It had to reconcile the divergent interests of *prestinari* and consumers, as well as those of its own members (who were only interested in the sale of wheat), and those of the owners of the bakeries leased to the *prestinari*. The breaking point was reached in 1766, when the Austrian government ordered the transfer of the financial management of the thirteen *prestini* from the *Banco di Sant'Ambrogio* ('St. Ambrose Bank', the public bank of the State of Milan) to the *Magistrato Camerale*, in order to "remove all the reasons that could contribute to making the price of bread exorbitantly high".[77]

Particularly explicit in this regard was Kaunitz who, writing to Firmian about what he thought was a malfunctioning of the Milanese *Annona*, attributed it to the fact that the *Tribunale di Provvisione* consisting "exclusively of patricians, who are driven, naturally, more by private interest than by patriotism".[78] These same elites also controlled the very powerful *Banco di Sant'Ambrogio*, a central institution in the financial and fiscal structure of the city, that gradually gained control of the most profitable municipal taxes and duties, including those related to bread-making. In 1662, the Municipality put the *Banco* in charge of the financial administration of ordinary real estate taxes, and the indirect taxes and duties on coal, meat, wine, poultry, and olive oil sales, and on cereals milling. These taxes and duties, in 1670, guaranteed in total an annual income of almost 900,000 Milanese *lire correnti*.[79] Then, in 1706, the same bank took over the tender for the thirteen *prestini*, and the collection of the tax of 2 *lire* for each *moggio* of wheat utilised.[80]

It is clear that, in such a situation, the opposition between victualling administration and the free market is a gross simplification. If on the one hand the *Annona* certainly reflected market logics and prices, it was on the other hand also a functional tool for the interests of the Milanese ruling elites. During the course of the Early Modern Age, these elites increasingly moved towards land ownership. Moreover, as we have endeavoured to show, the *Annona* and the regulated market in Milan were only a single cog, albeit a relevant one, in a much more complex machinery, composed of different markets and protagonists. We still need to understand if such a complex and particular supply structure was a Milanese prerogative, and whether that depended on the specific economic context of the State of Milan and its degree of development, or if it was instead a more generalised situation. Only a systematic comparison with other case studies would make it possible to draw conclusions in this regard.

Notes

1. Corritore (2012, p. 6). Here and below, all translations of original documents and works quoted are the authors'.
2. Parziale (2009, pp. 13–23).

3. This aspect is particularly clear in the Bolognese case, masterfully reconstructed by Alberto Guenzi (1982, pp. 4–12).
4. Mocarelli (2015, pp. 39–63).
5. In order to guarantee favourable prices for the owners even in the good harvest years, Venetian authorities in the eighteenth century decided to allocate the cereals surplus to the production of biscuits for the fleet (Vertecchi 2009, pp. 47–85).
6. The urbanisation rate of the Lombard area was over 20% higher. Almost double compared to the European average of the period, estimated in the order of 11.5% (Bairoch 1985, p. 230).
7. The State of Milan lost its independence in 1535. It was subjected to Spain from 1535 to 1706, to Austria from 1706 to 1733, to Piedmont from 1733 to 1736, to Austria again from 1736 to 1796. During the Napoleonic era, Milan was the capital city of the Transpadane Republic (1796–1797), the Cisalpine Republic (1797–1802), the Italian Republic (1802–1805), and the Kingdom of Italy (1805–1814).
8. Data on the surface area of the State and its population are derived from Romani (1949–1950, pp. 25, 43). Such data do not consider the territory around Mantua, as this was ultimately incorporated in the State of Milan only in 1785. In 1791 this territory had approximately 180,000 inhabitants in 1,984 square kilometres, 25,000 of whom were located in the city of Mantua.
9. Romani (1949–1950, p. 48). The highest population density levels were: 181 inhabitants per square kilometre in the rural district (*territorio*) of Como, 171 in that of Pavia (*principato*), and 169 in that of Lodi (*contado*). A level below 100 inhabitants per square kilometre could be observed only in the mountainous areas: the rural district (*contado*) of Como and the Val d'Intelvi (65 and 43 respectively).
10. Romani (1949–1950, p. 34). 23% was occupied by mountainous areas, and another 13% by hilly areas. In Belgium, on the other hand, in 1800 there were 41.9 inhabitants per square kilometre (Malanima 2002, p. 30).
11. Mocarelli (2001, pp. 67–81).
12. In a letter to Carlo Giuseppe of Firmian, plenipotentiary and governor general of Austrian Lombardy on 23 May 1774, the Austrian State chancellor and minister of foreign affairs, Wenzel Anton of Kaunitz-Rietberg observed that local cereals production covered the needs of the State of Milan only for thirteen and a half months, then adding: "I would have thought Lombardy's harvests to be more plentiful, as the land is known to be so fertile" ("io avrei ritenuto più ubertosi i raccolti della Lombardia, che ha il credito di essere tanto fertile in grani") (ASMI, ANPA, 33).
13. The *Broletto Nuovo* was the city hall, and the market in question took place in its courtyard.

14. Baldassarre Scorza was a Habsburg administration official in Lombardy. He was the author of the commercial budget of the State of Milan in 1778, the basis for the customs reform of Austrian Lombardy in 1786.
15. 1 Milanese *moggio* (plur. *moggia*) was divided into 8 *staia* and corresponded to approximately 146.23 cubic decimetres (Martini 1883, p. 350).
16. For a comment on Scorza's calculations, see Coppola (1982, pp. 135–136). On Cesare Beccaria, see Beccaria (1987, p. 406). Not unlike Scorza's proposal are the calculations of the *vicario di provvisione* regarding the consumption of bread in Milan: 319 *moggia* per day for white bread, and 69.6 for mixed-cereals bread (see his report dated 8 June 1773, in ASCMI, MA, 437). In the 1602 terms of understanding (ASMI, ANPA, 40), a per capita bread requirement of 25 *once* per day, corresponding to 246 kilos per year, was calculated (1 Milanese *oncia* ('ounce', plur. *once*) corresponded to approximately 27.23 grams, see Martini 1883, p. 351). The 1748 data are in annex D of the deliberation (*consulta*) of the *Magistrato Straordinario* dated 23 February (VBAMI, MS, L.42.inf.5).
17. The fact that almost everyone in Milan ate white bread, and that the use of lower-quality bread could not be imposed, not even in orphanages, seemed inconceivable to Kaunitz: see his harsh note, dated 7 March 1785, in response to a deliberation sent by Beccaria on 19 January, where he claimed that in Milan 90 people out of 100 consumed white bread (ASMI, ANPA, 39bis). It was so difficult to sell second-class bread (in printed regulations for the sale of second-rate bread in Milan from 1768 to 1770, its production was suspended "considering the lack of participation by the people" ("attesa la poca concorrenza del popolo"), see ASMI, ANPA, 40), that selling third-class bread was practically impossible. With regard to the countryside, we reference the incomplete documentation produced by the investigation carried out in a year of bad harvests, 1769, to learn about the production, consumption, and stocks of cereals in the parish churches of the State of Milan (ASCMI, MA, 437).
18. The data for 1769 and 1770 are found in ASCMI, MA, 438–439.
19. In 1759 they used 89,500 *moggia* (ASCMI, MA, 702), while in the three-year period between 1777 and 1779 they used an average of 87,462 *moggia* per year (ASCMI, MA, 707). It should also be noted that the seventeen *prestini* present in 1779 (until 1771 there had been only thirteen) were obliged to keep stocks of cereals and flour for 21,000 *moggia* (see the 13 July 1779 *Specifica delle scorte de' frumenti in grana ed in farina esistenti presso li prestinari di questa città di Milano*, in ASCMI, MA, 437).

20. See *Tabella generale del frumento e della segale introdotta dalle porte e tomboni della Città di Milano dal primo luglio 1774 a tutto giugno 1775*, which, however, is available only until March 1775 (ASCMI, MA, 436).
21. "[A]lle case degli stessi fittabili, ed ivi accaparare e contratare qualunque sorte di granaglie" (it was reported by the merchants of rice, maize, and other cereals on 27 August 1771, see ASCMI, MA, 437).
22. "[L]ungo la riva del Naviglio Maggiore di questa città ove sono luoghi in buon numero che chiamano *sostre* ove si sogliono riporre i grani di diversi mercanti per andargli poi vendendo a' compratori della città et specialmente a' farinari et prestinari" (see the 16 July 1601 deliberation of the *vicario di provvisione*, in ASCMI, MA, 436). *Navigli* was the name of Milan's canals.
23. Many of the requests pertaining to the period 1773–1777 are found in ASCMI, MA, 436. This also made it possible to obtain much lower prices than those of the *Broletto* market. On 4 July 1773, for example, the San Lorenzo *prestinaro*, Carlo Tognetti, asked to transport into the city 180 *moggia* of wheat. He had bought this on 21 June from the *Luogo Pio della Misericordia* (literally, 'Pious Place of Mercy') of Milan, paying 27 Milanese *lire correnti* per *moggio*, when the price on the *Broletto* market exceeded 40 *lire*. In the Milanese monetary system of account, 1 *lira corrente* (plur. *lire correnti*) was divided into 20 *soldi*, and 1 *soldo* into 12 *denari*.
24. "[M]oltissimi mercanti si son ritirati da quell'esercitio né più conducono quella copia de grani che prima solevano condurre"; "fanno per se stessi o per mezzo di suoi agenti mercanzia di grani" (*Alcuni pregiudicii e aggravi che da i capitoli del dacio de' prestini risultavano al pubblico in materia del pane*, ASCMI, MA, 692).
25. The list, along with numerous observations, is found in Beccaria (1990, p. 546).
26. Aldo Carera pointed out that the minimum distance that would allow a market to thrive was 3 miles in the most populated areas, and 5 in the least populated areas (Carera 1990, p. 48). 1 Lombard mile (*miglio*, plur. *miglia*) corresponded to approximately 1,784.81 metres (Martini 1883, p. 350).
27. In the Como market during the good harvest years, wheat was between 45% and 48% of cereals sold. In bad years, wheat was only between 35% and 37% of the total (these data are taken from ASCO, ASC, 396–411, and refer to the period 1808–1834).
28. It is derived from the aforementioned 1769 inquiry on cereals production, consumption, and stocks of the State's parish churches. The *Magistrato Straordinario*, in the aforementioned 1748 deliberation, estimated a consumption of only 80,894 *moggia* of wheat for the Milanese rural district

(*contado*), versus 940,017 of other cereals: therefore, not even 8% of the total.

29. Suffice it to note that, for instance, in a relatively small town like Sant'Angelo Lodigiano there were fourteen grocers (Beccaria 1987, p. 148). The retail trade of cereals happened in grocers' shops, and with street vendors (see the report sent by Commissioner (*commissario*) Giuseppe Giuliani to the *Magistrato Camerale* on 11 June 1772, in ASMI, ANPA, 49).
30. "[P]er seconda mano a prezzi sempre maggiori" (the quotation is taken from their 15 June 1773 plea in ASCMI, MA, 437). The data regarding 1795 are from a register containing the professions and conditions of the Milanese population (ASMI, POPA, 15).
31. "[D]i far rivivere l'antico sistema di giurisdizione dei prestinari e quindi non potessero essi [i postari] più godere della libertà loro accordata di provvedersi a loro talento da qualunque dei diciotto prestinari di meta" (see the 21 October report signed by Bossi, a *delegato alle vettovaglie* ('delegate for victuals'), in ASMI, ANPA, 39bis).
32. From 100,000 *moggia* of wheat approximately 88,000 *moggia* of bread were obtained. At 1.6 *moggia* per person, this equals to approximately 55,000 inhabitants, to which we must add the few thousand individuals who consumed the mixed-cereals bread produced with the cereals sold on the *Broletto*. Those who purchased the bread subject to the official setting of minimum weight, the so-called *pane da numero* ('bread sold by number'), were fewer. This is because approximately 20% of the bread sold in the *prestini* was *pane da staro* ('bread sold by *staio*', the *staio* being the aforementioned measure of volume), which was stable in weight and variable in price; on the contrary, the *pane da numero* was stable in price and variable in weight (in this regard, compare the *Memoriale dei prestinai e risposta della città* from 1640 with *Discorso di Filippo Bianchi prestinaro sopra i prestini della città*—undated, but datable to a period between 1600 and 1610—in ASCMI, MA, 692).
33. In 1795 nobles and rentiers amounted to 1,580 individuals, whereas servants both male and female amounted to 4,103 (ASMI, POPA, 15). According to the population registries for 1796, members of the clergy amounted to 3,490 (ASMI, POPA, 15).
34. This was the name of the bread that the *prestinari* were obliged to produce using the cereals supplied by their customers. Confirming the importance of this practice, an estimate from the mid-eighteenth century equated the quantity of wheat bought on the *Broletto* market from *prestinari* and flour sellers to that supplied by private individuals, valuing it in both cases at about 105,000 *moggia* (ASMI, ANPA, 39).
35. The data on consumption by nunneries are taken from Aiello (1996, pp. 162–164). See also Parziale (2009, pp. 145–155).

36. On 5 June 1773, for example, the *vicario di provvisione* ordered that convents and homes be inspected to look for cereals in storage, pending the now inevitable price increase. A note dated 10 July says that 364 *moggia* of cereals had already been seized in the Milanese monasteries (ASCMI, MA, 437).
37. The data are taken from Parziale (2009, pp. 158, 181–182). If we consider an average consumption of 2 litres of wine per day and of 2 *moggia* of cereals per year, it is evident that the quantities consumed by the Trivulzio were sufficient to feed between 400 and 500 people.
38. The surface of the lands owned by pious institutions is reconstructed in detail in Aiello (2013, p. 42). Regarding rents received in-kind on the rented portions of land belonging to pious institutions, see instead Bellettati (2013b, pp. 451–457).
39. Bellettati (2013a, pp. 125–127).
40. The data are derived from the ledger of the pious institution, and refers to the period 1764–1772 (ALPEMI, 254, 274, 278). A confirmation of these quantities comes from the fact that in the first eight months of 1749 the same *Luogo Pio della Misericordia* distributed 692 *moggia* of bread and 552 *brente* of wine (Bellettati 2013a, p. 122). 1 Milanese *brenta* (plur. *brente*) corresponded to approximately 75.55 litres (Martini 1883, p. 351).
41. See the meeting of the *Giunta d'Annona* on 12 September (ASMI, ANPA, 30).
42. It was precisely 9,260 hectares, of which only 380 were uncultivated. Grassland instead occupied 1,250 hectares, and woods 900 hectares (Chiodi 1937, p. 15).
43. Parziale (2009, p. 173).
44. Ferrario (1840, vol. II, pp. 468–470).
45. In the period between 1773 and 1789, the city's only prison averaged 200 inmates a year, who manufactured rough canvases, ropes, and moleskin, with excellent economic results (see the report of the *delegati* of the prison on 15 November 1794, in ASMI, AGPA, 258).
46. "[S]ia situata in pianura, la sua corte sia piccola, sebbene né il mare né nessun fiume navigabile crei il suo commercio e sia infine capitale di uno Stato, che oggi è poca cosa" (it was observed by Gilbert Burnet in 1687, quotation from Gozzoli 1993, p. 1593).
47. Rumi (2003, p. 104).
48. In this regard, see Mocarelli (2005, pp. 177–186).
49. Regarding the organisational and institutional structure of the Milanese *Annona*, see Auciello (1995, vol. I, pp. 302–310); Parziale and Puccinelli (2012, pp. 133–142).
50. Parziale and Puccinelli (2012, p. 139).

51. "[C]onservazione della pubblica abbondanza"; regarding the powers of the *Magistrato Straordinario*, see Benaglio (1711).
52. Orefice (1995, pp. 658–679).
53. Since 1598 the *Magistrato Straordinario* had been given the task of executing the *grida delle introduzioni dei grani a Milano* ('proclamations on cereals transportation into Milan'), removing it from the *Tribunale di Provvisione*, as it can be drawn from ASMI, ANPA, 29.
54. Parziale (2009, pp. 25–26). As remarked by Salvatore Pugliese (1924, p. 134): "The actual development of all municipal affairs was in fact in the hands of an even smaller group, namely the *Tribunale di Provvisione*. It already existed in the municipal period, it was elected by 60 people, and was presided by the vicar. The court had various tasks, including the supervision of the collection and use of taxes and duties, the regulation of provision, maintaining stable prices, and also the control of municipal employees". In this regard, see also Visconti (1913, pp. 402–420); Santoro (1968, pp. 75–78).
55. On the powers of the *Tribunale di Provisione* regarding victualling, see *Sommario delli ordini pertinenti al Tribunale di Provisione* (1657, especially the articles *Delle biade, farine, malossari de' grani, misuratori e conducenti* and *Delli pani, prestinari e molinari*, pp. 21–45).
56. *Sommario delli ordini pertinenti al Tribunale di Provisione* (1657, pp. 171–172).
57. Orefice (1995, pp. 674–675).
58. Parziale and Puccinelli (2012, pp. 140–141). See also Grab (1986, pp. 20–21).
59. Regarding price trends of the main cereals in Milan in the seventeenth and eighteenth centuries, we are currently conducting an analysis from the following source: *Nota delli prezzi de' grani fatti da' farinari et prestinari della città di Milano nell'ufficio della Camera de' Malossari de' Grani nel Broletto Nuovo della medema città di mese in mese quanto sia dal'anno 1600 in avanti* (VBAMI, MS, G.135.suss., fos. 30r–123v).
60. Exemplary in this regard appears to be the case of the Roman *Annona*, masterfully reconstructed by Strangio (2015, pp. 79–85).
61. They were forbidden from selling goods along the roads or the canals, even though the regulations regarding victualling, starting from 1612, allowed flour sellers to make purchases in November within 12 miles of the city walls, as can be gleaned from *Sommario delli ordini pertinenti al Tribunale di Provisione* (1657).
62. De Maddalena (1949, pp. 36–37).
63. The compensation for the *malossari* was fixed in 2 *soldi* per contracted *moggia*, and these were charged one to the seller and the other to the

buyer, unless the sale was made for the public cereals warehouse (De Maddalena 1949, p. 37).

64. They were: the *Libro delle vendite atte per mezzo delli malossari* ('Book of sales brokered by *malossari*', meaning wholesale sales), where the *malossari* would "report daily on the cereals sold, recording prices, quantities and quality, as well as the names and surnames of both sellers and purchasers" ("giornalmente si scrivono li grani che per mano de' malossari si vend[ono], con il prezzo, e quantità, e qualità del grano, e il nome, e cognome de' compratori e venditori"); the *Libro de' grani che non fanno prezzo* ('Book of cereals exchanges not considered for calculating market prices'), recording the exchanges of low-quality (*non mercanteschi*, literally 'not commercial') cereals, excluded from the *Broletto* market; the *Libro del mercato* (retail sales 'Market book'), which reported daily on the retail *Broletto* market prices of wheat, rye, and millet, whose prices would be the real ones of the day as given by public market measurers; furthermore, a fourth book reporting faithfully the cereals brought into the *Broletto* market, carefully indicating the type and quantities (*Sommario delli ordini pertinenti al Tribunale di Provisione* 1657, p. 30).
65. De Maddalena (1949, p. 19).
66. "[C]omprare in qualunque luogo ogni quantità di fromento per fornitura delli loro prestini" (see the *prestini* contract specifications for the three-year period 1603–1605, in ASMI, ANPA, 40).
67. "[S]e non si limita la possibilità per i prestinari di comprar grano, finisce che son loro a fare i prezzi"; "volendo un gentilhuomo vendere il suo grano a maggior prezzo del corrente, [il prestinaro può] intendersi con esso e quando il prestinaro lo va a comprare al mercato, paga uno o due moggia a quel prezzo e tutti vanno dietro" (see the anonymous writing from November that year, in ASMI, ANPA, 29).
68. "[P]rivare il padrone del libero arbitrio di vendere, consumare in casa propria, dar in pagamento o consumare a suo modo tali grani"; "pregiudiziale al medesimo pubblico, perché non havendo li particolari forma di far denari non ponno di conseguenza fare le spese, con le quali viene alimentata tanta plebe, quale pur cessando i lavoreri e i traffici, gli cessa del tutto il pane, et invece di proporre un rimedio, si incontrerebbe un maggior disordine" (see his speech during the *Giunta d'Annona* on 18 May, in ASMI, ANPA, 30).
69. The correspondence in this regard between the two high officials covers the period April 1767–August 1768 and is preserved in ASMI, ANPA, 33.
70. "[E]ssendo propriamente il Governo, quello che fa tener bassa la meta del pane, a fine di tenere contento il popolo, per ciò il pregiuditio che deriva a' prestinari e alla Città, tocca al Regio Erario a risarcirlo" (this is how the

vicario di provvisione expressed himself in the 5 May 1709 meeting of the *Giunta d'Annona*, in ASMI, ANPA, 31).

71. See, for instance, Van Zanden (1999, pp. 175–197); Allen (2001, pp. 411–447); and, in a global and comparative perspective, Allen et al. (2011, pp. 8–38).
72. It is very clearly shown in the numerous cases presented in Marin and Virlouvet (2004).
73. Between July 1772 and June 1775, the price of wheat went from 27 to 48 *lire*, while that of maize grew from 21 to 37 *lire* (ASCMI, MA, 439).
74. See the 23 May meeting of the *Tribunale di Provvisione* (ASMI, UCPA, 137) and the 24 May meeting of the *Congregazione del Patrimonio* ('Congregation of the Estate') (ASMI, UCPA, 151). Even more important was the intervention carried out in 1800, when the prices of cereals reached the highest point of the 1700–1860 period, due to the combined effects of bad weather, bad harvests, and French requisitions. Once again, the city's administration intervened in order to keep bread prices below their market value, pledging to pay the difference to the *prestinari*. In this case, the outlay was 100,000 *lire*, which weighed on the budget of the municipality of Milan for over ten years (in this regard, see Mocarelli 2012, pp. 99–100).
75. ASTO, MESAA, 1 (12). 1 Turinese *sacco* (plur. *sacchi*) was divided into 5 *emine* and corresponded to approximately 115.03 cubic decimetres (Martini 1883, p. 785). In the Piedmont monetary system of account, 1 *lira* was divided into 20 *soldi*, and 1 *soldo* into 12 *denari*.
76. BNBMI, MS, 14.16.C.17/14, 14.16.C.17/15. Although the document is bound in a single tome, two different signatures can be found inside: 14.16.C.17/14 (pp. 1–46) and 14.16.C.17/15 (pp. 47–63). There are two little books in a slightly different format. It is clear, however, that the subject matter is the same. Indeed, in the case of pages 32–42 and pages 50–51 and 55–61, these are copies of the same deeds—albeit in different order—which explains the decision to bring them together under the same title.
77. "[T]ogliere tutti i motivi che potessero contribuire a rendere esorbitante a danno de' nostri sudditi il prezzo del pan venale" (the 9 June 1766 decision and the related documents are in ASMI, COPA, 68).
78. "[D]a' soli patrizi, guidati, com'è naturale, più dal privato interesse che dal patriotismo" (his 9 April 1767 letter is in ASMI, UCPA, 136).
79. In this regard, see Cova (1972, p. 265). In any case, transferring revenues to cover extraordinary expenses was a consolidated practice that did not concern the city of Milan alone, as evidenced by the documentation kept in ASMI, SD, 49. On 18 December 1626, for example, the Senate was asked to authorise "the ability to transfer or mortgage many rural revenues

for the sum of 600,887 *lire* to be paid for military housing" ("poter vendere o hipotecare tanti redditi rurali per la somma di lire 600,887 da erogarsi nelle spese dell'alloggio militare").

80. The transaction was concluded on 13 February and the expected proceeds of the concession were valued at over 90,000 *lire* per year (it is calculated from *31 maggio 1767. Titoli con i quali il Banco possiede li detti fondi*, in ASMI, COPA, 69). In this manner, the elites increased their control over the entire system, because the contract could be unilaterally cancelled by the bank (see the text of the contract between the *prestinari* and the *Congregazione* ('Congregation') of the *Banco* for the three-year period 1761–1763, in VBAMI, MS, S.140.inf.).

Archival Sources

Archivio dei Luoghi Pii Elemosinieri di Milano (ALPEMI)
www.lombardiabeniculturali.it/archivi/soggetti-conservatori/MIAA0002D2

Archivio di Stato di Como (ASCO)
Archivio Storico Civico (ASC).
www.archiviodistatocomo.beniculturali.it

Archivio di Stato di Milano (ASMI)
Affari giudiziari parte antica (AGPA).
Annona parte antica (ANPA).
Commercio parte antica (COPA).
Popolazione parte antica (POPA).
Senato deroghe (SD).
Uffici civici parte antica (UCPA).
www.archiviodistatomilano.beniculturali.it

Archivio di Stato di Torino (ASTO)
Materie economiche seconda addizione, *Annona* (MESAA).
https://archiviodistatotorino.beniculturali.it

Archivio Storico Civico, Milano (ASCMI)
Materie (MA).
https://trivulziana.milanocastello.it

Biblioteca Nazionale Braidense, Milano (BNBMI)
Manoscritti (MS).
www.braidense.it

Veneranda Biblioteca Ambrosiana, Milano (VBAMI)
Manoscritti (MS).
www.ambrosiana.it

Published Sources

Beccaria, Cesare. 1987. *Edizione nazionale delle opere di Cesare Beccaria*, dir. by Luigi Firpo. Vol. VI: Atti di governo (serie I: 1771–1777), ed. by Rosalba Canetta. Milano: Mediobanca.

———. 1990. *Edizione nazionale delle opere di Cesare Beccaria*, dir. by Luigi Firpo and Gianni Francioni. Vol. VII: Atti di governo (serie II: 1778–1783), ed. by Rosalba Canetta. Milano: Mediobanca.

Benaglio, Giuseppe. 1711. *Relazione istorica del Magistrato delle Ducali Entrate Straordinarie nello Stato di Milano*. Milano: Marc'Antonio Pandolfo Malatesta.

Sommario delli ordini pertinenti al Tribunale di Provisione della città, et ducato di Milano, cominciato l'anno 1580, successivamente ampliato nel 1613 et finalmente perfettionato nell'anno 1657 con aggionta delli ordini seguiti sino al presente. 1657. Milano: Giulio Cesare Malatesta.

References

Aiello, Lucia. 1996. *I monasteri femminili di clausura nella Milano del Seicento (demografia, economia, problemi)*. Tesi di dottorato in storia economica e sociale, VII ciclo. Milano: Università Commerciale 'Luigi Bocconi'.

———. 2013. Introduzione al patrimonio fondiario dei Luoghi Pii Elemosinieri dal medioevo all'età moderna. In Aiello et al. 2013, 34–46.

Aiello, Lucia, Marco Bascapè, and Sergio Rebora, eds. 2013. *Il paese dell'acqua. I Luoghi Pii Elemosinieri di Milano e le loro terre: un itinerario nel paesaggio dal medioevo ai giorni nostri*. Como: Nodolibri.

Allen, Robert Carson. 2001. The great divergence in European wages and prices from the Middle Ages to the First World War. *Explorations in Economic History* 38 (4): 411–447.

Allen, Robert Carson, Jean-Pascal Bassino, Debin Ma, Christine Moll-Murata, and Jan Luiten Van Zanden. 2011. Wages, prices and living standards in China, 1738–1925: In comparison with Europe, Japan and India. *The Economic History Review* 64 (s1): 8–38.

Auciello, Fiammetta. 1995. Le istituzioni annonarie nello Stato di Milano fra Seicento e Settecento: gli sfrosi. In *Gli archivi per la storia dell'alimentazione* 1995, vol. I, 302–310.

Bairoch, Paul. 1985. *De Jéricho à Mexico. Villes et économie dans l'histoire*. Paris: Gallimard.

Bairoch, Paul, Jean Batou, and Pierre Chèvre. 1988. *La population des villes européennes. Banque des données et analyse sommaire des résultats, 800–1850*. Genève: Droz.

Bellettati, Daniela. 2013a. Dalla terra alla tavola. Un circuito virtuoso. In Aiello et al. 2013, 122–133.

———. 2013b. Il podere Niguarda, dispensa alimentare per la carità milanese. In Aiello et al. 2013, 451–457.

Carera, Aldo. 1990. I mercati della tradizione. In *I mercati e le fiere della provincia di Milano tra XVIII e XX secolo*, ed. by Maria Piera Bassi, 17–61. Milano: Provincia di Milano.

Chiodi, Cesare. 1937. *La proprietà terriera dell'Ospedale Maggiore di Milano. I progetti di bonifica edilizia ed idraulica.* Milano: Consiglio degli Istituti Ospitalieri di Milano.

Coppola, Gauro. 1982. Il commercio estero dei prodotti agricoli e lo sviluppo dell'agricoltura in età teresiana. In *Economia, istituzioni, cultura in Lombardia nell'età di Maria Teresa*, ed. by Aldo De Maddalena, Ettore Rotella, and Gennaro Barbarisi. Vol. I: Economia e società, 133–155. Bologna: il Mulino.

Corritore, Renzo Paolo. 2012. Un problema negletto. Per un riesame della questione annonaria nelle città di antico regime. *Storia Urbana* 36 (1/134): 5–9.

Cova, Alberto. 1972. *Il Banco di S. Ambrogio nell'economia milanese dei secoli XVII e XVIII.* Milano: Giuffrè.

De Maddalena, Aldo. 1949. *Prezzi e aspetti di mercato in Milano durante il secolo XVII.* Milano: Malfasi.

Ferrari, Maria Luisa, and Manuel Vaquero Piñeiro, eds. 2015. *"Moia la carestia". La scarsità alimentare in età preindustriale.* Bologna: il Mulino.

Ferrario, Giuseppe. 1840. *Statistica medica di Milano dal secolo XV fino ai nostri giorni.* Milano: Guglielmini e Redaelli.

Gli archivi per la storia dell'alimentazione. 1995. Roma: Ministero per i Beni Culturali e Ambientali, Ufficio Centrale per i Beni Archivistici.

Gozzoli, Maria Cristina. 1993. Milano nelle descrizioni dei viaggiatori stranieri. In *Storia illustrata di Milano*, ed. by Franco Della Peruta. Vol. V: Milano moderna, 1581–1600. Milano: Sellino.

Grab, Alexander I. 1986. *La politica del pane. Le riforme annonarie in Lombardia nell'età teresiana e giuseppina.* Milano: Angeli.

Guenzi, Alberto. 1982. *Pane e fornai a Bologna in età moderna.* Venezia: Marsilio.

Malanima, Paolo. 1998. Italian cities 1300–1800. A quantitative approach. *Rivista di Storia Economica*, new series 14 (2): 91–126.

———. 2002. *L'economia italiana. Dalla crescita medievale alla crescita contemporanea.* Bologna: il Mulino.

Marin, Brigitte, and Catherine Virlouvet, eds. 2004. *Nourrir les cités de Méditerranée. Antiquité-Temps modernes.* Paris: Maisonneuve et Larose/Aix-en-Provence: Maison Méditerranéenne des Sciences de l'Homme/Madrid: Universidad Nacional de Educación a Distancia.

Martini, Angelo. 1883. *Manuale di metrologia, ossia misure, pesi e monete in uso attualmente e anticamente presso tutti i popoli.* Torino: Loescher.

Mocarelli, Luca. 2001. Alle radici di un successo economico: l'area regionale lombarda in età moderna. *Geschichte und Region* 10 (1): 67–81.

———. 2005. The economy of a political periphery: Lombardy in a period of transition during the seventeenth and eighteenth centuries. In *Zones of fracture in modern Europe: The Baltic countries, the Balkans, and Northern Italy/Zone di frattura in epoca moderna: il Baltico, i Balcani e l'Italia settentrionale*, ed. by Almut Bues, 177–186. Wiesbaden: Harrassowitz.

———. 2012. Le crisi alimentari nello Stato di Milano tra metà Settecento e Restaurazione: una realtà di eccezione? In *Krisen: Ursachen, Deutungen und Folgen/Crises: causes, interprétations et conséquences*, ed. by Thomas David, Jon Mathieu, Janick Marina Schaufelbuehl, and Tobias Straumann, 97–109. Zurich: Chronos.

———. 2015. Ripensare le crisi alimentari: lo Stato di Milano nel secondo Settecento. In Ferrari and Vaquero Piñeiro 2015, 39–63.

Orefice, Isabella. 1995. La politica del pane a Milano fra XVI e XVIII secolo. In *Gli archivi per la storia dell'alimentazione* 1995, vol. I, 658–679.

Parziale, Lavinia. 2009. *Nutrire la città. Produzione e commercio alimentare a Milano tra Cinque e Seicento*. Milano: Angeli.

Parziale, Lavinia, and Elena Puccinelli. 2012. Un percorso tra le fonti per la storia dell'alimentazione e dell'approvvigionamento alimentare: le carte del fondo Annona dell'Archivio di Stato di Milano. *Storia Urbana* 36 (1/134): 133–142.

Pugliese, Salvatore. 1924. *Condizioni economiche e finanziarie della Lombardia nella prima metà del secolo XVIII*. Torino: Bocca.

Romani, Mario. 1949–1950. *Un secolo di vita economica lombarda, 1748–1848. Introduzione e parte prima*. Milano: Vita e Pensiero.

Rumi, Giorgio. 2003. La Lombardia: ragioni e limiti della scelta unitaria. In *Storia della Lombardia*, ed. by Livio Antonielli and Giorgio Chittolini. Vol. II: Dal Seicento a oggi, 101–112. Roma/Bari: Laterza.

Santoro, Caterina. 1968. *Gli offici del comune di Milano e del dominio Visconteo-Sforzesco (1216–1515)*. Milano: Giuffrè.

Strangio, Donatella. 2015. Ripensare le *food crises*: lo Stato Pontificio (1750–1800). In Ferrari and Vaquero Piñeiro 2015, 65–91.

Van Zanden, Jan Luiten. 1999. Wages and the standard of living in Europe, 1500–1800. *European Review of Economic History* 3 (2): 175–197.

Vertecchi, Giulia. 2009. *Il "masser ai formenti in Terra Nova". Il ruolo delle scorte granarie a Venezia nel XVIII secolo*. Roma: Università degli Studi Roma Tre.

Visconti, Alessandro. 1913. *La pubblica amministrazione nello Stato milanese durante il predominio straniero (1541–1796). Saggio di storia del diritto amministrativo*. Roma: Athenaeum.

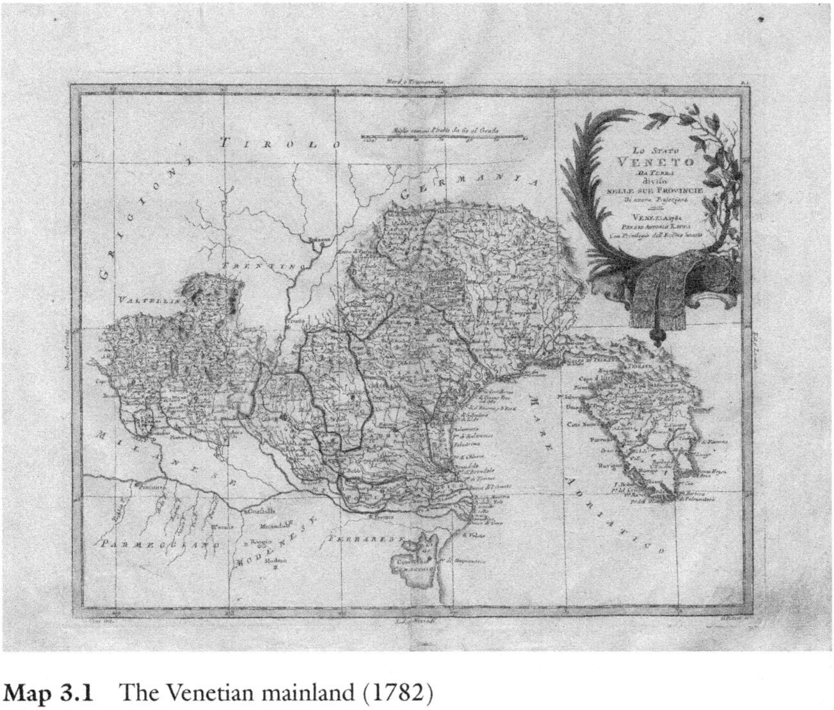

Map 3.1 The Venetian mainland (1782)

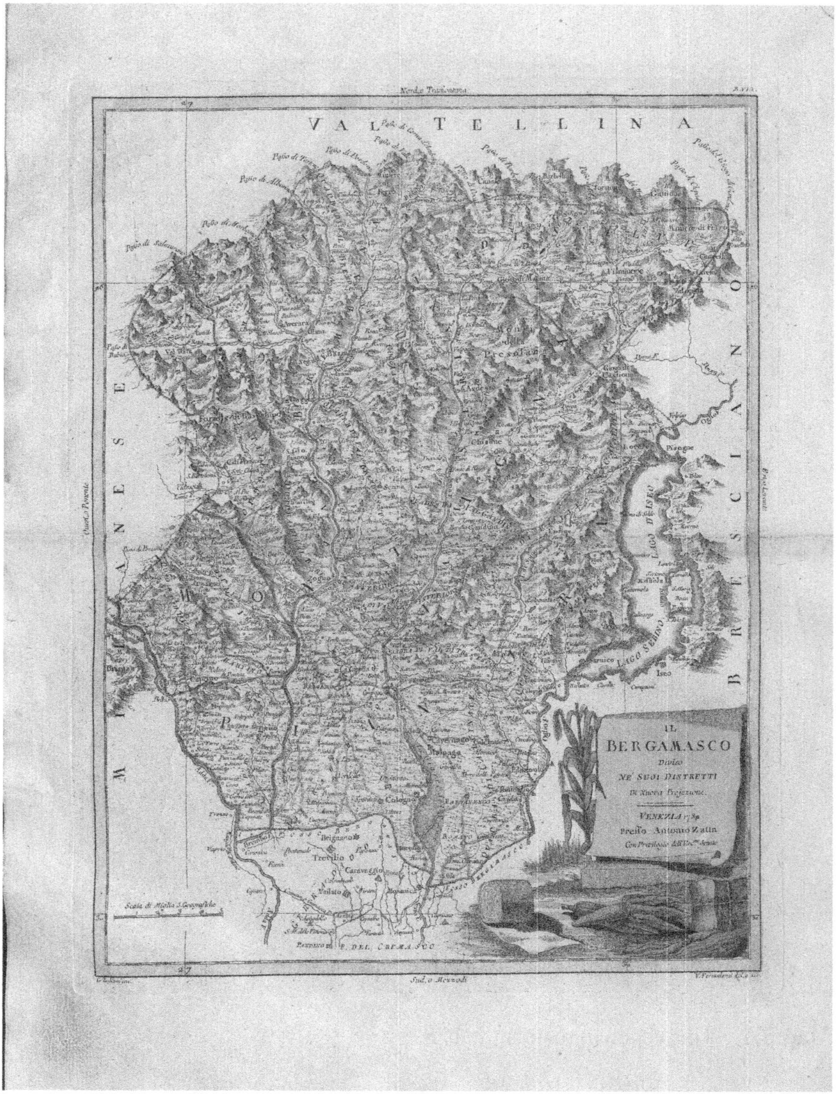

Map 3.2 The Bergamo province (1782)

CHAPTER 3

One City, Two Economic Areas: Wheat and Olive Oil Trade in Bergamo between Venice and Milan

Fabrizio Costantini

3.1 Introduction

In 1588, after almost thirty years, the construction of the city walls in Bergamo was completed: according to intentions, the structure should be a backward bastion to protect the Venetian territories, after a first line of defence consisting of fortified towns near the Adda and Oglio rivers. The city (since then a picturesque fortress overlooking the plain below) became the bulwark of the Republic of Venice against the nearby State of Milan, to the west, and the Grisons, just north.[1] A few decades earlier, the inhabitants of Bergamo had been estimated at 17,707, a third compared to Verona and Brescia, almost one-tenth of the capital city. In 1548 the entire province of Bergamo had about 122,500 inhabitants (7.9% of the population of the Venetian dominions in Italy) and in 1766 it was close to 200,000 (or 9.1% of the population).[2] The fiscal weight of the province was not proportionately much greater: in the sixteenth

F. Costantini (✉)
Università degli Studi di Milano, Milan, Italy
e-mail: fabrizio.costantini@unimi.it

L. Clerici (ed.), *Italian Victualling Systems in the Early Modern Age, 16th to 18th Century*, Palgrave Studies in Economic History,
https://doi.org/10.1007/978-3-030-42064-2_3

century, Bergamo paid about 8,000 of the 100,000 ducats required for the *sussidio ordinario* (literally, 'ordinary subsidy', a direct tax introduced in 1529 assigning to each province a fixed share of payment), and in 1679 Bergamo's *dazi* (indirect taxes and duties) yielded 9.2% of the total paid by the provinces of the Venetian *terraferma* ('mainland').[3] Between 1691 and 1732, the value was still between 11.0% and 12.9%.[4]

These quick references reveal what Bergamo meant to Venice between the sixteenth and eighteenth centuries: first of all, it was a frontier land, strategically fundamental but still far from the eyes and the main communication routes of the capital city; then, it was a secondary demographic and economic reality, albeit with a relative growth compared to the rest of the Republic. It was, however, enough populated and important to have a couple of *rettori* ('rectors') sent by the Republic for its government: a *podestà* ('podesta'), with mainly civil and judicial powers, and a *capitano* ('captain'), who had to deal with the control of the territory, the taxation, and the military sphere: however, such division of competences was not so clear nor rigidly defined.[5] Despite the relative marginality of the city—or rather, for this very reason[6]—the victualling system in Bergamo in the Early Modern Age deserves special attention. As this contribution will show, there were several elements that made this province an extremely interesting case study as regards its provisions: in fact, considering the insufficient production of cereals and other foodstuffs, Bergamo proposed very innovative solutions. First of all, a system for monitoring wheat transactions was delegated to the peripheral community of Romano di Lombardia, since it was located just a few kilometres away from the fertile Cremona plain in the State of Milan; secondly, the task of filling food shortages was entrusted to smuggling, incentives, and fiscal specifics. The result was the creation of an atypical victualling system which was, above all, much less binding than in other realities of the Republic and, in general, of the Old Regime.

In order to investigate these issues, the trade of cereals and olive oil will be taken into consideration, analysing in particular the documents of the *Giudici delle vettovaglie* ('judges for victuals'), *Deputati alle biade* ('deputies for crops'), and *Processi comunali* ('municipal trials') series kept in the civic archives of Bergamo. More specifically, the data provided by the substantial *Calmieri dei cereali* ('officially set cereals prices') subseries will be used, consisting of several documents recording the weekly trades on the markets in the Bergamo province between the seventeenth and eighteenth centuries.[7] This is a very promising source, because along with the closing prices of the transactions it also recorded traded quantities: this allows a closer look at the functioning of a victualling administration centre.[8] As for wheat, the rectors themselves, as explained later, certified in their reports the exceptionality of the province's victualling system. The centrality of olive oil, on the other hand, derived from the fortune of the local woollen mills, which until the beginning of the eighteenth century represented one of the most flourishing realities for the entire Venetian economy: they actually accounted for over 58% of the value of the province's exports.[9]

3.2 Urban Institutions and Local Authorities in a Deficit Area

Foodstuff transformation and trade in the Early Modern Age were under the authority of a significant number of bodies and offices. According to the seventeenth-century statutes of the Bergamo's *giudici delle vettovaglie*, it was this body, created in 1563, that had to supervise the work of bakers, millers, merchants and measurers of crops, butchers, charcuterie sellers, wine sellers, fishmongers, and olive oil traders. However, its duties went beyond the food sphere to include products that were fundamental for survival (such as wood), or to control the professions related to strategic sectors for the local economy (such as wool, silk, or linen fabrics, and the production of building stones). The last category under the monitoring of the *giudici* were the manufacturers of instruments designed for measuring and weighing what has just been listed.[10] The creation of the *giudici delle vettovaglie* was the final stage of a specialisation and institutional strengthening process starting in the fifteenth century: at that time, the urban space was under the control of the *giudici alle vettovaglie e strade* ('judges for victuals and roads'), who in 1563 were split into *giudici alle strade e incanti* ('judges for roads and auctions') and *giudici delle vettovaglie*. Until 1481 there were just two *giudici alle vettovaglie e strade* in the city: by the end of the sixteenth century there were already six *giudici delle vettovaglie* in service every year (nine from 1631). The office of *giudice delle vettovaglie* was often held by local noble families such as the Agosti, Albani, Calepio, Colleoni, and Secco Suardo, demonstrating how this body was, along with many others, a "point of intersection and mediation" of power between the capital city and the local ruling classes.[11]

Central authorities such as the *provveditori alle biave* ('superintendents for crops') or the *provveditori sopra oli* ('superintendents for olive oil') were to be informed.[12] Apart from the *giudici delle vettovaglie*, in the Bergamo province itself the rectors sent from Venice (especially the podesta) and other extraordinary authorities (such as the *deputati alle biade*) worked with victualling tasks. This last category, which seems to have been established only for special cases, worked alongside the incumbent podesta and captain, the *giudici delle vettovaglie*, the appointees of the local charities (above all, the *Monte dell'Abbondanza* and the *Consorzio della Misericordia Maggiore*), and agronomy experts, often relying on the collaboration of internationally renowned merchants. This deployment of forces and overlapping competences did not prevent local representatives and landowners from playing leading roles in the supply sector. The influence of peripheral actors was increased by the nature of the soil and the hydrographic structure of the territory. The Bergamo plain—whose extension covered 17% of the territory, compared to 70% of mountainous areas—could not produce enough wheat for the entire population and it was therefore necessary to import a quantity of cereals that in many years exceeded half of the total needs.[13] To the north of the city entire highly inhabited valleys, such as Val Brembana or Val Seriana, were almost completely unproductive in terms of cereals. According to the Venetian *provveditori alle biave*, the Bergamo province was one of the two areas chronically lacking in cereals, along with Istria.[14]

The testimonies on the sterility of the Bergamo province are countless. One of the few discordant voices is Francesco Sansovino, who in 1575 included Bergamo in the list of fertile cities in his work on the geography of Italy. Almost twenty years earlier, however, Leandro Alberti had described the province as a cold and harsh area, and Giovanni Botero, at the end of the sixteenth century, once again mentioned a vast territory without a satisfactory wheat production.[15] Rather than focusing on disorganised voices, we should first of all consider what was observed by local rulers. It is particularly useful, then, to look at what was put on paper by the Venetian rectors in their final reports. On this basis, in fact, it is possible to describe the sixteenth and early seventeenth centuries as a period with an actual obsession for victualling, at least up to the 1629–1631 Italian plague: twenty-six of the fifty-six reports for the period 1525–1630 reported approximate data on the food self-sufficiency of this province (not counting those, albeit numerous, that refer to a generic soil 'barrenness'). The unit of measurement used to express this deficit was the number of months the population could be fed with local crops. Of course, it would have been best to have crops for twelve months a year, or even something more: at the end of the eighteenth century, the State of Milan still considered itself a territory at risk because it produced sufficient cereals for thirteen and a half months a year (and therefore had only a slight food surplus).[16] The situation in the Bergamo province, as described by the local rectors, is shown in Table 3.1.

It is worth noticing that nearly all the rectors were unanimous in estimating a level of crops production that was sufficient for less than six months a year and some, especially around the middle of the sixteenth century, barely conceded three.[17] However, the data provided remain somewhat variable, which means that the rectors did not just wearily use a commonplace created by their predecessors. On the contrary, in the few cases where reports were published in the same year, the rectors had no hesitation in providing discordant observations; this happened—as can be seen in Table 3.1—in 1601, 1620, and 1627. Very curious is Captain Lorenzo Donà's report (1565): while focusing on a completely different

Table 3.1 Crops autonomy of the Bergamo province according to the rectors' reports (1542–1793)

Report's date	Autonomy (in months)	Report's date	Autonomy (in months)
30 January 1542	4	3 April 1610	5
23 May 1549	3	Year 1614	5
1 November 1553	3	31 October 1617	7.5
10 May 1555	4	2 May 1620	5
7 July 1560	4	10 October 1620	6
6 November 1561	4	12 August 1623	4
31 December 1565	3	12 January 1625	6
25 May 1572	6.5	12 June 1626	5
29 May 1579	4	15 May 1627	5.5
15 June 1591	4.5	27 November 1627	4
25 May 1593	4	22 January 1636	6
18 May 1595	4	19 July 1666	6
8 February 1601	3	4 February 1773	6
September 1601	5	23 October 1787	9
2 April 1605	6	14 November 1793	8
4 August 1606	5		

Source: Università di Trieste (1978, pp. 11, 19, 27, 32, 40, 60, 79, 102, 140, 183, 192, 212, 258, 274, 282, 297, 305, 346, 360, 374, 380, 414, 429, 435, 439, 452, 493, 551, 780, 791, 805)

matter (the defensive needs of the province), he noted that the inhabitants of Bergamo showed excellent military qualities due to a familiarity with weapons; this was the norm in the area precisely because of the spread of smuggling.[18] The import of crops was also acknowledged by ecclesiastical documents: in his reports on the state of the Bergamo diocese at the end of the sixteenth century, Bishop Giovanni Battista Milani stressed the low productivity of the province and talked about food that, especially in mountain areas, "consisted of milk, cheese, chestnuts, and imported wheat".[19]

After 1627 there were very few rectors' final reports with similar considerations. Only five rectors reported such data, and from this point on they always estimated that the food autonomy of the Bergamo province was equal to or greater than six months: this, either because of a lower demographic pressure, or thanks to the start of maize cultivation in the province, which took place around 1620.[20] One of the substantial changes occurring between the seventeenth and eighteenth centuries was precisely the diffusion of maize.[21] The data recorded in Bergamo and Romano di Lombardia show precisely the gradual reduction of trade in millet and the increasing weight of sales of maize (see Table 3.2). At the present stage of research, it is however not possible to explain why the trade of wheat in the urban market had already plummeted since the early eighteenth century (the data—in Table 3.3—will be discussed later on). The role of maize was probably to provide a viable alternative to wheat, especially when prices were rising. Such an alternative had several drawbacks: it required more irrigation and more peasant work, while nutritionally speaking it could cause avitaminosis diseases. It is difficult, however, to obtain precise data on the benefits that early modern victualling systems got from the introduction of maize, because this cereal had a high rate of self-consumption: even the records of the *Calmieri dei cereali* of the Bergamo province, moreover, only show the size of trade on the market (and just the legal one). It is clear, however, that the supply of the province was for the rectors an increasingly less pressing problem.

Foreign visitors provided partial confirmation of the chronic difficulties of agriculture in the area, as they noted in their diaries. Tourists and travellers moving between the State of Milan and the Republic of Venice noticed from time to time significant differences in the agricultural landscape. Montesquieu was certainly not a careless passenger when he travelled from Verona to Milan in September 1728. When he arrived in the village of Palazzolo he crossed the border between the Brescia and the Bergamo province and headed for Canonica, where he could enter the Milanese

Table 3.2 Cereals traded on the legal markets of Bergamo and Romano di Lombardia (1678–1778)

		Quantities (in Bergamo *some*)				Percentages			
Year	Market	Wheat	Maize	Millet	Total	Wheat	Maize	Millet	Total
1678	Bergamo	909.5	1,449.0	773.0	3,131.5	29.0	46.3	24.7	100
1688	Bergamo	1,094.5	896.0	921.0	2,911.5	37.6	30.8	31.6	100
1698	Bergamo	881.0	1,525.0	527.0	2,933.0	30.0	52.0	18.0	100
1708	Bergamo	136.5	464.0	301.0	901.5	15.1	51.5	33.4	100
1718	Bergamo	131.0	972.0	643.0	1,746.0	7.5	55.7	36.8	100
1728	incomplete data								
1738	Romano	2,258.0	2,167.0	1,226.0	5,651.0	40.0	38.3	21.7	100
1748	Romano	818.0	1,677.0	218.0	2,713.0	30.2	61.8	8.0	100
1758	Romano	1,132.0	1,869.0	109.0	3,110.0	36.4	60.1	3.5	100

Source: Elaboration on data from BCMBG, ASCGVCC, 1.2.18.10.5-29–143. 1 Bergamo *soma* (plur. *some*) was divided into 8 *staia* and corresponded to approximately 171.28 cubic decimetres (Martini 1883, p. 70)

Table 3.3 Cereals traded on the legal market of Bergamo (1678–1712)

	Quantities (in Bergamo *some*)				Percentages			
Five-year period	Wheat	Maize	Millet	Total	Wheat	Maize	Millet	Total
1678–1682	4,628.5	4,796.5	3,325.5	12,750.5	36.3	37.6	26.1	100
1683–1687	6,384.5	4,603.0	4,347.0	15,334.5	41.6	30.0	28.3	100
1688–1692	5,589.5	6,381.5	6,000.0	17,971.0	31.1	35.5	33.4	100
1693–1697	4,194.0	7,755.5	3,953.0	15,902.5	26.4	48.8	24.9	100
1698–1702	3,553.0	6,465.0	3,478.0	13,496.0	26.3	47.9	25.8	100
1703–1707	1,230.0	3,214.0	2,509.0	6,953.0	17.7	46.2	36.1	100
1708–1712	1,245.0	6,692.0	2,491.0	10,428.0	11.9	64.2	23.9	100

Source: Elaboration on data from BCMBG, ASCGVCC, 1.2.18.10.5-29–71

territory: he did not dedicate many words to the description of that of Bergamo, but he took note of the wide spread of vineyards and "scarce wheat plantations".[22] About forty years later the musician Charles Burney took the opposite path and, going from Milan to Brescia in July 1770, he noted that the territory beyond Canonica—then in the Bergamo province—was "burnt by drought" and that the countryside was well cultivated, but certainly not "as rich as that of Milan".[23] The deficit in cereals production was tenaciously confirmed by the observers Giovanni Maironi

Da Ponte and Ignazio Cantù: in the early nineteenth century, the two estimated that in the Department of Serio (not perfectly comparable to the Bergamo province in Venetian age) there would be a food autonomy for just seven or eight months at the most.[24] In short, whether they were local government bodies, ecclesiastical officials, local or foreign authorities, geographers, intellectuals, or simple travellers, it seems that in the Early Modern Age the Bergamo province gave everyone the impression of being highly deficient in terms of cereals supply.

Moreover, the considerable water shortage did not guarantee adequate support for either agricultural production or ease of transport. The prevalence of clayey soils in most of the flat area south of the city limited the effectiveness of canalisation and irrigation works.[25] The province was in a marginal position with respect to the Po river, holding back the potential use of this route for the transport of heavy and bulky goods such as wheat. Furthermore, the province was enclosed between the Adda, a navigable river completely managed by the State of Milan, and the Oglio: the latter was not always accessible by boat, especially after the excavation of the *Naviglio Pallavicino* in the early decades of the sixteenth century. The control of the Oglio river was disputed between the Republic of Venice and the State of Milan and this significantly limited its commercial use. Only through Lake Iseo could the people of the Bergamo province take advantage of transport via a waterway: thanks to this route, however, it was easier for food products to take the direction of Val Camonica, under control of nearby Brescia, rather than the Bergamo valleys. If crops traffickers wanted to go to Breno and its surroundings, they could benefit from the transport licences issued (illegally, according to the city of Bergamo) by the Calepio family, powerful local feudal lords always interested in controlling the trade and the taxes and duties gravitating around the port of Sarnico and Lake Iseo.[26]

As Captain Giovanni Da Lezze wrote at the end of the sixteenth century, specific environmental and political conditions had therefore pushed Bergamo to equip itself with a system of wheat supplies "completely different from other cities".[27] The province was characterised by an original victualling system, with no traditional instruments for the declaration of harvests nor a compulsory transportation into the city; such measures were in force for various reasons in central-northern Italy, thus also in all the other cities under Venetian rule.[28] On the contrary, Bergamo decided to rely on the free internal movement of foodstuffs and on import incentives. Nobody was normally required to inform the authorities—except during moments of intense crisis—of the quantity of seeds or the kind of expected production: there were also no strict rules that pushed the flow of cereals to be sold into the city. After being introduced into the urban market, in fact, the cereals could freely leave as long as they were sold within the province. In the words of Da Lezze, “although [Bergamo is] a very important fortress, no cereals are transported into it by obligation”:[29] the cereals transported into the city could be “exchanged outside without any obstacle [...], letting everyone sell them at whatever price they prefer”.[30] A much simpler victualling system was therefore created, similar—it has been written with some emphasis—to “precursor concepts” of free trade.[31]

Considering what happened elsewhere in the peninsula (e.g. in some areas of Apulia), the rejection of these obligations was not an innovative solution:[32] however, it was unusual for such a permissive system to be implemented in a province with no surplus cereals to sell, but rather foreign cereals to attract. This is another example of a solution that was “substantially based on an empiricism preventing an integral vision of the agrarian problem”,[33] an exclusively practical expedient that tried to fill an undeniable gap in wheat production (without the creation of any ideological structure to support a real free trade in foodstuffs). This is underlined in official proclamations by the linguistic persistence of the qualification of ‘smuggler’ (*contrabandiere*) for all those who imported wheat into the city: although such operation was appreciated, encouraged, and even supported by the legislator, it continued, etymologically speaking, to be considered a crime.[34] However, with regard to the free internal circulation of foodstuffs, Bergamo anticipated solutions that other cities under Venetian rule would implement much later in time (the very fertile Crema opened up free trade in foodstuffs only between 1732 and 1738) and that the Venetian Senate would adopt only between 1744 and 1769. In addition, the legislation of Venice, unlike that of Bergamo, reserved the right to reintroduce restrictions on free movement in case of sudden increases in agricultural prices.[35]

Despite the lack of rigid restrictions, the network of cereals markets in the Bergamo province consolidated along some routes, with the function of conveying food from abroad and from the plain to the city and the valleys, just like in other provinces of the Republic (e.g. that of Vicenza[36]). Many border towns with a few thousand inhabitants—such as Caprino, Romano di Lombardia, Sarnico, Lovere—found themselves playing a decisive role in guaranteeing adequate levels of crops imports. The three markets of Gandino, Vertova, and Clusone were concentrated in Val

Seriana: the entire valley was densely populated (it usually had more inhabitants than Bergamo) because of the numerous local manufacturing activities, and it needed a constant influx of food, even in the winter months when transportation could be a problem. However, local representatives did not monitor and manage just cereals routes: these communities were also often allowed to set their own minimum official weight for the bread loaves to be sold for a fixed price, different from the weight in force in Bergamo. Apart from the valleys, there were some market hubs intended to attract cereals from abroad and direct them to Bergamo: for example, the markets of Caprino and Romano di Lombardia were created for this very purpose. Another clearly identifiable route ran along the aforementioned Lake Iseo which, through Sarnico and Lovere, allowed the cereals from the plain to reach the Val Camonica area.[37]

The genesis and evolution of such a distribution network was not always peaceful or untroubled. Many crops markets had ancient origins and were already active in 1237: only the licences granted to Caprino (1431) and Sarnico (1566) seem more recent.[38] In the Early Modern Age, however, the city's institutions worked to regain the typically urban prerogatives as regards the victualling system and to reduce the importance of these local and peripheral markets. The attempt was not successful precisely because of the crucial role played by the smaller market hubs. In the seventeenth century there were numerous and very animated trials against Alzano, Sarnico, and Caprino, in order to try to take away from these small towns the right to host crops trades. Alzano, in particular, was located too close to Bergamo and was accused of depriving the city of a rich trade share: Caprino and Sarnico, on the other hand, were blamed for directing part of the cereals towards the Lecco area and Brianza (the first) and Val Camonica (the latter). These were mostly biased accusations, and none of them—except for Alzano—found a positive outcome in the trials that the city started against smaller towns.

The most important dispute, however, opposed Bergamo to Romano di Lombardia and focused on the choice of the marketplace designated for measuring the volume of cereals trades. In the Bergamo province, in fact, the process of recording prices and quantities of the wheat exchanged on the market was not dismissed: this task, however, continued to shift between Bergamo and the suburban communities throughout the whole Early Modern Age. The importance of Romano di Lombardia is confirmed by various sources dating back to the sixteenth century: between 1542 and 1553 Rectors Vincenzo Diedo and Francesco Bernardo had already indicated it as the main market hub in the province,[39] followed by similar statements from the *sindici inquisitori di Terraferma* (literally, 'Mainland inquisitors', itinerant Venetian officials) in 1555.[40] Unfortunately it is not so clear whether an analytical mechanism for transcribing the price of foodstuffs was already existing in the sixteenth century.

Observing the transcripts—available for most of the seventeenth and eighteenth centuries—it is possible to reconstruct the controversial relationship that linked and at the same time opposed Bergamo and Romano. The city was dependent on foreign crops and therefore on imports favoured by the peripheral markets, which were located a few miles from the fertile Cremona plain: at the same time, however, the city did not easily accept the need of granting these marketplaces some prerogatives in monitoring crops trade. The reports show that the reference market for cereals prices was Bergamo first (1619–1651), then Romano (1651–1678), Bergamo again (1678–1718) and, finally, Romano again (1718–1803, except for very short periods during some years of crisis). Echoes of the importance of suburban communities can be found in the notes of a French traveller in 1823: the geographer Jacques Barzilay wrote in that year that in Romano, "small town of the Bergamo province", a "great commerce of wheat" was held.[41]

In the third quarter of the seventeenth century the monitoring tasks were delegated to Romano without major impediments: at this stage, given the low demographic pressure caused by the plague, cereals prices were rather low and it was not perceived as a problem to rely on the information collected by Romano's *cancelliere* ('chancellor'). It is estimated, in fact, that the inhabitants of Bergamo and suburbs in 1630 were about 21,515, collapsing to 9,613 the following year: the impact of the epidemic on the rest of the province was less severe, with its population falling from 134,709 to 89,694.[42] This probably made it possible to tolerate the transfer of crops trade monitoring functions to the small town at the southern end of the province.

In 1678 Bergamo decided—for unknown reasons, perhaps linked to the demographic recovery—to reclaim the mechanism for monitoring cereals prices: for a more effective approach it was decided to move the urban market from the *città alta* ('upper city') to the so-called *Prato dell'Ospedale* ('Hospital's Field'), an area situated at the foot of the city walls in the *città bassa* ('lower city'). This was a place much easier to reach for crops traders and already well known by merchants for being the site of a very popular fair at the end of the summer.[43] This move was expected to attract more buyers and resellers, to support bargaining and to allow to calculate a reliable value of the average price of cereals. The number of exchanges, initially very satisfying, began to contract in 1694–1695, and then collapsed in the very first years of the eighteenth century (see Table 3.3).

The figures[44] gave the city's rectors no choice. Until 1699, at least 1,000 *some* of wheat per year circulated on the legal market in Bergamo, while the trading of maize and millet had greater fluctuations. Between 1702 and 1704, the average amount of wheat had already fallen to around 300 *some*, and there was no compensation in the increase of the trade of other cereals. In 1705, the minimum quantity of trade set by the regulations for calculating the average price of wheat (8 *some*) was reached on only ten occasions out of forty-nine. In 1710 sales rose again, maybe because of a particularly difficult climatic year which forced large segments of the population to turn to the market: in the months immediately following the 1709 'great frost', almost 2,300 *some* of maize and over 600 of millet were sold. The minimum peak of transactions was reached in 1713, when only 64 *some* of wheat, 779 of maize, and 250 of millet were traded.

In 1718, a quantitative comparison between the transactions on the Bergamo and Romano di Lombardia legal markets was ordered. The results were merciless: in Bergamo's *Prato dell'Ospedale* 131 *some* of wheat and 959 of maize were sold on the market, while under the arcades of Romano di Lombardia 2,235 *some* of wheat were traded (108 only on 18 July) and 1,282 of maize. Still in 1719, a few dozen *some* of wheat were sold in Bergamo, testifying a chronic and consolidated situation.[45] In short, over a dozen years it became clear that no regulatory intervention could reaffirm the centrality of the city's market: the rectors sent from Venice gave up and the task of supervising agricultural prices thus returned to the chancellor of Romano di Lombardia until the early nineteenth century, except for a handful of years. One of the peculiarities of the victualling system of the Bergamo province was therefore the ability to change the location used for the survey of cereals prices. An innovative element of the local crops supply was the absence of any centrality of the legal urban market, which had ceased to be the designated place for the concentration of crops trades. On the other hand, it was always possible for citizens to turn to another source, which was often invisible: the illegal market.

3.3 Systemic Recourse to Smuggling

When the demand for foreign cereals clashed with the export constraints imposed by the neighbouring states, one of the main actors in the local victualling system entered the scene: the smuggler. In the Bergamo province in fact this was a crucial figure not only for cereals, but also for wine and salt trade. As for wine, smuggling was the main means of exporting the surplus produced in Val Calepio to the State of Milan. Salt, on the other hand, was distributed in the Bergamo province through the auctions of the *cinque dazi di Lombardia* ('five taxes and duties of Lombardy', which grouped the provinces of Bergamo, Brescia, Crema, Salò, and Val Camonica): the 'white gold' was provided to the contractors by Venice itself, which also sold it to the State of Milan.[46] The first customs treaties in Bergamo report that as early as the fourteenth century this salt came from very distant supply basins, such as Ibiza and Cyprus, while in the sixteenth century the city had the privilege of getting salt from the African coasts.

At the borders of the Cremona province, however, there were various lands that had an agreement with fiscal authorities (such as the towns of Soncino or Calcio) and the salt was sold at less than half the price of the rest of the State of Milan; if in the eighteenth century the price of salt in the Cremona province was around 11–13 Milanese *lire correnti* per *staio*, in Soncino and Calcio it could be sold at 6 *lire* and 10 *soldi* and 3 *lire* and 15 *soldi* respectively.[47] The low prices in these towns generated a sort of 'return smuggling' from the privileged places of the Cremona province to the Venetian provinces of Brescia and Bergamo. Many communities beyond the Mincio river were therefore illegally supplied with salt coming from Spanish (until 1706) or Austrian (from 1706) Lombardy, which in turn had bought it from Venice. It is actually not surprising that in the eighteenth century the Milanese customs officials were stranded in long investigations to understand how intricate the circuits of salt smuggling in the border area between the State of Milan and the Republic of Venice were.[48]

The role of immunities and illicit trade for food supplies also emerges in the case of olive oil. The production in the Bergamo province was nearly non-existent—too few olive trees on the shores of Lake Iseo to meet the whole needs—but the demand remained very high until the first decades of the eighteenth century. The main cause, rather than food consumption, was the wool industry in Val Seriana; and unlike other areas of the Republic, this economic activity was still successful in the seventeenth century.[49] Olive oil was essential to strengthen the fibres of the finished products, but it was also a fundamental raw material for the soaps used by the wool mills themselves. Bergamo, with its 550,000 Venetian *libbre grosse* of soap imported from Venice, was the main consumer on the Mainland: as a comparison, Verona imported 260,000 *libbre grosse*, Brescia 126,000.[50] The price of olive oil and the taxes and duties imposed on it thus had a major impact on the competitiveness of the entire wool sector. In 1517 Bergamo and Crema were accorded the privilege of obtaining supplies, in case of need or high prices, not from Venice, but from the Republic of Genoa and Tuscany. This prerogative, originally linked to the supply difficulties caused by the previous wars, was however reconfirmed in 1532 and 1574.[51]

Venice had authorised these transits as long as the olive oil was directed along one of the following routes: the first consisted in circumnavigating the Italian peninsula, ascending the Adriatic Sea up to Venice and navigating the Po river; the second, instead, included the journey by mule from the Ligurian and Tuscan coasts to Pesaro, the passage through Venice and then the use of river navigation. The aim was, as always, to allow imported goods to be taxed in the port of Venice. It soon became clear that this was not enough to fully control the olive oil trade, for two reasons. First of all, the land route between Genoa and Bergamo—passing through Serravalle, Novi, Tortona, and Pavia or along the itinerary that crossed Sarzana, Lodi, and Crema or Cremona—was much more convenient. Secondly, the use of the Po river would favour olive oil smuggling in any case: once in Pontelagoscuro, barrels from Ferrara or the Papal States could easily be loaded with those from Genoa or Tuscany.[52] The loads were conveyed to the unreliable imperial outposts in the Duchy of Mantua—Castiglione delle Stiviere, Medole, Solferino—where the levels of taxation and control of the territory were very low, and from there they were carried to the Brescia and Bergamo provinces. The fiscal prerogative of the imperial feuds was thus transformed into a very valid cover for illegal activities.[53] However, the analysis of trading documents suggests that the woollen mills of the Bergamo province also turned with ease to other supply basins, such as Lake Garda or the Como province.[54]

The quantitative data available leave no room for interpretation: taking advantage of fiscal privileges and the black economy was something very widespread. In the second half of the seventeenth century, considering production needs and food consumption, Bergamo authorities estimated an olive oil demand of just over 800 Venetian *miara* per year: between 1664 and 1680, however, imports from Venice consisted of 303 *miara* per year on average and never exceeded the 440 *miara* recorded in 1677.[55] In the next century there were no significant changes: the data provided by Salvatore Ciriacono indicate for the years around 1740 an estimated consumption of 705 *miara* per year (about 400 for the wool industry alone), but imports from Venice for just 200–250 *miara*.[56] Desolating in this regard was the petition sent on 19 October 1674 by Iseppo Giacomazzi, the Bergamo olive oil customs official: in his opinion, fraud had become the real arbiter of trade in this sector, with illegal olive oil having no problem in penetrating from Ferrara into the lands of the Republic and, through the Duchy of Mantua, into the westernmost territories of the Republic. Giacomazzi also knew that Friuli and the Treviso province had to deal with the illicit trade carried on by the Istrian subjects. The smuggling of olive oil was everywhere associated with the trafficking of salt and other goods. According to him, the smugglers had become much braver in recent years; at the beginning of his contract they used to carry small saddlebags and sacks, while now they travelled undisturbed with entire wagons full of goods.[57] It was in the writer's interest to exaggerate and draw a gloomy picture of the damages suffered by him, but there is no doubt that Venice's ability to oppose the abuse of supply privileges was very limited.

Given the weight of supplies alternative to those guaranteed by the Republic of Venice, the *giudici delle vettovaglie* of Bergamo even tried to impose themselves as the only regulatory authority for monitoring and fixing olive oil prices. Their evidence, after all, was simple and logical. The other cities in the Mainland fixed their prices considering the average prices in Venice and adding transport costs and the taxes and duties paid to the various local fiscal offices (*camere fiscali*, literally, 'fiscal chambers') along the way. Given that a large share of the needs of the Bergamo province was covered by markets which were different from Venice, why would the city have had to join such a system? According to the *giudici*, moreover, accepting Venice prices would only have favoured fraud, and in particular it would have led to an artificial rise in the prices of bad olive oil. Our Bergamo sources (although we do not know how much biased) stated that the quality of the olive oil from Venice was actually better than that coming from Genoa or Tuscany, and therefore it was sold at a particularly high price; the adaptation to the Venetian price list would have caused a sudden and unjustified rise in the prices of foreign olive oils, with serious damage to consumers, wool mills, and city's privileges. Or, even worse, it could have pushed merchants and retailers to mix the different types, passing them off as coming from Venice.

Between 1653 and 1682 the merchants from the Bergamo province, the wool manufacturers from Val Seriana, Bergamo's *giudici delle vettovaglie*, and Venice's *provveditori sopra oli* confronted each other in a very long dispute concerning the structure of taxes and duties and the supply of olive oil in the province. The few city's merchants were particularly powerful and were accused of having realised disproportionate gains—1,000,000 Venetian *lire* instead of the lowest figure of 256,000 *lire*—with internal agreements and a mechanism for the calculation of prices which was independent from that of the Republic of Venice.[58] Vehement accusations came from wool manufacturers, who were instead in favour of anchoring the officially set prices in Bergamo to those of Venice: according to them, this solution (diametrically opposite to that of the *giudici delle vettovaglie*) would allow to lower the average price of olive oil and therefore it would increase the competitiveness of the manufacturers. This position may not have had a real foundation, but it led to the creation of two opposing sides, with the *provveditori sopra oli* defending wool mills, and the *giudici delle vettovaglie* siding with the Bergamo merchants (these latter two parts sharing the hope that the determination of prices would remain a task controlled by the city).[59]

In the second half of the seventeenth century all the aforementioned issues came to the fore. A charter of intent featured in the documents of the *giudici* listed the points that, according to Venice, needed to be clarified. It was necessary to determine how and why the merchants got rich so quickly, create detailed lists of the quantities of olive oil sent from Venice and understand whether they covered the needs of the Bergamo province, estimate the amount of demand from wool mills and investigate the suspicious transits via Po and via Mantua. The *giudici* relied on a single key point: unless anyone wanted to revolutionise the context of city's privileges (an aspect never on the negotiating table), they were the authority that could best establish the average prices. They could in fact control and verify the level of legitimate imports from abroad more easily than the Venetian officials. However, the valleys' wool producers and merchants could not accept that the fate of the most profitable sector in their territory was decided by a few people belonging to the urban aristocracy.

The first stage of the dispute ended in 1660, when the situation stabilised as follows: the Venetian olive oil prices in Bergamo were adjusted to those in Venice; there was no change for olive oil coming from Genoa and Tuscany as long as it had a regular licence and was subject to a new duty of 3 Venetian *soldi* per *libbra grossa* to be paid to the local fiscal office in

Bergamo (or in Crema, at most). The new regulations were also sent to both the resident envoy (*residente*) in Florence and the consul (*console*) in Genoa, who were directly interested in the new conditions imposed on the domains of the Republic of Venice.[60] However, small checks on the trend of the new-born duty, carried out in 1665 and 1670, suggested that it was constantly evaded: the refinement of strategies to avoid taxes and duties and the use of smuggling remained therefore constant in the supply of olive oil to the province.[61] The documents preserved in the Civic Library of Bergamo do not help to reconstruct the final outcome of the process: the records interrupt abruptly in 1682, just after a deep crisis of olive oil production in Genoa began.[62] The tensions between Bergamo and Venice were therefore alleviated and Bergamo itself decided to turn, at least for these years, to Venice rather than to Genoa. What is known, however, is that even in the following century, as already mentioned, the investigations of the *provveditori sopra oli* promoted by Venice continued to highlight the discrepancy between the olive oil Bergamo needed and the imports from the capital city's port.

The same decisive role was played by the uninterrupted flow of smuggled wheat. The proclamations issued by the Bergamo podestas were explicit: the smugglers who fraudulently imported wheat from abroad were not forced to direct it to the urban market or other authorised locations; they could instead sell it anywhere in the province without any restrictions. This powerful incentive was briefly suspended for some years in the second half of the seventeenth century, when the province went through low population density, low food demand, good product availability, and low agricultural prices. A second Venetian province where cereals smuggling was essential for food supply was the *Riviera* ('Shore') of Salò, on Lake Garda: this area too was characterised by a consolidated unproductiveness, but Desenzano had eliminated all the adjacent crops marketplaces becoming *de facto* the only hub for crops trading. The position of the market on the shores of a large lake, with a direct communication with the equally deficient mountain area of the Prince-Bishopric of Trent, had also suggested not radically abandoning (as happened in the Bergamo province) a pervasive system for the control of crops circulation.[63]

The normal supply circuit in the Bergamo province therefore included a massive and not always legal import of crops from the neighbouring State of Milan, and in particular from the province of Cremona (smaller lots could be channelled from the Brescia and Crema provinces and the

Duchy of Mantua). All this fed a parallel black market (on which archive documents can say little about), with a significant impact on the livelihoods of the entire province. "These smugglers must be caressed and favoured", wrote Da Lezze, adding that they had to be rewarded with the concession of a licence to bear arms and a warm welcome in the city.[64] This solution was obviously not the best when famine was accompanied by epidemic waves: the province was plunged into despair when, during the 1629–1631 Italian plague, there was a shortfall of 200,000 *some* of wheat for ordinary supply and, at the same time, foodstuffs could not be imported from the State of Milan both because cereals were lacking everywhere and because of health risks.[65]

In general, however, the system was structurally dependent on the recourse to a sort of 'legalised illegality': in fact, there was no lack of very harsh regulations issued by Venetian institutions in this regard, and on several occasions the authorities made reference to the extension of smuggling in Bergamo. Nevertheless, the possibilities to eradicate a now endemic and structural phenomenon with a simple proclamation were very scarce. One of the effects of this significant and constant transfer of crops from the Duchy of Mantua to the Lake Garda area and from the Cremona to the Bergamo province is visible in the direction of market integration: it has been demonstrated, in fact, that the trend of wheat prices in Venetian Lombardy was more similar to that in other Lombard territories than in the rest of the Venetian mainland.[66] In their action, smugglers were also supported by the presence of real power vacuum areas. This was the case, for example, of the Cerchietta area, a strip of land that included the surroundings of the large town of Treviglio that the Peace of Lodi in 1454 had not clearly attributed to either the State of Milan or the Republic of Venice. This created a fairly large territory—about 10 square kilometres—where it was unclear who had to exercise jurisdiction. All this had repercussions on fiscal and customs matters: in particular, given the fluidity of the situation, the landowners from Cerchietta were given the right to export and circulate at will the agricultural products from their fields. The result was an area with a specific fiscal system which was widely used to channel the flow of smuggled cereals from the Cremona to the Bergamo province. This situation of legal uncertainty was only partially overcome by the Treaty of Mantua in 1756.[67]

During difficult agricultural years the supply in the nearby State of Milan might not be enough, partly because most states used to impose laws that severely restricted the export of food. The city of Bergamo council therefore called for the creation of a special body (the *deputati alle biade*), whose sole purpose was to contribute to purchase cereals on the international market. Unfortunately, the documents produced by these officials are rather incomplete and fragmentary. In the second half of the sixteenth century, the delegates of the *deputati* were very active. A first expedition in 1562 took them to southern Piedmont and to the markets of Moncalieri and Casale Monferrato: the results were compromised by the simultaneous presence of envoys from Salò—which immediately made the price of wheat rise—and by the fact that Milan did not allow an easy passage of the foodstuffs purchased there. Other delegates then met in Morbegno, Chur, Zurich, and Baden in 1570: these unusual destinations were due to the absolute prohibition imposed by Venice to go and look for crops in the potential supply basins for the capital city. Thus, Bergamo could not go beyond the Garda line; since the city considered inappropriate to go back to Piedmont or Emilia (it was necessary to cross territories under Milan's jurisdiction even to reach Piacenza, Parma, or Modena), it decided to look at its northern neighbours. The mission was, of course, a failure, because there were very few loads of cereals available in the Alpine communities. Despite the traditional good economic relations that have always existed between Bergamo and the Swiss communities, prices for these supplies were very high. Finally, during the very difficult 1593 economic crisis, the *deputati* sent their emissaries to Ravenna, Ancona, and Senigallia. At least on this occasion Bergamo obtained 6,000 *some* of wheat, about 20% of the annual needs.[68]

However, at the end of the eighteenth century (another period with an available documentation from the *deputati*), a very serious dispute arose between some members of the institution. The information coming to Bergamo from Mantua and Ferrara, where some loads of wheat had been recovered, was not at all encouraging. According to local merchants, by the end of 1782 it was already clear the need to go as far as Styria or Hungary to find something to feed the population with. Among the *deputati*, however, opposite positions stood out: Giulio Cesare Agosti asked to turn to the few but safe low-cost supplies that Cremona and Mantua could promise, and Giacomo Vertova suggested instead going beyond the Adriatic and as far as the African coasts, if necessary.[69] Even the reference territories for wheat supply were therefore very variable: if the main expectations of the Bergamo institutions were generally met by the Milanese smugglers, in case of famine it was necessary to turn to every direction: to the west (Piedmont), to the east (Ferrara, March of Ancona), even to the Alpine territories (Chur, Zurich, Baden).

3.4 Conclusions

The analysis of the traffic of cereals and olive oil in the early modern Bergamo province makes it evident the ability of this province to take advantage of its border position, equidistant from the Ligurian Sea and the Gulf of Venice, in order to get the best supply conditions. The province, in fact, was close to what has been indicated as the fundamental discontinuity of the Po Valley, that is to say, the course of the Oglio river: according to Renzo Paolo Corritore, this river marked the division between two different regional economic basins, the first gravitating towards Milan and the second towards Venice.[70] Bergamo, although administratively belonging to the latter, was the Venetian province most deeply affected by the proximity to Milan. The people of this province were actually able to dialogue with two different economic systems, taking advantage of both according to their needs. As for wheat, the rectors and the *giudici delle vettovaglie* knew they could count more on smuggling from the State of Milan than on imports from the Venetian mainland or from Venice itself, which was too far away to effectively supply its westernmost province. Even olive oil was imported in significant quantities from one of the reference ports for Spanish Lombardy—Genoa—throughout the entire seventeenth century. At the same time, many local manufacturing and agricultural products—wool, silk, wine, wood—found their largest market in the State of Milan, just like weapons and textiles from the Brescia province.[71]

The incidence of an endemic phenomenon like smuggling only underlines one aspect: political (and fiscal) subdivisions did not reflect the economic influence. Monetary issues, the road system, import-export routes, and food-related links all show the presence of a Lombard economic region centred on Milan well before Bergamo, Crema, and Brescia would belong to it politically. According to Michael Knapton, these provinces in Venetian Lombardy "by the eighteenth century gravitated very largely towards the duchy of Milan and its international dealings".[72] Even family interests and personal career possibilities reflected this situation. A typical example is the Greppi family, whose members, originally from the Bergamo province, had always been part of the local wool mill industry; over the course of a few decades they found themselves at the head of the central indirect taxes and duties collection mechanism of the State of Milan, the *Ferma Generale*. What were the results of this 'hybrid' and 'minimal' structure? At first glance, they look pretty convincing. Analysing the data available for the Bergamo province, it is noticeable that the trend of cereals prices in the province did not suffer the effects of food crises more than Milan, Brescia, Desenzano, Padua, or Parma.[73] This would confirm what Podesta Alvise Priuli wrote in 1593 about the substantial alignment of the price of agricultural products from Bergamo with those from the surrounding territories, despite the poor production levels. In fact, going through the eighteenth century, it can be noticed that the rise of food prices during some difficult years—selected where data are available for a fair number of cities in central-northern Italy—was not different between Bergamo and other contexts.

Some examples: between 1730 and 1733 the price of wheat in Romano increased by 21.7%, in line with Milan (+19.0%) and Brescia (+19.3%). It was definitely more difficult, for example, for Padua, where prices rose by 30.3%. Among the worst trends in the whole northern Italy we can find Parma (with +41.0%), a city that was usually lacking in cereals and had not abandoned a substantial restrictive regime. Things were also rather difficult in Turin (+38.7%).[74] Since the early decades of the eighteenth century, therefore, the trend of wheat prices in Romano was more similar to that of other Lombard cities than to that of other cities of the Republic of Venice (such as Padua), or foreign cities with deficits (such as Parma). And if it is true that crises in the State of Milan were often less severe than elsewhere[75] (and the data collected seem to confirm this), then during famines there were never particularly serious consequences in the Bergamo province too. In the early 1770s, the increase of wheat prices in Romano (+40.9%) was similar to other major cities: Padua and Florence recorded increases of 37.0%, Mantua—whose territory was certainly among the most fortunate as for agriculture—exceeded Romano (+41.8%).[76] The nearby Brescia, which was usually quieter than Bergamo in terms of food prices, saw wheat prices rise by almost 50.0%. The 1782 famine in the Bergamo province was much more of concern, and it made the aforementioned Giacomo Vertova imagine exploring the African coasts in search of the much-needed wheat. In just one year, prices actually rose by 25.0%, but the situation in other Lombard cities was similar: Desenzano +19.1%, Milan +21.1%, and Brescia +22.7%.[77]

Nothing new, then, in the early nineteenth century, when the Bergamo province was incorporated into the Cisalpine Republic, then into the Kingdom of Italy, and finally into the Lombardo-Venetian Kingdom: the prices of wheat, maize, and rice were perfectly matching those recorded in the markets of other provinces considered more fertile, e.g. in Brescia, Cremona, and Mantua. Sometimes they were even lower in Bergamo: as early as 1801, for example, the average price of wheat recorded in the Department of Serio was just over 41 Italian *lire*, compared to 40 *lire* in the Upper Po and 42 *lire* in the Departments of Mincio, and Mella.[78] In the 1810s, the overall cereals production of the Department of Serio was in line with that of the most fertile provinces of Brescia, Cremona, and Mantua, while sectors such as breeding and silkworm production had grown disproportionately.[79] This shows that not only the price trend was now similar, but also its absolute level was in line with other provinces where the soil and water were undoubtedly more favourable.

As for olive oil, we can refer once again to the data provided by Salvatore Ciriacono, namely the volume of exports from Venice to Brescia and Bergamo. Considering the eighteenth century, the level of olive oil imports for Bergamo ranged from 187 Venetian *miara* imported in 1742 to 420 in 1745, while for Brescia—which had access to the production of the Garda olive oil—they ranged from 35 *miara* in 1727 to 716 in 1711. Bergamo was therefore able to efficiently manage its supplies, turning elsewhere as soon as the prices or quantities available on the Venetian market proved unsatisfactory and containing this way the fluctuations in imports from the capital city. This procedure made it possible to protect the main local manufacturing activity, ensuring an easy and convenient purchase of basic raw materials, such as wool (that from Spain was purchased in Genoa) and olive oil.[80]

The case of the victualling system of Bergamo therefore shows the results of a city characterised by a high level of demand for foreign wheat and olive oil and that chose (it was forced to choose) to open its market instead of relying on the local production. It is actually possible to say that, observing in particular what happened to cereals, the more the crisis was strong, the more the authorities went looking for faraway wheat. Even if Bergamo used to rely on Cremona, during the harvest crises of the sixteenth century it turned to Piedmont, Switzerland, and the Adriatic coast, and at the end of the eighteenth century it also considered that even North Africa could be a good source of livelihood for Bergamo. The ability shown by the inhabitants of Bergamo in turning their eyes to different supply basins was certainly favoured by the geographical position of the province, rather isolated but still at the centre of the Po Valley and ready to take advantage of all the connections derived from such a position. This flexibility allowed a very low level of social conflict even in a province where the food conditions were very difficult: as recalled by Giovanni Botero "nothing keeps the people more cheerful than a good market for bread"[81] and Bergamo, thanks to smuggling, was almost always well supplied.

Notes

1. For these considerations, see Cassinelli (1990).
2. Demographic data reworked by Lanaro (2006b, p. 62).
3. Pezzolo (2006, p. 169).
4. Pezzolo (2000, p. 234).
5. See what has been written on the competence of the rectors in Cappelluzzo (1992, pp. 28–29).
6. For Guido Alfani and Matteo Di Tullio (2019, pp. 38–41), the proximity to the state borders and the low land productivity were the main features of this Venetian province.
7. BCMBG, ASCGVCC, 1.2.18.10.5-29–143; ASCDP, 1.2.8.8.5-1–6; ASCPC, 22, 44, 250, 329, 347.
8. The same favourable condition applies to nearby Desenzano del Garda, also in the Republic of Venice, which has hundreds of available annals with prices and quantities of cereals exchanged on the Lake Garda market. For considerations on the Tuscan case, where such an abundance of data seems to be lacking to date, see Pult Quaglia (1990, p. 94).
9. Sella (2000, p. 86).
10. A summary of the *giudici*'s duties can be found in Calvi (1676, p. 183).
11. Knapton (2013, p. 94). Here and below, all translations of original documents are the author's.
12. For the creation of this last authority, see Costantini (1996).
13. See the reflections of Della Valentina (2015, pp. 37–39).
14. Jean Georgelin (1978, pp. 203–226, 245) talked extensively about the chronicity of poor food production in the Bergamo province.
15. See Cattini (1998, pp. 94–99).
16. On the city of Milan and its agricultural autonomy, see Mocarelli (2015).
17. Other rectors reported more peaceful situations for other provinces in the same years: in the Vicenza province, a context in many ways similar to that of Bergamo, Podesta Taddeo Contarini spoke of enough crops for the province's needs in the year 1600 (Università di Trieste 1976, p. 120).
18. The report stated that the population "was always carrying muskets and arquebuses, also thanks to smuggling and the continuous import of crops from foreign lands, of which the city and the territory of Bergamo most of the year used to relied on" ("sempre armat[a] de schiopi et archibusi rispetto anche delli contrabandi che fanno di continuo de estrazer biave per terre aliene, delle qual vive la maggior parte dell'anno et la città et il territorio bergamasco") (Università di Trieste 1978, p. 76).
19. "Lacte, caseo et castaneis consistit et frumento utuntur inportato". This report is transcribed in Camozzi (1992, quotation from p. 178).
20. This indicative date is suggested in Moioli (1983, p. 694).

21. On the debate on its gradual spreading through the territory of the Republic of Venice, see Messedaglia (2008); Coppola (1979); Fassina (1982); Gasparini (2002); Della Valentina (2015).
22. "[T]rès peu de terre à bled" (Montesquieu 1894–1896 [1728–1729], vol. I, p. 91).
23. Bellazzi and Cantone (2017, pp. 57–58).
24. For these data, see Maironi Da Ponte (1803, p. 48); Cantù (1859, p. 29).
25. Della Valentina (2006, pp. 22–23).
26. Costantini (2016b, pp. 75–78).
27. "In tutto differente dalle altre città": this is the famous and frequently mentioned expression used in 1596 by the captain of Bergamo (Da Lezze 1988 [1596], p. 148).
28. Just as an example, Alessio Fornasin wrote that "the legislative measures [...] demonstrate the precise political will to make Udine the centre where most of the local foodstuffs converge and to force within its walls as many wheat negotiations as possible" (Fornasin 2000 [1999], pp. 34–35). In Verona there was a "mechanism of compulsory supply of the city's markets [which was] divided into a series of variously burdensome obligations" (Vecchiato 1979, p. 38). The Desenzano market, on the other hand, had a more tolerant structure; however, there was also the problem of smuggling to the Prince-Bishopric of Trent and the requests for loosening the existing restrictions were also not lacking (Rossini and Zalin 1985, pp. 138–139). In order to understand how, within the same political structure, the productive and legislative conditions could differ from place to place, it is worth analysing the detailed study by Paolo Macry (1974) on the Kingdom of Naples.
29. "Benché fortezza importantissima, non si introducono grani per obbligo né per limitatione" (Da Lezze 1988 [1596], p. 148).
30. "Relassar[e] fuori senza alcuno impedimento [...] lasciando che ognuno li venda a che precio possono" (Da Lezze 1988 [1596], p. 148).
31. The expression was used in Vecchiato (1979, p. 171).
32. Elena Papagna stated that, especially during periods of abundant production, the "government policy is oriented towards opening up to the international market" through the reduction of the cost of export licences (Papagna 1990, p. 44).
33. Vertecchi (2009, p. 89).
34. On the fluidity of the spaces and the lawful and illicit agents of an urban economy, see Montenach (2011).
35. The topic of the liberalisation of the cereals trade in the Republic of Venice was addressed in Zalin (1972).
36. See for example Clerici (2001, p. 41).
37. Costantini (2016b, pp. 79–80).

38. The reconstruction of the geography of cereals markets in the Bergamo province can be found in Cantù (1859, pp. 54–55).
39. Università di Trieste (1978, pp. 11–12, 27).
40. Some reports by the *sindici inquisitori* were published in Melchiorre (2013). On the market of Romano, they stated that "[t]his place is very convenient for the Bergamo province because it is a refuge for Milanese smugglers, who carry here crops at night. This is a safe place, and then these crops are headed to the Bergamo province. This can be defined as the granary of the Bergamo province" ("Questo loco è molto comodo al Bergamasco per essere il reduto delli contrabandieri milanesi, quali conduceno biave et le portano de notte in questo loco. Nel qual le sono secure et son poi condute sul Bergamasco per loro comodità, de sorte che questo loco se puol reputar che sia il graner del Bergamasco") (Melchiorre 2013, p. 114).
41. "[P]etite ville du Bergamasque"; "grand commerce de grains" (see the travel reports published in Moretti 2009, p. 61).
42. Data used by Saba (1995, p. 232).
43. Colmuto Zanella and Zanella (1995).
44. However, it should be considered that until 1774, whereas the markets used to take place three times a week, it was a custom to record the trades of just a single market day on a sample basis.
45. Costantini (2016b, pp. 85–86).
46. On salt, see Hocquet (1982 [1978–1979]); Caizzi (1992).
47. BCMBG, ASCPC, 1.2.19.1-22 is dedicated to the supply of salt in the Bergamo province. In the Milanese monetary system of account, 1 *lira corrente* (plur. *lire correnti*) was divided into 20 *soldi*, and 1 *soldo* into 12 *denari*. 1 Milanese *staio* (plur. *staia*) corresponded to approximately 18.279 cubic decimetres (Martini 1883, p. 351).
48. On the *Ferma Generale* (literally, 'General Contract', the institution created for the indirect taxes and duties collection in the State of Milan) and its role in the fight against smuggling, see Gregorini (2003).
49. On the wool production of the Bergamo province in the Venetian scenario, see Panciera (1996); Pizzorni (2005); Demo (2006).
50. Ciriacono (1975, p. 133). 1 Venetian *libbra grossa* ('thick pound', meaning heavy; plur. *libbre grosse*) corresponded to approximately 477.00 grams; 1,000 *libbre grosse* constituted a *miaro* ('one thousand') (Martini 1883, p. 818).
51. Events reconstructed in BCMBG, ASCPC, 1.2.19.1-250.
52. Back in December 1522, in fact, a Senate decision addressed to the rectors of Bergamo invited them to especially monitor olive oil and soap smuggling (the legislative intervention can be found in Cappelluzzo 1992, pp. 134–135).

53. Costantini (2016a).
54. This is reported in the business documents analysed in Pizzorni (2005, p. 87).
55. BCMBG, ASCPC, 1.2.19.1-44.
56. Data from Ciriacono (1975, pp. 146–150).
57. "In these times, the roads are more popular among smugglers than other people: from Ferrara they head to Carpi through the Adige river, and then they move to the Padua, Vicenza, Verona, and Cologna provinces without fear or respect. Passing through Castiglione delle Stiviere, Solferino, Medole, and other border areas, they are transported and distributed in the Brescia, Cremona, and Bergamo provinces. It is not news their transport from Istria throughout Friuli or the Treviso province [...]. And God wanted the evil to stop here, so His Serenity did not suffer more damage, but olive oil is accompanied by salt and still many other goods [...]. [Smugglers are now] so audacious that the initial small tools hidden in bags, are replaced by whole wagons" ("Le stradde a questi tempi sono più battute da contrabandieri che da altre persone: dal Ferrarese si conducono a Carpi su l'Adice e poi vengono distribuiti nel Padovano, Vicentino, Veronese e Colognese senza timore, o rispetto alcuno medesimamente fatti passar a Castion, Solferino, Medole et altri luochi di confine, vengono trasportati, e distribuiti per il Bresciano, Cremonese et Bergamasco. Dalla parte dell'Istria non è nuovo il trasporto di essi per tutta la Patria del Friuli, o per il territorio trevisano [...]. E Dio volesse che il male si fermasse in questo solo datio, acciò Sua Serenità non risentisse maggiori pregiuditii, ma con l'olio s'accompagna il sale e s'accompagnano ancora molte altre mercantie [...]. [I contrabbandieri sono ora] tanto arditi che da piccioli arnasi o baghe nascoste nei sacchi sono riddotti a carri carrichi intieri") (BCMBG, ASCPC, 1.2.19.1-329).
58. BCMBG, ASCPC, 1.2.19.1-44.
59. BCMBG, ASCPC, 1.2.19.1-347. On 15 December, 1682, the wool producers of Gandino wrote that "it would be a great profit for woollen clothes, which would be produced in this valley in large quantities if the price of olive oil, which is excessive, was more moderate and regulated by the authorities of the Most Serene Dominant City" ("Sarebbe di gran profitto alla fatica delle pannine, che si fabricano in questa valle in gran quantità se il prezzo dell'oglio, qual si vende con prezzi eccessivi, fosse più moderato et regolato dalli calmieri della Serenissima Dominante").
60. The issue in BCMBG, ASCPC, 1.2.19.1-329.
61. On 3 September 1682, however, the *provveditori sopra oli* in Venice admitted that "officially set maximum prices of olive oil are common practice in all the cities on this side, and on the other side of the Mincio river, apart from Bergamo" ("il calamiero dell'oglio si pratticca in tutte le città di qua,

e di là dal Menzo, tolto Bergamo"). Also in this case, therefore, the city had peculiar features compared to the other cities under Venetian rule.

62. See Raggio (1982).
63. This market hub was studied by Rossini and Zalin (1985).
64. "Tali contrabandieri deveno esser accarezzati et favoriti" (Da Lezze 1988 [1596], p. 148).
65. Ulvioni (1989, pp. 127–132).
66. This is evident in Pezzolo (2002, p. 25).
67. Costantini (2017).
68. Costantini (2016b, pp. 58–62).
69. Costantini (2016b, pp. 64–65).
70. This is the conclusion of Corritore (1997).
71. Mocarelli (1996); Bowd (2010).
72. Knapton (2013, p. 115).
73. Costantini (2016b, pp. 112–115).
74. Author's elaboration on data from De Maddalena (1974, p. 379), for Milan; Bettoni (2008, pp. 222–223), for Brescia; Gullino (1984, pp. 490–495), for Padua; Bargelli (2013, p. 215), for Parma; Bulferetti (1963, p. 94), for Piedmont.
75. As stated in Parziale (2009, p. 17).
76. On Mantua, see Vivanti (1967, p. 423); on Florence, see Gori (1989, p. 525).
77. On Desenzano, see Ferlito (2006, pp. 682–688).
78. Cova (1977, p. 216).
79. Canetta (1979, pp. 108–109, 137–139).
80. The link with Genoa was also very close thanks to the dockers, who were largely from the Bergamo province. This seasonal emigration was itself also a response to the difficult food conditions in the province and represented an effective outlet (see Acerbis and Invernizzi 2009).
81. "[N]issuna cosa tien più allegro il popolo, che il buon mercato del pane" (Botero 1588, p. 79).

Archival Sources

Biblioteca Civica 'Angelo Mai', Bergamo (BCMBG)

Archivio Storico Comunale, Antico Regime, Giudici delle vettovaglie, Calmieri dei cereali (ASCGVCC).

Archivio Storico Comunale, Antico Regime, Deputati alle biade (ASCDP).

Archivio Storico Comunale, Antico Regime, Processi comunali (ASCPC).

www.bibliotecamai.org/patrimonio-e-cataloghi/archivio-storico-comunale

Published Sources

Botero, Giovanni. 1588. *Delle cause della grandezza delle città libri tre*. Roma: Giovanni Martinelli.

Calvi, Donato. 1676. *Effemeride sagro profana di quanto di memorabile sia successo in Bergamo, sua diocese, et territorio da' suoi principii sin al corrente anno*. Vol. I. Milano: Francesco Vigone.

Camozzi, Ermenegildo. 1992. *Le visite* ad limina apostolorum *dei vescovi di Bergamo (1590–1696)*. Bergamo: Provincia di Bergamo.

Cappelluzzo, Giovanni. 1992. *Lo statuto del podestà di Bergamo. Commissione dogale per Lorenzo Bragadin, 1559*. Bergamo: Amministrazione Provinciale di Bergamo.

Da Lezze, Giovanni. 1988 [1596]. *Descrizione di Bergamo e suo territorio, 1596*, ed. by Vincenzo Marchetti and Lelio Pagani. Bergamo: Provincia di Bergamo.

Maironi Da Ponte, Giovanni. 1803. *Osservazioni sul Dipartimento del Serio*. Bergamo: Alessandro Natali.

Montesquieu, Charles-Louis de Secondat, baron de. 1894–1896 [1728–1729]. Voyage en Italie. In *Voyages de Montesquieu*, ed. by Albert Montesquieu. Vols. I, 17–276, and II, 1–126. Paris: Picard/Bordeaux: Gounouilhou.

Università di Trieste, Istituto di Storia Economica, ed. 1976. *Relazioni dei rettori veneti in Terraferma*. Vol. VII: Podestaria e capitanato di Vicenza. Milano: Giuffrè.

———, ed. 1978. *Relazioni dei rettori veneti in Terraferma*. Vol. XII: Podestaria e capitanato di Bergamo. Milano: Giuffrè.

References

Acerbis, Eliana, and Nazzarina Invernizzi. 2009. *Huomeni Societatis Caravanae. La compagnia dei Caravana tra Genova e Bergamo*. Bergamo: Fondazione per la Storia Economica e Sociale di Bergamo Istituto di Studi e Ricerche.

Alfani, Guido, and Matteo Di Tullio. 2019. *The Lion's share: Inequality and the rise of the fiscal state in preindustrial Europe*. Cambridge: Cambridge University Press.

Bargelli, Claudio. 2013. *Dal necessario al superfluo. Le arti alimentari parmensi tra medioevo ed età moderna*. Milano: Angeli.

Bellazzi, Valeria, and Valeria Cantoni, eds. 2017. *Viaggiatori stranieri in Lombardia*. Genova: De Ferrari.

Bettoni, Barbara. 2008. Aspetti dell'economia agricola bresciana nei secoli XVII e XVIII: assetti fondiari, produzioni, tecniche colturali, contratti e mercati. In *Storia dell'agricoltura bresciana. Dall'antichità al secondo Ottocento*, ed. by Carlo Marco Belfanti and Mario Taccolini, 167–230. Brescia: Fondazione Civiltà Bresciana.

Bowd, Stephen. 2010. *Venice's most loyal city: Civic identity in Renaissance Brescia.* Cambridge/London: Harvard University Press.

Bulferetti, Luigi. 1963. *Agricoltura, industria e commercio in Piemonte nel secolo XVIII.* Torino: Istituto per la Storia del Risorgimento Italiano.

Caizzi, Bruno. 1992. Sale e fiscalità nel ducato milanese. *Archivio Storico Lombardo*, 11th series 9/118: 129–181.

Canetta, Rosalba. 1979. Materiali statistici sulle produzioni agricole della Lombardia nella prima metà dell'Ottocento. In *Questioni di storia agricola lombarda nei secoli XVIII–XIX. Le condizioni dei contadini, le produzioni e l'azione pubblica*, ed. by Sergio Zaninelli, 97–218. Milano: Vita e Pensiero.

Cantù, Ignazio. 1859. *Bergamo e il suo territorio.* Milano: Corona e Caimi.

Cassinelli, Bruno. 1990. Dalle fortificazioni venete di pianura alle mura cittadine. In *1588–1988. Le mura di Bergamo*, 21–33. Bergamo: Edizioni dell'Ateneo.

Cattini, Marco. 1998. Verso l'individualismo agrario. Campagne bergamasche nei sec. XV–XVI. In *Storia economica e sociale di Bergamo.* Vol. III: Il tempo della Serenissima. Part II: Il lungo Cinquecento, ed. by Marco Cattini and Marzio Achille Romani, 91–119. Bergamo: Fondazione per la Storia Economica e Sociale di Bergamo Istituto di Studi e Ricerche.

Ciriacono, Salvatore. 1975. *Olio ed ebrei nella Repubblica veneta del Settecento.* Venezia: Deputazione di Storia Patria per le Venezie.

Clerici, Luca. 2001. Fiere e mercati del Vicentino nel tardo medioevo e in età moderna. *Società e Storia* 24 (1/91): 11–77.

Colmuto Zanella, Graziella, and Vanni Zanella. 1995. "*Città sopra monte excellentissime situada*": evoluzione urbana di Bergamo in età veneziana. In De Maddalena et al. 1995, 59–151.

Coppola, Gauro. 1979. *Il mais nell'economia agricola lombarda (dal secolo XVII all'Unità).* Bologna: il Mulino.

Corritore, Renzo Paolo. 1997. Una fondamentale discontinuità padana: la linea dell'Oglio (secoli XVI–XVIII). In *La Lombardia spagnola. Nuovi indirizzi di ricerca*, ed. by Elena Brambilla and Giovanni Muto, 139–153. Milano: Unicopli.

Costantini, Fabrizio. 2016a. "Un popolo che non vorrebbe sentire nominare dazi". Esenzioni, privilegi e traffici illeciti tra Brescia, Cremona e Mantova nel Settecento. *Studi Storici Luigi Simeoni* 66: 55–65.

———. 2016b. *"In tutto differente dalle altre città". Mercato e contrabbando dei grani a Bergamo in età veneta.* Bergamo: Centro Studi e Ricerche Archivio Bergamasco.

———. 2017. La stagione dei trattati confinari tra Milano e Venezia. Controllo del territorio e criminalità di frontiera negli anni Cinquanta del XVIII secolo. In *Tra polizie e controllo del territorio. Alla ricerca delle discontinuità*, ed. by Livio Antonielli and Stefano Levati, 197–223. Soveria Mannelli: Rubbettino.

Costantini, Massimo. 1996. L'olio della Serenissima, dal commercio alla produzione. Per una storia dell'uso produttivo di un territorio d'oltremare in una strategia mercantilista. In *Levante veneziano. Aspetti di storia delle isole Ionie al tempo della Serenissima*, ed. by Massimo Costantini and Aliki Nikiforou, 11–19. Roma: Bulzoni.

Cova, Alberto. 1977. *Aspetti dell'economia agricola lombarda dal 1796 al 1814.* Milano: Vita e Pensiero.

Della Valentina, Gianluigi. 2006. L'agricoltura si rinnova. Si impongono gelso e granoturco. In *Storia economica e sociale di Bergamo.* Vol. III: Il tempo della Serenissima. Part IV: Settecento, età del cambiamento, ed. by Marco Cattini and Marzio Achille Romani, 17–73. Bergamo: Fondazione per la Storia Economica e Sociale di Bergamo Istituto di Studi e Ricerche.

———. 2015. *Storia delle campagne bergamasche dal Settecento a oggi.* Bergamo: Fondazione per la Storia Economica e Sociale di Bergamo.

De Maddalena, Aldo. 1974. *Prezzi e mercedi a Milano dal 1701 al 1860.* Milano: Banca Commerciale Italiana.

De Maddalena, Aldo, Marco Cattini, and Marzio Achille Romani, eds. 1995. *Storia economica e sociale di Bergamo.* Vol. III: Il tempo della Serenissima. Part I: L'immagine della Bergamasca. Bergamo: Fondazione per la Storia Economica e Sociale di Bergamo Istituto di Studi e Ricerche.

De Maddalena, Aldo, Marzio Achille Romani, and Marco Cattini, eds. 2000. *Storia economica e sociale di Bergamo.* Vol. III: Il tempo della Serenissima. Part III: Un Seicento in controtendenza. Bergamo: Fondazione per la Storia Economica e Sociale di Bergamo Istituto di Studi e Ricerche.

Demo, Edoardo. 2006. Wool and silk. The textile urban industry of the Venetian mainland (15th–17th centuries). In Lanaro 2006a, 217–243.

Fassina, Michele. 1982. L'introduzione della coltura del mais nelle campagne venete. *Società e Storia* 5 (1/15): 31–57.

Ferlito, Carmelo. 2006. Per un'analisi del costo della vita nella Verona del Settecento. *Studi Storici Luigi Simeoni* 56: 631–688.

Fornasin, Alessio. 2000 [1999]. Il mercato dei grani di Udine. Indagine per una storia dei prezzi in Friuli (secoli XVI–XVIII). New ed. In *La Patria del Friuli in età moderna. Saggi di storia economica*, by Alessio Fornasin, 33–60. Udine: Forum.

Gasparini, Danilo. 2002. *Polenta e formenton. Il mais nelle campagne venete tra XVI e XX secolo.* Sommacampagna: Cierre.

Georgelin, Jean. 1978. *Venise au siècle des Lumières.* Paris/La Haye: Mouton/Paris: École des Hautes Études en Sciences Sociales.

Gori, Orsola. 1989. Mercato e prezzi del grano a Firenze nel XVIII secolo. *Archivio Storico Italiano* 147 (3/541): 525–623.

Gregorini, Giovanni. 2003. *Il frutto della gabella. La Ferma generale a Milano nel cuore del Settecento economico lombardo.* Milano: Vita e Pensiero.

Gullino, Giuseppe. 1984. *I Pisani Dal Banco e Moretta. Storia di due famiglie veneziane in età moderna.* Roma: Istituto Storico Italiano per l'Età Moderna e Contemporanea.

Hocquet, Jean Claude. 1982 [1978–1979]. *Le sel et la fortune de Venise.* 2nd ed. Lille: Université de Lille III.

Knapton, Michael. 2013. The *terraferma* state. In *A companion to Venetian history, 1400–1797*, ed. by Eric R. Dursteler, 85–124. Leiden/Boston: Brill.

Lanaro, Paola, ed. 2006a. *At the centre of the Old World. Trade and manufacturing in Venice and the Venetian mainland, 1400–1800.* Toronto: Centre for Reformation and Renaissance Studies.

———. 2006b. At the centre of the Old World. Reinterpreting Venetian economic history. In Lanaro 2006a, 19–69.

Macry, Paolo. 1974. *Mercato e società nel Regno di Napoli. Commercio del grano e politica economica nel Settecento.* Napoli: Guida.

Martini, Angelo. 1883. *Manuale di metrologia, ossia misure, pesi e monete in uso attualmente e anticamente presso tutti i popoli.* Torino: Loescher.

Melchiorre, Matteo. 2013. *Conoscere per governare. Le relazioni dei sindici inquisitori e il dominio veneziano in terraferma (1543–1626).* Udine: Forum.

Messedaglia, Luigi. 2008. *La gloria del mais e altri scritti sull'alimentazione veneta.* Costabissara: Colla.

Mocarelli, Luca. 1996. *Le industrie bresciane nel Settecento.* Milano: Cuesp.

———. 2015. Ripensare le crisi alimentari: lo Stato di Milano nel secondo Settecento. In *"Moia la carestia". La scarsità alimentare in età preindustriale*, ed. by Maria Luisa Ferrari and Manuel Vaquero Piñeiro, 39–63. Bologna: il Mulino.

Moioli, Angelo. 1983. Una grande azienda del Bergamasco durante i secoli XVII e XVIII. In *Agricoltura e aziende agrarie nell'Italia centro-settentrionale (secoli XVI–XIX)*, ed. by Gauro Coppola, 599–724. Milano: Angeli.

Montenach, Anne. 2011. Formal and informal economy in an urban context: The case of food trade in seventeenth-century Lyons. In *Shadow economies and irregular work in urban Europe, 16th to early 20th centuries*, ed. by Thomas Buchner and Philip R. Hoffmann-Rehnitz, 91–106. Wien/Berlin: Lit.

Moretti, Isidoro. 2009. *Viaggiatori francesi a Bergamo e dintorni nel periodo romantico (1815–1850).* Gorle: Velar.

Panciera, Walter. 1996. *L'arte matrice. I lanifici della Repubblica di Venezia nei secoli XVII e XVIII.* Treviso: Fondazione Benetton Studi Ricerche/Canova.

Papagna, Elena. 1990. *Grano e mercanti nella Puglia del Seicento.* Bari: Edipuglia.

Parziale, Lavinia. 2009. *Nutrire la città. Produzione e commercio alimentare a Milano tra Cinque e Seicento.* Milano: Angeli.

Pezzolo, Luciano. 2000. Fiscalità e congiuntura in città e nel territorio (1630–1715). In De Maddalena et al. 2000, 217–235.

———. 2002. I prezzi cerealicoli nel Veneto in età moderna: problemi di una ricerca in corso. In *Prezzi, redditi, popolazioni in Italia: 600 anni (dal secolo XIV al secolo XX)*, ed. by Marco Breschi and Paolo Malanima, 23–30. Udine: Forum.

———. 2006. *Una finanza d'*ancien régime. *La Repubblica veneta tra XV e XVIII secolo.* Napoli: Edizioni Scientifiche Italiane.

Pizzorni, Geoffrey. 2005. *La Marcantonio Bonduri di Gandino. Un'impresa laniera in controtendenza tra Sei e Settecento.* Milano: Angeli.

Pult Quaglia, Anna Maria. 1990. *"Per provvedere ai popoli". Il sistema annonario nella Toscana dei Medici.* Firenze: Olschki.

Raggio, Osvaldo. 1982. Produzione olivicola, prelievo fiscale e circuiti di scambio in una comunità ligure del XVII secolo. *Atti della Società Ligure di Storia Patria* 22: 123–162.

Rossini, Egidio, and Giovanni Zalin. 1985. *Uomini, grani e contrabbandi sul Garda tra Quattrocento e Seicento.* Verona: Università degli Studi di Verona, Facoltà di Economia e Commercio, Istituto di Storia Economica e Sociale.

Saba, Franco. 1995. La popolazione del territorio bergamasco nei secoli XVI–XVIII. In De Maddalena et al. 1995, 215–273.

Sella, Domenico. 2000. Le attività manifatturiere nelle valli bergamasche. In De Maddalena et al. 2000, 83–97.

Ulvioni, Paolo. 1989. *Il gran castigo di Dio. Carestia ed epidemie a Venezia e nella Terraferma (1628–1632).* Milano: Angeli.

Vecchiato, Francesco. 1979. *Pane e politica annonaria in Terraferma veneta tra secolo XV e secolo XVIII. (Il caso di Verona).* Verona: Università degli Studi di Padova, Facoltà di Economia e Commercio in Verona, Istituto di Storia Economica e Sociale.

Vertecchi, Giulia. 2009. *Il "masser ai formenti in Terra Nova". Il ruolo delle scorte granarie a Venezia nel XVIII secolo.* Roma: Università degli Studi Roma Tre.

Vivanti, Corrado. 1967. I prezzi di alcuni prodotti agricoli a Mantova nella seconda metà del XVIII secolo. In *I prezzi in Europa dal XIII secolo a oggi. Saggi di storia dei prezzi*, ed. by Ruggiero Romano, 421–436. Torino: Einaudi.

Zalin, Giovanni. 1972. La politica annonaria veneta tra conservazione e libertà. *Rivista di Storia dell'Agricoltura* 12 (3–4): 389–423.

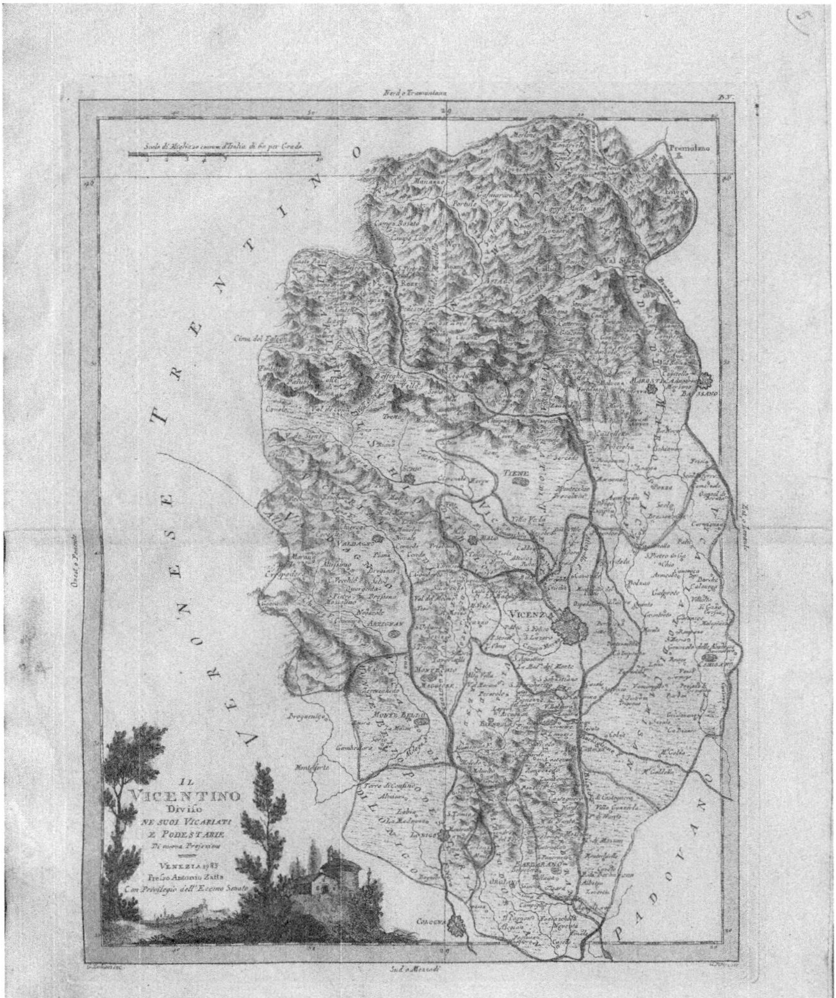

Map 4.1 The Vicenza province (1783)

CHAPTER 4

Provisioning a Medium-Sized City in a Polycentric State: Vicenza and Venice, 1516–1629

Luca Clerici

4.1 Introduction

The Republic of Venice, including many important and populous cities, was a noteworthy example of a polycentric state in early modern Italy. The degree of autonomy given by Venice to the cities under its rule has been the subject of ample debate in the last decades: in its essence, autonomy was limited to local administration, but with a certain degree of wiggle room.[1] The inland territorial expansion of Venice had begun in 1339, with the conquest of Treviso (Vicenza would willingly submit in 1404), and had reached its apex at the beginning of the sixteenth century. This had triggered the reaction of the League of Cambrai, gathered by Pope Julius II in 1508, which included the Holy Roman Empire, France, Spain, and some Italian states.[2] After the peripheral losses caused by the subsequent war, by 1517 the surface of Venetian dominions in Italy amounted

L. Clerici (✉)
Università degli Studi di Padova, Padua, Italy
e-mail: lclerici@unipd.it

L. Clerici (ed.), *Italian Victualling Systems in the Early Modern Age, 16th to 18th Century*, Palgrave Studies in Economic History,
https://doi.org/10.1007/978-3-030-42064-2_4

to 32,177 square kilometres, and remained so until the fall of the Republic in 1797.

These territories extended from eastern Lombardy to Friuli and, in the mid-sixteenth century, they were inhabited by no less than 1,614,000 people, including those living in the city of Venice. Ten cities and towns had no less than 10,000 inhabitants, and five of them were among the twenty most populous cities of Italy: Venice itself, Verona, Brescia, Padua, and Vicenza. Venice, in particular, was the third most populous European city after Paris and Naples.[3] In this context, the case of Vicenza from 1516 (when the city ultimately returned under the Venetian rule, after having been occupied and plundered several times by enemy troops) to 1629 (at the eve of the great plague epidemic, which upset previous economic and social equilibria) is particularly interesting.[4] This is due both to this city's wealth (thanks to wool and silk manufacture[5]) and to the rapid growth of its population (almost doubling between 1557 and 1617, something unparalleled in other cities of the Republic[6]).

4.2 The Commercial Heart of the City: Market Squares and Municipal Shops

The attraction exerted by Venice on the resources of the inland had already begun before its military conquest. After the territorial expansion at the beginning of the fifteenth century, the internal circulation and trade of wares had initially been left free, in order to favour the provisioning of cities (and, in particular, of the capital city), as well as to increase fiscal revenues. Nevertheless, engrossing and smuggling had led—soon, and with increased strength after the food crisis of the middle of the century—to increased regulation and reinforcement of the primacy of Venice's provisioning.[7] Subsequent developments intersected with the greater administrative and military control exercised by Venice over the Mainland after the 1509–1516 war.[8] The need for general regulation of trade in those territories was widespread, and central authorities were engaging in the reorganisation of commercial circuits, which had sprawled uncontrolled during the war. In his report submitted to the Venetian Senate in 1524, the outgoing podesta of Vicenza, Marco Antonio Contarini, assessed the necessity of reducing the number of weekly markets in the rural district. In fact, he attributed to their recent proliferation the increase in smuggling, the reduction in foodstuffs supply to the city's weekly markets, and the consequent decline of the proceeds of customs dues, transit fees, tolls, and taxes on the sale of goods (collectively called *dazi*).[9]

More generally, Vicenza was facing a threefold issue: a need to repair material damages caused by military occupations; a need to restore the city's laws and regulations, which had been lost in a fire to a great extent; and a need to reconstruct the economic fabric of the city, worn out by depopulation and plundering. This produced a unitary and systematic process, which comprised three lines of intervention: the restoration and enhancement of commercial spaces (market squares and municipal shops), the reorganisation of the layout of weekly markets, and the systematisation of the regulation of crafts and trades. By the middle of the century, the regulation of crafts and trades was progressively strengthened, in order to cope with the rapid growth of urban population. At the same time, growing difficulties in wheat provisioning led to the establishment of a new line of intervention: the regularisation of the compulsory transportation into the city of a part of the wheat surplus produced in the rural district.

The interventions on commercial spaces resumed the process of monumental transformation of public buildings, enlargement of public squares, and regulation of market areas, which had spread in northern and central Italy from mid-fifteenth century, and which had been interrupted by the war in the cities of the Venetian mainland.[10] In Vicenza, the first interventions regarded the municipal shops and stands existing in the city-hall vaults. At the end of the war, the flight of merchants and dealers, or their capture by enemy troops, had left these spaces in a state of neglect: shops had been plundered and damaged, and some conflicts had arisen regarding the occupation of stands. In 1518, two members of the executive board of the city's eight *deputati alle cose utili* ('deputies of useful things') were charged with assessing the expenses borne by the new tenants for repairing the damages suffered by shops; later in the same year, three other citizens were charged with arranging and allotting stands. In 1521, shops alienated at the beginning of the war in order to face financial needs but subsequently abandoned by the new owners, were restored to the Municipality.

In 1522, attention was extended to weekly markets, and three *deputati* were charged with revising the arrangement of the various categories of dealers in the market squares. This originated a new municipal office, subsequently called the office of the *presidenti*, *prefetti*, or *provveditori delle piazze* ('presidents', 'prefects', or 'superintendents of the squares'). In 1526, they published the first organic regulations of Vicenza's weekly markets, which in the following decades were republished several times with variations and additions, taking their final form in 1553.[11] Afterwards, urban authorities devoted themselves to the systematisation of crafts and trades regulation, at least in those areas which central bodies did not reserve for themselves.[12] In 1554, the rectors and the *deputati* published the first regulations of the office of *cavaliere di Comun* ('municipal knight'), the official in charge of monitoring crafts and trades.[13] These regulations too were republished several times in the following decades, constantly expanding and transforming from the initial form of the proclamation to the more solemn one of the volume compiled in 1587.[14]

The compilation of weekly-markets regulations was accompanied by the repaving of the central market area: *Piazza delle Biade* ('Crops Square') in 1524–1526, *Piazza delle Pescherie Vecchie* ('Old Fish Market Square') and maybe also *Piazza del Pesce Minuto* ('Small Fish Square') in 1532–1535 and 1547–1551, *Piazza delle Erbe* or *della Frutta* ('Herbs'—meaning vegetables—or 'Fruit Square') in 1535–1537, and other minor works here and there in 1545–1548. Furthermore, the port of the so-called *Isola* ('Island', an area situated at the confluence of the Bacchiglione and Retrone rivers), that had been filled by soil for quite a long time, was refurbished in 1535–1548.[15] During the same years, the Municipality erected a series of new masonry shops under public buildings: five under the Podesta's palace in 1527–1528, twenty under the city hall in 1534–1535, and some others under the Captain's palace in 1543–1544.[16] Their construction was dictated also by financial needs, often mentioned when the decision was taken. Shops were indeed much more profitable than stands: in the city-hall vaults in 1517, for instance, the rent of a shop was on average four times and a half that of a stand.[17]

The clearest example in this regard was the decision—taken in 1534 by the city's council, the *Consiglio dei Cento* ('Council of the One Hundred')—to build ten shops in those vaults, in the place occupied by the stands of women selling vegetables from their food gardens (*hortulane*, 'gardeners').[18] But if, on the one hand, shop rents contributed to feed municipal coffers, on the other hand the presence of hucksters increased and diversified the supply—also contributing to lower prices—to the benefit of buyers and, in particular, of the consumer population.[19] The Council took into account both aspects, and distinguished, on the one hand, the 'city's utility' (*civitatis utilitas*, that is to say, that of the Municipality), connected with shop rents collection, and, on the other hand, 'public utility' (*publica utilitas*, that is to say, that of buyers), associated with the preservation of vegetables supply, by allotting a suitable place to direct sellers. Consequently, it was decided that a market hall for greengrocers and fruiterers be built in the middle of Herbs Square, even if the project was soon abandoned and, instead, ten basement shops were built for them in 1535 under the city hall, on the side giving onto Herbs Square.[20]

4.3 Competing Categories of Foodstuffs Sellers: Cheese

Shops and stands were not only the location for different categories selling different goods, but also for different categories selling the same goods. When this happened, and goods were provided in abundance, public authorities usually limited themselves to preventing any contact between those categories, in order to preserve the variety of supply channels and protect buyers from collusion among sellers, engrossing, and speculation. This was the case of fruit, vegetables, poultry, eggs, and dairy products. Special attention was paid to resellers, in particular when they resided in the city, because they could be easily accused of causing unnecessary rises in prices, simply by buying and selling goods without either transporting or transforming them.[21] Vicenza's municipal statutes prohibited them in particular from buying foodstuffs outside the market squares and before noon (*nona hora*, that is to say, between 3 p.m. and 4 p.m., in nowadays terms).[22]

In 1339, Vicenza's foodstuffs resellers (*revendiculi* or *zavascarii*, 'greengrocers', from their main trade) were already organised in a guild, just like—among food trades—grocers, millers, fishmongers, taverners, butchers, and bakers.[23] These resellers—mostly hucksters—traded a large range of goods, and the sixteenth-century weekly-markets regulations subdivided them in four groups, each having a specific place in the market squares, different from that of the direct sellers trading the same goods. These four groups respectively sold crops, vegetables, fruit, and a heterogeneous set of goods including game, poultry, eggs, cheese, butter, and other goods (such as olive oil, lard, tallow candles, salt meat, and kids).[24] Regulations concerning the last set of goods were very complex, since many of them were sold not only by the guild of resellers and by direct sellers, but also by the members of another guild, that of grocers (*casolini* or *casolarii*, 'cheesemongers'—from their main trade—mostly shopkeepers). This complex situation, and the frequent conflicts between the different groups involved in the same trade, offers an interesting vantage point for better understanding the dynamics of urban provisioning through market and competition.[25]

The statutes of the guild of grocers in force at the end of the war dated to 1479 and had been confirmed several times in the following years.[26] They made guild membership compulsory for anyone wishing to sell goods traded by grocers (chiefly cheese, butter, olive oil, lard, salt meat, and tallow candles) in the centre of the city, in the *borghi* ('suburbs'[27]), and in the *colture* ('cultivated lands'[28]). This was regardless of where they may stand and sell (in private or municipal shops, on public ground with tables or simple sacks, or elsewhere), and regardless of their provenance (the city, the district, or other territories they came from). Symmetrically, on market days (Tuesday, Thursday, and Saturday) anyone was allowed to sell their goods in the market squares, although only wholesale and until noon (with a few exceptions concerning olive oil and salt meat).[29] The guild of grocers enjoyed a twofold benefit: first, hucksters (whether or not they were already members of the guild of resellers) had to enter the grocers' guild and pay a fee; secondly, shopkeepers were admitted to the market squares, and were not explicitly forbidden from selling also elsewhere.[30] But this potentially compromised the transparency of exchanges, both because of the spatial dispersion of sellers (which made them less controllable) and because of the intermingling of the different categories (which made them less distinguishable).[31] In the following years, several solutions were tested by the city's rectors and *deputati* to solve these problems.

After the war, in 1521, the members of the grocers' guild were allowed to sell only in private or municipal shops, or in the stands on public ground, and were forbidden from selling elsewhere, including market squares (clearly, if they did not rent a stand). Therefore, in order to adequately supply the weekly markets, it was necessary to allow some other sellers not to enter the grocers' guild. These were the 'foreigners' (*forenses*), here defined as those who, although not being enrolled in the guild, brought into the city and sold the kind of goods traded by grocers. These sellers were prescribed to stay in the eastern part of the Grand Square.[32] Actually, this was not a true definition of the term *forensis*, but a distinction among the many different sellers coming from outside of the city:[33] those who were not enrolled in the grocers' guild were admitted to the market squares, but only there, being thus excluded from itinerant trade in other parts of the city, like the members of the guild. Nevertheless, the measure did not state on which basis certain sellers coming from outside of the city were exempted from entering the guild. The answer is contained in a sentence pronounced in 1518 in favour of some of such sellers, men and women declaring they were "poor and powerless".[34] Therefore, the eastern part of the Grand Square was reserved to those sellers not residing in the city who, because of their condition of particular need,[35] were exempted from entering the guild, as well as from paying for the stallage to the Municipality, contrary to what resellers normally had to do in order to stay and sell in the market squares.[36]

The measure taken in 1521, while solving some problems, also created others. In fact, among the poor sellers coming from outside of the city, there were both resellers and direct sellers. In 1533 and 1539, only resellers coming from outside of the city were prescribed to stay and sell in the eastern part of the Grand Square, but it was added that they had to enter the grocers' guild (manifestly, without being obliged to rent a shop). At the same time, both "citizens and peasants" were allowed to sell anywhere—ostensibly without entering the guild—the butter and cheese produced with the milk of their own animals, on condition that they were not "resellers or merchants".[37] The 1521 measure was thus largely altered. Nevertheless, even the separation between direct sellers and resellers coming from outside of the city was not free from problems, because the condition of the latter was intrinsically ambiguous.

On the one hand, regardless of their provenance, all resellers based their gains on the difference between the buying and the selling price of the goods. From this point of view, resellers not residing in the city were considered on par with those residing in it, and public authorities preferred to separate them from direct sellers, in order to prevent the eventuality that resellers, exploiting spatial proximity, may unlawfully buy and resell at higher prices the goods sold by direct sellers. On the other hand, regardless of the nature of their trade, all sellers not residing in the city fed an additional provisioning channel, different from that controlled by resellers residing in it, and thus increased urban supply. From this point of view, resellers coming from outside of the city were considered on par with direct sellers having the same provenance (from whom it was moreover often difficult to distinguish them). Thus, always in order to avoid regrating, public authorities preferred to separate them from resellers residing in the city.

In the following decades, the city's rectors, *deputati*, and *presidenti delle piazze*—responding also to the pressures exerted by the various categories involved—fluctuated between these two solutions. One of their main concerns was safeguarding the plurality of the categories selling the same goods, in order to diversify supply channels to the city, and not to rely on a single channel. Moreover, they tried to take advantage of competition among these categories, siding alternatively sometimes with one group, sometimes with another. Therefore, resellers coming from outside of the city were sometimes prescribed to stay and sell in the square allotted to resellers residing in it (usually Herbs Square, but also—due to the works on the arcades of the city hall[38]—Crops Square, Old Fish Market Square, and Small Fish Square), and sometimes in the eastern part of the Grand Square.[39]

As early as 1540, the latter had become again the site for direct sellers coming from outside of the city; in 1549 and 1553 weekly-markets regulations, they were respectively called "poor men and women coming from villages" and "the poor from villages".[40] It seems that—as in 1518—poverty implied the exemption from the obligation of enrolment in the grocers' guild (at least for direct sellers, for whom this was specified in 1555[41]). It is likely that small direct sellers were considered as the quintessential poor, and that they had been brought back to the Grand Square because the 1533 and 1539 measures had exposed their goods, more than before, to regrating and reselling. This situation was further complicated because of the presence of another group of sellers, the milkmen (*lactarii*), who sold milk and fresh dairy products in Herbs Square, at the foot of the city hall. On the one hand, grocers alleged that the prohibition of selling on holydays, prescribed by the statutes of their guild, applied to milkmen too. On the other hand, milkmen replied by invoking the opposite custom, which they asserted was observed since more than sixty years before, but was not acknowledged by grocers.[42]

Any solution adopted by public authorities entailed specific conflicts. Resellers coming from outside of the city went often to the eastern part of the Grand Square, even when they were forbidden from doing so. Resellers residing in the city did the same, especially when those not residing in the city were instead admitted in that square, since they did not accept being subjected to different rules compared to their colleagues. The grocers' guild—who safeguarded the interests of its most influential members, shopkeepers—constantly denounced all transgressors, even when they were members of the guild. Sometimes resellers recurred to subterfuge to elude the law: for instance, in 1543 Cristoforo Ghezzi, a merchant who came from Piacenza (in western Emilia) and had been residing in Vicenza since one year before, did so. He should have entered the guild and rented a shop, but he had instead hired a servant coming from the district, who was thus entitled to stay and sell in the Grand Square.[43]

In this as in other cases, grocers complained that they paid shop rents and taxes, but were forbidden from staying and selling in the market squares. In other words, they reminded public authorities that they had a common interest, because part of their earnings fed public coffers: indeed this argument was reused by public authorities when ordering enforcement of the guild's statutes, as for instance in 1550.[44] Nevertheless, the interests of public authorities and grocers could diverge also on this matter. When in 1573 the city's council built five rows of wooden shops in the eastern part of the Grand Square and leased one row to butter and cheese sellers, the grocers' guild objected to this decision, because the row had been assigned to some resellers residing in the city, a category which in those years was not allowed to stay and sell in that square.[45] In other cases, the efforts of the guild were focused towards obtaining the authorisation for all its members—thus not only hucksters residing in the city, but also shopkeepers—to stay and sell in the market squares. In 1542 and 1555, for instance, they were admitted in the same square allotted to resellers coming from outside of the city (respectively, the eastern part of the Grand Square—with direct sellers—and Herbs Square).[46]

However, these were only exceptional and temporary measures. In fact, the power of the grocers' guild was not only limited by the action of public authorities, but also opposed by resellers, both residing and not residing in the city. It is worth noting that resellers not residing in the city—and particularly those of the district—demonstrated both the ability to adopt forms of self-organisation and representation, and the possession of a certain economic and political weight, even in the absence of a specific guild. In fact, it is well documented that the district's resellers produced some significant personalities (in particular, the members of the Poveretto family, from Castelnovo, between the 1550s and the 1570s), who bore the burden of the actions brought against those resellers by the grocers' guild. They were able to represent their colleagues not only in the first degree of judgement before the city's *deputati* and in the appeal before the podesta, but also in the following degrees of judgement before the Venetian magistracies of the *auditori novi* ('new auditors') and of the *Collegio dei Venti Savi* ('Board of the Twenty Wisemen').[47]

In 1570, when resellers coming from outside of the city were admitted in the eastern part of the Grand Square, and resellers residing in the city were not, a mixed group of them justified their presence there by declaring that they charged lower prices than grocers (i.e. shopkeepers), adding that this fostered the 'city's utility' (*civitatis utilitas*, that is to say—in this case—that of buyers).[48] This price difference was justified by the different costs met by shopkeepers and hucksters, costs of which the grocers' guild—as previously seen—constantly reminded public authorities. It is likely that resellers charged lower prices than shopkeepers in Herbs Square too, since the rent of a stand was much lower than that of a shop. Nevertheless, the prices charged by direct sellers in the Grand Square were plausibly the lowest, since they did not have to pay neither for the stallage to the Municipality, nor the fee to the grocers' guild, nor the costs of professional intermediation.

Consequently, the eastern part of the Grand Square was attractive for resellers (and shopkeepers) for many reasons. On the one hand, as it was often complained, they illegally bought goods from direct sellers and resold them at higher prices (although probably still lower than those charged in shops). On the other hand, in the Grand Square resellers did not have to pay for the stallage and had the opportunity to intercept the clientele of direct sellers. More generally, since all major public buildings overlooked the Grand Square, one could there benefit from larger passer-by traffic, as it can be argued by the fact that resellers stood and sold there even outside market days and even in its western part (on front of the main side of the city hall), where trade was forbidden. At the same time, since lower prices attracted buyers to the market squares rather than to grocers' shops, the prohibition of retail selling in the squares was aimed at balancing this situation. Protecting (to a certain extent) grocers who were running a shop was meant to benefit not only public coffers (through the taxes and rents they paid), but also buyers (thanks to the daily and regular supply ensured by shopkeepers, albeit at higher prices).

4.4 Urban Provisioning and Officially Set Maximum Prices: Meat and Fish

The situation was different when health concerns were combined with difficulties in ensuring regular supplies to the city: this was the case of meat and fish. The managing of the four city butcheries—where animals were slaughtered, and their meat sold—was let out on contract each year. The system of contracts is clearly attested in its fullest form until 1550.[49] The contractor undertook to ensure the activity of the butcheries and to pay a rent to the Municipality; in his turn, he allotted to butchers the licences for fresh meat retailing and let them the butchery stalls. Since stalls were not numerous (ten or so in the central butchery, and one in each of the three butcheries located in the suburbs[50]), allocation of contracts was accompanied by the official fixing of the maximum selling prices of fresh meat for the whole year, and by very detailed anti-collusive and anti-speculative regulations. These measures were aimed at ensuring an adequate supply at reasonable prices, even if—in general—this kind of measures was not necessarily always successful, given groups that were able to systematically get the contract.[51]

Apart from the general obligation to keep the stalls well-stocked, contract specifications covered only exceptionally the supply of a given quantity.[52] Nevertheless, it was in every respect a contract for provisioning the city, with exclusive rights of sale at given maximum prices. Contracts were allocated by public auction. The city's *deputati* announced the contract after having defined its specifications—which also contained the maximum prices to be observed—and let the contract to the highest bidder. Sometimes, if nobody made a bid, the *deputati* softened some conditions, or at worst proceeded to engage in private negotiations. The contractor was usually a butcher, or a company of butchers, and only rarely an outsider wishing to invest in this sector. The latter was the case of the patrician Paolo Dal Gorgo, who took the contract in 1544 and 1545 and tried to enforce contract specifications about selling, but was hindered by the butchers' guild; he took the contract again in 1547, but gave it up only eleven days after.[53]

Price setting regarded fresh beef, mutton, lamb, veal, and (not always) kid. The price of fresh pork—which was sold not only by general butchers, but also by pork-butchers and sausage-makers—was set in specific proclamations addressed to these three categories.[54] In compliance with the period's ideal of price stability—important for the political legitimation of rulers[55]—maximum prices were officially set at a constant level for long periods. Nonetheless, public authorities were aware that excessively low prices—although in themselves advantageous for buyers—could produce short supply for the butchery stalls and an expansion of the illegal market. This would have entailed the undesirable consequence of both hitting exactly the buyers who were supposed to be protected (especially the poor), and damaging public finances (due to low contract rents and low fiscal yield).[56] Therefore, official maximum prices were set at a level that normally guaranteed both a satisfying margin of profitability to contractors and butchers, and adequate public revenues, thus mediating among the interests of all the actors involved and ensuring the effectiveness of the system.

Given the stability of officially set maximum prices, public authorities recovered a certain margin for manoeuvre in the short run by frequently modifying other clauses of contract specifications which influenced the contractor's and the butchers' gains, in order to allow them to deal with changing costs. These clauses regarded the distinction between locally-bred and imported animals; the length of the periods (varying between 0 and even 167 days, usually in Lent and summer, when sales were lower) during which it was allowed to charge an overprice of 6 Venetian *denari* per Vicentine *libbra grossa*[57] (corresponding to a price increase of 14.3–25.0%, depending on the kind of meat and on the year);[58] the kinds of animals whose meat should not be sold in the butcheries (sows, cows, bulls, ewes, she-goats, and he-goats); the less valuable parts of the animals (*zonte*, 'additions': entrails, heads, and shins) that butchers might or might not add to muscle meat and sell at the same price; the weight limit between calves—whose meat was dearer—and steers (varying between 120 and 200 Vicentine *libbre grosse*, sometimes further distinguishing between small and large calves). A margin of flexibility was also left to butchers, who could sell the meat of some animals, or some parts and by-products of slaughtering (e.g. skins and tallow[59]) at unregulated prices.[60] The effect of the exogenous variations in the yearly revenues and expenses expected by contractors and butchers was partially absorbed through the aforesaid channels. The part which was not absorbed in that way influenced the bids made by tenderers when contracts were allocated, due to the competitive mechanism of auctions. The importance of this factor is demonstrated by the wide range of variation in contract rents, which oscillated between 26 and 380 Venetian *ducati* from 1517 to 1550 (see Fig. 4.1).[61]

Similar considerations apply to the fish market. The managing of the stone stalls located in Old Fish Market Square—whose economic importance was much lower than that of the butcheries—was also let out on contract each year.[62] Nonetheless, contrary to the case of the butcheries, contract specifications were not recorded in the books of measures of the *deputati*, probably because the norms regulating fish trade were already included in the municipal statutes.[63] Another difference was more important: official maximum fish prices were not necessarily set at the moment of the contract's announcement. The reason was probably that the stone stalls constituted only a part of the fish market, which stretched from Old Fish Market Square to Small Fish Square. Furthermore, official maximum fish prices were set without any regularity and often more than once a year, using classifications which changed continuously and hampered a simple and immediate comparison between old and new prices (distinguishing, or not distinguishing, between saltwater or freshwater, alive or dead, and large-sized or small-sized fish, at times further specifying qualities and sizes). Thanks to this method, it was possible to introduce a margin of

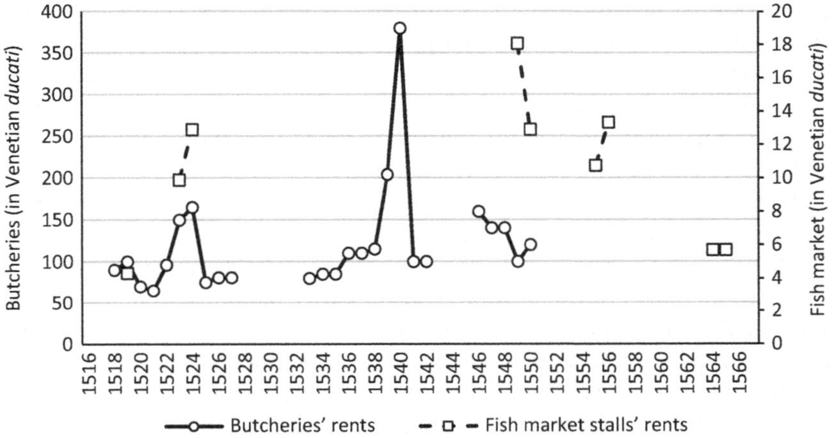

Fig. 4.1 Annual contract rents for Vicenza's butcheries (1518–1550) and fish market stone stalls (1519–1565). (Sources: Elaboration on data from BCBVI, AT, 795–802, 804. Data regarding fish market stalls' rents, originally in Vicentine *lire*, have been converted into Venetian *ducati* for ease of comparison)

flexibility also in setting official maximum fish prices. Contract rents were also volatile—even if less than those for the butcheries—oscillating between 20 and 84 Vicentine *lire* (i.e. between 4.30 and 18.06 Venetian *ducati*) from 1519 to 1565 (see Fig. 4.1).[64]

The connection between the official setting of maximum prices and the provisioning of the city became more evident during Lent, when the precept of abstaining from meat increased the demand for fish,[65] creating a tension towards price rise.[66] The *deputati* then settled specific agreements with fishmongers—usually without auctions—for provisioning the city with fish at given prices, that were also valid as officially set maximum prices for all sellers.[67] Regarding 1519, for instance, the contract for the managing of fish market stalls for the whole year was let out on contract to Domenico Vendramin, a weaver from Grossa (a village in Vicenza's district), while that for the fish provisioning for Lent was let to Battista Matto, a fishmonger from Padua.[68] In 1554, the *deputati* convened two important fishmongers of the city: Belforte Spinella, from Padua (who had already been the contractor for fish market stalls in 1550, and would again be in 1555 and 1556[69]), and Gianmaria Bruschi, from Trissino (another village in Vicenza's district), acting also on behalf of their partners. They agreed with the *deputati* on official maximum fish prices for Lent and undertook to provision the city during this period. Nevertheless, since they demanded to have exclusive rights of sale in the city, and fish was on short supply, the city's council decided to allocate a new contract, also offering a loan to the contractor. It seems that negotiations were not easy: only a month later the *deputati* agreed on new prices with Battista Matto, and other fishmongers represented by him.[70]

Information about the functioning of the system of contracts for the managing of the butcheries is fragmentary after 1550. On the one hand, yearly notices of auctions and allocation of contracts disappeared from the books of measures of the *deputati*; on the other hand, the rental of single stalls by the Municipality to butchers is sometimes attested, as well as the allocation of specific contracts for Lent. Contract specifications were inserted in the regulations of the office of *cavaliere di Comun* in 1570, 1587, and 1622, thus remaining unchanged for long periods. Overprices were no longer mentioned in these specifications, maybe because of the allocation of a different contract for Lent.[71] The origin of these changes must be found in a conflict which had pitted Venice against the cities of the Mainland in the previous decades.[72] In 1529, Turkish military campaigns had forced the Senate to replace previous cattle imports from Eastern Europe, and each province of the Mainland was obliged to supply the capital city with a yearly quota.[73] This duty had been supported one year later by a twofold measure, aimed at making the Venetian market more attractive for sellers. Firstly, the *Collegio delle Beccarie* ('Butcheries' Board') had allowed anybody to freely sell meat in Venice's butcheries, without the usual authorisation from the collector of the tax on meat sales and without paying any rent for the stalls. Secondly, the Board had set the official maximum prices for veal and beef in the Mainland at 2 Venetian *denari* per *libbra grossa* less than in Venice (corresponding to 6.6% less for veal and 8.5% less for beef).[74]

These prescriptions had endangered the provisioning of Mainland cities and provoked the reaction of urban authorities, both municipal bodies and Venetian rectors. The opposition to compulsory provisions had continued for almost three decades—until 1557—when the burden had been progressively reduced.[75] At the same time, urban authorities had succeeded in reneging on the rule about prices. It had been necessary to repeat the order several times—and to go as far as to threaten rectors with a fine of 100 Venetian *ducati* in case of non-execution[76]—before it was finally obeyed in 1558.[77] By then, prices were once again stable for thirty years, but the system of contracts in Vicenza dramatically changed. Since official maximum prices were set by Venice, and by 1570 contract specifications were crystallised in the regulations of the office of *cavaliere di Comun*, Vicenza's *deputati* lost the discretionary power that in the past had allowed them to adapt contract specifications to circumstances and to attract meat supplies to Vicenza, even in competition with Venice.[78]

4.5 Compulsory Transportation and Public Provisioning: Wheat

At the end of the 1509–1516 war, Vicenza had no permanent body or office specifically in charge of crops provisioning. Before the Venetian rule, Mainland cities were characterised by municipal and—most of all—seigneurial granaries (*fontici*, 'warehouses', or *canipae*, 'cellars'), which had been pivotal for economic policies regarding crops. These included not only gathering and distributing crops to the city's people, but also granting agrarian loans, monitoring stocks, and trading surpluses on both a domestic and an international scale. Nevertheless, these institutions had been dismantled after the Venetian conquest, partly because of their connection with previous rulers, partly because they would have hampered the free internal circulation of goods initially introduced by the Republic. New institutions of this kind (also called *montes*, 'mounts', by analogy with the mounts of piety) were established in the Mainland only with the demographic recovery of the second half of the fifteenth century, but their function was reduced to ensuring subsistence for the city's people and, in particular, the poor.[79]

In Vicenza, their presence—often opposed by patrician landowners[80]—is discontinuously attested during the sixteenth and seventeenth centuries. In 1539, a year of scarcity, the preaching of a Dominican friar inspired the foundation of the *Monte di San Giovanni Battista* ('Mount of St. John the Baptist'). Its objective was to buy wheat, transform it into flour and bread, and sell these to the needy at lower prices than those offered by private sellers. This institution still existed in 1557, but it disappeared before 1589, when a harsh food crisis hit the city. The city's council then instituted a new *Fontico Generale di Farine* ('General Warehouse of Flours'), on the strong impulse of the city's rectors, who wrote its regulations. It was reserved for poor families, which could buy crops and flours within the limits of their weekly consumption needs. Despite the prescription of selling at purchase price, plus operating costs and a slight mark-up, the practice of selling at a loss, and the concomitant undercapitalisation, progressively led to the crisis of the *Fontico*, the last mention of which dates to 1613.[81]

Another measure which was still exceptional at the end of the 1509–1516 war, was represented by the compulsory transportation of crops from the rural district to the city. The first attestations regarding surveys (*descriptiones*) of the crops harvested in the district of Vicenza date to the end of the thirteenth century, and those about their compulsory transportation into the city (*impositiones*) to the first half of the fourteenth century.[82] After the Venetian conquest, carrying out annual surveys in Mainland provinces was the podesta's duty. The amount of disposable surplus was estimated by deducting from the amount of wheat harvested in summer what was necessary for the following year's sowing and for peasants' alimentation until the autumn harvest of other crops, and its trade was subjected to the podesta's authorisation. The execution of crops surveys (*descrizioni*), together with the control over their trade, was aimed at giving central offices an up-to-date picture of the stocks existing in the Mainland, from which it would be possible to draw in case of need.[83] Moreover, these surveys were the basis for ordering compulsory transportation (*condotte*) into the city of a part of the surplus, after quantification of the duty (*limitazioni*, 'definitions').

This caused conflicts between the podesta—concerned with the stable provisioning of the city—and the owners of wheat, residing both in the city and in the district—who wished to freely dispose of their crops—.[84] In 1543, the outgoing podesta of Vicenza Bernardo Venier asked the Senate to render wheat compulsory transportation annual, also in order to contrast smuggling and to support the revenue from taxes and duties on transport and trade.[85] The institution of a regular system of surveys and compulsory transportation was not immediate and it can be dated to 1561: on the one hand, they are only sporadically attested until the mid-1550s; on the other hand, it also happened—as in 1530—that the podesta ordered transportation without having previously carried out any surveys.[86] In the more populous city of Verona, an obligation to supply wheat to the *Mercato Vecchio* reserved for the poor had already been established in 1549, and the system of annual surveys and compulsory transportation into the city was introduced in 1562.[87]

On the local level, the institution of annual wheat transportation reinforced the position of the Venetian rectors against the cities' patriciates regarding the power of disposal of the surplus harvested in the rural districts, and this engendered new conflicts. On the one hand, owners tried to escape the obligation, searching for more profitable outlet markets.[88]

On the other hand, podestas used their discretionary powers to introduce additional obligations. In Vicenza, once wheat had been transported into the city in due time and manner, owners were to be free to use it as they pleased. Despite this, the podesta occasionally ordered the transportation of wheat to the market square for selling, and exceptionally imposed maximum selling prices. Some other times, he ordered to transport into the city even wheat exceeding the amount due.[89] On the state level, the conflict between central and local bodies was fuelled by the ancient obligation, for Venetians receiving agricultural rents, to each year report to central authorities their crops surplus, and to transport it into Venice.[90] The problem was that, while compulsory transportation into Mainland cities was imposed on the wheat harvested in their respective districts, regardless of where the owners resided, compulsory transportation into Venice was imposed on the wheat owned by Venetians, regardless of where it had been harvested. Since compulsory transportation into Venice had priority status, the provisioning of Mainland cities was hampered by the expansion of Venetian landholding. As a consequence, compulsory transportation into Venice was opposed not only by the councils of subject cities, but also by the Venetian rectors, who were frequently threatened with severe punishments by central bodies regarding this subject.[91]

All these transformations can be understood in the framework of the more general Italian and Mediterranean situation. In mid-sixteenth century, the growth of Italian crops production—which for a century was accompanying and supporting the demographic growth of the peninsula—was increasingly impeded by the cultivation of marginal lands, the reduction of yields, and the competition of more profitable cultivations, such as grapevine and olive tree.[92] At the same time, the development of territorial states was increasingly hampering long-distance crops trade.[93] The course of these trade routes was very important for a city like Venice, which around 1550 imported half of its crops requirements from overseas.[94] During the 1550s, the expansion of crops trade with the Levant had compensated for the effects of the increased cost of export licences from Sicily, imposed in 1546. Nevertheless, the Ottoman Empire forbade crops export by the time of the 1560 agrarian crisis, which had hit the entire Mediterranean basin area.[95]

The difficulties in provisioning Venice from overseas increased the interest in Mainland dominions, and the victualling concerns of the Republic intersected with the will of its patriciate to invest in a sector which the century-long increase in crops prices had made very lucrative. The office of the *provveditori sopra beni inculti* ('superintendents for uncultivated lands')—competent on the subject of reclamation and irrigation—which had been created in 1545, was reinforced in 1556, and in 1562 the first land-reclamation syndicates appeared. The office of the *provveditori sopra beni comunali* ('superintendents for municipal lands')—supervising the lands left for the collective use of rural communities—was created in 1574.[96] Available data show the effects of these transformations: between 1566 and 1595, the amount of crops imported into Venice from overseas was characterised by a descending linear trend of 1.36% per year, while those coming from the Mainland by an ascending trend of 1.71%. On average, crops imported from overseas amounted to 189,740 Venetian *staia* per year, and those coming from the Mainland to 270,046 (see Fig. 4.2).[97]

As regards Vicenza, between 1572 and 1593, wheat compulsory transportation presented a substantially flat trend—increasing by only 0.02%

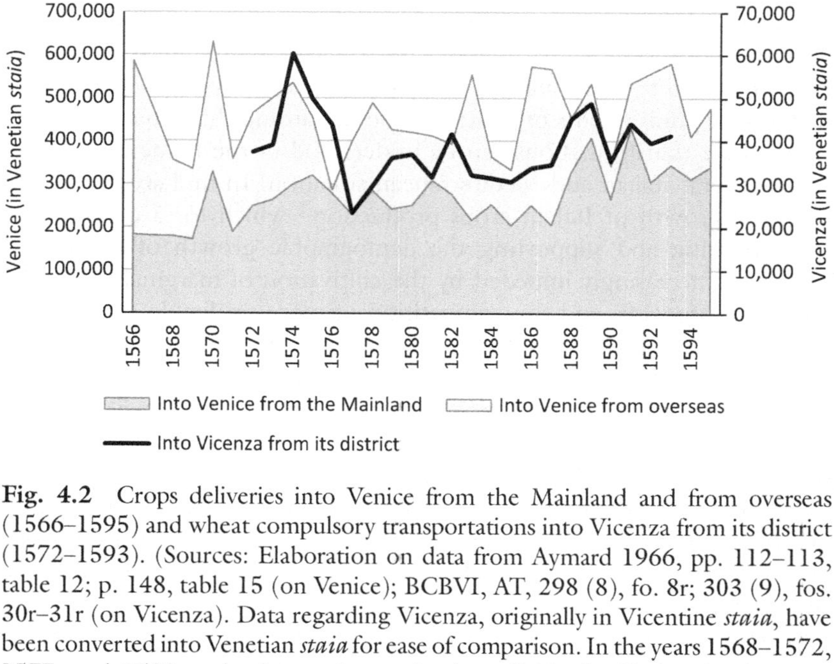

Fig. 4.2 Crops deliveries into Venice from the Mainland and from overseas (1566–1595) and wheat compulsory transportations into Vicenza from its district (1572–1593). (Sources: Elaboration on data from Aymard 1966, pp. 112–113, table 12; p. 148, table 15 (on Venice); BCBVI, AT, 298 (8), fo. 8r; 303 (9), fos. 30r–31r (on Vicenza). Data regarding Vicenza, originally in Vicentine *staia*, have been converted into Venetian *staia* for ease of comparison. In the years 1568–1572, 1577, and 1580, only the total quantity is available for Venice; in the years 1572–1575 and 1577, data regarding Vicenza are incomplete; missing data have been estimated through ordinary least squares)

per year—and amounted on average to 118,402 Vicentine *staia* per year (corresponding to 38,431 Venetian *staia*) (see Fig. 4.2).[98] In 1590, the annual wheat consumption of Vicenza was estimated to approximately 300,000 Vicentine *staia*:[99] since the city's population could have then amounted to approximately 30,000 inhabitants,[100] it follows that the annual consumption per person amounted on average to 10 Vicentine *staia*.[101] Estimating that in those two decades the city's population approximately increased from 27,000 to 31,000 inhabitants, it follows that compulsory transportation covered on average 41% of the city's yearly consumption.[102] After the harsh 1589–1591 food crisis, articulated regulations of wheat surplus surveys and compulsory transportation were established. In 1594, a general proclamation concerning crops was issued, reviving a previous one from 1567 and adding new norms, in particular regarding surveys and compulsory transportation. By 1602, these norms were extracted from the general proclamation and became the subject of a second, specific and more detailed proclamation. It appears that these proclamations were issued yearly, even if not all specimens have been preserved.[103] The system of compulsory transportation was enhanced also in Venice, where in 1590 specific *provveditori* in charge of surveys were created, thus replicating the system already in use in Mainland cities, instead of relying on owners' declarations as before.[104]

A third form of provisioning Vicenza with crops went through the intervention of the Municipality in times of scarcity. The decision was taken by the city's council. Purchases usually regarded wheat, and sometimes other crops, for the city, and only exceptionally—as in 1587 and 1600—other crops for the district. For such a purpose, the Council appointed specific *presidenti ai frumenti* or *alle biade* ('presidents for wheat' or 'for crops'), usually three in number.[105] First of all, the *presidenti* had to find the money needed to finance the operation. The sources for financing were various: in addition to the ordinary revenues of the Municipality—sometimes increased by new rentals of its properties, but rarely sufficient to meet the need—the *presidenti* drew from the fixed deposits set aside by the Municipality at the Mount of Piety for emergency situations, with the obligation of restoring them. In exceptional cases, the municipal patrimony was sold. Nevertheless, before coming to this point, the *presidenti* tried to borrow money from citizens and merchants, from the Mount of Piety or, in extreme cases, from the city's rectors or from central bodies of the Republic, mortgaging the properties of the Municipality. Sometimes, forced loans were imposed on the basis of the general assessments (named *estimi*, 'evaluations') of the contributing capacity of the city's population. Nevertheless, a more frequent solution was to resort to loans in favour of the Municipality, which were provided for by the procedure of appointment of some municipal officials.

The *presidenti* could also be charged with seeking, buying, transporting, storing, and selling crops, but it was usually private contractors who—following the example of Venice—were entrusted with these operations.[106] Contract terms were also similar to those fixed by the Venetian *Collegio delle Biave* ('Crops Board').[107] In Vicenza, contractors were sometimes granted a loan for executing the purchases, sometimes they received an import bounty, rarely both.[108] The Municipality (and sometimes even the podesta) was usually obliged to provide contractors with the licence (named *tratta*, 'bill') necessary for exporting crops or transiting with them from Venice, on penalty of nullifying of the contract.[109] Sometimes, the Municipality also bore a part of its cost.[110] Among the terms of the contracts concluded by Vicentine *presidenti alle biade*, the clause of buying crops from foreign countries—or at least not from Vicenza's district—was recurrent. Crops trade was a very complex business,[111] and entering commercial circuits beyond the local dimension could present some difficulties for relatively inexperienced individuals. Taking this into account, to rely on contractors allowed the *presidenti*—who were usually members of the local patriciate and were not necessarily involved in trade[112]—to take advantage of merchants' experience and acquaintances in the circuits of crops trade. Furthermore, by doing so, the *presidenti* could avoid the need to find large amounts of money and to bear the risks of the operations, especially when contractors were simply bestowed import bounties, and did not receive loans for effecting the purchases.

The importance of these factors is demonstrated by the fact that, when contractors were merchants specialised in crops trade, their relationship with the Municipality went on for years: this was the case of Sebastian Auer, in 1540 and 1555; of Gabriele, in 1559, and Tommaso, Barana, in 1581, 1586, and 1587; and of Stefano, in 1562, and Giacomo, Magrè, in 1581. Moreover, in 1540 the Municipality had recourse to the keepers of the *Monte di San Giovanni Battista*, both as negotiators and as suppliers.[113] In other cases, the usual business of contractors—even if they were merchants—was not crops trade. Despite this, the prospect of a profitable deal could lead them to get into that trade: this was the case of the wool merchant Pietro Pizzoni and his nephews, in 1562; of the silk merchant Girolamo Mazzi, in the same year; and of the linen merchants Francesco and Pietro Dal Bo, in 1586 and 1587.[114] The *presidenti* took advantage of the collaboration of members of the business community even when they did not find anybody willing to take the contract, being thus obliged to provision the city personally. In 1560, they sent the wool merchant Antonio Zorzi to buy crops in Venice as their agent. In the same capacity, the silk merchant Ottavio Moro dealt not only with the purchase, but also with the distribution of wheat in 1600–1601.[115]

Lack of experience in crops trade could cause some problems also to merchants. It was for this reason that Francesco and Pietro Dal Bo took the contracts—probably contributing with their capital—in partnership with Tommaso Barana. He was a merchant specialised in crops, who kept contacts with the *presidenti* and dealt with commercial operations. On the contrary, Pietro Pizzoni and his nephews were less foresighted and encountered various complications, despite the later participation in the initiative by two merchants specialised in sea trade, Marco Attavanti and Pellegrino Brunaccini. To safeguard itself against the risk of contract breach, the municipality of Vicenza—not unlike the *Collegio delle Biave* in Venice—asked contractors to give due guarantees, usually a suretyship. Sometimes, the guarantor too was interested in the deal: this can be argued, for instance, from the fact that, when in 1581 the contract of Giuseppe Lodi and Giulio Campana was cancelled for breach, their guarantor—the silk merchant Giacomo Magrè—took a new contract.[116] In addition to the obligation of giving a guarantee, the terms of the contract provided also for the penalties to apply when the delivery dates were not observed, or when the quality of crops was not good. Controversies between the Municipality and contractors were not infrequent. The most important lawsuit was that against Giacomo Magrè, charged with several irregularities. It extended from 1582 to 1591 and ended with an arbitration agreement.[117]

Differing from the Venetian pattern—where the State bought at a predefined price the crops imported by contractors, and it controlled the distribution channels[118]—the contracts let in Vicenza provided that contractors would also deal with selling the crops. Having renounced direct management of the distribution of crops, the Municipality safeguarded itself against the risk of price speculations by contractors by obliging them to sell crops within a few days from their arrival. Conditions regarding selling prices varied. Sometimes contractors were left free to sell crops at current prices, sometimes the selling price was fixed in advance, on the basis of market conditions at the moment of the letting of the contract. In the latter case, contractors' earnings would be limited whenever current prices would rise again, but they would be protected in case of price reductions. Lastly, some other times it was specified that the selling price should be equal to the purchase price, with the addition of operating costs and a mark-up (the contractors' gain).

Entrusting crops distribution to contractors allowed the Municipality to transfer to them some specific risks connected with these operations: for instance, the risk of exceedingly low selling prices preventing the recovery of purchase expenses, or the risk of crops quality being inadequate, which—in the best case scenario—would require them to be sifted again, with the consequent loss of mass. Moreover, the conversion of the coins collected during the distribution of crops into valuable coinage or scriptural money necessary to reconstitute the initial capital, often entailed the payment of an agio, and sometimes entailed even more difficulties. In 1601, for instance, the Mount of Piety refused to accept the petty coins presented by the agent of the *presidenti*, Ottavio Moro, in restitution of the not negligible sum of 150 Venetian *ducati*.[119] On the one hand, when crops were bought wholesale and sold retail, it was necessary to systematically give valuable coinage or scriptural money, and mostly accept petty coins. On the other hand, even if crops were not directly sold retail, counterparts having a strong bargaining power—like the bakers' guild—could force their suppliers to accept the petty coins they received from their customers. Moreover, the current quotation of valuable currencies in terms of money of account was variable: this could cause not only a loss, but also a gain. The latter case occurred, for instance, in 1629: firstly, the Spanish *doppie* received by the *presidenti* in Vicenza were spent at a higher rate when wheat was bought by the city's permanent representative (*nunzio*, 'messenger') in Venice, Giovanni Biagio Macchiavelli; moreover, other *scudi* spent to buy wheat in Venice were recovered at a lower rate when selling crops in Vicenza.[120]

Until the 1580s, resorting to contracts for crops provisioning during years of scarcity was the habitual solution, but it came to an end after the institution of the *Fontico* in 1589, and the strengthening of the regulations for compulsory transportation by 1594. As a matter of fact, the institutive deliberation of the *Fontico* mentioned the aim to liberate the Municipality from attending to crops provisioning, and especially from dealing with contractors.[121] It is likely that the problems experienced with contractors—especially with Giacomo Magrè in the 1580s—contributed to this decision. Only in cases of particular scarcity, the *presidenti* still procured crops, directly or through their agents.

4.6 Conclusions

Victuals provisioning in Vicenza—as in all early modern cities—followed different patterns for different goods and in different times, adapting to circumstances in a flexible and pragmatic manner. In this chapter, three paradigmatic cases have been considered. As regards cheese, abundantly supplied by many different categories of sellers, public authorities limited themselves to fostering competition among these categories, without officially setting maximum prices, and relying on the spatial separation or aggregation of sellers in the market area. As regards meat and fish, more delicate foodstuffs both from the point of view of health safety and of the regularity of the supply, the managing of the four butcheries and of the fish market stalls was let out on contract each year, with very detailed specifications, including officially set maximum prices. As regards wheat, the most strategic foodstuff at the time, a wide variety of measures were adopted as long as self-consumption and market supply were insufficient, including: the creation of specific institutions devoted to gathering and selling wheat on favourable terms to the poor; the establishment of compulsory transportation of a part of the surplus produced in the rural district into the city; and the allocation of contracts or the effectuation of direct purchases by the Municipality during years of scarcity. In all these cases, the negotiation between public authorities and the various categories provisioning the city emerges as a distinctive feature of early modern societies end economies. To a certain extent, negotiation was also possible between Vicenza and Venice, even if available options were limited by the priority given to the needs of the capital city.

Notes

1. Cozzi (1986, pp. 205–221); Law (1992, pp. 159–174); Ventura (1993 [1964], pp. 39–47); Viggiano (1993, pp. 3–50); Mallett (1996a, pp. 212–240).
2. Lane (1973, pp. 225–234, 242–245); Cozzi (1986, pp. 3–47, 65–95); Mallett (1996a, b). The new territories formed the *Stato da Terra* ('Mainland State'), which did not include the lagoonal strip forming the *Dogado* ('Duchy') since the Early Middle Ages. Overseas dominions formed the *Stato da Mar* ('Sea State'). The border between the *Stato da Terra* and the *Stato da Mar* was ambiguously defined: most of times, Istria was attributed to the latter (Arbel 1996, pp. 954–955).
3. Vicenza and its district stretched for 2,672 square kilometres. 40% of this area was mountainous, 31% hilly, and 29% was flatland. At the time of the

first (albeit to some extent incomplete) census of the Venetian *Stato da Terra*, in 1548, the area was populated by 144,708 people, with a not unremarkable—especially considering the nature of the territory—average density of 56 inhabitants per square kilometre (for comparison, the *Stato da Terra* and the *Dogado*, including Venice, had an average density of 50). Venice had 158,069 inhabitants in 1552. In 1548, Verona had 52,109 inhabitants, Brescia had 42,660, Padua 34,075, Vicenza 21,268, Bergamo 17,707, Udine 14,579, Treviso 11,798, Crema 10,689, and Chioggia, in 1561, approximately 11,500. Considering these ten cities and towns, the rate of urbanisation was 23%. On the population of the Republic of Venice, see Beloch (1994 [1937–1961], pp. 389–501) (slightly different data can be found in Beltrami 1954, pp. 68–70; 1961, pp. 169–173); on its surface and pedology, see Beltrami (1961, pp. 174–175, 178–184). Elaborations on data provided by these sources are the author's.

4. On Vicenza in the Early Modern Age, see Franzina and Pozza (1980); Grubb (1988); Barbieri and Preto (1989, 1990); Gullino (2014); on its economy, see Fontana and Clerici (2004).
5. On the dynamics of these two sectors, see Demo (2001, 2004, 2006, 2012); Vianello (2004a, b, 2006); Prandin (2015, 2019).
6. Sources of different origins record 19,000 inhabitants in 1483, 21,268 in 1548, 19,899 in 1557, 26,346 in 1569, 29,540 in 1585, 32,668 in 1603, 36,547 in 1617, 31,897 in 1629, and 19,000 in 1631 (Franzina and Pozza 1980, pp. 221–222; Mometto 1989, pp. 4, 8–11; Vianello 2004a, pp. 43–44; on the famine and the plague which hit Vicenza respectively in 1627–1629 and 1630–1631, see Mometto 1989, pp. 12–15; Ulvioni 1989, pp. 177–185). A necessary caveat is that it is not always clear whether or not these figures include the population of the so-called *colture* (literally, 'cultivated lands'), the rural area surrounding the city within a radius of up to five Venetian miles, directly depending from the city's administration (De Biase 1981, pp. 1039–1040; Università di Trieste 1976, pp. 91, 175). 1 Venetian mile (*miglio*, plur. *miglia*)—the mile also used in Vicenza—corresponded to 1,738.67 metres (Martini 1883, p. 817).
7. Ventura (1993 [1964], pp. 256–257); Faugeron (2006); (2014, pp. 260–281, 328–376).
8. Knapton (1984, pp. 47–55).
9. Università di Trieste (1976, p. 5). The podesta (*podestà*) and the captain (*capitano*)—the rectors (*rettori*)—were the representatives sent by Venice to administrate the most important cities of its dominions; the powers of the podesta were mainly civil and judiciary powers, mainly military those of the captain. On Vicenza's system of administration, see BCBVI, MS,

572, year 1426; Varanini (1988, pp. 144, 148, 151); Grubb (1988, pp. 49–62, 82–85); Ventura (1993 [1964], pp. 89–94). On Venetian general administration in the Early Modern Age, see Maranini (1931); Gullino (1996); on victualling administration, see Faugeron (2014, pp. 36–89). On Mainland's commercial networks, see Ciriacono (1986); Lanaro (1999); more specifically, on Venetian afterwar policies on this subject, see Lanaro (1999, pp. 86–90); (2003, pp. 21–51).

10. Zucconi (1989, p. 29); Calabi (1997b, pp. 10–15, 20–27); Degrassi (2003, pp. 470–479). Within the vast literature concerning Renaissance Vicenza, see, for a general frame of reference, Motterle (1973); Barbieri (1987); Moretti (1997).
11. BCBVI, AT, 795–797, 800–801. See also Clerici (2015, pp. 40–47, 50–51); for a detailed analysis of the markets' layout in 1553, see Clerici (2001, pp. 66–69).
12. Vecchiato (1979, pp. 36–38); Grubb (1988, p. 114).
13. The *cavaliere di Comun* shared his authority with the *cavaliere del podestà* ('podesta's knight').
14. BCBVI, AT, 802–805, 783–784. The 52 articles from 1554 became 117 in 1587 and 247 in 1622 (plus other regulations and dispositions transcribed in these volumes).
15. BCBVI, AT, 796–798, 800–801, 863.
16. BCBVI, AT, 796–801; Zorzi (1937, pp. 99–100, 134–138, 149–150, 168–169). See also Clerici (2015, pp. 47–50).
17. The average annual rent of a shop was 15.63 Venetian *ducati*, while that of a stand was 15.93 Vicentine *lire* (i.e. 3.43 Venetian *ducati*) (BCBVI, AT, 795, fos. 12r, 35v–36r). The rental of public shops was very profitable also in Venice (Calabi 1987b, pp. 74–78). In the Venetian account system of the *lira di piccoli*, linked to silver coinage, 1 *lira* (plur. *lire*) was divided into 20 *soldi*, and 1 *soldo* into 12 *denari* or *piccoli*. A *ducato* of account belonging to this system and worth 124 *soldi* progressively spread in the second half of the fifteenth century, when the gold *ducato* constantly maintained this quotation. The Vicentine *lira di piccoli* was a money of account derived from the Veronese monetary system, equally divided into 20 *soldi* or 240 *denari*. On the basis of the exchange rate fixed at the moment of the submission of Verona and Vicenza to Venice, the Vicentine *lira* was worth four-thirds of the Venetian *lira* (Lane and Mueller 1985, pp. 616–617; Mueller 1997, pp. 620–622). If not otherwise stated, all monies mentioned are monies of account.
18. BCBVI, AT, 797, fo. 856v. In general, vegetables were sold both by women and men (BCBVI, AT, 796, fo. 390v, year 1526).
19. On the role of hucksters, see, more generally, Montenach (2009, pp. 213–215, 240–243); Abad (2002, pp. 618–621).

20. BCBVI, AT, 797–798, 800, years 1533 to 1547; ES, 37, year 1564; Zorzi (1937, pp. 99–100, 149–150).
21. Todeschini (2002, pp. 176–177); Martinat (2004, pp. 42–43, 56, 74, 110); Todeschini (2005, p. 189); Prodi (2009, pp. 35–36); Davis (2012, pp. 34–136).
22. BCBVI, MS, 572, fos. 180v–181r, year 1426. On the correspondence between the pre-modern and the modern system of counting hours in Vicenza, which varied depending on the season, see *Tabelle perpetue delle ore che si osservano in Vicenza* (1797, pp. 7–24).
23. BCBVI, MS, 569, fo. 145v. This norm, prescribing the order to be observed by the twenty-four guilds of the city during religious processions, highlighted the very different rank of the grocers' and the resellers' guild, respectively occupying the fifth and the twenty-second place (first and last place among the guilds trading in food).
24. BCBVI, AT, 801, fos. 695v–697v, year 1553.
25. See also Clerici (2015, pp. 53–67).
26. BCBVI, MS, 182, fos. 33r–35v, years 1479–1500.
27. These were areas with buildings grown along roads outside of the medieval city walls, and then enclosed in subsequent wall rings.
28. These were the rural area surrounding the city (see note 6).
29. BCBVI, MS, 182, fo. 5r. Sausage-makers, who in general constituted a different category, were mentioned as members of the guild of grocers in 1568 and 1569 (BCBVI, MS, 182, fos. 16v–17r). In general, the prescription to enter the grocers' guild was obeyed: its register included a large number of members (495 were recorded in little more than a century); almost all (491) were men, and their main occupations—often different from that of grocer—were the most diverse (BCBVI, MS, 182, fos. 8v–25r, years 1479–1583). Pluriactivity was a common feature in late medieval and early modern economies (Montenach 2009, pp. 158–162; Faugeron 2014, pp. 558–562).
30. For shopkeepers, this constituted an opportunity both for expanding their clientele, and for selling off low-quality products (Montenach 2009, pp. 248, 253–256; 2011, p. 98). It is uncertain to which extent open-air trade was subjected to enrolment in the guild of resellers, since their statutes—if any existed—have not been preserved.
31. The two distribution circuits of shopkeepers and hucksters were at the same time complementary and rival systems (Montenach 2000, pp. 36–39; 2009, pp. 60–65; Petrowiste 2015, pp. 139–140).
32. BCBVI, MS, 182, fo. 48r. The distinction between sellers residing and not residing in the city was a common feature (Petrowiste 2015, pp. 140–141).

33. Usually, the inhabitants of the district (*districtuales*) were distinguished from those of other territories (*forenses*) (BCBVI, MS, 182, fo. 5r). Here, the term *forenses* was used in a broader sense to include both.
34. "[P]auperes et impotentes" (BCBVI, MS, 182, fo. 47r). Here and below, all translations of original documents are the author's.
35. In 1410 Venice, the 'poor and powerless' clandestinely sold Mainland wines (Faugeron 2014, p. 673). In 1622 Verona, the 'powerless' were those who, among the 'poor' having access to the monitored *Mercato Vecchio* ('Old Market'), were exempted from the obligation to carry away by themselves the sacks of crops they bought (Vecchiato 1979, pp. 148–149).
36. This can be argued from the fact that in 1543—when information about the rental of stands in the market squares is available—it regarded Herbs Square, the area of Old Fish Market Square and Small Fish Square, and Crops Square, but not the eastern part of the Grand Square; moreover, in Herbs Square a convenient space was reserved to the women coming and selling vegetables from the suburbs, the *colture* and other places, i.e. direct sellers of the produce from their food gardens (BCBVI, AT, 863, fo. 164r–v). Exemption from the payment for the stallage for these categories was widespread (see, for instance, Nada Patrone 1981, p. 140; Calabi 1987a, pp. 82–83).
37. "[C]itadini o contadini", "compravendi atque merchadanti" (BCBVI, MS, 182, fos. 50v–51r; AT, 798, fos. 952r–953r).
38. See, for instance, BCBVI, AT, 804, fo. 790v, year 1554.
39. BCBVI, AT, 799, 801–802; MS, 182; years 1540–1555.
40. "[P]overetti et poverette done da villa", "poveri da villa" (BCBVI, AT, 801, fos. 3r, 696r).
41. BCBVI, MS, 182, fo. 60v.
42. BCBVI, AT, 796, 798, 801, 804; MS, 182; years 1526–1563.
43. BCBVI, MS, 182, fo. 44v.
44. BCBVI, MS, 182, fo. 56v.
45. BCBVI, AT, 806–807, 865; MS, 182; years 1573–1578.
46. BCBVI, MS, 182, fos. 42r–v, 60r–v.
47. BCBVI, AT, 803–804, 806–808; MS, 182; years 1558–1583. On the general degrees of judgement in Vicenza, see Grubb (1988, pp. 136–148); on the particular jurisdiction in the case of foodstuffs, see BCBVI, AT, 1779, fo. 78v, year 1606.
48. The maximum price of the goods sold by grocers was not officially set in Vicenza during the sixteenth century, except for olive oil and tallow candles (BCBVI, AT, 797 ff., years 1534 ff.). Official maximum prices were imposed on butter and rice in 1603, and on cheese and charcuterie (in

addition to sausages, whose price was already set together with that of fresh pork) in 1632 (BCBVI, AT, 99).

49. BCBVI, AT, 795–801, years 1493–1550. See also Clerici (2012, pp. 468–471); (2017, pp. 310–312, 320–321, 323–325).
50. Two of the three butcheries in the suburbs were private property until, respectively, 1558 and 1559 (BCBVI, AT, 803); nevertheless, butchers had to get the licence from the general contractor.
51. Nada Patrone (1981, p. 245).
52. The system in use in Vicenza depended on the fact that the beneficiary of the tax on meat sales was the Republic (Grubb 1988, pp. 118–119), while that of the butcheries' contract rents was the Municipality. In the case of Venice, instead, official maximum meat prices were set when the collection of meat tax was let out on contract. In the second half of the fifteenth century, import of oxen, calves, and wethers in Venice was almost completely controlled by the collectors of this tax: a part of the butchery stalls were allotted to them and they were responsible for their provisioning. By the end of the century, the collection of the tax and the managing and provisioning of the butcheries were unified in a single contract, let to a livestock wholesaler (Faugeron 2014, pp. 96–97, 440–449, 626–627, 652).
53. BCBVI, AT, 799–800, 863, years 1543–1547.
54. BCBVI, AT, 795 ff., years 1525 ff.
55. Martinat (2004, pp. 73, 103); de Vries (2019, pp. 10–11); with reference to the price of meat in Venice, see Faugeron (2014, p. 652); Tucci (1975, p. 156).
56. In late medieval Venice, for instance, officially set maximum meat prices were sometimes increased for these reasons (Faugeron 2014, pp. 238–239, 651–653). Cases of short supply due to low prices occurred again during the sixteenth century (Tucci 1975, p. 156).
57. 1 Vicentine *libbra grossa* (literally, 'thick pound', meaning heavy; plur. *libbre grosse*)—used for weighing most of the goods, especially the heaviest and cheapest—corresponded to approximately 486.54 grams (Martini 1883, p. 823).
58. This expedient is already attested in late medieval Venice (Faugeron 2014, pp. 239 and 651–652, note 76).
59. Stouff (1970, p. 165); Tucci (1975, pp. 156, 159); Faugeron (2014, p. 621).
60. The importance of these earnings was not negligible (see, on early modern Bologna, Guenzi 1985, pp. 547–549).
61. Annual rents are not always comparable, because contracts sometimes did not cover the entire year or all of the city butcheries. Considering only complete contracts, the range of variation in annual rents extended

between 65 and 380 Venetian *ducati*. They were on average equal to 120.08 *ducati*, with a coefficient of variation of 0.52. Their growing linear trend of 1.57% per year is explained by the debasement of Venetian silver coinage by only 0.48% (calculations on data from Papadopoli Aldobrandini 1907, pp. 87–230).

62. BCBVI, AT, 794–804, years 1518–1565. See also Clerici (2012, pp. 468–471); (2017, pp. 321–324). On the fishmongers' guild in sixteenth-century Venice, see Shaw (2002).
63. BCBVI, MS, 572, fos. 188v–189v, year 1426.
64. Annual rents were on average 48.33 Vicentine *lire* (i.e. 10.39 Venetian *ducati*), with a coefficient of variation of 0.41. Their growing linear trend of 0.09% per year did not even compensate the effect of the debasement of Venetian silver coinage, amounting to 0.34% (calculations on data from Papadopoli Aldobrandini 1907, pp. 87–292). In the years for which the contract rents of both butcheries and fish market stalls are known (1519, 1523–1524, 1549–1550), contract rents for the butcheries were on average equal to almost eleven times those for the fish market stone stalls (127.00 Venetian *ducati* instead of 54.00 Vicentine *lire*, i.e. 11.61 Venetian *ducati*).
65. Montanari (1993, pp. 98–103).
66. Also provoking the growth of the illegal market for meat (Montenach 2001).
67. Agreements for fish provisioning during Lent were settled also elsewhere (Stouff 1970, p. 205; Montenach 2012, pp. 15–16).
68. BCBVI, AT, 795, fos. 262v, 310r.
69. BCBVI, AT, 801, fo. 145v; 802, fos. 434v, 627v. The identity of the contractor for 1554 is not known.
70. BCBVI, AT, 802, fos. 153v–154v, 172r; 863, fo. 561v. It is not possible to determine if this Battista Matto was the same person as in 1519 or not.
71. BCBVI, AT, 783–784, 802, 804–807, 809–811, 865, years 1554–1622.
72. Lecce (1958, pp. 20–51); Tucci (1975, pp. 156–159).
73. ASVE, SDT, 25, fo. 211r–v.
74. ASVE, SDT, 26, fos. 30v–31v. In Venice, the officially set maximum price of veal was 3.5 Venetian *soldi* and that of beef 2.5 Venetian *soldi* per *libbra grossa*. Percentages are calculated considering that prices were set in local *libbre grosse*, which differed: that of Venice was lighter than that of Vicenza and corresponded to approximately 477.00 grams (Martini 1883, p. 818).
75. Lecce (1958, pp. 20–51).
76. In 1533 for Vicenza, again (BCBVI, AT, 57, fo. 136r), in 1542 and 1558 for the whole Mainland (ASVE, SDT, 41, fo. 128r–v). In 1558, officially set maximum prices in Venice were raised at 5 Venetian *soldi* for veal and

for beef 3 Venetian *soldi* per *libbra grossa*; the unchanged difference of 2 Venetian *denari* per *libbra grossa* became thus less significant in percentage: 5.2% less for veal and 7.4% less for beef.

77. BCBVI, AT, 803, fo. 583r.
78. The policy for prices on the scale of the whole State changed when the flows of goods went from the centre to the periphery, as in the case of olive oil. Here, it was a matter of distributing the oil imported into Venice from abroad in the Mainland, and officially set maximum prices in Vicenza were connected with current wholesale prices in Venice, increased by transportation costs, taxes and duties, and sellers' earnings (BCBVI, AT, 784, fos. 92v–93v, 97r–98v, years 1580, 1605. See also Clerici 2017, pp. 325–328).
79. Collodo (1999 [1990], pp. 59–67); Faugeron (2014, pp. 278–279). On Vicenza, in particular, see Varanini (1988, pp. 156–157, 169–170); Collodo (1999 [1990], pp. 59–61). On Venice's *fontici* of crops and flours, see Faugeron (2014, pp. 485–496, 681–689).
80. Povolo (1981, p. 420); Pezzolo (1989, p. 141). The same happened in Treviso (Vecchiato 1979, p. 44).
81. BCBVI, AT, 798, 863–867; Università di Trieste (1976, pp. 22, 121, 202, 225). On the 1589–1591 food crisis, see Mometto (1989, pp. 6–8). On Verona's *fontici* of crops and flours in the Early Modern Age, see Vecchiato (1979, pp. 207–250).
82. Varanini (1988, pp. 169–170); Collodo (1999 [1990], p. 53).
83. ASVE, CFC, 6, fos. 4r, 22r, 37v, [years 1404–1413]; BCBVI, AT, 779, fo. 13r, year 1558.
84. On Vicenza, see BCBVI, AT, 57, years 1530–1540.
85. Università di Trieste (1976, p. 27). These were the same reasons alleged by his colleague Marco Antonio Contarini when asking, in 1524, for the reduction of the number of weekly markets in the rural district.
86. BCBVI, AT, 57, fo. 45r.
87. Vecchiato (1979, pp. 57, 156–157, 177–202). Compulsory transportation was instituted in all Mainland cities, with the noteworthy exception of Bergamo, as shown by a survey of Vicenza's *deputati* in 1654 (BCBVI, AT, 303 (16); on Bergamo, see also Costantini 2016).
88. Vecchiato (1979, pp. 36–46, 149–158). On Vicenza, in particular, see Università di Trieste (1976, p. 120).
89. See, for instance, BCBVI, AT, 298, year 1568. Following a widespread pattern (Braudel 1979 [1967], pp. 112–113), normally the maximum price of crops—which constituted most of the agricultural rents received by the urban patriciate, eager to realise their value—was not officially set in Vicenza; instead, the minimum weight of the bread loaf to be sold for a given price was. On officially set minimum weight of bread in Vicenza,

see Clerici (2017, pp. 304–305, 317–320); in Verona, see Vecchiato (1979, pp. 97–121); on the much more complex system in force in Venice, see Faugeron (2014, pp. 691–701); Mattozzi (1983); Mattozzi et al. (1983).

90. The obligation is first attested in 1351 (Faugeron 2014, pp. 260–261), and the control over its enforcement increased during the sixteenth century (Aymard 1966, pp. 78–79, 114; Vecchiato 1979, pp. 151–152, 252–255).
91. Vecchiato (1979, pp. 36–37, 253–254).
92. Braudel (1966 [1949], vol. I, pp. 540–542, 548).
93. Aymard (1966, p. 34).
94. Aymard (1966, p. 64).
95. Aymard (1966, pp. 125–137).
96. Nevertheless, it must be noticed that Venetian efforts were focused more on the reclamation of marshes than on the irrigation of arid lands, contrary to what was happening in the more advanced agriculture system of the State of Milan (Aymard 1966, pp. 36–37, 150–151; Ventura 1970, pp. 528–534; Ciriacono 1994, pp. 29–39, 49–52, 85–88).
97. 1 Venetian *staio* (plur. *staia*) corresponded to approximately 83.317 cubic decimetres (Martini 1883, p. 818). Supplies from the Mainland were more stable than imports from overseas: their coefficients of variation were 0.24 and 0.48 respectively.
98. 1 Vicentine *staio raso* ('level' *staio*)—used for measuring well dried wheat in the granary or on the marketplace—corresponded to approximately 27.043 cubic decimetres (Martini 1883, p. 823). The coefficient of variation of wheat compulsory transportations from Vicenza's district to the city was 0.21. In that period, they were moderately correlated with crops supplies from the Mainland to Venice: their Pearson correlation coefficient was 0.59. This fact does not surprise, since the extension of the production areas concerned was much different.
99. BCBVI, AT, 298 (1), fo. 16r. According to the equivalence used for assessing the official minimum weight of the bread loaf in 1560, 4 Vicentine *staia* of wheat weighed 169 Vicentine *libbre grosse* (BCBVI, AT, 864, fo. 134r); thus, 10 *staia* weighed 422.5 *libbre grosse*, approximately corresponding to 205.56 kilos.
100. Calculations on the data reported in note 6.
101. 10 Vicentine *staia* approximately corresponded to 270.43 cubic decimetres. This datum is consistent with those regarding Verona (6–7 Veronese *minali* per person, corresponding to 229.31–267.52 cubic decimetres) and Venice (3 Venetian *staia* per person for common people, corresponding to 249.95 cubic decimetres, and 4 *staia* per person for the wealthy, corresponding to 333.27 cubic decimetres) (Vecchiato 1979, pp. 65–67;

Mattozzi et al. 1983, p. 280; on the Veronese *minale* (plur. *minali*), see Martini 1883, p. 822).

102. In Verona, compulsory transportation (called *comandà*, 'impositions') covered 53% of the overall wheat consumption in 1595 and 32% in 1600 (Vecchiato 1979, pp. 67, 69).
103. BCBVI, AT, 299, years 1594 ff.
104. Aymard (1966, p. 79).
105. BCBVI, AT, 300, 796–818, 863–868, 1464, years 1526–1629. See also Clerici (2009).
106. On the evolution of Venetian crops provisioning, see Faugeron (2014, pp. 225–236, 250–292, and, on the sources of financing, 105–170); Aymard (1966, pp. 78–101). On the preference for contracts instead of direct purchases during the sixteenth century, see, in particular, Aymard (1966, pp. 81–82, 99–101). On contracts for crops provisioning in Verona in the same century, see Vecchiato (1979, pp. 43–44, note 68). In Vicenza, contracts of this kind were also habitually assigned for firewood provisioning through timber floating on the Astico river (BCBVI, AT, 57, 797 ff., 863 ff., years 1532 ff.).
107. Aymard (1966, pp. 80–81).
108. Between 1587 and 1588, for instance, import bounties corresponded to approximately 6.5–8.2% of the final selling prices provided for by contract terms (BCBVI, AT, 865, fo. 578v; 300 (4), fo. 1bisv). In Venice, import bounties usually corresponded to 5–15% of current domestic prices (Aymard 1966, p. 81).
109. In general, the *tratte* were issued by exporting countries and by countries of transit; they were necessary also for exporting crops from Venice to the Mainland (Aymard 1966, pp. 71, 81).
110. Aymard (1966, pp. 81, 118).
111. Braudel (1966 [1949], vol. I, pp. 518–524).
112. It must be noticed, however, that the patriciate of Vicenza was more involved in economic activities than those of other Mainland cities. On Vicentine merchants, see Demo (2001, 2004, 2006, 2012); Vianello (2004a, b, 2006); Prandin (2015, 2019).
113. BCBVI, AT, 300 (3, 5, 13, 15), 863, 865.
114. BCBVI, AT, 300 (2, 15), 865.
115. BCBVI, AT, 300 (7), 1464.
116. BCBVI, AT, 300 (3).
117. BCBVI, AT, 300 (3).
118. Aymard (1966, p. 81). Moreover, the predefined price was in fact a minimum guaranteed price, because merchants were allowed to freely sell their loads whenever current prices were higher.

119. BCBVI, AT, 300 (7), fo. 63r.
120. BCBVI, AT, 300 (9), fos. 4v–5r, 23v.
121. BCBVI, AT, 865, fos. 623v–624r.

Archival Sources

Archivio di Stato di Venezia (ASVE)
Collegio, Formulari di commissioni (CFC).
Senato, Deliberazioni, Terra (SDT).
www.archiviodistatovenezia.it

Archivio di Stato di Vicenza (ASVI)
Estimo (ES).
www.archiviodistatovicenza.beniculturali.it

Biblioteca Civica Bertoliana, Vicenza (BCBVI)
Archivio Torre (AT).
Manoscritti (MS).
Stampati antichi (SA).
www.bibliotecabertoliana.it

Published Sources

Tabelle perpetue delle ore che si osservano in Vicenza, principiando da mezzanotte, ridotte alle ore europee o di Francia, e del ragguaglio delle ore francesi colle italiane. 1797. Vicenza: Stamperia Rossi (BCBVI, SA, Gonz. 294.3).

Università di Trieste, Istituto di Storia Economica, ed. 1976. *Relazioni dei rettori veneti in Terraferma*. Vol. VII: Podestaria e capitanato di Vicenza. Milano: Giuffrè.

References

Abad, Reynald. 2002. *Le grand marché. L'approvisionnement alimentaire de Paris sous l'Ancien Régime*. Paris: Fayard.

Arbel, Benjamin. 1996. Colonie d'oltremare. In *Storia di Venezia dalle origini alla caduta della Serenissima*. Vol. V: Il Rinascimento. Società ed economia, ed. by Alberto Tenenti and Ugo Tucci, 947–985. Roma: Istituto della Enciclopedia Italiana Fondata da Giovanni Treccani.

Aymard, Maurice. 1966. *Venise, Raguse et le commerce du blé pendant la seconde moitié du XVIe siècle*. Paris: Sevpen.

Barbieri, Franco. 1987. *Vicenza città di palazzi*. Vicenza: Banca Popolare di Vicenza/Milano: Silvana.

Barbieri, Franco, and Paolo Preto, eds. 1989. *Storia di Vicenza*. Vol. III: L'età della Repubblica veneta, 1404–1797. Part I. Vicenza: Accademia Olimpica/Pozza.

———, eds. 1990. *Storia di Vicenza*. Vol. III: L'età della Repubblica veneta, 1404–1797. Part II. Vicenza: Accademia Olimpica/Pozza.

Beloch, Karl Julius. 1994 [1937–1961]. *Storia della popolazione d'Italia*, ed. by the Società Italiana di Demografia Storica. Italian translation. Firenze: Le Lettere.

Beltrami, Daniele. 1954. *Storia della popolazione di Venezia dalla fine del secolo XVI alla caduta della Repubblica*. Padova: Cedam.

———. 1961. *Forze di lavoro e proprietà fondiaria nelle campagne venete dei secoli XVII e XVIII*. Venezia/Roma: Istituto per la Collaborazione Culturale.

Braudel, Fernand. 1966 [1949]. *La Méditerranée et le monde méditerranéen à l'époque de Philippe II*. 2nd ed. Paris: Colin.

———. 1979 [1967]. *Civilisation matérielle, économie et capitalisme, XV*e*–XVIII*e *siècle*. Vol. I: Les structures du quotidien: le possible et l'impossible. New ed. Paris: Colin.

Calabi, Donatella. 1987a. Città e spazi di mercato nella Repubblica veneta. In laguna: un'isola, i luoghi, le fabbriche. *Eidos*, new series 1 (1): 76–87.

———. 1987b. Le fabbriche. In *Rialto: le fabbriche e il Ponte, 1514–1591*, by Donatella Calabi and Paolo Morachiello, 3–170. Torino: Einaudi.

———, ed. 1997a. *Fabbriche, piazze, mercati. La città italiana nel Rinascimento*. Roma: Officina.

———. 1997b. La "plathea magna": il disegno, il committente, l'architetto. In Calabi 1997a, 9–32.

Ciriacono, Salvatore. 1986. Venise et ses villes. Structuration et déstructuration d'un marché régional, XVIe–XVIIIe siècle. *Revue Historique* 276 (2/560): 287–307.

———. 1994. *Acque e agricoltura. Venezia, l'Olanda e la bonifica europea in età moderna*. Milano: Angeli.

Clerici, Luca. 2001. Fiere e mercati del Vicentino nel tardo medioevo e in età moderna. *Società e Storia* 24 (1/91): 11–77.

———. 2009. Sul ruolo dei mercanti nell'approvvigionamento cerealicolo urbano durante gli anni di scarsità. Vicenza, XVI–XVII secolo. In *Imprenditorialità e sviluppo economico. Il caso italiano (secc. XIII–XX)*, ed. by Franco Amatori and Andrea Colli, 1553–1569. Milano: Egea.

———. 2012. Market, civic virtues, and civic bargaining in the medieval and early modern age: Some evidence from sixteenth century Italy. *International Review of Economics* 59 (4): 459–475.

———. 2015. L'approvisionnement du marché urbain: conflits et négociations (Vicence, XVIe siècle). In Fondazione Istituto Internazionale di Storia Economica 'F. Datini' 2015, 39–68.

———. 2017. Le prix du bien commun. Taxation des prix et approvisionnement urbain (Vicence, XVIe–XVIIe siècle). In *I prezzi delle cose nell'età preindustriale/The prices of things in pre-industrial times*, ed. by the Fondazione Istituto Internazionale di Storia Economica 'F. Datini', 293–332. Firenze: Firenze University Press.

Collodo, Silvana. 1999 [1990]. Il sistema annonario delle città venete: da pubblica utilità a servizio sociale (secoli XIII–XVI). New ed. In *Società e istituzioni in area veneta. Itinerari di ricerca (secoli XII–XV)*, by Silvana Collodo, 47–67. Fiesole: Nardini.

Costantini, Fabrizio. 2016. *"In tutto differente dalle altre città". Mercato e contrabbando dei grani a Bergamo in età veneta*. Bergamo: Centro Studi e Ricerche Archivio Bergamasco.

Cozzi, Gaetano. 1986. Politica, società, istituzioni. In *Storia d'Italia*, dir. by Giuseppe Galasso. Vol. XII: La Repubblica di Venezia nell'età moderna. Part I: Dalla guerra di Chioggia al 1517, by Gaetano Cozzi and Michael Knapton, 1–271. Torino: Utet.

Davis, James. 2012. *Medieval market morality: Life, law and ethics in the English marketplace, 1200–1500*. Cambridge: Cambridge University Press.

De Biase, Luca. 1981. Rilevazioni e problemi sull'evoluzione demografica della "Coltura di Lisiera" nel XVIII secolo. In *Lisiera. Immagini, documenti e problemi per la storia e cultura di una comunità veneta. Strutture-congiunture-episodi*, ed. by Claudio Povolo. Vol. II, 1037–1080. Vicenza: Parrocchia di Lisiera.

Degrassi, Donata. 2003. Potere pubblico ed edilizia nella Terraferma veneziana (secolo XV). In *Pouvoir et édilité. Les grands chantiers dans l'Italie communale et seigneuriale*, ed. by Élisabeth Crouzet-Pavan, 461–481. Rome: École Française de Rome.

Demo, Edoardo. 2001. *L'"anima della città". L'industria tessile a Verona e Vicenza (1400–1550)*. Milano: Unicopli.

———. 2004. Le manifatture tra Medioevo ed Età moderna. In Fontana and Clerici 2004, 21–126.

———. 2006. Wool and silk. The textile urban industry of the Venetian mainland (15th–17th centuries). In Lanaro 2006, 217–243.

———. 2012. *Mercanti di Terraferma. Uomini, merci e capitali nell'Europa del Cinquecento*. Milano: Angeli.

de Vries, Jan. 2019. *The price of bread: Regulating the market in the Dutch Republic*. Cambridge: Cambridge University Press.

Faugeron, Fabien. 2006. De la commune à la capitale du *Stato di Terra*: la politique annonaire et la constitution de l'État de Terreferme vénitien (1re moitié du XVe siècle). In *Les villes capitales au Moyen Âge*, ed. by the Société des Historiens Médiévistes de l'Enseignement Supérieur Public, 97–111. Paris: Publications de la Sorbonne.

———. 2014. *Nourrir la ville. Ravitaillement, marchés et métiers de l'alimentation à Venise dans les derniers siècles du Moyen Âge*. Rome: École Française de Rome.

Fondazione Istituto Internazionale di Storia Economica 'F. Datini', ed. 2015. *Il commercio al minuto. Domanda e offerta tra economia formale e informale. Secc. XIII–XVIII/Retail trade: Supply and demand in the formal and informal economy from the 13th to the 18th century*. Firenze: Firenze University Press.

Fontana, Giovanni Luigi, ed., and Luca Clerici, assistant ed. 2004. *Storia dell'economia vicentina*. Vol. II: L'industria vicentina dal Medioevo a oggi. Padova: Cleup.

Franzina, Emilio, in cooperation with Neri Pozza. 1980. *Vicenza. Storia di una città, 1404–1866*. Vicenza: Pozza.

Grubb, James S. 1988. *Firstborn of Venice: Vicenza in the early Renaissance state*. Baltimore/London: The Johns Hopkins University Press.

Guenzi, Alberto. 1985. La carne bovina: consumi, prezzi e controllo sociale nella città di Bologna (secc. XVII e XVIII). In *Popolazione ed economia dei territori bolognesi durante il Settecento*, ed. by the Istituto per la Storia di Bologna, 537–551. Bologna: Istituto per la Storia di Bologna.

Gullino, Giuseppe. 1996. L'evoluzione costituzionale. In Tenenti and Tucci 1996, 345–378.

———, ed. 2014. *Storia di Vicenza. Dalla preistoria all'età contemporanea*. Sommacampagna: Cierre/Vicenza: Istituto Storico della Resistenza e dell'Età Contemporanea della Provincia di Vicenza.

Knapton, Michael. 1984. Il Territorio vicentino nello Stato veneto del '500 e primo '600: nuovi equilibri politici e fiscali. In *Dentro lo "Stado Italico". Venezia e la Terraferma fra Quattro e Seicento*, ed. by Giorgio Cracco and Michael Knapton, 33–115. Trento: Gruppo Culturale Civis/Biblioteca Cappuccini.

Lanaro, Paola. 1999. *I mercati nella Repubblica Veneta. Economie cittadine e stato territoriale (secoli XV–XVIII)*. Venezia: Marsilio.

———. 2003. Periferie senza centro. Reti fieristiche nello spazio geografico della terraferma veneta in età moderna. In *La pratica dello scambio. Sistemi di fiere, mercanti e città in Europa (1400–1700)*, ed. by Paola Lanaro, 21–51. Venezia: Marsilio.

———, ed. 2006. *At the centre of the Old World: Trade and manufacturing in Venice and the Venetian mainland, 1400–1800*. Toronto: Centre for Reformation and Renaissance Studies.

Lane, Frederic Chapin. 1973. *Venice: A maritime republic*. Baltimore/London: The Johns Hopkins University Press.

Lane, Frederic Chapin, and Reinhold Christopher Mueller. 1985. *Money and banking in medieval and Renaissance Venice*. Vol. I: Coins and moneys of account. Baltimore/London: The Johns Hopkins University Press.

Law, John Easton. 1992. The Venetian mainland state in the fifteenth century. *Transactions of the Royal Historical Society*, 6th series 2: 153–174.

Lecce, Michele. 1958. Le condizioni zootecnico-agricole del territorio veronese nella prima metà del '500. *Economia e Storia* 5 (1): 20–51.

Mallett, Michael Edward. 1996a. La conquista della Terraferma. In Tenenti and Tucci 1996, 181–244.

———. 1996b. Venezia e la politica italiana: 1454–1530. In Tenenti and Tucci 1996, 245–310.

Maranini, Giuseppe. 1931. *La costituzione di Venezia dopo la serrata del Maggior Consiglio*. Venezia/Perugia/Firenze: La Nuova Italia.

Martinat, Monica. 2004. *Le juste marché. Le système annonaire romain aux XVIe et XVIIe siècles*. Rome: École Française de Rome.

Martini, Angelo. 1883. *Manuale di metrologia, ossia misure, pesi e monete in uso attualmente e anticamente presso tutti i popoli*. Torino: Loescher.

Mattozzi, Ivo. 1983. Il politico e il pane a Venezia (1570–1650). Le tariffe dei calmieri: semplici prontuari contabili o strumenti di politica annonaria? *Studi Veneziani*, new series 7 (1/7): 197–220.

Mattozzi, Ivo, Francesco Bolelli, Carmen Chiasera, and Daniela Sabbioni. 1983. Il politico e il pane a Venezia (1570–1650): calmieri e governo della sussistenza. *Società e Storia* 6 (2/20): 271–303.

Mometto, Giovanni. 1989. Per una storia della popolazione in età moderna. In Barbieri and Preto 1989, 1–27.

Montanari, Massimo. 1993. *La fame e l'abbondanza. Storia dell'alimentazione in Europa*. Roma/Bari: Laterza.

Montenach, Anne. 2000. La boutique au cœur du commerce alimentaire à Lyon au XVIIe siècle: entre économie légale et marchés parallèles. In *La boutique et la ville. Commerces, commerçants, espaces et clientèles, XVIe–XXe siècle*, ed. by Natacha Coquery, 31–44. Tours: Université François Rabelais, Centre d'Histoire de la Ville Moderne et Contemporaine.

———. 2001. Esquisse d'une économie de l'illicite. Le marché parallèle de la viande à Lyon pendant le Carême (1658–1714). *Crime, Histoire et Sociétés/Crime, History and Societies* 5 (1): 7–25.

———. 2009. *Espaces et pratiques du commerce alimentaire à Lyon au XVIIe siècle. L'économie du quotidien*. Grenoble: Presses Universitaires de Grenoble.

———. 2011. Formal and informal economy in an urban context: The case of food trade in seventeenth-century Lyons. In *Shadow economies and irregular work in urban Europe, 16th to early 20th centuries*, ed. by Thomas Buchner and Philip R. Hoffmann-Rehnitz, 91–106. Wien/Berlin: Lit.

———. 2012. Le marché du poisson à Lyon au XVIIe siècle. Contrôle et enjeux d'une filière et d'un espace marchand. *Rives Méditerranéennes* 43: 13–25.

Moretti, Silvia. 1997. Vicenza: XV–XVII secolo. Tra volontà di riscatto e 'normalizzazione'. In Calabi 1997a, 224–254.

Motterle, Ettore. 1973. In *Il "peronio" di Vicenza nel 1481*, ed. Franco Barbieri. Vicenza: Ente Fiera Vicenza.

Mueller, Reinhold Christopher. 1997. *Money and banking in medieval and Renaissance Venice*. Vol. II: The Venetian money market: Banks, panics, and the public debt, 1200–1500. Baltimore/London: The Johns Hopkins University Press.

Nada Patrone, Anna Maria. 1981. *Il cibo del ricco ed il cibo del povero. Contributo alla storia qualitativa dell'alimentazione. L'area pedemontana negli ultimi secoli del Medio Evo*. Torino: Centro Studi Piemontesi.

Papadopoli Aldobrandini, Nicolò. 1907. *Le monete di Venezia*. Vol. II: Da Nicolò Tron a Marino Grimani, 1472–1605. Venezia: Tipografia Libreria Emiliana.

Petrowiste, Judicaël. 2015. Définir et sanctionner le commerce informel dans une petite ville de la fin du Moyen Âge: Saint-Jean-d'Angély aux XIVe–XVe siècles. In Fondazione Istituto Internazionale di Storia Economica 'F. Datini' 2015, 131–151.

Pezzolo, Luciano. 1989. Uomini e istituzioni tra una città soggetta e Venezia: Vicenza 1630–1797. In Barbieri and Preto 1989, 115–146.

Povolo, Claudio. 1981. Crimine e giustizia a Vicenza. Secoli XVI–XVII. Fonti e problematiche per l'approfondimento di una ricerca sui rapporti politico-giudiziari tra Venezia e la Terraferma. In *Venezia e la Terraferma attraverso le relazioni dei Rettori*, ed. by Amelio Tagliaferri, 411–432. Milano: Giuffrè.

Prandin, Ruggero. 2015. *La Magnifica Città e la mercatura della seta. Ascesa economica, grandezza e stagnazione di Vicenza nei secoli XVI e XVII*. Sommacampagna: Cierre.

———. 2019. *La Magnifica Città e la borghesia produttiva. Storia economica di Vicenza nel XVIII secolo*. Sommacampagna: Cierre.

Prodi, Paolo. 2009. *Settimo non rubare. Furto e mercato nella storia dell'Occidente*. Bologna: il Mulino.

Shaw, James E. 2002. Retail, monopoly, and privilege: The dissolution of the fishmongers' guild of Venice, 1599. *Journal of Early Modern History* 6 (4): 396–427.

Stouff, Louis. 1970. *Ravitaillement et alimentation en Provence aux XIVe et XVe siècles*. Paris/La Haye: Mouton.

Tenenti, Alberto, and Ugo Tucci, eds. 1996. *Storia di Venezia dalle origini alla caduta della Serenissima*. Vol. IV: Il Rinascimento. Politica e cultura. Roma: Istituto della Enciclopedia Italiana Fondata da Giovanni Treccani.

Todeschini, Giacomo. 2002. *I mercanti e il tempio. La società cristiana e il circolo virtuoso della ricchezza fra Medioevo ed Età Moderna*. Bologna: il Mulino.

———. 2005. La riflessione etica sulle attività economiche. In *Economie urbane ed etica economica nell'Italia medievale*, ed. by Roberto Greci, 151–228. Roma/Bari: Laterza.

Tucci, Ugo. 1975. L'Ungheria e gli approvvigionamenti veneziani di bovini nel Cinquecento. In *Rapporti veneto-ungheresi all'epoca del Rinascimento*, ed. by Tibor Klaniczay, 153–171. Budapest: Akadémiai Kiadó.

Ulvioni, Paolo. 1989. *Il gran castigo di Dio. Carestia ed epidemie a Venezia e nella Terraferma, 1628–1632*. Milano: Angeli.

Varanini, Gian Maria. 1988. Vicenza nel Trecento. Istituzioni, classe dirigente, economia (1312–1404). In *Storia di Vicenza*. Vol. II: L'età medievale, ed. by Giorgio Cracco, 139–245. Vicenza: Accademia Olimpica/Pozza.

Vecchiato, Francesco. 1979. *Pane e politica annonaria in Terraferma veneta tra secolo XV e secolo XVIII. (Il caso di Verona)*. Verona: Università degli Studi di Padova, Facoltà di Economia e Commercio in Verona, Istituto di Storia Economica e Sociale.

Ventura, Angelo. 1970. Considerazioni sull'agricoltura veneta e sulla accumulazione originaria del capitale nei secoli XVI e XVII. In *Agricoltura e sviluppo del capitalismo*, ed. by the Istituto Gramsci, 519–560. Roma: Editori Riuniti/Istituto Gramsci.

———. 1993 [1964]. *Nobiltà e popolo nella società veneta del Quattrocento e Cinquecento*. 2nd ed. Milano: Unicopli.

Vianello, Francesco Maria. 2004a. *Seta fine e panni grossi. Manifatture e commerci nel Vicentino, 1570–1700*. Milano: Angeli.

———. 2004b. Mercanti, imprese e commerci nel Cinque e Seicento. In Fontana and Clerici 2004, 187–229.

———. 2006. Rural manufactures and patterns of economic specialization: Cases from the Venetian mainland. In Lanaro 2006, 343–366.

Viggiano, Alfredo. 1993. *Governanti e governati. Legittimità del potere ed esercizio dell'autorità sovrana nello Stato veneto della prima età moderna*. Treviso: Fondazione Benetton/Canova.

Zorzi, Giangiorgio. 1937. *Contributo alla storia dell'arte vicentina nei secoli XV e XVI. Il preclassicismo e i prepalladiani*. Venezia: Regia Deputazione di Storia Patria per le Venezie.

Zucconi, Guido. 1989. Architettura e topografia delle istituzioni nei centri minori della Terraferma (XV e XVI secolo). *Studi Veneziani*, new series 13 (1/17): 27–49.

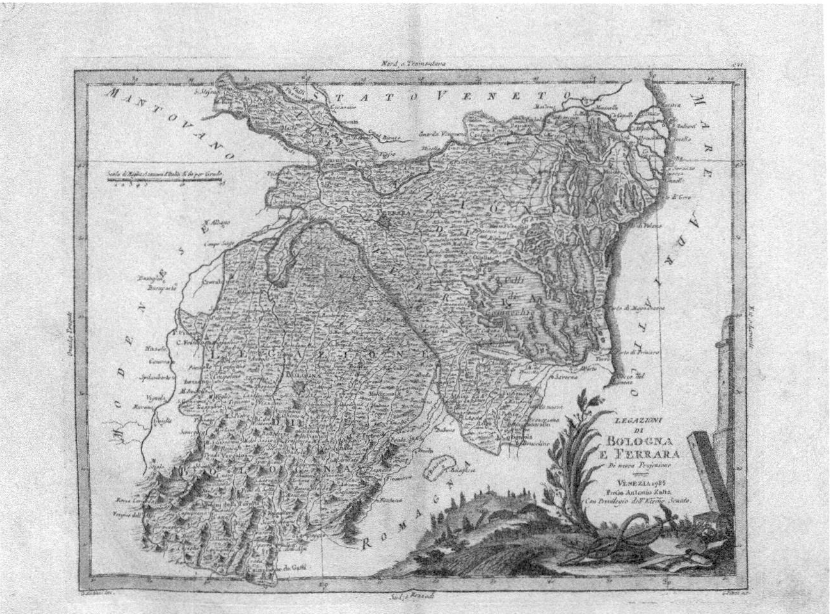

Map 5.1 The Legations of Bologna and Ferrara (1783)

CHAPTER 5

Managing Abundance: Victualling Offices and Cereals Merchants in Eighteenth-Century Ferrara

Giulio Ongaro

5.1 Introduction

This chapter describes the details and functioning of the victualling system and the cereals market in eighteenth-century Ferrara, focusing on the important intervention of public institutions in managing cereals stocks in an area characterised by significant agricultural productivity. It also underlines the strong relationship between merchants, producers, and public institutions. Public regulation (by way of the victualling office and authorisations for the import/export of cereals) was strongly affected by, and in

Special thanks go to the personnel of the Historical Archives of the Municipality of Ferrara: it would have been impossible to collect the documents used to prepare this chapter without their courtesy, competence, and willingness to assist.

G. Ongaro (✉)
Università degli Studi di Milano-Bicocca, Milan, Italy
e-mail: giulio.ongaro@unimib.it

L. Clerici (ed.), *Italian Victualling Systems in the Early Modern Age, 16th to 18th Century*, Palgrave Studies in Economic History,
https://doi.org/10.1007/978-3-030-42064-2_5

turn had an effect on, the behaviour of the economic players. Eighteenth-century Ferrara is emblematic as a case study of the complex relationship between victualling institutions and the cereals market in the Early Modern Age.

Ferrara became a member of the Papal States in the eighth century. For a considerable period, it operated as a ducal fief of the d'Este family; however, the year following Duke Alfonso II d'Este's death without heirs in 1597, the territory once again came under the direct control of the pope. Ferrara was a medium-sized city (a more complete demographic analysis will follow later) at the centre of an area corresponding roughly to the modern-day province of Ferrara (2,650 square kilometres), along with some parts of the modern-day provinces of Rovigo (such as Ariano, Crespino, and Ficarolo) and Ravenna (the so-called 'Romagnola', south of Ferrara).[1] This territory was situated in the eastern Po Valley, seaward on the Adriatic, and entirely flat, with a substantial bipartition between arable land and swampland, including the Comacchio lagoonal area. A strong relationship with water was, and still is, a peculiar trait of the province. Since the Middle Ages, swamp reclamation projects have been conducted to increase the cultivable land area, such as constructing drains and banks to contain the flow of a thick net of rivers: the Po di Lombardia, the Po di Primaro, the Po di Volano, the Tartaro, the Panaro, the Castagnaro, and the Reno. In addition to their role in irrigating the Ferrara plain, these rivers—especially the Po—were fundamental channels for commerce between northern Italy and the Adriatic Sea, the Mediterranean, and international trades routes.[2]

Although the area had relatively high agricultural productivity in the Italian peninsula, the Legation of Ferrara maintained a victualling institution, the *Congregazione dell'Abbondanza* (literally, 'Congregation of Abundance', henceforth *Congregazione*), from the beginning of the seventeenth century throughout the entire Early Modern Age. This may at first appear anomalous, considering that the function of victualling offices was to ensure availability of food to the population in areas where agricultural production or market dynamics did not adequately meet the demand. Furthermore, the neighbouring Legation of Bologna, which experienced chronic shortages in cereals availability, never established a similarly stable institution, the exact theoretical function of which was to solve food supply issues.[3] Why, then, according to this recalled perspective, did fertile Ferrara consistently maintain its institution, even after the French conquest at the end of the eighteenth century, despite the absence of supply problems beyond specific years of general scarcity?[4]

The apparent anomaly can be explained by looking to the functioning of the victualling system and the profiles of the people directly involved in its administration and creation of regulating rules. Indeed, for many economic players in Ferrara's cereals market, public control and intervention were fundamental, particularly in managing cereals stocks (less so in the definition of prices and direct purchases by public institutions).[5] After a short introduction to the research context, this chapter analyses the functioning of the victualling system in eighteenth-century Ferrara and the interaction between public and private interests, stressing their strong reciprocal penetration. It is important to note that the term 'cereals' does not refer exclusively to wheat. By the seventeenth century, other cereals such as maize had already permanently entered both rural and urban diets, contributed to the agricultural diversification of the Italian and European countryside, and occupied an important place in local, regional, national, and international cereals markets.[6]

5.2 The Legation of Ferrara and the Cereals Market in the Papal States

A description of the agricultural sector and cereals market in Papal States and the Legation of Ferrara is fundamental to understand the context of regulation and public intervention, such as the economic interests of various parts of society. "We should be grateful that, if other populations [...] cultivate hard and thankless lands [...], we have around us for immense spaces excellent terrains, from which we can obtain immeasurable fruits".[7] Thus wrote Francesco Containi (a figure to whom we will return in the following pages) and described the province of Ferrara in 1767: an almost completely flat area, rather densely populated relative to the urbanisation standards of northern Italy, with an economy long centred on agricultural production.[8] Various surveys, more or less reliable, have described the population of the city and the overall Legation (see Table 5.1). For a general idea, it must be considered that, estimating a territory of around 3,000 square kilometres and an average population of approximately 200,000 people, the population density was around 67 inhabitants per square kilometre: completely in line with the average for northern and

Table 5.1 The population of the city and of the Legation of Ferrara (1680–1797)

Year	Ferrara	Legation
1680		198,544
1701	27,326	
1720	25,907	
1740	28,185	206,780
1754	28,017	
1764		176,899
1767–1768	27,129	210,000
1770	27,675	
1781	31,253	
1784		235,324
1787	27,677	
1797	25,569	

Sources: Angelini (1979, pp. 34, 44); Containi (1995 [1767], pp. 7, 75); Beloch (1994 [1937–1961], pp. 255–256); Sani (2001, p. 27); ASCFE, FXVIII, 81, fo. 220r

central Italy during that period, but considerably lower than, for example, the 110 inhabitants per square kilometre in the neighbouring State of Milan.[9] Furthermore, the population in the neighbouring Legation of Bologna, which was characterised by lower agricultural production than Ferrara, was almost a third higher, at approximately 270,000 people.[10]

Wheat production (data on other cereals are unavailable) certainly exceeded the food needs of the population, at least in years of good harvest.[11] According to a document produced by the *Congregazione dell'Abbondanza* in 1769,[12] even if the 6,000 Ferrara *moggia* of wheat brought into the city were insufficient to nourish the population,[13] it would not be a problem, because additional amounts would be transported to Ferrara according to need, without taking into account the flour purchased by bakers and pasta producers in the countryside; furthermore, the lowest strata of the population subsisted on "Venetian bread, and on maize flour".[14] Therefore, the situation was not at all alarming, thanks to the availability of maize in addition to wheat. The same document reports that, in the District of Ferrara alone[15] (that is to say, not in the entire Legation), that year's harvest amounted to 720,000 Ferrara *staia* of wheat (approximately 22,387 cubic metres[16]); estimating a monthly consumption of one *staio* per person, that amount was more than double the amount needed to nourish the city of Ferrara, which was by far the most populous settlement in the Legation.[17]

Certainly, the cereals needed for seeding must be subtracted from that amount, but Ferrara's agricultural production was among the most prosperous in the Italian peninsula. Werther Angelini himself, quoting a source dated a few years before (1767), wrote that in the entire Legation, 24,000 *moggia* of wheat—the main agricultural product of the area—were seeded, and 120,000 *moggia* were produced, showing a relationship of one to five between seeding and output. After subtracting 70,000 *moggia* from this amount for nourishment of the inhabitants, 26,000 *moggia* remained available for commerce. Furthermore, wheat was not the only cereal harvested: 3,000 *moggia* of maize were seeded, 100,000 harvested, 51,000 seeded again or used for the food needs of the population, and 49,000 available for trading.[18] The overabundance of agricultural production in the Ferrara province is also testified by its role as a 'granary' for the neighbouring Legation of Bologna, which was constantly deficient in production.[19] In this sense, it is emblematic that as late as July 1797, when the revolutionary armies conquered the city, French authorities linked the choice of whether to limit the export of wheat from Ferrara to the food needs of the army and "to the need of the inhabitants of Bologna, your brothers".[20]

This was likely one reason why, despite frequent overabundance in cereals production in the Ferrara province, only 6.4% of cereals exports allowed under the *tratte* system[21] were sold abroad from the Legation between 1741 and 1776, whereas 65.5% were exported from the March of Ancona and 25.2% from Romagna.[22] In contrast, Ferrara's exports were sold to other areas of the Papal States: first Bologna, but also Rome itself.[23] This does not mean that production from Ferrara was absent from the international market. According to Valentino Sani, ships departing from the port of Goro on the Adriatic Sea carried wheat and other products to Trieste, Venice, Ancona, Civitavecchia, Leghorn, Genoa, the commercial hubs in the Kingdom of Naples, Nice, and the French ports of Toulon and Marseille.[24] However, the flow of cereals towards other areas of the Papal States was predominant, both before and after the establishment of the free circulation of cereals within the State in 1749 (a rule that was often suspended when there was risk of significant modifications to cereals prices and in their availability, or when the risk became reality).[25] A flourishing smuggled cereals market also affected the Legation, involving both millers on the Po river, small merchants across the borders of the territory towards the Republic of Venice and the territory of Mantua, and large cereals merchants.[26] The enormous amount of cereals illegally exported from the Legation in 1739 (more than 12,440 cubic metres) is emblematic of the problem; indeed, the responsible party was Graziadio Coen—at that time treasurer of the customs—with the connivance of local nobles and papal officials themselves.[27]

We may thus contextualise the case of the Ferrara province—in summary, an area with average population density and high agricultural production, which was allocated to the neighbouring province of Bologna and abroad—within the eighteenth-century Papal States. As in many other states at that time, cereals commerce in the Papal States was subject to strict control.[28] With respect to the free circulation of cereals, the reformist spirit that characterised the papal authority in the eighteenth century led to gradual progress towards free commerce of cereals within the State which, as noted, was definitively ratified in 1749; however, in truth, the cereals market was never completely liberalised. Exports outside the State remained subject to the *tratte* system. We must also consider that, ultimately, the legate of Ferrara could directly intervene to safeguard both the food needs of the population and the interests of merchants and producers. For example, in June 1703, the papal legate prohibited the export of wheat outside the Legation; prohibitions were also made in July 1718, September 1728, and 1730 (with the exception of merchants with specific permissions); in September 1749 (a few months after the *motu proprio* by Pope Benedict XIV); in August 1755; and in 1759, 1762, 1763, 1765, 1766, 1767, and 1768.[29] In other instances, the legate reiterated the prohibition to export wheat abroad[30] or, on the contrary, opened to free commerce with other provinces of the Papal States, as in 1712, 1717–1727, 1730, 1731, 1734, 1737, 1756, and 1760.[31]

5.3 The *Congregazione dell'Abbondanza* and the Cereals Supply of Ferrara

The previous section clearly demonstrates that, besides the state legislation, the real management of the food supply and cereals market lay in the hands of the legate of Ferrara. This official, appointed by the pope after the incorporation of the area into the Papal States, substantially appropriated the main functions of decision-making and supervision of the food supply and cereals market, although some tasks were still formally assigned to specific municipal offices.[32] During the d'Este period, public intervention in the functioning of the cereals market was basically limited to the presence of two communal institutions, the *iudex bladorum* (literally, 'judge for crops') and the *consoli alle vettovaglie* (literally, 'consuls for victuals'); from a political and economic perspective, the duke did not intervene in the cereals market beyond sustaining the *Camera Ducale* (literally, 'Ducal Chamber', that is to say the Treasury) with taxes on bread and creating the general contract for the production of ordinary bread.[33] Only in 1590, during a famine that affected almost all of Europe,[34] did Duke Alfonso II d'Este create a true victualling institution to face the emergency.[35]

It was Legate Giacomo Serra who created the *Congregazione dell'Abbondanza* in 1616. This institution, without prejudice of the authority of the legate on this topic, gradually divested the municipal authorities of the management of everything related to the food supply of Ferrara and its territory: from purchases of wheat to defining the price of bread, from controlling all the steps of the wheat transformation process to deciding the amount of eels that should be imported into the city.[36] The new *Congregazione* included a judge, two of the ten *savi del Maestrato* (literally, 'wisemen of the Magistrate'), one of the *consoli alle vettovaglie*, and two nobles of Ferrara;[37] assemblies were held in the city's castle, the dwelling place and symbol of the legate's power. The composition of the *Congregazione* itself demonstrated the interests at the table: both the food-related interests of the city and the commercial interests of the noble landowners and merchants.

These two entities, the legate of Ferrara and the *Congregazione*, were the cornerstones of the Ferrara victualling system. They controlled, managed, and made decisions regarding the cereals market—and, more broadly, overall food issues—throughout the Legation. This control was extremely pervasive, at least in intention, implying minute regulation and careful surveillance of the entire process of food supply in the city, from cultivated fields to bakers' shelves. In the eighteenth century, the situation was not unlike that of the previous century, described by Franco Cazzola:[38] the system of declaration regarding cereals harvested by the landowners was maintained, to provide at least an approximate idea of food availability year after year.[39] In critical situations, public authorities could also ask merchants to provide notice of the wheat they owned, or declarations by cereals owners could be followed by specific surveys commanded by the victualling institutions to verify the private declarations and real availability of cereals; this was done, for example, during the famine of 1764.[40]

In the eighteenth century, as in the seventeenth, after providing notice of their cereals production, landowners (aside from those who enjoyed specific exemptions) were obligated to transport a third of their harvest into the city, after deducting seeds and products allocated to field workers.[41] Based on the availability of products and the market prices, the *Congregazione* was tasked with officially establishing the *calmiere* of bread (that is to say, the minimum weight of the loaves to be sold for a fixed price) and, upstream, the price of wheat.[42] It is important to note that the officially set price of wheat did not affect all the transactions, but only purchases by the *Congregazione* and by bakers, and thus did not directly affect trade between private parties. Following trials (*scandagli*) using various samples of wheat to verify the output in terms of flour and bread, then calculating the costs for the bakers and their licit profit, the *Congregazione* officials established how heavy the bread sold in the city had to be, along with the price of wheat to be purchased by the bakers and, potentially, by the *Congregazione* itself.[43] A similar procedure was implemented in Bologna,[44] intended to avoid excessive fluctuation in bread weight. We must keep in mind, however, that most baking was done within private homes, and therefore the public bakers primarily supplied the lowest strata of the population, who did not have an oven (or cereals stores) in their homes.

The *Congregazione* itself maintained some stocks of wheat, purchased from the landowners and merchants of Ferrara according to the officially set price; these reserves, according to orders issued in 1619, should amount to 2,500 *moggia* (i.e. 50,000 *staia*),[45] which at the time corresponded to the food needs of the city for approximately two months. Therefore, it was not a small amount, especially considering that Ferrara was located in a highly overabundant territory with respect to cereals production. However, over the years, there were significant fluctuations in the *Congregazione*'s reserves owing to the availability or scarcity of cereals or, on the contrary, the possibility of distributing the stores to the bakers. In the eighteenth century, the stocks of the *Congregazione* included maize as well as wheat, and flour as well as unrefined cereals. Many examples of purchases by the *Congregazione* in the years of 'normal' harvests can be found (purchases in years of famine will be discussed later), and they help to shed light on the role this institution played in the cereals market of Ferrara.

First, it is interesting to note the amounts purchased: in December 1776, the bookkeeper of the *Congregazione* reported that in the eighteen years since 1759, the institution had purchased 24,308.5 *moggia* (486,170 *staia*) of local wheat at various prices, on average 13–14 Roman *scudi* per *moggio*.[46] A considerable amount, but importantly, not an exaggerated one: assuming the previous production estimate of 720,000 *staia* in the District of Ferrara alone in 1769, the *Congregazione* purchased an average of only 27,000 *staia* each year, a very small part of the entire harvest. The amount could appear more significant considering that it corresponded to the food needs of the city of Ferrara for one month; moreover, if we consider it in light of the commercialised portion of the harvest (which, according to the aforementioned calculations by Angelini—144,000 *staia* in 1769—was around 20%), the products that flowed into the granaries of the *Congregazione* amounted to around 18.75% of the total commercial production of the District of Ferrara. The percentage is high with respect to the urban market but not to the entire Legation, which undoubtedly produced and commercialised much greater amounts.

The lists of sources from whom the *Congregazione* purchased wheat year after year demonstrate that its reserves were assembled through hundreds of small purchases (rarely more than 20 *moggia*, almost always under 6) from many different sellers, although important landowner families were also listed, such as the Massari, the Bevilacqua, the Gnoli, the Cremona, the Novara, the Rocci, and the Bottoni.[47] The low inclination of landowners to sell large amounts of cereals to the *Congregazione* (especially in years when prices were high) is also testified by the fact that in some cases, the legate himself had to intervene to force landowners to cede part of their harvest; for example, in October 1767, Legate Niccolò Serra ordered that in addition to transporting a third of the harvest into the city, landowners must sell another third to the *Congregazione* at the officially set price of 16 *scudi* per *moggio*.[48]

Circumstances were different when harvests were scarce, and corresponding amounts had to be purchased to supply the urban bakers. In such cases, the lots purchased by the *Congregazione* were quite significant, and the sellers were large merchants or important landowners who took advantage of the situation to obtain even more significant earnings.[49] In 1705, Sigismondo Gavassini, a member of a noble family of Ferrara, who would become a member of the *Giudice dei Savi* (literally, 'Judge of the Wisemen', an important municipal body) in 1721, sold to the *Congregazione* 1,500 *moggia* of wheat.[50] Between 1735 and 1736, the

Congregazione purchased 3,823 *moggia* of wheat in Venice, Trieste, and Ancona, among which 140 *moggia* sold by the Jewish Vida family and 60 by the Bottoni and Rocci company.[51] A total of 12,000 *moggia* of wheat was also collected in the ports of the northern Adriatic Sea (coming from London, Holland, and Dalmatia) and purchased for the *Congregazione* by Angelo Moretti, a "public trader" from Ferrara, owner of the *Banco Moretti* ('Moretti Bank') and a financier of the *Congregazione* itself.[52]

In 1740, Angelo Moretti again made 2,000 *scudi* available to purchase wheat in the Romagna province.[53] In 1764, a member of the Jewish Hanau family sold to the *Congregazione* 150 *moggia* of wheat, which was then distributed to the bakers, for 17.5 to 18 *scudi* per *moggio*.[54] Such examples illustrate the role played by the important merchant families (often Jewish[55]) in supplying the *Congregazione*, such as, even if in a different way, the opportunities for earnings coming from the requests of credit by the public institution to the private banks. In the following decades, the circumstances remained unchanged: in August 1773, during a significant crops shortage, the Felice Coen company imported 191 *moggia* of wheat into Ferrara from the March of Ancona;[56] between May and July 1783, the *Congregazione* purchased nearly 170 *moggia* of wheat from the Bottoni and Rocci company, 80 from the Vida family (although they signed an agreement for 160 *moggia* of wheat at 30 *scudi* each), and 370 from Francesco Massari, a member of one of Ferrara's most important families.[57]

In summary, in addition to routine small purchases from a large number of the laic and ecclesiastic landowners of Ferrara, the important families (Hanau, Coen, Vida, and Massari, among others) supplied the *Congregazione* in periods of food shortage. Such names belonged to a class of bankers and merchants that, according to Sani, strongly opposed the traditional nobility of Ferrara and gained an increasingly important role (in both public offices and landownership) in the eighteenth century, first by introducing French revolutionary ideas into Ferrara, then by supporting the arrival of the Napoleonic army, and finally by playing important roles in the new revolutionary administration.[58] These merchants operated on an international as well as a regional level: in 1763, for example, the victualling office of Bologna (the *Assunteria di Abbondanza*) purchased 20,000 Bolognese *corbe* of wheat from the Coen family, and 16,000 more in 1766, consisting of 10,000 "foreign grain from the sea" and 6,000 "from Germany".[59] In 1764, on behalf of Filippo Coen, a merchant from Trieste, Grassin Vita Levi, sent 2,300 Trieste *staia* of wheat to

Civitavecchia, 4,200 to Ancona, and 2,375 to Rome.[60] In May 1767, the Bottoni and Rocci company sold to the *Assunteria di Abbondanza* of Bologna between 7,000 and 8,000 *corbe* of wheat ("all foreign") and 4,500 of maize ("all from Mantua"), in addition to thousands of additional *corbe* during the same year and 3,000 *corbe* of wheat in December 1772.[61] The Massari family too is present in the documents of the *Assunteria di Abbondanza*, having supplied the city with 5,000 *corbe* of wheat in 1767.[62]

Once cereals were purchased by the *Congregazione dell'Abbondanza* of Ferrara, whether directly from the landowners or through local cereals merchants, their conservation was entrusted to a *granarista* ('granary-keeper'), who managed both the public and rented private[63] granaries in Ferrara and Pontelagoscuro.[64] The financing for purchases came from three main channels: sale of the cereals and flour to merchants and bakers,[65] the latter of which were sometimes almost forced to purchase from the *Congregazione*;[66] credit supplied by public *monti* (the Mount of Piety and other similar charitable institutions); or credit supplied by private banks or financers, often Jewish.

Sales to merchants, in particular, are an important element by which to understand the interaction between the public victualling institution, private economic players, and the overall market: not only could cereals merchants rely on the *Congregazione* as an important buyer in periods of scarcity, they could also purchase products from it when the *Congregazione* decided to sell out wheat purchased in surplus in case of small harvests or food shortages. In such cases, the prices proposed by the *Congregazione* were usually quite conservative, with relevant consequences on the debts accumulated by the institution (that did not recouped the money spent for the purchases of the cereals), but also with an important possibility of earnings for the merchants. Indeed, they could later resell the cereals in more lucrative markets with higher prices. The names of such purchasers in historical records are familiar: in 1738, the Coen family paid the *Banco Moretti* for 50 Ferrara *moggia* of wheat obtained from the *Congregazione*,[67] and in May 1786 the Massari company purchased 4,500 *moggia* to resell "outside the State".[68] This was not an extemporaneous purchase, given that the previous year the Massari obtained 2,156 *moggia* of wheat from the *Congregazione*.[69]

Banks and *monti* also played a fundamental role in guaranteeing credit for regular purchases and extraordinary purchases in years of scarcity. In eighteenth-century Ferrara, various *monti* lent money at an interest rate of around 6%: along with the traditional Mount of Piety (*Monte di Pietà*), there were the *Monte delle Farine* (literally, 'Flours Mount'), the *Monte Comunità* ('Community Mount'), the *Monte Sanità sesta erezione* ('Health Mount, sixth refinancing'), the *Monte Difesa* ('Defence Mount'), the *Monte Riparazione seconda erezione* ('Restoration Mount, second refinancing'), the *Monte Gualengo* ('Gualengo Mount'), and the *Monte Bentivoglio* ('Bentivoglio Mount').[70] The Mount of Piety and the *Monte delle Farine* (established in 1543) served as the primary economic foundation of the *Congregazione*, particularly the Mount of Piety, which the *Congregazione* deposited its assets into, drew from to purchase cereals, and used to receive sums due from bakers and merchants.[71] In April 1740, for example, money made available by the legate (approximately 10,000 *scudi*) was deposited into the Mount of Piety and used to supply urban bakers.[72] In 1772, Ercole Rossi (probably a member of the namesake Jewish family of Ferrara)[73] lent the *Congregazione* 1,500 *scudi* through the Mount of Piety, at a yearly payment of 50 *scudi* in interest,[74] to purchase wheat from the March of Ancona. An additional 2,500 *scudi* for this purpose was lent by Count Lorenzo Soderini, governor of the papal army in Ferrara, at a yearly payment of 125 *scudi* in interest.[75]

In January 1773, the Massari and the Guitti families, along with other important names among Ferrara's nobility, bourgeoisie, and private bank owners deposited funds to purchase wheat into the Mount of Piety,[76] and in the 1780s, the *Congregazione* proposed selling the shares in the *Monte Sanità* and *Monte Comunità* to compensate for the absence of assets in its treasury.[77] Nor was that the first time the victualling administration had relied on the *Monte Sanità* to purchase cereals: when Pope Benedict XIV allowed the establishment of the *Monte Frumentario* in Ferrara in 1714, a wheat reserve managed by the *Congregazione* for the production of bread for the urban population, 20,000 *scudi* for purchasing were collected through the creation and sale of 200 shares in the *Monte Sanità*, sixth refinancing.[78] An additional 200 shares were sold in 1744 to finance the purchase of cereals.[79] Sold shares were acquired by the families of Ferrara, but the *Congregazione* itself could also take advantage of the credit market to replenish its treasury. For example, in 1778, at the end of the mandate of Legate Scipione Borghese, the *Congregazione* held over 8,300 *scudi* deposited in the Mount of Piety; approximately 834 *moggia* of wheat in its granaries (an approximate value of 10,670 *scudi*); joint participation in the contract for the production of high-quality *pan di fiore* (a value of 4,000 *scudi*); 25,900 *scudi* in shares in the Mount of Piety (with a 3% interest rate); and around 260 *scudi* from the interest earned on these shares, immediately reinvested in other similar shares. Speculative operations such as joint participation in the *pan di fiore* contract and purchase of shares were promoted by the legate himself, with the aim to guarantee stable earnings for the *Congregazione*.[80]

Nevertheless, the Mount of Piety lay at the foundation of the *Congregazione*'s day-to-day functions and accounting. Other *monti* were used in exceptional financing cases, such as the creation of the *Monte Frumentario*, and so were private banks. Indeed, the public *monti* were not the only sources of credit for the *Congregazione* to purchase cereals; in periods of scarcity, private banks also intervened to supplement the *Congregazione*'s insufficient assets. According to Sani, in 1783 there were five private banks in Ferrara, managed respectively by the Bottoni and Rocci company, the Guitti brothers, the Massari brothers, Antonio M. Lugo and partners, and Mosè Vita Coen.[81] Over the course of the century, other similar banks represented the credit market in Ferrara; however, the aforementioned names are most interesting as they also appear in the records of cereals production and purchases and sales to and from the *Congregazione*. As previously noted, the *Banco Orsini*[82] and the *Banco Moretti* played a fundamental role during the famine of the 1730s.[83] Documents from April 1739 show that the *Banco Merli* played a similar role in that period.[84] In addition to the sale of *monti* (*Sanità* or *Comunità*) shares and the credit provided via deposits by private entities into the Mount of Piety, credit supplied by private banks was fundamental in compensating for the *Congregazione*'s chronic deficiency in assets. As with the withdrawal of capital in the Mount of Piety, private bank loans were repaid using money owed to the *Congregazione* by bakers and merchants, deposited directly into the lending bank.

5.4 Public Interests, Merchants, and Producers

The chapter's description thus far of the functioning of the victualling system in Ferrara, focusing on cereals, helps to illustrate some observations on the role played by public institutions (in this specific case, the *Congregazione dell'Abbondanza*) in the cereals market, and on the interaction between the organisation of the victualling system and the behaviour of the economic players. First, unlike circumstances in other areas (such as Venice), the *Congregazione*'s purchases had a relatively limited effect on the demand for cereals, and therefore on the functioning of the cereals market, in years of normal or abundant harvests; in years of scarcity, their role was far more important. In contrast, the role played by the *Congregazione* and the legate in setting the official price of wheat and weight of bread can be characterised differently. As Cazzola indicated, the public institutions could pursue a real policy of agricultural price support, to use modern terms.[85] However, as illustrated by the data in Fig. 5.1, the situation appears to have been somewhat different: the official price of wheat established in Ferrara roughly followed trends in market prices in the neighbouring areas (unfortunately, data on market prices in Ferrara are unavailable), without substantial modifications of increases or decreases. Correlation coefficients between officially set wheat prices in Ferrara and market wheat prices in Padua and Desenzano are quite high (0.76 and 0.74, respectively).

In addition to the strong correlation between the three series, Fig. 5.1 shows that Ferrara's prices had clear variations, even slightly higher than those of the two neighbouring markets (coefficients of variation are 0.30

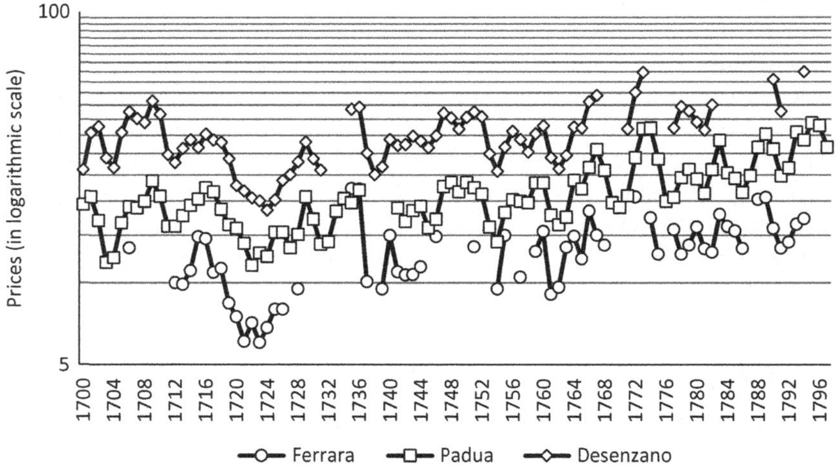

Fig. 5.1 Officially set wheat prices in Ferrara and market wheat prices in Padua and Desenzano (1700–1797). (Sources: Cazzola 1971, pp. 554, 560–561 (on Ferrara); Bertoni 2014, pp. 15–54 (on Desenzano); sincere thanks are due to Professor Luciano Pezzolo, who kindly provided the data on Padua. Original prices for Ferrara are in Roman *scudi* per Ferrara *moggio*; for Padua, in Venetian *lire di piccoli* per Paduan *staio*; for Desenzano, in Venetian *lire di piccoli* per Brescia *soma*)

for Ferrara, 0.29 for Padua, and 0.25 for Desenzano). Although we cannot tell how much the market prices in Ferrara differed from these figures, it is evident that the officially set price did not have a significant preventative effect on sharp increases or decreases in wheat prices, which would have produced a more regular movement with lower fluctuations. This characteristic is not unique to Ferrara; comparison of officially set prices in Ferrara and Bologna shows similar dynamics, with a Pearson correlation coefficient of 0.77 (see Fig. 5.2).

In summary, officially set wheat prices in eighteenth-century Ferrara—aside from negotiation between producers, public authorities, and bakers[86]—tended to follow market prices, perhaps mitigating some high or low extremes. However, as Fig. 5.2 shows, this mitigating effect was much less evident than in neighbouring Bologna: the coefficient of variation in prices is 0.30 for Ferrara but only 0.18 for Bologna. Therefore, we can assume that the intervention of the public institutions was focused more on the fixation of bread weight than of wheat prices, with the intention of guaranteeing food availability for the

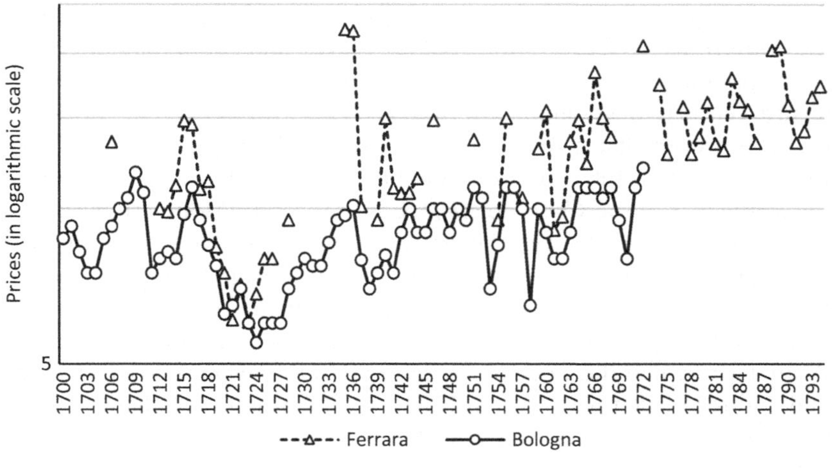

Fig. 5.2 Officially set wheat prices in Ferrara and Bologna (1700–1794). (Sources: Cazzola 1971, pp. 554, 560–561 (on Ferrara); Mocarelli and Ongaro 2019b, p. 51 (on Bologna). Original prices for Bologna are in Bolognese *lire* for Bolognese *corba*)

population. From an economic point of view, the importance of public intervention, particularly that of the *Congregazione dell'Abbondanza*, is more evident in purchases of cereals during periods of scarcity, when these goods could play a significant role both in economic terms and in guaranteeing food availability for the population. The major merchant families (Coen, Bottoni, Rocci, Massari, etc.) interacted with the *Congregazione* by selling wheat during famines, purchasing it for resale in other markets when the *Congregazione* decided to renew its stocks, offering significant amounts of products for sale at limited prices. The same families also 'invested' in the *Congregazione* through the credit market, granting loans through either the Mount of Piety or their own banks. It is interesting to note that the economic players who operated in the cereals market (in addition to other fields, given the strong diversification of their investments) adapted their behaviour based on the functioning of the *Congregazione* and participated in its management.

A clear example is Francesco Containi, the author of *Ferrara felice*, who came from a family of important landowners and served as a member of the *Congregazione*.[87] When the *Congregazione* sought to purchase large quantities of wheat from the March of Ancona in 1772, Containi, described in the documents as *abbondanziere*, was appointed to secure the needed funds and sign loan contracts in the *Congregazione*'s name.[88] Furthermore, the *Giudice dei Savi*, one of the *savi* themselves, and two nobles of Ferrara were appointed to manage the *Congregazione*'s functioning in the eighteenth century, maintaining the nobility's control of it. This does not mean, however, that cereals merchants, especially the Jewish merchants, were excluded. In July 1762, for example, Mosè Vita Coen guaranteed for the *granarista* of the *Congregazione*, Carlo Antonio Pisoni, establishing a clear and potentially very lucrative connection with one of the *Congregazione*'s functions (that is to say conservation of food stocks), given the merchants' opportunity to acquire lots to be sold out.[89] Pisoni may even have been a representative for Coen himself; similarly, Giacomo Pisoni represented the Coen in the *conciera* ('tanning') tax contract of the mid-eighteenth century,[90] and in 1771, the Coen family purchased various lands and estates in Ferrara and Pontelagoscuro through Baldassarre Baldassarri and none other than Carlo Pisoni himself.[91]

It is also interesting to observe that contemporary opinions of the *Congregazione* were far less negative than might be expected based on coeval publications in favour of free commerce. Certainly, the functioning of the *Congregazione* created problems with respect to debt in the public treasury, and payments to producers appear to have been consistently delayed, to the point of continuous reprimands from the legate.[92] However, essays focusing on the reform of Ferrara's economy in the eighteenth century—with respect specifically to the agricultural sector and cereals commerce—made no calls for radical change. For example, Containi's manuscript *Ferrara felice* makes no mention of the *Congregazione*. The author certainly complained that, despite Ferrara's high agricultural production and access to important river and sea communication lines, commerce failed to flourish.[93] The chapter *Del commercio de' grani* ('On cereals commerce') immediately expressed the correlation between "a very good and abundant harvest, that quickly leads to a significant scarcity";[94] however, Containi did not link these difficulties to the presence of the *Congregazione* or to the officially set wheat prices. Rather, he attributed the restricted growth of cereals commerce in Ferrara to the excessive limitation on movement of cereals within and outside the State.

Containi proposed taking the Republic of Venice as an example,[95] ensuring that all could export their products where they preferred, only prohibiting exports when the prices would be too high in the Legation of Ferrara. In other words, he proposed basing freedom of commerce on fixation of a maximum price, under which the market would be completely free; in this way, he claimed Ferrara would never lack cereals stocks, and landowners would have the assurance that they could sell their stocks abroad if prices in the Legation were low, or within the state borders if domestic prices were higher. Such a solution would satisfy both the food needs of consumers and the economic needs of the producers and the state Treasury. Containi asked himself why it was not pursued, and his answer involved problems linked to freedom of the cereals market, pushes towards its general liberalisation, and the diverse interests of those involved. According to Containi, the merchants, especially those who enjoyed specific privileges linked to cereals commerce, opposed this solution.[96] This brings to light a fundamental opposition between the interests of the cereals producers (who sought greater freedom in cereals commerce) and the major merchants (who often monopolised export permissions[97] and benefitted from a restricted market), where, therefore, it was possible only for a few of them to seek financial returns on the asymmetries between the various areas.

5.5 Conclusions

The previous section demonstrated the complexity of the interests involved in cereals commerce, which affected the evolution of public regulation in the sector. In conclusion, victualling systems were both an arena of interaction between these interests and a variable for merchants and producers to consider when planning their strategy. However, compared to other areas in which public intervention played a fundamental role (e.g. officially set prices in Bologna or huge purchases of cereals for the fleet by the Venetian government), public regulation of the cereals market in eighteenth-century Ferrara had some specific traits: officially set wheat prices tended to follow market prices, without having any particular effect on sharp increases or decreases; similarly, purchases made by the *Congregazione* were limited and did not significantly affect the overall demand for cereals. Demand was generally sustained not by the internal market but by the necessity to supply the Legation of Bologna. However, this does not indicate that the *Congregazione* was an irrelevant institution: from the victualling perspective, it maintained food stores to meet the city's needs for around a month, and given the strongly surplus character of agriculture in the area, this indicated great prudence by the institution.

Moreover, the *Congregazione* was important to the economic players in the cereals market, as testified by the desire of merchants and producers to hold controlling positions and offices. Besides the fact that the institution could potentially affect prices and purchases, it was also an interesting field for investments (via loans made through the Mount of Piety or private banks), and it was both a major customer for merchants in periods of scarcity and an occasional seller of low-cost products that could be resold in more profitable markets. It is also interesting that the same bourgeois families that gained increasing political and economic influence in the eighteenth century (Massari, Containi, Bottoni, Rocci, etc.) took the advantage of the public institution to inform their economic behaviour and gradual growth in the context of Ferrara—or at least took it into account to the point of participating in its management.

Similarly important is that, despite apparent search for greater freedom of the market and abolition of the privileges and restrains of the Old Regime, the arrival of the French at the end of the century did not lead to substantial changes. The aforementioned families did gradually overtake the nobility of Ferrara in terms of political and economic influence (although without drastic reform of the public institutions), but with respect to the victualling system, changes were limited. First, public control of the import and the export of the cereals was maintained based on the food needs of Ferrara, Bologna, and the army, in addition to military-diplomatic dynamics (entailing recurring restrictions of commerce with Austria and England). Second, the *Congregazione dell'Abbondanza* was not only maintained but supported by the provisional government with the establishment of a *Comitato di Annona* ('Victualling Committee') involving, among others, the Bevilacqua and Massari families.[98]

Notes

1. Containi (1995 [1767], p. 7) (publication of the manuscript dated 1767 and preserved in the *Biblioteca Comunale Ariostea* in Ferrara); Sani (2001, pp. 27–29).
2. Containi (1995 [1767], pp. 8–9); Sani (2001, pp. 28–29); Cazzola (2003, pp. 18–22); (2018, pp. 71–78).
3. Dal Pane (1969, pp. 37–39); Guenzi (1977, 1978, 1981, 1982).
4. In the province of Ferrara, major famines occurred in 1739, 1764, and 1772–1774. Other problems affecting the cereals supply arose in the first and last decades of the eighteenth century as a result of military circumstances impacting the province.
5. Regarding the contrasting interests of landowners and small, medium-sized, and large cereals merchants in the Papal States, see Ongaro (2019).
6. Cazzola (1991); Mocarelli (2015, pp. 57–59); Gasparini (2002); Appleby (1979).
7. "Noi per altro specialissima gli abbiamo obbligazione per ciò, che laddove altri popoli [...] coltivano terreni duri ed ingrati [...], noi tutto v'abbiamo per ispazi immensi terreno ottimo, e da trarne frutto anche immenso" (Containi 1995 [1767], p. 139). Here and below, all translations of original documents and works quoted are the author's.
8. Containi (1995 [1767], pp. 7, 13–15); Cazzola (2003, pp. 39–42); Sani (2001, pp. 45–49).
9. Mocarelli and Ongaro (2019a, pp. 25–26).
10. Dal Pane (1969, pp. 8, 20–21).
11. Regarding the significance of Ferrara's agricultural production, see also Containi (1995 [1767], pp. 13–14); Cazzola (2003, pp. 39–42).
12. On the 1769 survey, see also Angelini (1973, pp. 176–177).
13. 1 Ferrara *moggio* (plur. *moggia*) was divided into 20 *staia* and corresponded to approximately 621.86 cubic decimetres (Martini 1883, p. 205).
14. "[P]ane veneziano, e della farina di formentone" (ASCFE, FXVIII, 82, fo. 385r).

15. After the incorporation of the former Duchy d'Este into the Papal States, the domain of Ferrara in the territory of the newborn Legation was considerably reduced. Seven *podesterie* were created (Bondeno, Ficarolo, Francolino, Garofalo, Migliaro, Massafiscaglia, and Portomaggiore), which were administered by officials appointed by the city of Ferrara's *Consiglio Centumvirale* (literally, 'Council of the One Hundred Men'), and fifteen districts ruled by governors nominated directly by the supreme court of the *Sacra Consulta* in Rome (Argenta, Ariano, Bagnacavallo, Cento, Codigoro, Comacchio, Cotignola, Crespino, Lugo, Massalombarda, Melara, Pieve di Cento, Sant'Agata, Conselice, and Trecenta). The territory of the District of Ferrara (not to be confused with the entire Legation) included 109 communities in the administrative region of Ferrara and the *podesterie*; the remaining 65 communities in the Legation were called *extradistrettuali* (Sani 2001, p. 31). It is not possible to calculate the precise extension of the two areas.
16. Available data on the specific weight of wheat in those years' Ferrara are very variable.
17. ASCFE, FXVIII, 82, fo. 385v.
18. Angelini (1979, pp. 33–34).
19. See Dal Pane (1969, pp. 37–39); Guenzi (1977, 1978, 1981, 1982); Mocarelli and Ongaro (2019b, pp. 37–51). Many documents related to purchases by the *Assunteria di Abbondanza*—the victualling office—of Bologna are preserved in ASBO, AAD, 3, fos. 291r–293r; 4, fos. 266r–268r; 7, fos. 172r–173r, 449r–v.; AAN, 1, fo. 52r; 2, fos. 386r–387r; 3, fos. 112r–115v, 396r–436v.
20. "[E] al bisogno de' Bolognesi vostri fratelli" (ASBO, AAN, 100bis, fo. 245v).
21. The *tratte* were temporary export permissions for specific amounts and types of products. They were granted to merchants by the pope or the Congregation of Cardinals (in the case of a vacant seat), either for free or, more often, against payment (Dal Pane 1939).
22. Dal Pane (1939, p. 108).
23. ASCFE, FXVIII, 97, fos. 502r, 559r–v.
24. Sani (2001, p. 50).
25. Dal Pane (1939); (1965, pp. 386–405).
26. Cazzola (1971, pp. 559–560); Angelini (1973, pp. 49–51, 148).
27. Angelini (1973, pp. 364–369, 403–414); Containi (1995 [1767], pp. 25, 97–98).
28. On these topics, see Dal Pane (1939, 1965, 1969).
29. ASCFE, PA, 241 (65), 272 (8), 296 (73), 301 (39, 48, 55), 343 (1), 355 (7), 362 (49), 369 (4, 12), 371 (13), 376 (3), 377 (24), 379 (4), 382 (13, 26).

30. ASCFE, PA, 303 (4), 338 (109), 343 (1), 372 (197), 373 (2, 17), 376 (7), 382 (26).
31. ASCFE, PA, 257 (48), 269 (22), 274 (2), 275 (50), 277 (46), 279 (34), 283 (16), 285 (63), 288 (11), 292 (7), 294 (39), 301 (39, 48), 303 (52), 311 (26), 316 (52), 356 (17b), 364 (37).
32. Cazzola (1971, p. 548).
33. On the general contracts for production of the *pan di fiore* (higher-quality bread), *pan venale* (ordinary bread), and *pan da munizione* (bread for soldiers), see Cazzola (1971, p. 549).
34. Clark (1985); Alfani (2013 [2010]).
35. Cazzola (1971, p. 549).
36. Cazzola (1971, p. 551).
37. Cazzola (1971). On the organisation of political institutions in Ferrara, see Containi (1995 [1767], p. 9); Sani (2001, pp. 30–31).
38. Cazzola (1971, p. 551).
39. ASCFE, PA, 263 (19), 265 (58), 273 (57), 318 (12), 331 (13, 67), 362 (50), 372 (11); FXVIII, 81, fos. 61r–70r, 127r–224r; 96, fos. 596r–611r.
40. ASCFE, FXVIII, 81, fos. 227r, 332r–v.
41. ASCFE, PA, 253 (6), 301 (47), 343 (2), 347 (8).
42. Cazzola (1971, pp. 554, 560–561).
43. Many *scandagli* and *calmieri* exist in the archival collection of the *Congregazione dell'Abbondanza* of Ferrara. See ASCFE, FXVIII, 76–86, 88, 90–94, 96–98, 100, 110bis.
44. Regarding this topic, see Guenzi (1977, 1978, 1981, 1982).
45. Cazzola (1971, pp. 555, 558–559).
46. ASCFE, FXVIII, 84, fo. 309r. In the Roman monetary system of account, extended to the Papal States, 1 *scudo* (plur. *scudi*) was divided into 10 *giuli* or *paoli*, and 1 *giulio* or *paolo* into 10 *baiocchi* (Balbi De Caro and Londei 1984, pp. 55, 61, 89, 127; Londei 1990, pp. 308, 311–318).
47. ASCFE, FXVIII, fo. 524r; 85, fos. 105r–110v, 728r–734r, 875r–876r; 86, fos. 326r–329r; 87, fos. 153r–v, 322r–323r; 89, fos. 356v–364r; 90, fos. 3r–4v, 250r–v, 377r–380v; 93, fos. 578r–580r, 585r–587r; 95, fos. 455r–458r.
48. ASCFE, FXVIII, 100bis, fo. without number.
49. Angelini (1973, pp. 19–20).
50. Angelini (1973, pp. 20–21); (1979, p. 105).
51. ASCFE, FXVIII, 78, fo. 434r.
52. "[P]ublico negotiante" (ASCFE, FXVIII, 78, fos. 349r–414r; PA, 314 (5)).
53. ASCFE, FXVIII, 79, fo. 108r–v.
54. ASCFE, FXVIII, 81, fo. 103r.

55. On the significant economic role played by the populous Jewish community in Ferrara, see Cazzola (2003, pp. 34–38); Sani (2001, pp. 43–45); and especially Angelini (1973).
56. ASCFE, FXVIII, 83, fo. 610r; Angelini (1973, pp. 180–182).
57. ASCFE, FXVIII, 89, fo. 46r; 90, fo. 402r. On the Massari family, see Sani (2001, pp. 22, 158, 182, 241, 265–267, 390–392).
58. Sani (2001, especially pp. 41–42, 49, 80, 109–115, 158, 182, 250, 257). On the Bottoni and Rocci families, see Sani (2001, pp. 22, 82, 132–134, with specific references to their involvement in the cereals market); on the Containi family, see Sani (2001, pp. 22, 25–26, 89, 158); on the Vida family, see Sani (2001, p. 378). For similar considerations on cereals merchants in the Republic of Venice, with a specific focus also on the Jewish Vivante family, see Ongaro (2018).
59. "[G]rani forestieri di mare", "di Germania" (Mocarelli and Ongaro 2019b, p. 45; ASBO, AAI, 3, fos. not numbered). 1 Bolognese *corba* (plur. *corbe*) was divided into 2 *staia* and corresponded to approximately 78.645 cubic decimetres (Martini 1883, p. 92, where 8 instead of 2 *staia* are erroneously indicated).
60. Andreozzi (2019, p. 59). 1 Trieste *staio* (plur. *staia*) corresponded to approximately 86.812 cubic decimetres (Martini 1883, p. 794).
61. "[T]utto forestiero", "tutto mantovano" (ASBO, AAI, 3, fos. not numbered).
62. ASBO, AAI, 3, fos. not numbered.
63. In 1754, the lease of granaries owned by the duke of Modena in *Via Gioco del Pallone* was renewed, and in July 1759, a reference was made to the "restoration of the public granaries in San Lorenzo, paid for the moment by the *Abbondanza*" ("rifacimento de' granai da San Lorenzo, del publico, da farsi a spese per ora dell'Abbondanza") (ASCFE, FXVIII, 79, fo. 539r). In October 1772, the *Congregazione* rented granaries in Pontelagoscuro owned by Count Cornelio Pepoli, originally of Bologna but residing in Venice (ASCFE, FXVIII, 82, fo. 536r). In addition to some permanent warehouses where the *Congregazione* stored long-term provisions, some buildings—such as the granaries in Pontelagoscuro—were temporarily rented during the harvest period to store cereals to be distributed to the bakers within a short time. A document dated 1780 lists granaries rented "because of the harvest" ("a comodo del raccolto"), referring to a total of twenty-nine buildings, partially located with a fixed fee, partially according to the amounts of cereals stored (ASCFE, FXVIII, 85, fo. 882r–v). Similar lists from 1782, 1783, 1784, and 1786 exist (ASCFE, FXVIII, 88, fo. 331r; 90, fos. 463r, 465r; 91, fo. 253r; 92, fo. 6r). Regarding the office of the *granarista* and its election, see the *Accettazione di Carlo Pisoni in granarista de' formenti della pubblica Abbondanza*, dated 1759 (ASCFE,

FXVIII, 80, fos. 537r–546r). See also Cazzola (1971, p. 558). On the complex (and costly) process of cereals conservation, see the observations of Gérard Béaur (2019) on the French case, which are also valid for the Italian case.

64. Pontelagoscuro was a port on the Po river, where merchandise from the Adriatic Sea bound to Ferrara or other areas of northern Italy were transferred from the seafaring ships to river transports. On the significant role played by Pontelagoscuro, see Peron and Savioli (1987); Balzani (1993); Cazzola (2003, pp. 289–291); Containi (1995 [1767], pp. 14–15); and, for a broad perspective, Angelini (1979).
65. Examples of distribution of wheat and flour to bakers, such as receipts of their payments to the Orsini and Moretti banks, are numerous: see ASCFE, PA, 254 (18); FXVIII, 78–87, 89–98.
66. In January 1766, a regulation established that bakers must purchase wheat from the *Congregazione* and were prohibited from obtaining it elsewhere, and additionally obligated them to purchase 120 *moggia* of flour from the *Congregazione* (ASCFE, FXVIII, 79, fo. 541v). A decree of Legate Serra, dated October 1767, prohibited bakers from purchasing wheat other than the amounts they were obliged to obtain from the *Congregazione*, and paid them through the Mount of Piety (ASCFE, FXVIII, 100bis (1), fo. 1r).
67. ASCFE, PA, 318 (22).
68. "[F]uori Stato" (ASCFE, FXVIII, 92, fos. 92r–94r).
69. ASCFE, FXVIII, 91, fo. 755r.
70. Containi (1995 [1767], p. 12); Angelini (1973, p. 52); Sani (2001, pp. 36–37). On the role played by the *monti* in the *Congregazione*'s financing, see also Cazzola (1971, p. 577).
71. In addition to the following examples, see also ASCFE, FXVIII, 86, fos. 326r–329r; 97, fo. 478r.
72. ASCFE, PA, 79, fo. 67r–v.
73. Angelini (1979, p. 55); (1973, pp. 64–65, 73, 153).
74. ASCFE, FXVIII, 82, fos. 558r–559r, 590r–591v.
75. ASCFE, FXVIII, 82, fos. 601r–604r.
76. ASCFE, FXVIII, 83, fos. 4r–8v, 61r–80r. Near the end of the century, the Massari family also lent 6,000 *scudi* to the victualling administration of Rome, demonstrating their involvement in such business even outside the Legation of Ferrara (Sani 2001, p. 23).
77. ASCFE, FXVIII, 85, fo. 751r–v.
78. ASCFE, FXVIII, 84, fo. 808r; 79, fo. 539r.
79. ASCFE, FXVIII, 84, fo. 808r; 79, fo. 539r.
80. ASCFE, FXVIII, 84, fos. 809v–810r.
81. Containi (1995 [1767], p. 82).

82. ASCFE, PA, 254 (18); FXVIII, 77, fos. 91r–104r, 152r.
83. ASCFE, PA, 318 (22); FXVIII, 78, fos. 33r, 344r, 400r–414r.
84. ASCFE, PA, 79, fo. 8r.
85. Cazzola (1971, p. 553).
86. Cazzola (1971, pp. 562–563, 565).
87. Containi (1995 [1767], pp. 35–45).
88. ASCFE, FXVIII, 82, fo. 646r.
89. ASCFE, FXVIII, 80, fo. 544r–v. On the importance of management of food stores in terms of both economics and food supply, see also Ronsijn et al. (2019).
90. Angelini (1973, p. 138). The *conciera* tax, as the term itself suggests, was imposed on leather tanning (Containi 1995 [1767], p. 81).
91. Sani (2001, p. 44).
92. ASCFE, FXVIII, 87, fos. 32r–33r; 89, fo. 366r; 95, fo. 572r; 97, fo. 804r.
93. Containi (1995 [1767], p. 161).
94. "[U]na lietissima ricolta ed abbondanza di quelli talor si fa passaggio repentino a tanta scarsezza" (Containi 1995 [1767], p. 162). On this topic, see also Vertecchi (2012, 2013).
95. Dal Pane (1946).
96. Containi (1995 [1767], pp. 162–163). On these topics, see also Angelini (1979, pp. 297, 317).
97. Dal Pane (1939, pp. 139–140).
98. Sani (2001, pp. 166–168, 240, 248, 258, 359).

Archival Sources

Archivio di Stato di Bologna (ASBO)
Assunteria di Abbondanza, Diversorum (AAD).
Assunteria di Abbondanza, Instrumenti (AAI).
Assunteria di Abbondanza, Notizie (AAN).
www.archiviodistatobologna.it

Archivio Storico Comunale di Ferrara (ASCFE)
Finanziaria XVIII (FXVIII).
Patrimoniale (PA).
https://archibiblio.comune.fe.it/272/archivio-storico-comunale

Published Sources

Containi, Francesco. 1995 [1767]. *Ferrara felice. Ovvero della felicità dello Stato di Ferrara di Francesco Containi*, ed. by Valentino Sani. Roma: Vecchiarelli.

References

Alfani, Guido. 2013 [2010]. *Calamities and the economy in Renaissance Italy: The grand tour of the Horsemen of the Apocalypse*. English translation. Basingstoke: Palgrave Macmillan.

Andreozzi, Daniele. 2019. "L'aggravio dei dazi". Norme, mercato e concorrenze nei circuiti del grano della Trieste settecentesca. In Clemente and Russo 2019, 53–71.

Angelini, Werther. 1973. *Gli Ebrei di Ferrara nel Settecento. I Coen e altri mercanti nel rapporto con le pubbliche autorità*. Urbino: Argalia.

———. 1979. *Economia e cultura a Ferrara dal Seicento al tardo Settecento*. Urbino: Argalia.

Appleby, Andrew B. 1979. Grain prices and subsistence crises in England and France, 1590–1740. *The Journal of Economic History* 39 (4): 865–887.

Balbi De Caro, Silvana, and Luigi Londei. 1984. *Moneta Pontificia (da Innocenzo XI a Gregorio XVI)*. Roma: Quasar.

Balzani, Roberto, ed. 1993. *Le cronache di Pontelagoscuro di Antonio Dolcetti (1796–1801)*. Bologna: Analisi.

Béaur, Gérard. 2019. Preventing subsistence crisis: The state and granaries of abundance in Old Regime France. In Ronsijn et al. 2019, 193–210.

Beloch, Karl Julius. 1994 [1937–1961]. *Storia della popolazione d'Italia*, ed. by the Società Italiana di Demografia Storica. Italian translation. Firenze: Le Lettere.

Bertoni, Rodolfo. 2014. Il mercato a Desenzano in epoca veneta. In *Il mercato a Desenzano in epoca veneta e l'odierna agricoltura*, ed. by the Associazione Culturale Noialter de la Ria del Lac, 15–54. Bedizzole: Bontempi.

Cazzola, Franco. 1971. Il problema annonario nella Ferrara pontificia: il Legato Serra e la Congregazione dell'Abbondanza (1616–1622). *Annali della Facoltà di Lettere e Filosofia dell'Università di Macerata* 3–4: 541–578.

———. 1991. L'introduzione del mais in Italia e la sua utilizzazione alimentare (sec. XVI–XVIII). *Pact. Revue du Groupe Européen d'Études pour les Techniques Physiques, Chimiques et Mathématiques Appliquées à l'Archeologie* 26: 109–127.

———. 2003. *La città, il principe, i contadini. Ricerche sull'economia ferrarese nel Rinascimento, 1450–1630*. Ferrara: Corbo.

———. 2018. Acque, fiumi e lavoro umano nella costruzione della bassa pianura emiliano-romagnola. In *Lucio Gambi, Ravenna e la Romagna. Un geografo per la storia*, ed. by Dante Bolognesi and Carla Giovannini, 71–78. Bologna: Bononia University Press.

Clark, Peter, ed. 1985. *The European crisis of the 1590s: Essays in comparative history*. London: Allen and Unwin.

Clemente, Alida, and Saverio Russo, eds. 2019. *La* polizia de' grani. *Mercati, regole e crisi di sussistenza nelle economie di Antico Regime*. Soveria Mannelli: Rubbettino.

Dal Pane, Luigi. 1939. Il commercio dei grani nello Stato Pontificio nei secoli XVII e XVIII. *Annali della Facoltà di Economia e Commercio dell'Università di Bari* 2: 61–150.

———. 1946. La politica annonaria di Venezia. *Giornale degli Economisti e Annali di Economia*, new series 5 (5–6): 331–353.

———. 1965. La Congregazione economica istituita da Benedetto XIV e la libertà di commercio. *Rivista di Storia dell'Agricoltura* 5 (4): 371–418.

———. 1969. *Economia e società a Bologna nell'età del Risorgimento. Introduzione alla ricerca*. Bologna: Zanichelli.

Gasparini, Danilo. 2002. *Polenta e formenton. Il mais nelle campagne venete tra XVI e XX secolo*. Sommacampagna: Cierre.

Guenzi, Alberto. 1977. Il "calmiero del formento": controllo del prezzo del pane e difesa della rendita terriera a Bologna nei secoli XVII e XVIII. *Annali della Fondazione Luigi Einaudi* 11: 143–201.

———. 1978. Un mercato regolato: pane e fornai a Bologna nell'età moderna. *Quaderni Storici* 13 (1/37): 370–397.

———. 1981. Il frumento e la città: il caso di Bologna nell'età moderna. *Quaderni Storici* 16 (1/46): 153–167.

———. 1982. *Pane e fornai a Bologna in età moderna*. Venezia: Marsilio.

Londei, Luigi. 1990. La monetazione pontificia e la zecca di Roma nell'età moderna (secc. XVI–XVIII). *Studi Romani* 38 (3–4): 303–318.

Martini, Angelo. 1883. *Manuale di metrologia, ossia misure, pesi e monete in uso attualmente e anticamente presso tutti i popoli*. Torino: Loescher.

Mocarelli, Luca. 2015. Ripensare le crisi alimentari: lo Stato di Milano nel secondo Settecento. In *"Moia la carestia". La scarsità alimentare in età preindustriale*, ed. by Maria Luisa Ferrari and Manuel Vaquero Piñeiro, 39–63. Bologna: il Mulino.

Mocarelli, Luca, and Giulio Ongaro. 2019a. *Work in early modern Italy, 1500–1800*. Cham: Palgrave Macmillan.

———. 2019b. La gestione dei rifornimenti granari in periodi di scarsità: Milano e Bologna a confronto (XVIII sec.). In Clemente and Russo 2019, 37–51.

Ongaro, Giulio. 2018. Military food supply in the Republic of Venice in the eighteenth century: Entrepreneurs, merchants, and the state. *Business History*. https://doi.org/10.1080/00076791.2018.1520211.

———. 2019. Free ports in a controlled market: The role of Ancona, Livorno, Genova and Trieste in the grain trade in eighteenth-century Italy. Paper presented at the conference *The construction of free ports: Political communication, commercial development and administrative control*, Venice, 29–30 April.

Peron, Marica, and Giacomo Savioli, eds. 1987. *Il Lago-Scuro Ponte per la città*. Ferrara: Arstudio.

Ronsijn, Wouter, Niccolò Mignemi, and Laurent Herment, eds. 2019. *Stocks, seasons and sales: Food supply, storage and markets in Europe and the New World, c. 1600–2000*. Turnhout: Brepols.

Sani, Valentino. 2001. *La rivoluzione senza rivoluzione. Potere e società a Ferrara dal tramonto della legazione pontificia alla nascita della Repubblica Cisalpina (1787–1797)*. Milano: Angeli.

Vertecchi, Giulia. 2012. Dal grano al biscotto. Elementi per una storia della politica annonaria di Venezia fra XVII e XVIII secolo. *Storia Urbana* 36 (1/134): 57–74.

———. 2013. L'"eccessiva abbondanza si converte in miserabil penuria": i provvedimenti del governo veneziano nel XVIII secolo. In *Quando manca il pane. Origini e cause della scarsità delle risorse alimentari in età moderna e contemporanea*, ed. by Luca Mocarelli, 237–252. Bologna: il Mulino.

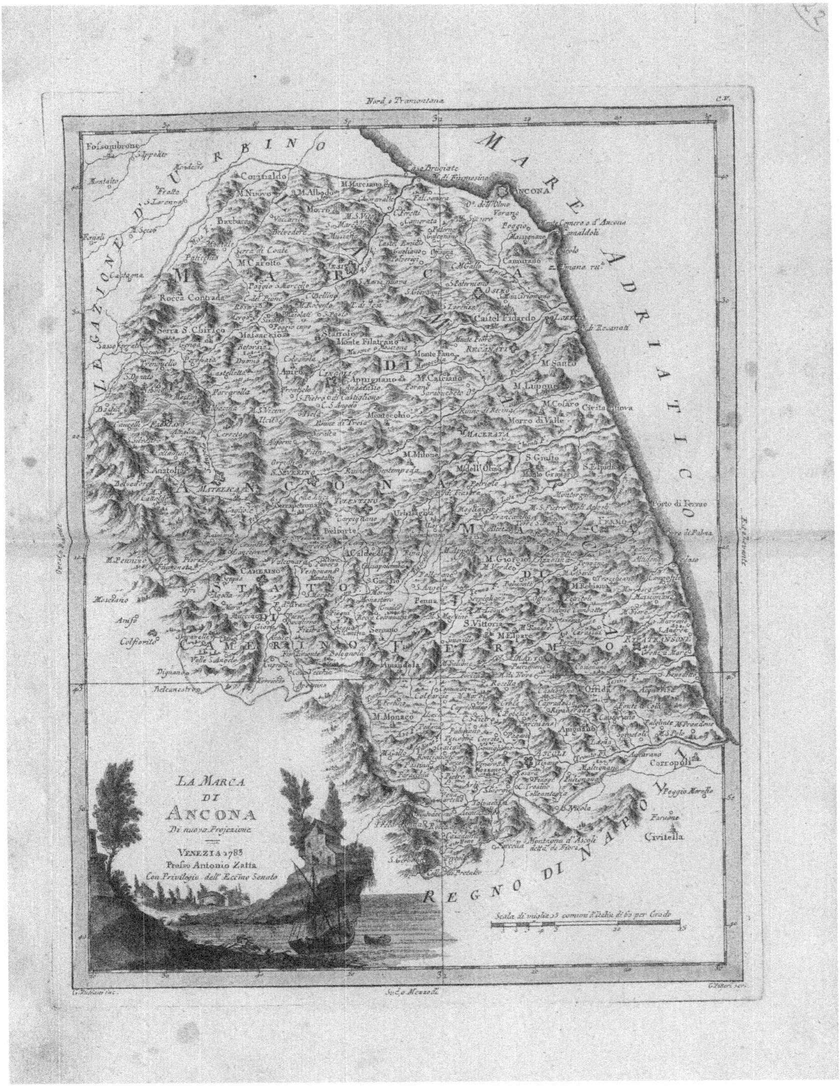

Map 6.1 The March of Ancona (1783)

CHAPTER 6

The Wealth of Periphery? Food Provisioning, Merchants, and Cereals in the Papal States: The Case of the March of Ancona

Luca Andreoni and Marco Moroni

6.1 Introduction

The purpose of this chapter is the reconstruction of the fundamental traits of the provisioning system of the March of Ancona in the Papal States (or simply the March—*Marca*—in the heart of today's Marche region), during the Early Modern Age. That is to say, to try to understand the mechanisms of the administration and the practices put in place to achieve the ideal of the good remuneration for producers and the market access for consumers. As said by Steven Laurence Kaplan for the twentieth-century French case (proof of the long duration of these problems), this ideal could be

This chapter is the result of a common reflection by the two authors. However, Sects. 6.1, 6.7, 6.8, and 6.9 were written by Luca Andreoni, while Sects. 6.2, 6.3, 6.4, 6.5, and 6.6 were written by Marco Moroni. Section 6.10 was written together.

L. Andreoni (✉) • M. Moroni
Università Politecnica delle Marche, Ancona, Italy
e-mail: l.andreoni@univpm.it

L. Clerici (ed.), *Italian Victualling Systems in the Early Modern Age, 16th to 18th Century*, Palgrave Studies in Economic History,
https://doi.org/10.1007/978-3-030-42064-2_6

summarised as follows: "the good (rather high) price of wheat and the low price of bread".[1] In more details, the following pages address the most relevant issues concerning wheat provisioning. After an overview of the functioning of the system in some small or medium-sized cities as Osimo, follows a discussion of certain major conurbations.

This kind of study is justified by the existence of a strong, homogeneous character of this territory. This harmony existed both from an institutional point of view, and from the point of view of agricultural systems (and also the urban-rural porosity, the conformation of the territory, which are not detailed here, but occasionally called up, if deemed appropriate).[2] Here, it suffices to mention the characteristics of the political integration pursued by the Holy See between the fourteenth and sixteenth centuries, founded on the multiple local level compromise, also with the feudal lords.[3] Institutional bodies, such as the *Congregazione del Buon Governo*, created in the late sixteenth century to serve as a connection structure, did not completely succeed in limiting the stratified and heterogeneous character of the Papal States. They were divided into large provinces *immediatae subiectae*, directly dependent on the Holy See. As for the Marche region, they were: the Duchy of Urbino, the Governorship (*Governo*) of the March of Ancona (which had the head office in Macerata), the Duchy of Camerino, the State of Fermo, the State of Ascoli, the *Presidiato* of Montalto, the Governorships of Fano, Ancona, Fabriano, Jesi, Loreto, San Severino, and Matelica. From these large provinces differed the *mediatae subiectae* that consisted of estates, villas, castles, which were under the rule of the *immediatae subiectae*.[4] The *governatore generale della Marca* ('governor general of the March') had jurisdiction over a wide territory, which included medium-sized cities and towns such as Macerata, Recanati, Osimo, but, paradoxically, not Ancona, demographically larger, that in the late eighteenth century reached almost 18,000 inhabitants.[5]

It seems appropriate to divide our analysis in three parts, devoted to the different institutional and economic aspects that the polysemy of the research object implies.[6] First, the organisational structures of the victualling system are taken into account, starting from certain specific cases (Sects. 6.2, 6.3, and 6.4). After this 'horizontal' and comparative analysis conducted on the municipal statutes and official regulations instituting the victualling offices, in the second part a 'vertical' analysis follows, in which the mechanism of cereals accumulation and distribution in the region is analysed in detail. Rejecting any rigid dichotomous contraposition between private initiatives (market) and regulatory constraints managed by local authorities, we investigate some of the concrete ways in which the 'market principle' and the 'marketplace' articulated in practice.[7] In this part, after a rapid survey about the existence and the role of the *monti frumentari* (literally, 'mounts of wheat', the charitable institutions which granted interest-free loans of wheat, or even made free distributions to the poor in years of scarcity) (Sect. 6.5), we deal with the main actors of the cereals trade. In order to explain the intersection between control intentions and planning of the urban institutions and the personal trajectories of merchants, lords, or businessmen seeking profits, two complementary and interrelated directions are considered. In the first instance, we investigate the production levels of the March, in order to delineate the place of the agriculture of the region in the supply dynamics of the Papal States (Sect. 6.6); second, the focus is on some stories of hoarders. In this perspective, we analyse two case studies, Macerata and Ancona, whose important port is a privileged vantage point for tracing the geographical network of cereals imported and exported to and from the region (Sects. 6.7, 6.8, and 6.9). In the third and final part, instead, we suggest some concluding reflections on the role of trade in this victualling system (Sect. 6.10).

6.2 *Annona*: Origins and Structures in Pontifical Periphery

In the cities of the pontifical March of Ancona, since the Late Middle Ages, even with different times, a system of boards and offices was set up to regulate the supply and distribution of foodstuffs, in particular cereals. At the central level, the repeated measures introduced during the fifteenth century to prevent serious food crises led to the establishment of the *Annona* office, ordered by Pope Sixtus IV in 1476.[8] These measures, in addition to creating a regulated and protected cereals market, favoured the construction of an increasingly complex and powerful victualling administration.[9] The significance acquired by it is attested by the fact that the *Annona* in the sixteenth century became part of the central governmental bodies of the State.[10] In the capital city, the supply (*sfamo*) of a population in strong growth had to be guaranteed; the measures that were taken had precisely the objective of guaranteeing the Roman market, so that the bakeries were regularly supplied and the citizens had bread at controlled prices.[11] The authority of the prefect of the *Annona* was exercised directly on a very large territory that included a large part of Lazio.[12] By the second half of the sixteenth century, with the further demographic increase of the capital city, while heavy restrictions were imposed on the exports and transport of cereals within the State, it was established that the provinces of Romagna and of the March of Ancona should contribute to the supply of Rome.[13] An analogous structure was achieved neither in the other provinces nor in the March; with various and in-depth research, Alberto Guenzi showed that a city like Bologna, even if belonging to the Papal States, had no victualling offices.[14]

The governor general of the March had among its competences also those related to victualling administration. In fact, however, he did not exercise them, within the framework of the wide autonomy left to the cities and the free municipalities (*terre*) of this pontifical province.[15] This means that the victualling administration was managed by the individual communities, based on the rules approved in the general councils. Between one city and another the differences were not lacking, but since the analogies prevailed, it is opportune to analyse an exemplary case for which the norms are preserved, approved before the great famine that at the end of the sixteenth century would upset the victualling system of the entire region. The exemplification is that offered by the chapters of the *Abbondanza*, the victualling office of the city of Osimo for the year 1575.[16] Naturally, as it happened at a central level and in the urban context of Rome itself, also the structure and the characteristics of the system of Osimo were the result of a long series of interventions, probably introduced since the thirteenth century, when the inhabitants of the city lived a strong phase of growth, to the point that already in that century the construction of a new wall was necessary.[17] The first known provision is the *Ordinamenta prostumi* approved on 24 January 1311, with which, to guarantee the food supply of the population, it was forbidden to export (*estrarre*) from the city and its rural district "wheat, barley, cereals, spelt, broad beans, chickpeas and wild peas, and any kind of other crops, legumes, or flour", and also figs, nuts, cheese, eggs, chickens, and other animals.[18] Giovanni Mira pointed out that, in the course of the fourteenth century, even more restrictive measures were taken in Umbria and, in particular, in Perugia.[19]

At the centre of the victualling system of the March was the *Congregazione dell'Annona* ('Congregation of *Annona*', henceforth *Annona*). In the case of Osimo, it was composed of four *deputati* ('deputies'), who were elected by the general council. They held office for one year, from 1 September to 31 August of the following year. Among them two *deputati super pane* (literally, 'deputies for bread') and two others *super carnibus* ('for meat') were distinguished. The two *deputati super pane* had the task of "establishing the quantity of wheat to be supplied and the price of it". They also had to check the activity of the mill and supply the municipal bakery with wheat. Finally, they had to watch the wheat market scrupulously.[20] The amount of wheat needed was calculated on the basis of the so-called *assegne* (literally, 'assignments'), sworn declarations that the producers sent to the secretary of the prior (*priore*) of the city, immediately after the harvest. In addition to the harvest, the *assegne* also indicated the number of *bocche* (literally 'mouths', i.e. people) in the family and the quantities of wheat to be set aside for sowing and for family consumption. It was thus possible to define the quotas that the owners had to keep "at the disposal of the *abbondanzieri*, both for the marketplace and for the public bakery" (the *abbondanzieri* were the officials of the victualling administration).[21] On all this surplus the Municipality reserved the right of pre-emption. Being aware of the total number of people to feed, ascertained by parish priests in their periodic censuses (called *stati delle anime*), the *abbondanzieri* could calculate the wheat needed for the *sfamo* of the entire population.

The names of the owners, subjected to the quota system, were inserted in a ballot box and then drawn monthly, taking into account the needs of the bakery and of the marketplace. This also avoided storing the wheat: a complex problem that could lead to significant losses if the chosen location was not completely dry. In the March there were few large buildings used as wheat stores. In Ancona, there was a building named, significantly, *Palazzo della Farina* (literally, 'Flour Palace'). More often the wheat was stored in ditches, made both by private individuals and by the municipality, with sophisticated construction techniques: these were "underground compartments" of different sizes, "buried just below street level"; they were made "with bricks arranged head-to-head, well tightened together so as to guarantee perfect sealing and good insulation from moisture".[22] Such ditches were found in Corinaldo, Gradara, Castel Colonna, and other cities and towns of the March; in the case of Corinaldo they had been built by a private person in the mid-fifteenth century. In Ancona, in the mid-sixteenth century, in a period of economic splendour, the ditches for depositing cereals were themselves the object of a rental market. This is demonstrated by the case of the Jews Levi Sancton and Ioseph Oeff, who rented three pits from Vincenzo Nappi in 1553.[23] A large crops pit was instead built in Castelfidardo in 1618, at the expense of the Municipality, in the square in front of the palace of the Prior.[24]

To the owners who paid their quota, the wheat was paid at the current price, also calculated on the basis of the price charged in the surrounding cities and towns; sometimes, especially in the event of rapidly increasing prices, the owners refused to deliver the quota of wheat on the grounds that the *abbondanzieri* were not prompt in payments, but in reality because it was convenient for them at those moments to sell to private individuals rather than to the *Annona*.[25] In general it was not necessary to arrive at this refusal. Being based on declarations, this system could be circumvented: the owners tended to declare harvests lower than what was true in order to reduce the quota assigned to them. Those who were able to obtain export licences (the so-called *tratte*) could, however, do the opposite: inflate the harvest data, obtain good *tratte*, buy wheat from other local producers, and then sell it in export markets.[26] As will be seen in more detail, these difficulties were then joined by those linked to the presence on the market of operators capable of speculating on prices; the *Annona* tried to control the activity of profiteers and hoarders, but often with poor results.

6.3 Making Bread: The Municipal Mill and Bakery

The other columns of the victualling system of Osimo were the municipal mill and bakery. A study by Giovanni Cherubini concerning the Late Middle Ages showed that the municipalities of the March very soon operated to gain control of private mills. Cherubini distinguished three phases: in the early communal period, there was still a seigneurial control; then, almost everywhere the municipal control was established; finally, especially in the cities, the privately owned mills spread.[27] In the Early Modern Age, in almost all limited-size cities and towns, the mill was a municipal property and had the monopoly on milling. The exception was the Holy House (*Santa Casa*) of Loreto: during the sixteenth century, the power of the sanctuary grew to such an extent that its administrators not only succeeded in obtaining substantial privileges from the cities of Recanati and Osimo, but they came to purchase the mill of Castelfidardo.[28]

In Osimo, as in many other cities of the March, there was a mill owned by the Municipality, that was rented for three years to the highest bidder; but in an urban reality of almost 10,000 inhabitants there were also other private mills: the statutes of the early fourteenth century mention at least six.[29] For the municipal mill, the three-year rent formula was maintained until the last decade of the eighteenth century; only in 1794, during a period of serious difficulties for the *Congregazione dell'Annona*, it was decided to grant it in third-generation emphyteusis, as had long been done for some municipal properties, but this choice soon proved to be unfortunate because in 1797 the conductor, overburdened with debts, decided to terminate the contract with serious consequences for the budget of the *Annona*.[30] Fraud and counterfeiting were also possible in processing wheat; the most common consisted of mixing wheat flour with poorer-quality ones. Precisely in order to control these counterfeits, in 1794 the figure of the *ministro venditore delle farine* ('flour seller minister') was established, to whom the task of supervising wheat milling was entrusted.[31]

Like the mill, the municipal bakery was also leased for three years "to those who make the best conditions".[32] In Osimo the *Annona* managed a single bakery, called the bakery of the *pan venale* (literally, 'bread for sale', meaning ordinary bread), but there were other places where bread was sold: in the 1308 statutes, bakers were allowed to sell bread, but only in the places assigned to them by the municipal authorities.[33] In the Early Modern Age information on this subject is scarce, but the presence of some bakers who did not practice retail trade is attested. They limited themselves to baking the bread for individual people: in 1666 they protested with the governor of the March because the authorities of Osimo had burdened them with a "new toll".[34] Certain is also the activity of the other bakers: in 1733, when wheat was becoming scarce, the first of the measures taken was the closure of all the bread shops with the exception of one, so as to be able to better control the sale.[35] In the minutes of the eighteenth-century city council meetings, many contracts stipulated with the baker of the *pan venale* are preserved. The Municipality required substantial capital and good entrepreneurial qualities from the bakery's contractor, because he not only had to pay the miller for milling, but also had to dispose of the necessary capital for purchasing the wheat used in the bakery.

It is possible to understand this mechanism on the basis of the documents of the governor of the March and from the chapters transcribed in the municipal laws; for example, both from a dispute with the *abbondanzieri* that broke out in 1658 and from the chapters agreed in 1715, at the time of the tender, it appears that the purchase of the necessary wheat in the bakery was a specific task of the baker. The wheat, as we have seen, was set aside by the owners on the basis of the quotas imposed by the Municipality; but the baker was charged to buy the wheat from the

Annona, which, as also happened in the case of Rome, analysed in various studies by Jacques Revel, tried to stabilise the market by selling wheat at a uniform and constant price.[36] When the *Annona* had exhausted its supplies or the wheat had poor quality, as it happened in 1765,[37] the contractor could decide to buy wheat on the market, but had to obtain the assent of the *deputati* of the *Annona*; in any case he was not allowed to sell bread or wheat outside the city of Osimo.[38] At the end of the eighteenth century, the contractor of the bakery obtained not having to buy the wheat: starting from this moment, the wheat was supplied directly by the *abbondanzieri*; but this concession would further weaken the victualling system and, as will be seen, would lead to the collapse.[39]

6.4 Inside the System: Cereals Supply between the Sixteenth-Century Crisis and That of the Late Eighteenth Century

The functioning mechanisms of a typical victualling system of the March of Ancona described in the previous pages were valid in 'normal' years. In years of famine, these mechanisms could also be radically modified by the new provisions introduced to deal with the emergency. In this regard, a valid point of analysis is the famine of the years 1590–1593, which in various European regions lasted until 1596 and which is considered the largest food crisis in Europe in the Early Modern Age.[40] The crisis of the late sixteenth century was undoubtedly a turning point from various points of view: not only for its gravity and duration, but also for the breadth and quality of the responses put in place: new supply routes were opened (for example, the Genoese came to import wheat from the Baltic, and also the Venetians turned occasionally to it, before coming back to the Adriatic and the Levant[41]); the production and distribution of all foodstuffs were subjected to a stricter control; smuggling was fought more harshly; interventions by cities were intensified; subsidies were offered and free food aid was distributed. Faced with such a terrible test, the most advanced agrarian systems, such as the Emilian, failed, and thus did also the systems that usually produced strong cereals surpluses, such as that of the March.[42]

In the March, as soon as the first signs of crisis occurred, the public institutions of all cities and towns, large and small, from Osimo to Camerino, from Fabriano to Recanati, from San Ginesio to Ripatransone, reacted in a traditional way. It was forbidden to transport cereals outside the municipal area; wheat was bought within the State, where it could be found, and was sold at controlled prices; bread began to be rationed, limiting its weight to a certain number of ounces apiece; it was prescribed to pack the bread with a mixture of other cereals, such as barley, broad beans, and millet.[43] In 1591, however, faced with a new fall in the harvest, those measures were no longer enough; then wheat was purchased in the Kingdom of Naples, in Sicily, and in Dalmatia. When the coffers of the *Annona* ran out, money was borrowed; regulations were passed against speculators and smugglers, and armed guards were sent to the countryside to monitor fraud, smuggling, and other illegal activities; special ration cards (called *bollette*) were issued to rigidly ration the sale of bread to each family; all the poor were counted so as to distribute the bread for free only to the real poor; it was decided to survey all the 'foreigners' (*forastieri*) and expel them from the cities; an order was made to make a type of bread, called *pane di mescolanza* ('mixture bread'), also using acorn flour.[44]

In 1592 and 1593, the following two years of poor harvests found the victualling systems now powerless in the face of the explosion of famine: the cities got into debt by borrowing other money and distributing the wheat for free. The confraternities did the same, but hunger and petechial typhus were now rampant, causing a very high number of deaths. For many cities and especially for the inland areas of the March, the great famine of the late sixteenth century was a real demographic catastrophe.[45] In particular for the Apennine economies, which until that moment had been rich and dynamic, the crisis marked a sharp reversal of the trend, causing a clear and definitive overturning of the relationship between mountain and plain;[46] as Girolamo Allegretti wrote, from that crisis the mountain of the Marche region "comes out forever reduced and wounded".[47]

Going back to Osimo, at the end of the eighteenth century, the contractor of the bakery obtained not having to supply the wheat; at a particularly difficult time, as cereals reached the price of 15 Roman *scudi* per *rubbio*,[48] the *abbondanzieri* were forced to purchase the missing wheat. For some time, in the occasion of food crises, the *Annona* had worked to control the price of bread, selling wheat at a lower price than that paid to the owners; in this way, with the coffers now empty, debt had grown. Not only in the 1760s, the 'years of hunger',[49] but also in 1772–1773, and then during the 1783–1784 crisis, it was necessary to resort to large loans. By 1793 the budget of the *Annona* was out of control; the financial disruption was such that in 1795, in combination of other critical points, the debt of the municipality of Osimo touched the enormous sum of 30,000 *scudi*.[50] The dynamics was similar to that of many other local cases. In the same years the collapse of the victualling system of numerous communities of the March, or at least of those that in the previous years did not constitute a small hoard of savings able to cope with the years of scarcity, was consummated. Even the sanctuary of the Holy House of Loreto, which could boast extensive possessions and remarkable privileges that made it one of the leading exporters in the region, found itself facing a serious crisis.[51]

Further north, on the border with the territories of Romagna, the small community of the Republic of San Marino had to face the same difficulties. However, this poor territory, which had made small land ownership and border trade its economic fundamentals,[52] had managed to overcome the darkest years of 1762 and 1765–1766 thanks to a shrewd policy of setting aside money, which came in handy in moments of greatest difficulty. The main loans were settled within a short time. The peak of the more than 8,883 *scudi* borrowed in 1766 was covered in part within the year (6,577.95 *scudi*) and without further loans. This allowed to contain the total debt on the 4,000 *scudi*, a significant figure for the parameters of the Republic, since it corresponded to four or five times the annual collection of the *Camerlengato* (the Treasury) in those years. Nevertheless, an irreparable failure did not occur. The trouble came (or increased) over the course of the century. The financial difficulties combined with the negative effects of the expulsion of the peasantry, the growing demographic pressure, the pressure on consumption, the monetary devaluation.[53] Here then appeared on urban markets a bread of worse quality.[54]

6.5 On the Threshold of the Market: The *Monti Frumentari*

Victualling institutions acted as a powerful intermediary between the needs of all the parties involved: great owners, farmers, merchants, bakers, and consumers.[55] The *Annona* was thus revealed, as a scholar wrote, "the most important intermediary between producers and consumers".[56] However, it was not the only one. At the end of the fifteenth century, in the area of the today's Umbria and Marche regions, the mounts of piety (*monti di pietà*, charitable funds which were part of a political framework of the Christian elites of the early modern states in the Italian peninsula[57]) were joined by the first *monti frumentari* (literally, 'mounts of wheat'), which arose with the specific purpose of providing wheat to the poorest peasants.[58] The initiatives of Foligno and Macerata, born by the will of the Observant Franciscans, engaged in the same years in the diffusion of the mounts of piety, had a short duration.[59] In the case of Macerata, after the approval of the statutes obtained by Friar Marco da Montegallo, the *monte* did not even start. The real pioneer was Friar Andrea da Faenza, who in the last decade of the fifteenth century, in addition to that of Foligno, founded other *monti frumentari*, first in Sulmona, Rieti, Spoleto, Terni, Orvieto, and Annifo (a village near Foligno), then also in Carpi, in Cremona, and in Castell'Arquato, near Piacenza.[60]

The *monti* of central Italy were limited to the loan of wheat, while those of northern Italy also lent barley, beans, and other crops, which is why they often took the name of *monti delle biade* (literally, 'mounts of crops'). In agreement with the local authorities, civil and ecclesiastical, the initial patrimony was raised with a collection sponsored by the preacher himself and then increased with other quests carried out during the Holy Week or on the feast day of their patron saint.[61] It was in the second half of the sixteenth century and especially during the seventeenth century that, thanks to the impulse coming from the Council of Trent and the commitment of the new order of the Capuchin friars, a wide diffusion of the *monti frumentari* was realised. Those who in the years of famine were forced to use for their subsistence also the stocks set aside for sowing, could resort to the *monti frumentari*, as long as they undertook to give back after the harvest the wheat received. In some cases a pledge was required for the value of at least one-third higher than that of the wheat borrowed, while in others the guarantee offered by a guarantor was sufficient; this means that, in general, the paupers could not obtain wheat from the *monti* and had to turn to other charitable institutions, public or private. In the most dramatic moments, however, many *monti frumentari* also made free wheat distributions in favour of the poorest.[62]

In Osimo the first *monte frumentario*, named after San Leopardo, was founded in 1498 on the initiative of Bishop Antonio Sinibaldi and was then managed by the chapter of the canons of the cathedral.[63] Almost a century later, in 1596, after the terrible experience of the early 1590s, at the request of the municipal authorities, Pope Clement VIII approved the establishment of a *monte frumentario* powered by the surplus of the *Annona* and governed by representatives of the city's council.[64] In the following century, the *monte* was managed by two *deputati* and by the *abbondanzieri*.[65] Also in Roccacontrada (today's Arcevia) the decision was taken by the municipal authorities, who established the *Monte Charitativo da Grani* ('Charitable Mount of Cereals') in the 16 April 1581 council meeting.[66] At the birth of the *monte* of Treia, which arose in 1574, a joint initiative was reached by the bishop, the Municipality and two local confraternities.[67] In the seventeenth century, throughout the entire March, many confraternities, particularly those of the Most Blessed Sacrament, gave life to their own *monti frumentari*, sometimes to the advantage of the brethren alone.[68] In Osimo in 1707, as many as seventeen are reported, some in the city and several others scattered in the parishes of the countryside. In general they were small institutions, but they were used by a large number of farmers and day labourers: in Castelfidardo in 1768, after the strong crisis of the years 1764–1767, the *monte frumentario* of the *Compagnia del Santissimo Rosario* ('Company of the Most Holy Rosary') counted more than 300 debtors, to be accurate 280 men and 45 women.[69]

6.6 Inside the Market: Places and Players of the Exchange

Sales did not always take place in the location assigned to the mercantile exchange—i.e. the market square—for a number of reasons. It is well known that in the Early Modern Age self-consumption was very high; it is believed that perhaps only a quarter of the population turned to the market.[70] If we consider the wheat that was not consumed for family food, only a portion of the marketed wheat went through the municipal market; this is because in part the wheat was exported or taken away from the market through smuggling, but also because many wheat merchants (named *farinelli*, from *farina*, 'flour') bought it directly from the producers who kept it in their barns. In the Papal States the wheat market was not left to the wheels of the commerce;[71] every kind of transaction and the export market were all included in a binding context. Every year the March of Ancona had to send large quantities of wheat in the direction of Rome.[72] Despite the constraints placed on the free circulation of foodstuffs, in the March, a great producer of cereals, the wheat trade was large, even if it is difficult to quantify it: in normal years the wheat in surplus was exported, but there were sales even in the most difficult years, both through the widespread smuggling, and thanks to the *tratte* system.[73]

It is certainly true that smuggling should not be overrated.[74] However, the concern for the spread of this phenomenon often emerges from the correspondence the governor general of the March entertained with the municipalities, even if it does not seem that the measures taken have had concrete effects.[75] In the March, the most frequented place for smuggling activities was Case Bruciate, located at the mouth of the Esino river, on the border between the suburbs of Jesi and Ancona, in a sort of nobody's land.[76] A similar role was also played by the beach of Sentina, at the mouth of the Tronto river, near the 'port' of Ascoli.[77] In that border area between the Papal States and the Kingdom of Naples, smuggling was a widespread activity, even if difficult to document; often intertwined with other illegal practices, it took then the form of banditry. The gangs that made the Tronto Valley dangerous were fought successfully in the late sixteenth century, but illegal activities did not cease.[78] The authorities of the Kingdom of Naples in the seventeenth century openly complained about the situation.[79] Still in the second half of the eighteenth century, according to what the Neapolitan consul in Trieste reported, the ship owners of southern March continued to use the mouth of the Tronto to practise, on a large scale, the smuggling of wheat, oil, and other foodstuffs.[80]

As for legally authorised exports, for a fee or not, many of the privileged institutions and the main landowners, thanks to the *tratte*, managed to export considerable quantities of cereals. Certainly, the licences were granted annually, but the wheat production of the March generally guaranteed substantial surpluses. Luigi Dal Pane published a report on the March's harvest and consumption of cereals in 1751.[81] From this analysis it emerges with evidence that, despite the oscillations on the estimate of global consumption, the territory was able to produce large surpluses, ready to be exported. In 1751 the surplus was 44,000 *rubbia*, while the previous year it was 75,000 *rubbia*.[82] Wheat exports are also attested in the years of great scarcity, such as the 1760s. Dal Pane documented it analytically for the period 1710–1776.[83] The data collected by him confirm that in the first half of the eighteenth century the March was still the 'granary' of the State; together with Romagna, the March covered 90% of the Papal States' cereals trade.

From the ten-year averages, obtained by processing those data, the tendency to an increase in exports emerges starting from the 1730s, albeit with a strong fall in the 1740s and then in the 1760s.[84] Until the middle of the century, three-quarters of the wheat exports of the State came from the March; in the 1730s this percentage reached even 80%. After the

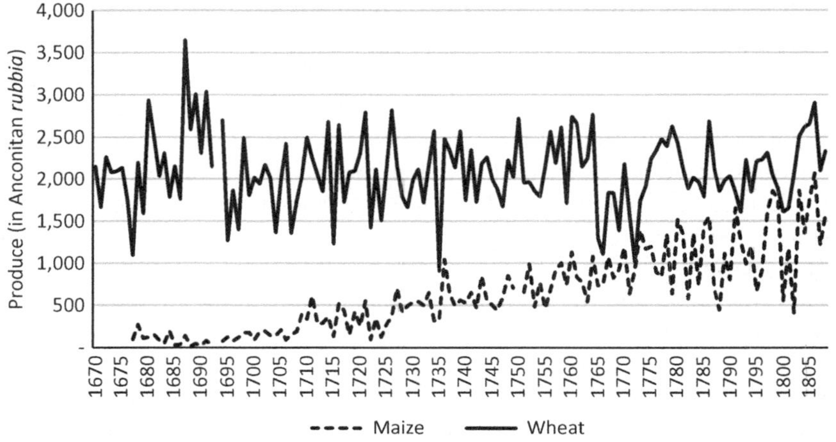

Fig. 6.1 Cereals production of the Holy House of Loreto's farms (1670–1808). (Source: Elaboration on data from Moroni 2016, pp. 109–113; see also pp. 102–103 for references on double diet)

middle of the century, instead, the weight of Romagna grew from 16% of total exports in the first forty years, to more than 26% during the following twenty-five years, authorised with the *tratte* system. The surge in exports was made possible by the progressive and pervasive establishment of a double diet: maize was reserved for peasants; wheat, released from the need to serve as a basic foodstuff of the regime of a large slice of the population, rose to the rank of a valuable trade product. The documents reporting the pacts of sharecropping (the most common contract in this area), and the data on production of the lands of the Holy House of Loreto, one of the greatest producers in the March, amply demonstrate it (see Fig. 6.1).

6.7 The Wealth of the Periphery: A Wealth for All? The Case of Macerata

To understand how the victualling system worked, it is necessary to move the analysis to a micro level. To cope with the overall consumption of wheat, which was estimated in 1753 in 9,000 *rubbia* per year, the *Annona* of the city of Macerata, where the governor general of the March had his headquarter, was organised as follows: the contractor of the public bakery, which prepared bread for the urban population, had the task of preparing the bread for a total of 1,000 *rubbia* of wheat per year. For the most part (about 541 *rubbia*) the bakery was supplied by the properties of the Municipality (land and municipal mill), and for the rest by the bakery's contractor.[85] To these were added the 534.6 *rubbia* of wheat made available to the six *monti frumentari* operating in the city, for "the need of the peasants, and other poor people who usually live with cereals loans".[86] The rest of the wheat needed to be passed through the two weekly markets: "For retail sales, supplies are sufficient in the two weekly markets; the cases were very rare, in which the landowners had to send their own wheat to sell in the marketplace for lack".[87] Taking into account the urban population, the per capita consumption fluctuated between 0.75 and 0.83 *rubbia* per year,[88] a non-lean ration, but certainly not abundant.[89]

The available data allow some evaluations, as far as they present objective difficulties of treatment. The *Annona* of Macerata sure enough recorded the productions that fell in its own territory and that were subject to its own jurisdiction in case of need. For this reason, the productions that the citizens of Macerata and, in particular, the great owners had in the neighbouring countryside, which fell under the jurisdiction of the neighbouring communities, were not calculated. These productions, however, once the minimum wheat requirements of the smaller municipalities had been fulfilled, although not counted accurately by the *Annona* of Macerata, flowed most of the time into the owners' warehouses in the city, actually increasing the availability of wheat of Macerata itself. The apparent lack of wheat for the marketplace thus often turned into overabundance and into opportunities for mercantile gain. As Secretary Filippo Ranaldi wrote in 1753: "The narrow territory of Macerata cannot give more harvest. But, since almost all the landowners of this city possess external territory to it, it follows that Macerata not only remains abundantly supplied, but that there is still surplus for this reason, and for the other, that cereals continually concur there from nearby places, which keep the marketplace abundant".[90] Municipal authorities, however, required all landowners, following the central directives, to keep a certain amount of wheat at the disposal of the *Annona*, just in case. By 1752, this amounted to 445 *rubbia*, distributed among seventy-five landowners.[91]

This distribution of land and this social structure also determined another consequence, the differentiation of consumption levels. As we have seen, the produce did not always remain in the territory: it was moved to the city or was sold; for this reason, the countryside suffered more than the city. A confirmation of these dynamics comes from one of the most productive territories of the March, that of the city of Jesi. Despite the relatively high values of average theoretical wheat availability, on the basis of the work of Luigi Dal Pane, the real paths of access to resources kept the countryside of Jesi in a difficult situation, to such an extent that the demographic progress of the countryside around the city had noticeably slower rhythms than those of the city of Jesi, as Carlo Vernelli showed.[92] Once the need to guarantee the wheat to all citizens had been fulfilled (even if, as we have seen, in different ways, according to the territory of origin), the rest of the production could take the route of trade. The calculation of the *assegne* for the year 1751 allows us to appreciate the overall production of the rural district of Macerata, which amounted to 7,164 *rubbia*. To this quantity, it is necessary to add 387.75 *rubbia* of the previous year, for a total of 7,551.75 *rubbia* available. At the time the declarations were delivered by the landowners, 649.50 *rubbia* had already been sold, while just 1,525.75 *rubbia* had been set aside for sowing the following year.[93]

As shown in Table 6.1, the wheat trade was a bargain for few. Just under 15% of landowners held over 60% of the wheat production in Macerata's rural district and over 90% of the wheat that had already been

Table 6.1 Distribution of the wheat produced, stored, and sold among the landowners in Macerata (1751)

Production range (in Anconitan *rubbia*)	Number of landowners	Percentage of landowners	Percentage of wheat produced	Percentage of wheat in warehouse	Percentage of wheat traded	Average consumption of wheat per capita (in Anconitan *rubbia*)
0–50	227	85.9	39.0	30.3	7.1	1.3
51–100	22	8.3	21.9	14.1	6.6	1.8
101–150	9	3.4	16.0	16.0	20.1	2.0
151–200	2	0.8	4.5	1.5	0.0	1.5
201–250	0	0.0	0.0	0.0	0.0	0.0
251–300	1	0.4	3.9	0.8	15.4	9.5
301–350	1	0.4	4.5	0.0	0.0	2.5
351–400	2	0.8	10.3	37.3	50.8	2.5

Source: Elaboration on data from ASMC, CAG, 557 (3), *Spoglio delle assegne date in Macerata l'anno 1751*. Discrepancies on totals are due to the averages of single ranges; the particularly high anomalous figure of the per capita consumption of wheat in the 251–300 *rubbia* range is determined by a single value, belonging to a specific family, that of the Marefoschi

introduced into the commercial circuits. The two major owners, the college of the Barnabite Fathers and Marquis Amico Ricci, controlled more than half of the wheat on the market. Immediately behind were the main houses of the urban elite and religious congregations: Ignazio Compagnoni, Monsignor Marefoschi, the *Congregazione di San Filippo*, Antonio Lazzarini, Benedetto Costa, the monastery of Santa Chiara, and the Jesuit college.[94] The possibility of selling their own wheat was also made possible by the massive stocks they could count on, useful for the sowing of the following year and to guarantee satisfactory food levels.[95] These availabilities also allowed an average consumption of wheat almost double compared to the rest of the city's population. However, these disparities were situated in a context of sufficient and constant availability of wheat.

6.8 Merchants and Speculators: The Case of Ancona

The privileged interlocutors of these great producers were the wheat merchants who populated the territory in search of lots of cereals. Since the sixteenth century the most active speculators were the *farinelli*, who exported wheat from the largest port in the province, Ancona. Although there were also the small ports (often at the mouth of a river) of Pesaro, Fano, Senigallia, Case Bruciate and the smaller landing places south of Ancona, from the port of Recanati to that of Fermo, Ancona was the site of a constant and lively cereals trade. After the establishment of the free port, deliberated in 1732, it acquired the function of a centre of gravity.[96] The *farinelli* of Ancona hoarded wheat in the nearby cities and towns, often provoking protests of the local 'poor'; in Castelfidardo, faced with their growing presence on the local market, in the second half of the seventeenth century the local authorities first turned to the governor general of the March and then, at the end of the century, to the supreme court of the *Sacra Consulta* in Rome. The results, however, were disappointing.[97]

In the sources the name *farinelli* refers to distinct merchants and behaviours, although sometimes superimposed by the protagonists themselves. At the first degree of this polysemy, this name identified those who had to reduce the wheat to flour.[98] With this epithet, however, documents were also referring to those who hoarded wheat, amassing flour, in fact. To the simple description of the activities, in this second case, mistrust, rivalry, and cutting remarks, typical of the political battle, overlapped. The *farinelli* unhinged the bonds of solidarity of the community seeking the profit deriving from stockpiling in the March of Ancona. To the political battle, the language of morality provided the interpretative schemes, helping to define these merchants as those responsible for the crisis of availability and price increases. The presence of foreign *farinelli*, understood here as hoarders, grew during the eighteenth century, after the establishment of the free port in 1732, which favoured, as seen, the commercialisation of agriculture and made Ancona the largest point of embarkation of the cereals of the March. The merchant class of the city came to control much of the production of the hinterland, determining its fate.[99] In July 1735, a year of scarce production, in Osimo it came to appoint four *deputati* charged with watching "over the sale of wheat in the marketplace".[100]

Wheat coming out, wheat coming in. When the signs of poor harvests reached the authorities, the alarm mechanisms were set in motion, first on a local scale and then, sometimes with mistrust, in Rome. Economic factors and political factors, in this case, touched each other until they were confused. The pressures of the great merchants, who were often also local notables, members of the city's congregations, pushed for a liberalisation of the *tratte*. Once the faculty was obtained from the central authority, the communities, for their part, began to go hunting for wheat, no matter whether at the cost of hindering or damaging the nearby community.[101] The great merchants could therefore deploy all their influence. Their networks now became strategic. The need to fill the granaries and appease the citizens' passions pushed the authorities to turn to the great protagonists of the trade of the city, starting from the wealthiest and most representative of them, Francesco Trionfi.[102] Among them there were also some of the main Jewish merchants of Ancona, who in this way rendered a great service to local governments, receiving in exchange a *de facto* co-optation—being the legal co-optation forbidden by the laws—in the ranks of the urban economic elite. It was during 1735 that Moisè Coen, son of Rafael, one of the most active merchants on the two shores of the Adriatic, got 735 *rubbia* of wheat from Leghorn on the ship *Gerusalem* and another 824 *rubbia* on the ship *Fenice*.[103]

The role of Jewish merchants in the wheat trade is a relevant and little studied fact. In 1711, for example, Venanzo Giamagli and Giovanni Antonio Vincenti intervened as peacemakers between the two Jewish owners of the *Società di Negozio dei Grani d'Albania* ('Trading Company of Albania's Cereals').[104] In 1715, Moisè Fermi, son of Iacob, one of the protagonists of the trade activity of the city, was one of the trustees to whom the Municipality entrusted itself in order to find the wheat necessary to face the serious shortage of that year.[105] A few years later, in 1747 (a year of crisis), the French vice-consul of Senigallia noted that a substantial load of cereals came from the port of Ancona, "hoarded by the Jew Morburgue of Ancona": almost 10,000 *rubbia* of wheat and almost 1,000 *rubbia* of "wheat of Turkey" took the road to Mantua.[106] For the Morpurgo, the wheat trade was certainly not an occasional activity. On the contrary, it demonstrates the presence of a network of contacts and support also with the political authorities of the time, a network that extended outside the Papal States.[107] Not by chance, the commitment of the Morpurgo family of Ancona in this sector emerged also in the following years. In the years of the great 1764–1767 famine, the company *Eredi di Sanson Morpurgo* ('Heirs of Sanson Morpurgo') completed numerous purchases for the community of Ancona in different marketplaces, such as Ferrara and Trieste.[108]

6.9 Crisis, Commerce, and Prices: Ancona in the First Half of the Eighteenth Century

Despite the mediating action of the *Annona*, the price of wheat flour was noticeably affected by the crisis events of the first half of the eighteenth century (see Fig. 6.2). In September 1735, on the marketplace of Ancona a peak was reached. The closest precedent was that of 1715, a year of great suffering. If it is difficult to accurately assess the weight of the speculative component and that deriving from the decrease in production, the role of the port franchise in determining in the medium term an upward trend in prices appears instead evident. The great landowners and the main merchants of the city managed always greater quantities of cereals, mostly destined for export. The price dynamics that began in 1732 reflected a growing demand. Foodstuffs sold better and better. They pushed farms in the hinterland towards an extensive production, which sacrificed the food regime of the peasants, who were forced to eat the poorest cereals, to reserve wheat for national and foreign markets. This predominance of the market, in a high-level production area like the March of Ancona, and more in general the Marche region, has been identified as the main cause of the increase in prices in local markets and, consequently, as the fundamental reason for the moments of subsistence crisis.[109] The case of Ancona seems to fit into this trend.

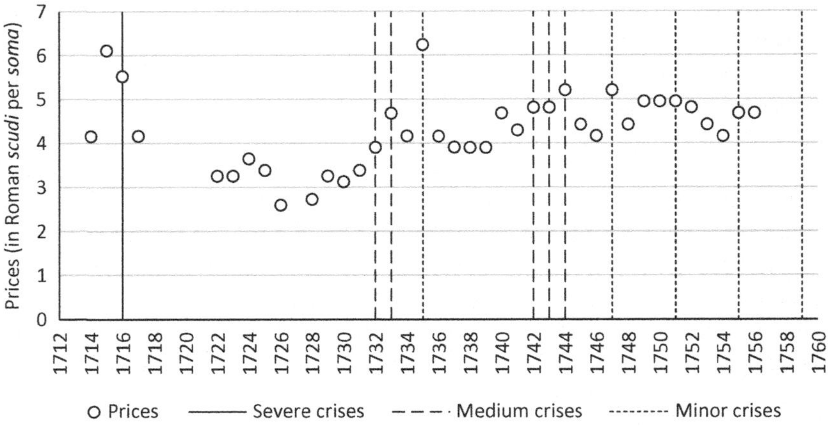

Fig. 6.2 Price of wheat flour in Ancona (1714–1756). (Sources: Elaboration on data from ASAN, ACARAN, *Tariffe del pane, grano e altri generi*, 5–7 (on prices); Dal Pane 1959 [1939], pp. 564–567; Sori 2005, p. 16 (on *tratte* and mortality). Data on prices were collected in September of each year. High mortality and no *tratte* during severe crisis; no official *tratte* during minor crisis)

6.10 Conclusions: A World of Merchants in the Central Adriatic Area?

The wheat trade did not only animate the port of Ancona. South of it, the fertile hills of the small and medium-sized cities facing the coast were targeted by the great hoarders. In Recanati we find Angelo Massucci and Giuseppe Carradori, while in Castelfidardo the administrators of the Holy House of Loreto or the merchants of Ancona had a dominant role: the sources register in their name large quantities of 'extracted'—that is to say exported—wheat.[110] When it was not the great merchants of Ancona sweeping up all the wheat available, the local landowners and the governors general of the March had free hand. In 1671, in Castelfidardo, the local *Congregazione dell'Abbondanza* ordered Carlo Guarnieri and Marquis Ciccolini not to export their remaining wheat to avoid the depletion of municipal granaries for their benefits.[111] Thirty years later, the merchant Agostino Tartaglino, Captain Pietro Carelli, and the landowner Anton Angelo Borgia, all of Castelfidardo, were caught hoarding large quantities of wheat, to be sold then in Ancona.[112]

The same type of censorship, however, was never made to the administrators of the Holy House of Loreto. In fact, as already mentioned, the Loreto sanctuary could count on considerable fiscal exemptions and specific privileges; among these there was the faculty to sell large quantities of cereals without too many administrative encumbrances.[113] The progressive growth of landed property, and the exceptional regulatory framework, made the Holy House of Loreto one of the main mercantile players in the region. Average annual export levels were around 1,800 *rubbia* of wheat, up to a peak of over 3,800 *rubbia* in 1731.[114] However, the sale of foodstuffs was not reserved for a closed and exclusive circle. In an expanding market, which offered narrow but progressively wider spaces of economic affirmation, hoarding and selling wheat was one of the privileged grounds for social ascent. Some families of Porto San Giorgio and Grottammare, today in the province of Fermo, found a way to enter these Adriatic circuits. Their fortune was built thanks to the establishment of a triangulation with the Dalmatian area, in which the wheat of the Kingdom of Naples, the manufactured products and the produce of specialised agriculture of southern March, and the salted fish of Istria and Dalmatia were circulating.[115]

We can conclude with some considerations. In the first place, the presence of a binding regime is evident; but this regime, in practice, had much wider links than is commonly assumed on the basis of rigid theoretical schemes, based exclusively on the official regulatory framework of the time. This was in connection with the data on the productive levels of the Papal States, of which the March of Ancona was, for most of the period examined here, one of the principal granaries. The two factors just mentioned—and this is the second acquisition—explain the pressures that came from the great owners and the great food merchants. They aimed to obtain continuous renewal of export licences, but their action does not appear to have significantly disturbed the procurement process of the cities of the March. Finally, from the documentation it appears that their turnover was fuelled in both directions, both by selling excess wheat abroad in periods of abundance and by buying wheat in the years of scarcity, as soon as the import *tratte* were ‘opened’ (that is to say, when the permission to export freely was granted), in Albania, Turkey, Provence (through the port of Leghorn), or the Adriatic basin, in order to subsequently sell it in the March.

Notes

1. Kaplan (2008, p. 89), quoted in Chatriot (2016, p. 2). Here and below, all translations of original documents and works quoted are the authors'. On the Early Modern Age, see Kaplan (1976, 1984).
2. Anselmi (1989); Moroni (2003).
3. Zenobi (1979, 1982).
4. Fioretti (1987, pp. 37–38); Cecchi (1978, p. 66); Zenobi (1991, p. 18).
5. Zenobi (1994).
6. Corritore (2012).
7. This division is the well-known idea of Kaplan (1984), from which we quote here.
8. Delumeau (1959, pp. 626–633).
9. On the origin of the cereals supply system in Rome, see Palermo (1990, pp. 13–60).
10. Strangio (2015, p. 72).
11. Strangio (1998).
12. Strangio (2015, p. 77).
13. Paci (1975, pp. 110–112). Ciuffetti (2019, pp. 74–81) stressed the importance of the centre-periphery relationship in the papal victualling system during the Early Modern Age.
14. Guenzi (1978).
15. Zenobi (1991, pp. 38–40).
16. ASCOS, AB, 1, *Capitoli dell'Abbondanza per l'anno 1575.*
17. Moroni (1991, pp. 135–136).
18. "[G]ranum, ordeum, annonam, speltam, fabas, cicera et cicerchia vel alia biada seu legumina vel farinam cuiuscumque generis" (Cecchi 1991, pp. 520–527, quotation from p. 520).
19. Mira (1957, p. 516; 1971).
20. "[S]tabilire la quantità di grano da provvedersi et il prezzo di esso" (Ribechi 1996, pp. 112–115, quotation from p. 112).
21. "[A] disposizione degli abbondanzieri, sì per la piazza che per il pubblico forno" (Ribechi 1996, p. 113).
22. Gregorini (1987, p. 120).
23. Leoni (2011, doc. 906, p. 946).
24. Moroni (2015, p. 110).
25. ASMC, GM, 647, *Protesta dei proprietari che hanno consegnato il grano all'Annona*, 15 April 1678.
26. Paci (1975, pp. 109–115).
27. Cherubini (1985).
28. Moroni (2015, pp. 136–138).
29. Cecchi (1991, pp. 303, 389, 475–476, 486).

30. Ribechi (1996, pp. 114–115).
31. ASCOS, AN, 3, 26 August 1794.
32. "[A] chi ne facesse migliori condizioni" (ASCOS, AB, 2, 2 August 1759).
33. Cecchi (1991, pp. 725–726).
34. "[N]uovo pedaggio" (ASMC, GM, 644, *Protesta dei fornari casalini di Osimo*, 19 June 1666).
35. Ribechi (1996, p. 115).
36. Revel (1972, 1975).
37. ASCOS, RI, *1757–1769*, fo. 211, 13 November 1765 meeting.
38. ASCOS, RI, *1705–1717*, fo. 210, *Capitoli per il fornaro dell'anno 1715*.
39. Ribechi (1996, pp. 116–117).
40. Clark (1985).
41. Grendi (1970, 1971); Aymard (1966, pp. 155–168).
42. Alfani (2015, pp. 142–143).
43. Fioretti (1986); Ribechi (1996); Tallè (1998, pp. 72–83).
44. Moroni (1986); Bagalini (1998).
45. Di Stefano (1986, p. 74).
46. Paci (1986, pp. 13–14).
47. Allegretti (1987, p. 504).
48. In the Roman monetary system of account, used in the Papal States, 1 *scudo* (plur. *scudi*) was divided into 10 *giuli* or *paoli*, and 1 *giulio* or *paolo* into 10 *baiocchi* (Balbi De Caro and Londei 1984, pp. 55, 61, 89, 127; Londei 1990, pp. 308, 311–318). The Anconitan *rubbio* (plur. *rubbia*) corresponded to approximately 280.65 cubic decimetres (Martini 1883, p. 33); it was also called *soma*, plur. *some* (Paci 1978, p. 530); the weight of 1 *rubbio* of wheat corresponded to approximately 2.1 quintals (Anselmi 2001, p. 54).
49. Venturi (1973).
50. Ribechi (1996, pp. 115–117).
51. Moroni (2000, pp. 129–133).
52. Moroni (1994).
53. Andreoni (2012, pp. 134–158).
54. Andreoni (2012, pp. 159–160).
55. Revel (1972, pp. 214–217). See also Strangio (1999); Reinhardt (1990); (1991, pp. 361–411).
56. Strangio (2010, p. 130).
57. Todeschini (2016).
58. Sensi (1971, 1972, 1980); Battaglini (1976); Bonazzoli (1999); Checcoli (2015).
59. Sensi (1971).
60. Sensi (1972).
61. Sensi (1980).

62. Bellagamba (1991, pp. 303–308); Sensi (1972, pp. 201–205).
63. ASCOS, AB, 1; Grillantini (1985, vol. II, pp. 726–727).
64. ASCOS, BB, 9 April 1596.
65. ASCOS, AB, 1, *Rogiti di quelle persone che prenderanno grano dal Monte Frumentario* (they are preserved from 1660).
66. ASCAR, DI, *Capitoli fatti da' signori deputati de ordine nel pubblico Consiglio della magnifica comunità de Roccha Contrada, celebrato il 16 di aprile 1581 sopra l'ordine, modo e governo da tenersi sopra il Monte Charitativo da Grani.*
67. ASCTR, MF, *1574–1652*, fo. 1.
68. Sensi (1980); see also Battaglini (1976). In the Synod of Ancona celebrated in 1674 by Cardinal Giannicola Conti, it is possible to read an *Istruzione per l'amministrazione de' monti frumentarii.*
69. ASSCL, AC, *Materie diverse*, *Stato della Compagnia del Santissimo Rosario nell'anno 1768.*
70. Mocarelli (2015, pp. 46–47).
71. Strangio (1998, p. 173).
72. Paci (1962); see also Strangio (2010).
73. Paci (1975, pp. 111–115).
74. Mocarelli (2015, p. 45).
75. ASMC, GM, 1085, 1 July 1620; see also Napolioni (1991, pp. 88–89).
76. Moroni (2009, p. 106).
77. Ascoli did not have direct access to the sea. As in most of the region, however, the projection on the coast of cities and towns close to it, had allowed the birth of landing places and beaches in strong dependence with the respective centres of urban gravitation (Moroni 2006, pp. 1041–1056).
78. Moroni (2006); Loggi (1992, pp. 157–158).
79. Moroni (2006); Bulgarelli Lukacs (1998, p. 264).
80. Moroni (2006); Romano (1951, p. 88).
81. Dal Pane (1959 [1939], pp. 573–574).
82. Moroni (1997, p. 57).
83. Dal Pane (1959 [1939], pp. 566–567).
84. Dal Pane (1959 [1939], pp. 566–567); Moroni (1997, pp. 68–69).
85. ASMC, CAG, 557 (2), account of Secretary Filippo Ranaldi, year 1753.
86. "[I]l bisogno de' contadini, et altre povere persone che sogliono vivere colle prestanze de' grani" (ASMC, CAG, 557 (1), account of Secretary Filippo Ranaldi, year 1753).
87. "Per la piazza bastantemente suppliscono gl'affluenti nelli due mercati che si fanno in ogni settimana, e rarissimi sono stati li casi, ne' quali i possidenti hanno dovuto mandare a vendere li propri grani in piazza per mancanza" (ASMC, CAG, 557 (1), account of Secretary Filippo Ranaldi, year 1753).

88. This fluctuation derives from the availability of data on the population of Macerata, limited to two years around 1753, in a context of constant growth in the eighteenth century: in 1736 it amounted to 10,892 inhabitants, while in 1769 to 11,979 (Beloch 1994 [1937–1961], p. 233; Cioci 1977, p. 341).
89. Remembering what Fernand Braudel wrote, a quintal of wheat was 300,000 kilocalories. Therefore, the estimated consumption, between 1.58 and 1.74 quintals per year, provided between 1,298 and 1,430 kilocalories per day. In general, cereals made up a large part of the daily diet, which could reach three-quarters of the daily calorie intake, more easily reaching around 50% (Braudel 1967, pp. 97–100; Flandrin 1997, p. 429).
90. "L'angusto territorio di Macerata non può dare raccolto maggiore. Ma sicome quasi tutti li possidenti di detta città possiedono in alieno territorio, così ne viene che non solamente resti soprabondantemente proveduta del bisogno, ma che vi sia del sopravanzo ancora per tal motivo, e per l'altro, che del continuo concorrono li grani da' luoghi vicini, che mantengono abbondante la piazza" (ASMC, CAG, 557 (2), account of Secretary Filippo Ranaldi, year 1753).
91. ASMC, CAG, 557 (3), *Spoglio delle assegne date in Macerata l'anno 1751.*
92. Dal Pane (1959 [1939], p. 573); Vernelli (1993).
93. ASMC, CAG, 557 (3), *Spoglio delle assegne date in Macerata l'anno 1751.*
94. On landowners in Macerata, see Troscé (1972); on the Compagnoni Marefoschi family, see Domenichini (2010, 2011).
95. ASMC, CAG, 557 (3), *Spoglio delle assegne date in Macerata l'anno 1751.*
96. Caracciolo (2002 [1965], pp. 197–236).
97. Moroni (2015, pp. 110–111).
98. ASAN, ACARAN, *Mandati di acquisto di grano e farina* (1).
99. Caracciolo (2002 [1965], pp. 104–135).
100. Ribechi (1996, p. 113).
101. Caracciolo (2002 [1965], p. 217).
102. Caracciolo (1962).
103. Andreoni (2019, p. 220). On this merchant, see also Andreoni (2013).
104. ASAN, ANAN, *Secolo XVIII, Notaio Filippo Franchi*, 1787, fo. 253v. The existence of this partnership and this documentation was reported by Angelini (1989, p. 24). On this kind of general partnership, see Bonazzoli (1998); Trivellato (2009, pp. 139–152).
105. ASAN, ACARAN, *Libri di entrata e uscita dell'Abbondanza Frumentaria*, 16, years 1715–1716.
106. "[E]ncepté par le juif Morburgue d'Ancône", "bled de Turquie" (ANP, AE, microfilm B.I.1015, 6 April 1747). On the French consular network in the Adriatic, see Nardone (2013); Biagianti (2016).

107. Angelini (1982). On the Republic of Venice, see Ongaro (2018).
108. ASAN, ACARAN, *Mandati di acquisto di grano e farina*, 2, years 1755–1782.
109. Ciuffetti (2013, pp. 177–178).
110. Moroni (2015, p. 148).
111. Moroni (2015, p. 111).
112. Moroni (2015, p. 111).
113. Moroni (2016, pp. 95–98).
114. Moroni (2000, pp. 66–70); Termite (1986a, b).
115. Moroni (2006); Gobbi (2004, pp. 112–113).

Archival Sources

Archivio Storico del Comune di Arcevia (ASCAR)
Diplomatico (DI).
https://siusa.archivi.beniculturali.it/cgi-bin/pagina.pl?TipoPag=cons&Chiave=4524&RicDimF=2&RicProgetto=reg-mar

Archivio Storico del Comune di Osimo (ASCOS)
Abbondanza (AB).
Annona (AN).
Bolle e brevi (BB).
Riformanze (RI).
https://siusa.archivi.beniculturali.it/cgi-bin/siusa/pagina.pl?TipoPag=cons&Chiave=6557&RicVM=ricercasemplice&RicSez=conservatori&RicDimF=2&RicProgetto=reg%2dmar&RicFrmRicSemplice=osimo

Archivio Storico del Comune di Treia (ASCTR)
Monte frumentario (MF).
https://siusa.archivi.beniculturali.it/cgi-bin/siusa/pagina.pl?TipoPag=cons&Chiave=9236&RicFrmRicSemplice=treia&RicVM=ricercasemplice&RicDimF=2&RicProgetto=reg%2dmar&RicSez=conservatori

Archivio Storico della Santa Casa di Loreto (ASSCL)
Atti di Castelfidardo (AC).
www.anagrafebbcc.chiesacattolica.it/anagraficaCEIBib/public/VisualizzaScheda.do?codice_cei=CEI456A00001

Archivio di Stato di Ancona (ASAN)
Archivio del Comune di Ancona, *Antico regime*, *Sezione II*, *Annona* (ACARAN).
Archivio Notarile di Ancona (ANAN).
www.archiviodistatoancona.beniculturali.it

Archivio di Stato di Macerata (ASMC)
Camerlenghi, Annona e grascia (CAG).
Governatore della Marca (GM).
www.archiviodistatomacerata.beniculturali.it

Archives Nationales, Paris (ANP)
Affaires étrangères (AE).
www.archives-nationales.culture.gouv.fr

Published Sources

Cecchi, Dante, ed. 1991. *Il Codice osimano degli Statuti del secolo XIV*. Osimo: Fondazione Don Carlo Grillantini.

References

Alfani, Guido. 2015. Alcune riflessioni sulle cause delle carestie in Italia settentrionale (XV–XVII secolo). In Ferrari and Vaquero Piñeiro 2015, 129–150.

Allegretti, Girolamo. 1987. Marchigiani in Maremma. In Anselmi 1987, 504–522.

Andreoni, Luca. 2012. *I conti del camerlengo. Finanza ed economia a San Marino fra Sette e Ottocento*. San Marino: Centro Sammarinese di Studi Storici.

———. 2013. Riscatto degli schiavi cristiani e intermediari ebrei. Un caso di studio tra Ancona e Ragusa (sec. XVIII). *Dimensioni e Problemi della Ricerca Storica* 2: 107–130.

———. 2019. *"Una nazione in commercio". Ebrei di Ancona, traffici adriatici e pratiche mercantili in età moderna*. Milano: Angeli.

Angelini, Werther. 1982. Riflessioni sopra un'incetta cerealicola degli anni 1772–73 nella Marca. In *La fascia costiera della Marca*, ed. by the Centro di Studi Storici Maceratesi, 175–201. Macerata: Centro di Studi Storici Maceratesi.

———. 1989. Tra Cinquecento e tardo Settecento: preparazione e maturità dell'attività mercantile degli ebrei ad Ancona. In *The Mediterranean and the Jews: Banking, finance and international trade, XVI–XVIII centuries*, ed. by Ariel Toaff and Simon Schwarzfuchs, 11–38. Ramat Gan: Bar Ilan University.

Anselmi, Sergio, ed. 1987. *Storia d'Italia. Le regioni dall'Unità a oggi. Le Marche*. Torino: Einaudi.

———. 1989. Un insediamento resistente: mezzadria e reticolo urbano nell'Italia centrale. In *L'ambiente nella storia d'Italia: studi e immagini*, ed. by the Fondazione Lelio e Lisli Basso/Issoco, 39–56. Venezia: Marsilio.

———. 2001. *Agricoltura e mondo contadino*. Bologna: il Mulino.

Aymard, Maurice. 1966. *Venise, Raguse et le commerce du blé pendant la seconde moitié du XVIe siècle*. Paris: Sevpen.

Bagalini, Sabina. 1998. Carestie e carità a Ripatransone nei secoli XVI e XVII. *Proposte e Ricerche. Economia e Società nella Storia dell'Italia Centrale* 21 (2/41): 53–70.

Balbi De Caro, Silvana, and Luigi Londei. 1984. *Moneta Pontificia (da Innocenzo XI a Gregorio XVI)*. Roma: Quasar.

Battaglini, Gelsimo. 1976. I Monti frumentari della diocesi di Ancona nel secolo XVIII. *Atti e Memorie. Deputazione di Storia Patria per le Marche*, 8th series 10: 7–24.

Bellagamba, Velia. 1991. I Monti frumentari. In *La Marca e le sue istituzioni al tempo di Sisto V*, ed. by Pio Cartechini, 303–308. Roma: Ministero per i Beni Culturali e Ambientali.

Beloch, Karl Julius. 1994 [1937–1961]. *Storia della popolazione d'Italia*, ed. by the Società Italiana di Demografia Storica. Italian translation. Firenze: Le Lettere.

Biagianti, Annalisa. 2016. Recrutement et pratiques en chancellerie consulaire. Le cas du consulat de France à Ancône et des viceconsulats de l'Adriatique (1726–1814). *Mélanges de l'École Française de Rome. Italie et Méditerranée Modernes et Contemporaines* 128 (2): 335–348.

Bonazzoli, Viviana. 1998. *Adriatico e Mediterraneo orientale. Una dinastia mercantile ebraica del secondo '600: i Costantini*. Trieste: Lint.

———. 1999. Banchi ebraici, Monti di pietà e Monti frumentari in area marchigiana: un insieme di temi aperti. In *Monti di pietà e presenza ebraica in Italia (secoli XV–XVIII)*, ed. by Daniele Montanari, 181–214. Roma: Bulzoni.

Braudel, Fernand. 1967. *Civilisation matérielle et capitalisme (XVe–XVIIIe siècle)*. Vol. I: Le possible et l'impossible: les hommes face à leur vie quotidienne. Paris: Colin.

Bulgarelli Lukacs, Alessandra. 1998. Mercati e mercanti in Abruzzo (secc. XV–XVIII). In *Abruzzo. Economia e territorio in una prospettiva storica*, ed. by Massimo Costantini and Costantino Felice, 225–336. Vasto: Cannarsa.

Caracciolo, Alberto. 1962. *Ricerche sul mercante del Settecento*. Vol. II: Francesco Trionfi capitalista e magnate d'Ancona. Milano: Giuffrè.

———. 2002 [1965]. *Il porto franco di Ancona nel XVIII secolo. Crescita e crisi di un ambiente mercantile*, ed. by Carlo Vernelli. Italian ed. Ancona: Proposte e Ricerche.

Cecchi, Dante. 1978. Dagli stati signorili all'età post-unitaria: le giurisdizioni amministrative in età moderna. In *Economia e società: le Marche tra XV e XX secolo*, ed. by Sergio Anselmi, 61–92. Bologna: il Mulino.

Chatriot, Alain. 2016. *La politique du blé. Crises et régulation d'un marché dans la France de l'entre-deux-guerres*. Paris: Comité pour l'Histoire Économique et Financière de la France.

Checcoli, Ippolita, ed. 2015. *I Monti frumentari e le forme di credito non monetarie tra Medioevo ed Età contemporanea*. Bologna: il Mulino.

Cherubini, Giovanni. 1985. Lo sfruttamento dell'acqua negli statuti della Marca meridionale. In *Arti e manifatture nella Marca nei secoli XIII–XVI*, ed. by the Centro di Studi Storici Maceratesi, 27–40. Macerata: Centro di Studi Storici Maceratesi.

Cioci, Lorenzo. 1977. Appunti sulle vicende economiche e sociali. In *Storia di Macerata*, ed. by Aldo Adversi, Dante Cecchi, and Libero Paci. Vol. V, 304–389. Macerata: Biemmegraf.

Ciuffetti, Augusto. 2013. Scarsità delle risorse, dinamiche demografiche e percorsi economici nella provincia pontificia in età moderna. In *Quando manca il pane. Origini e cause della scarsità delle risorse alimentari in età moderna e contemporanea*, ed. by Luca Mocarelli, 163–178. Bologna: il Mulino.

———. 2019. Mercati del grano, consumi e carestie nella provincia pontificia tra XVIII e XIX secolo. In *La* polizia de' grani. *Mercati, regole e crisi di sussistenza nelle economie di Antico Regime*, ed. by Alida Clemente and Saverio Russo, 73–89. Soveria Mannelli: Rubbettino.

Clark, Peter, ed. 1985. *The European crisis of the 1590s: Essays in comparative history*. London: Allen and Unwin.

Corritore, Renzo Paolo. 2012. Un problema negletto. Per un riesame della questione annonaria nelle città di antico regime. *Storia Urbana* 36 (1/134): 5–9.

Dal Pane, Luigi. 1959 [1939]. Il commercio dei grani nello Stato pontificio nei secoli XVII e XVIII. New ed. In *Lo Stato pontificio e il movimento riformatore del Settecento*, by Luigi Dal Pane, 557–607. Milano: Giuffrè.

Delumeau, Jean. 1959. *Vie économique et sociale de Rome dans la seconde moitié du XVIe siècle*. Vol. II. Paris: de Boccard.

Di Stefano, Emanuela. 1986. La crisi del Seicento nell'area appenninica: il territorio camerte. *Proposte e Ricerche. Rivista di Storia dell'Agricoltura e delle Società Rurali Marchigiane* 9 (2/17): 73–85.

Domenichini, Roberto. 2010. Fonti documentarie locali per la storia della Compagnia di Gesù: l'archivio Compagnoni Marefoschi. In *Ordini e congregazioni religiose dal concilio di Trento alla soppressione napoleonica*, ed. by the Centro di Studi Storici Maceratesi, 193–233. Macerata: Centro di Studi Storici Maceratesi.

———. 2011. Note sull'archivio Compagnoni Marefoschi di Potenza Picena. In *Palazzo Compagnoni Marefoschi di Macerata. Palazzo rosso di Potenza Picena*, ed. by Adele Piergallini and Umberto Santori Compagnoni Marefoschi, 213–227. Recanati: Bieffe.

Ferrari, Maria Luisa, and Manuel Vaquero Piñeiro, eds. 2015. *"Moia la carestia". La scarsità alimentare in età preindustriale*. Bologna: il Mulino.

Fioretti, Donatella. 1986. Risorse alimentari e crisi demografica nel Fabrianese, tra Cinque e Seicento. *Proposte e Ricerche. Rivista di Storia dell'Agricoltura e delle Società Rurali Marchigiane* 9 (1/16): 19–28.

———. 1987. Persistenze e mutamenti dal periodo giacobino all'Unità. In Anselmi 1987, 35–119.

Flandrin, Jean-Louis. 1997. I tempi moderni. In *Storia dell'alimentazione*, ed. by Jean-Louis Flandrin and Massimo Montanari, 427–448. Roma/Bari: Laterza.

Gobbi, Olimpia. 2004. Porti e commercio marittimo a Marano e Grottammare nei secoli XVI e XVII. In *Fermo e la sua costa. Merci, monete, fiere e porti fra tardo Medioevo e fine dell'età moderna*, 101–132. Cupra Marittima: Laboratorio Didattico di Ecologia del Quaternario.

Gregorini, Eros. 1987. Le fosse da grano di Corinaldo. In *L'architettura popolare in Italia. Marche*, ed. by Sergio Anselmi and Gianni Volpe, 118–120. Roma/Bari: Laterza.

Grendi, Edoardo. 1970. Genova alla metà del Cinquecento: una politica del grano? *Quaderni Storici* 5 (1/13): 107–160.

———. 1971. I Nordici e il traffico del porto di Genova, 1590–1666. *Rivista Storica Italiana* 83 (1): 25–73.

Grillantini, Carlo. 1985. *Storia di Osimo*. Recanati: Tecnostampa.

Guenzi, Alberto. 1978. Un mercato regolato: pane e fornai a Bologna nell'età moderna. *Quaderni Storici* 13 (1/37): 370–397.

Kaplan, Steven Laurence. 1976. *Bread, politics and political economy in the reign of Louis XV*. The Hague: Nijhoff.

———. 1984. *Provisioning Paris: Merchants and millers in the grain and flour trade during the eighteenth century*. Ithaca/London: Cornell University Press.

———. 2008. *Le pain maudit. Retour sur la France des années oubliées, 1945–1958*. Paris: Fayard.

Leoni, Aron di Leone. 2011. *La nazione ebraica spagnola e portoghese di Ferrara (1492–1559). I suoi rapporti col governo ducale e la popolazione locale ed i suoi legami con le Nazioni Portoghesi di Ancona, Pesaro e Venezia*, ed. by Laura Graziani Secchieri. Firenze: Olschki.

Loggi, Saturnino. 1992. *Monteprandone porto d'Ascoli. Storia di un territorio*. Acquaviva Picena: Cassa Rurale e Artigiana di Acquaviva Picena e Monteprandone.

Londei, Luigi. 1990. La monetazione pontificia e la zecca di Roma nell'età moderna (secc. XVI–XVIII). *Studi Romani* 38 (3–4): 303–318.

Martini, Angelo. 1883. *Manuale di metrologia, ossia misure, pesi e monete in uso attualmente e anticamente presso tutti i popoli*. Torino: Loescher.

Mira, Giuseppe. 1957. Il fabbisogno di cereali in Perugia e nel suo contado nei secoli XIII–XIV. In *Studi in onore di Armando Sapori*. Vol. I, 500–517. Milano: Istituto Editoriale Cisalpino.

———. 1971. Un aspetto dei rapporti fra città e campagna nel Perugino nei secoli XIII e XIV: l'approvvigionamento dei generi di prima necessità. In *Storia e arte in Umbria nell'età comunale*, ed. by the Facoltà di Lettere e Filosofia dell'Università degli Studi di Perugia. Vol. II, 311–352. Gubbio: Centro di Studi Umbri.

Mocarelli, Luca. 2015. Ripensare le crisi alimentari: lo Stato di Milano nel secondo Settecento. In Ferrari and Vaquero Piñeiro 2015, 39–63.

Moroni, Marco. 1986. Recanati nella carestia del 1591. *Proposte e Ricerche. Rivista di Storia dell'Agricoltura e delle Società Rurali Marchigiane* 9 (1/16): 29–43.

———. 1991. Il codice degli Statuti del XIV secolo e l'economia di Osimo nella prima metà del Trecento. In Cecchi 1991, vol. I, 135–151.

———. 1994. *L'economia di un "luogo di mezzo". San Marino dal basso Medioevo all'Ottocento*. San Marino: Centro Sammarinese di Studi Storici.

———. 1997. *Tra Romagna e Marche. Le campagne feretrano-romagnole in età moderna*. San Marino: Centro Sammarinese di Studi Storici.

———. 2000. *L'economia di un grande santuario europeo. La Santa Casa di Loreto tra basso Medioevo e Novecento*. Milano: Angeli.

———. 2003. *L'Italia delle colline. Uomini, terre e paesaggi nell'Italia centrale (secoli XV–XX)*. Ancona: Proposte e Ricerche.

———. 2006. Tra "relitti di mare" e paludi costiere: nascita di una comunità di pescatori a San Benedetto del Tronto (secc. XVI–XVIII). In *Ricchezza del mare, ricchezza dal mare (secc. XIII–XVIII)*, ed. by Simonetta Cavaciocchi, 1041–1056. Firenze: Le Monnier.

———. 2009. Reti commerciali e spazi costieri: il caso di Ancona fra XVII e XVIII secolo. In *Acque, terre e spazi dei mercanti. Istituzioni, gerarchie, conflitti e pratiche dello scambio dall'età antica alla modernità*, ed. by Daniele Andreozzi, Loredana Panariti, and Claudio Zaccaria, 85–112. Trieste: Editreg.

———. 2015. *Castelfidardo da castello a città*. Fermo: Livi.

———. 2016. Mezzadria, mercato e redditività nei beni fondiari della Santa Casa di Loreto. *Marca/Marche. Rivista di Storia Regionale* 4 (2/7): 87–114.

Napolioni, Angiola Maria. 1991. Legati e Governatori generali della Marca. In *La Marca e le sue istituzioni al tempo di Sisto V*, ed. by Pio Cartechini, 79–92. Roma: Ministero per i Beni Culturali e Ambientali.

Nardone, Paola. 2013. Diplomacy and international commerce in the 18th century Adriatic: The case of the French consulate in the port of Ancona. *The Journal of European Economic History* 42 (1–3): 165–207.

Ongaro, Giulio. 2018. Military food supply in the Republic of Venice in the eighteenth century: Entrepreneurs, merchants, and the state. *Business History*. https://doi.org/10.1080/00076791.2018.1520211.

Paci, Renzo. 1962. *Agricoltura e vita urbana nelle Marche. Senigallia fra Settecento e Ottocento*. Milano: Giuffrè.

———. 1975. Rese, commercio ed esportazione dei cereali nella Legazione d'Urbino nei secoli XVII e XVIII. *Quaderni Storici* 10 (1/28): 87–150.

———. 1978. Una rivoluzione agraria mancata. In *Una città adriatica. Insediamenti, forme urbane, economia, società nella storia di Senigallia*, ed. by Sergio Anselmi, 481–544. Jesi: Cassa di Risparmio di Jesi.
———. 1986. Demografia, disponibilità alimentari e crisi di mortalità nelle Marche tra XIV e XVIII secolo. *Proposte e Ricerche. Rivista di Storia dell'Agricoltura e delle Società Rurali Marchigiane* 9 (1/16): 9–18.
Palermo, Luciano. 1990. *Mercati del grano a Roma tra Medioevo e Rinascimento.* Vol. I: Il mercato distrettuale del grano in età comunale. Roma: Istituto Nazionale di Studi Romani.
Reinhardt, Volker. 1990. Il prezzo del pane a Roma e la finanza pontificia dal 1563 al 1762. *Dimensioni e Problemi della Ricerca Storica* 3 (2): 109–134.
———. 1991. *Überleben in der frühneuzeitlichen Stadt. Annona und Getreideversorgung in Rom, 1563–1797.* Tübingen: Niemeyer.
Revel, Jacques. 1972. Le grain de Rome et la crise de l'Annone dans la seconde moitié du XVIIIe siècle. *Mélanges de l'École Française de Rome. Moyen Âge, Temps Modernes* 84 (1): 201–281.
———. 1975. Les privilèges d'une capitale: l'approvisionnement de Rome à l'époque moderne. *Mélanges de l'École Française de Rome. Moyen Âge, Temps Modernes* 87 (2): 461–493.
Ribechi, Donatella. 1996. L'Amministrazione dell'Annona in un comune della Marca anconitana nel XVIII secolo. *Proposte e Ricerche. Economia e Società nella Storia dell'Italia Centrale* 19 (2/37): 111–121.
Romano, Ruggiero. 1951. *Le commerce du Royaume de Naples avec la France et le Pays de l'Adriatique au XVIIIe siècle.* Paris: Colin.
Sensi, Mario. 1971. Tre monti frumentari del secolo XV. In *Civiltà del Rinascimento nel Maceratese*, ed. by the Centro di Studi Storici Maceratesi, 285–305. Macerata: Centro di Studi Storici Maceratesi.
———. 1972. Fra Andrea da Faenza istitutore dei Monti frumentari. *Picenum Seraphicum* 9: 162–257.
———. 1980. Monti frumentari. In *Dizionario degli istituti di perfezione*, ed. by Guerrino Pelliccia and Giancarlo Rocca. Vol. VI, 115–119. Milano: Edizioni Paoline.
Sori, Ercole. 2005. Le Marche tra '600 e '700: congiunture economiche e demografiche. *Proposte e Ricerche. Economia e Società nella Storia dell'Italia Centrale* 28 (1/54): 7–31.
Strangio, Donatella. 1998. Di fronte alla carestia in età preindustriale. *Rivista di Storia Economica*, new series 14 (2): 161–192.
———. 1999. *Crisi alimentari e politica annonaria a Roma nel Settecento.* Roma: Istituto Nazionale di Studi Romani.
———. 2010. Mercato del grano e mercanti nello Stato pontificio tra età moderna e contemporanea: la normativa giuridica e la gestione del grano a Macerata.

Proposte e Ricerche. Economia e Società nella Storia dell'Italia Centrale 33 (2/65): 126–143.

———. 2015. Ripensare le *food crises*: lo Stato Pontificio (1750–1800). In Ferrari and Vaquero Piñeiro 2015, 65–91.

Tallè, Tania. 1998. La carestia del 1590–1592 nella terra di San Ginesio. *Proposte e Ricerche. Economia e Società nella Storia dell'Italia Centrale* 21 (1/40): 72–83.

Termite, Elena. 1986a. Il commercio del grano nelle Marche del Settecento: la Santa Casa di Loreto. *Proposte e Ricerche. Rivista di Storia dell'Agricoltura e delle Società Rurali Marchigiane* 9 (1/16): 44–61.

———. 1986b. Produzione e vendita di grani nell'azienda della Santa Casa di Loreto. *Proposte e Ricerche. Rivista di Storia dell'Agricoltura e delle Società Rurali Marchigiane* 9 (2/17): 58–66.

Todeschini, Giacomo. 2016. *La banca e il ghetto. Una storia italiana*. Roma/Bari: Laterza.

Trivellato, Francesca. 2009. *The familiarity of strangers: The Sephardic diaspora, Livorno, and cross-cultural trade in the early modern period*. New Haven/London: Yale University Press.

Troscé, Mariella. 1972. Governanti e possidenti nel XVI e nel XVII secolo a Macerata. *Quaderni Storici* 7 (3/21): 827–850.

Venturi, Franco. 1973. 1764–1767: Roma negli anni della fame. *Rivista Storica Italiana* 85 (2): 514–543.

Vernelli, Carlo. 1993. L'incremento demografico del contado jesino tra XVI e XVIII secolo. In *La popolazione delle campagne italiane in età moderna*, ed. by the Società Italiana di Demografia Storica, 305–325. Bologna: Clueb.

Zenobi, Bandino Giacomo. 1979. *Dai governi larghi all'assetto patriziale. Istituzioni e organizzazioni del potere nelle città minori della Marca dei secoli XVI–XVIII*. Urbino: Argalia.

———. 1982. I caratteri della distrettuazione di antico regime nella Marca pontificia. In *Scritti storici in memoria di Enzo Piscitelli*, ed. by Renzo Paci, 61–106. Padova: Antenore.

———. 1991. L'assetto territoriale dal XV al XVIII secolo. In *La Marca e le sue istituzioni al tempo di Sisto V*, ed. by Pio Cartechini, 15–31. Roma: Ministero per i Beni Culturali e Ambientali.

———. 1994. *Le ben regolate città. Modelli politici nel governo delle periferie pontificie in età moderna*. Roma: Bulzoni.

Map 7.1 The Papal States (1786)

CHAPTER 7

The Roman *Annona* and Its Market in the Eighteenth Century

Donatella Strangio

7.1 Introduction: The Historical Formation of the Roman Victualling System

Fifteenth-century Rome enjoyed an abundant food supply thanks to the papal victualling system, the principles of which had initially been outlined in two documents dating back to 1283 and 1299. Luciano Palermo highlighted the importance of these plans for fulfilling Roman political and geographical needs.[1] They materialised in the formation and growth of a centralised and politically controlled system of circulation of foodstuffs, particularly wheat. The internal organisation that this sector of the state administration acquired during the fifteenth century endured through the following centuries, thanks partly to some innovative interventions.[2] Charles Tilly's general observation, which attributes the origin of the public oversight of wheat policies as a response to growth in demand and consequent market shifts, is applicable to the Roman context.[3] Since the

D. Strangio (✉)
Sapienza Università di Roma, Rome, Italy
e-mail: donatella.strangio@uniroma1.it

L. Clerici (ed.), *Italian Victualling Systems in the Early Modern Age, 16th to 18th Century*, Palgrave Studies in Economic History,
https://doi.org/10.1007/978-3-030-42064-2_7

Late Middle Ages, the market for all foodstuffs, especially wheat, had been closely controlled and protected. In practice, this resulted in a dynamic interplay between the political interest of ruling groups and the economic interest of merchants because wheat was more than just a potential source of enrichment for its dealers, it was fundamental to the very survival of all. Braudel defined wheat as "the outstanding product of the pre-industrial economies in Europe, and indeed their measure".[4]

The secondary cereals (such as barley and oats) represented, respectively, about 5% and 8% of the supplies of Rome and its immediate surroundings,[5] and the predominance of wheat was so rooted in the taste of the public as to render even low-level rice and maize production a waste of time until about the middle of the nineteenth century.[6] While other food sectors, chief among them salt, had also been gradually subjected to the control of the authorities, only wheat had acquired strictly economic characteristics alongside its social dimension: demand was relatively inelastic for the sector, which could not always respond to upward variations in consumption levels, even at times of increased production. The demand for foodstuffs, led by wheat, performed a very significant economic function between the Middle Ages and the Early Modern Age, one that remained evident until the early nineteenth century, when substitute assets became established on the market, primarily in Rome.[7]

In the fourteenth century, the fear of sudden famine and the attendant risk of having to import wheat from abroad prompted ecclesiastical bodies to set up controls for crops production from sowing to consumption and made sure that the vast majority of wheat was destined for the Roman market. As Palermo stated, it was much easier for the authorities to take possession of what had already been produced and to direct it towards their own goals rather than push for increased production in short windows;[8] it was very difficult to control and then try to increase crops production in the first place because the land under cultivation was not producing high yields. This constituted an objective limit of the productivity of the Roman countryside. Furthermore, landowners fiercely protected their own interests, which did not often coincide with those of the government.[9] Therefore, it was vital to preserve a store of wheat from one year to the next in the public warehouses of the city's victualling office, the *Abbondanza* (literally, 'Abundance'). Maintaining an adequate stock in this way was a safeguard against famine. But to store wheat it was necessary to know the quantities produced, the most fertile and suitable lands for sowing, and the usual consumption levels of the population; this called for the investment of financial and administrative resources.

If immediate increases in production were not possible during emergencies, the State had to be able to intervene speedily to make the exchange system more effective and to increase supply levels. However, it should be pointed out that archival sources indicate that not all agricultural produce was sent to the market and that not all consumption of agricultural goods occurred through market demand. The specific path of expansion of the mercantile economy in the Papal States[10] underscored this distinction. Production could not and did not necessarily go towards market supply (at least not at the local level, or not immediately): it could be partly consumed by the producers themselves, stored or even hoarded in anticipation of rising prices; alternatively, it could be exported to the markets of other cities or regions offering higher crops prices. But the opposite could also happen in certain circumstances, namely that in the event of serious local shortages, provisions could be imported from other markets.

This chapter aims to contribute to the debate on food supply and the role played by victualling systems, with a special emphasis on the Roman case. The spotlight will be on agents and wheat circuits, the analysis of whose workings furthers our general understanding of the phenomenon. In this regard, the work will be structured in line with its focus on the following subjects: documenting the *Annona*: the organisation of the *Annona* in the eighteenth century; the political and public function of wheat reserves; the export licences and actors of the wheat circuits. Having presented the evidence, some conclusions will be presented.

7.2 Documenting the *Annona*: The Organisation of the *Annona* in the Eighteenth Century

The jurisdiction of the *monsignor prefetto dell'Annona* ('monsignor prefect of the *Annona*') extended up to the Tuscan coast, and includes 103 villages in the provinces of Sabina, Lazio, and Campagna and Marittima. There were commissioners of the Roman *Annona* in Tivoli, Velletri, Sabina, Toscanella, Civitavecchia, Corneto, and Sutri. In all these places, farmers were reliant on the cash of the *Annona*.[11] These places constituted the territorial circuit within which Roman jurisdiction was activated during the eighteenth century, according to a letter sent by Giovanni Battista Zanoperti (a lawyer) and Marco Antonio Canazzoni to the particular *congregazione* ('congregation') delegated by Pope Pius VI in 1777 to investigate the work of the prefect of the *Annona*, Nicola Bischi.[12] Despite the close contemporary recording of the functioning of the *Annona*, and the preservation of a vast archive, the interest of historians has been limited. The earliest works on the subject remain valid points of reference, primarily the volumes by Cesare De Cupis and Alberto Canaletti Gaudenti. The second contains the unpublished fourth volume of Nicola Maria Nicolai's work.[13] The research of Jacques Revel, although confined to the late eighteenth century and the financial crisis that put an end to the Roman system, analysed the abundant quantitative data available on the *Annona Frumentaria*. Donatella Strangio's work analysed the quantitative data of the *Annona* of the eighteenth century, linking famine, lack of wheat supply, and public debt to reveal a model that was unique in the European panorama. Renata Sabene's recent work enriched our knowledge of the Roman victualling system in the eighteenth century through its deployment of new archival sources, such as those on the *Fabbrica di San Pietro* and the labour market.[14]

The *Annona Frumentaria* was an organisation structured on a pyramidal basis, which had as its vertex the *camerlengo* ('chamberlain'). This official supervised the activity of the prefect of the *Annona*, who was nominated from among the clerics of the Apostolic Chamber and controlled the crops policy of the entire territory of the Papal States: extensive powers were conferred on the prefect of the *Annona* by Pope Paul IV in 1557 and by Pope Gregory XIII with the 18 December 1577 *motu proprio*. From 1572 the *Tribunale dell'Annona* ('Tribunal of the *Annona*') supported the prefect in establishing prices, selecting officials, collecting quantitative information, and arbitrating on disputes.[15] At the foundation of this system was a large group of commissioners (*commissari*)[16] who resided, sometimes permanently, in the provinces bordering the capital city and within the *Districtus Urbis* ('City District', the land area around Rome to a radius of 40 miles—approximately 60 kilometres—and including Tivoli, Frascati, Albano, Ardea, Palestrina, Porto, and Ostia).[17] The commissioners were in charge of buying the wheat production of the provinces and of funnelling it towards Rome, the most populous market of the State. The District had its own character and features in terms of taxation and victualling policy: it represented a breakdown useful for the imposition of certain taxes.[18] In the city, the officials of the *Abbondanza* took care of registering arrivals, paying transport costs and storing wheat in barns and then distributing them in the monitored marketplace of

Campo de' Fiori and to bakers. The officials were mainly Roman and performed their tasks as bookkeepers, measurers, and overseers, positions which became permanent during the eighteenth century (in 1750 there were about 100 such officials).

The centralisation of victualling administration in the Papal States, under the joint authority of the prefect and the chamberlain, was virtual and did not mask the tensions existing between the provinces over the fact that certain *legazioni* ('legations', seats of a papal legate) enjoyed special privileges and did not fall within the jurisdiction of Rome as regarded victualling. In the Papal States there was no other victualling system comparable to the institution of Rome, whereby the *Annona*'s set of magistrates, competences, and structures tightly regulated crops trade. For example, in a large city like Bologna, where the local political elite had adopted a policy of control and orientation of the urban market in order to ensure the maximum possible guarantee to urban consumers, a public granary was never built and the victualling system concentrated on price manipulation and regulation of the urban market.[19] Several communities, large and small, administered their own *Abbondanza*, which was used as a warehouse for stocks preserved for times of crisis. In the more organised communities, specific institutions called *monti frumentari* (literally, 'mounts of wheat') were established.[20] Municipal councils elected one or more highly productive farmers as wheat custodians, charged with managing supplies and maintaining steady levels of consumption.[21] However, the *Sacra Congregazione del Buon Governo* ('Sacred Congregation of Good Government') acted as a wide-ranging supreme tribunal in all municipalities and had final say over all subjects, including wheat.[22]

The *Annona*, especially in times of crisis, enjoyed incontestable prerogatives and a broad range of action, exercised through the intermediation of the *Congregazione*. It constituted a point of reference and a link between all the communities of the country and the government of Rome.[23] The prefect of the *Annona* was head of the *Congregazione* and had the title of superintendent general of the Papal States, or prime minister of the temporal state. The reorganisation of the *Congregazione* in 1701 substantially strengthened its control instruments: interventions, such as the *visite* (literally, 'visits') by dedicated officials, became a tool for managing community administrative management and eventually, over the course of a century, for the equalisation of fiscal burdens.[24] The *Annona* administration was part of the central government.[25] The officials of the *Annona* had to prevent produce hoardings and remove all barriers to the concentration of essential commodities in Rome. These tasks were facilitated by a legislation characterised by constraints, prohibitions, restrictions, and inhibitions.

7.3 The Political and Public Function of Wheat Reserves

Among the main tasks of the *Annona Frumentaria*, in addition to the issuing of laws on sowing, was the purchase of large quantities of wheat directly from producers. The *Annona* set prices based on scarcity and distance from the place of harvesting. The wheat was amassed in numerous granaries and large stocks were maintained (this was one of the most important public functions of the State, reflecting the religious, moral, and political conception of royal absolutism).[26] Wheat reserves performed a variety of functions, chief among them the reassurance of the population that the threat of famine was offset.[27] Almost as important as that was price stability at a level affordable for less affluent social strata. This was achieved by the release of wheat to the market at appropriate times or, indeed, by the restriction of supply if that was necessary. The *Annona* also had to provision the bakeries of the city. The psychological function fulfilled by the measures of the *Annona* proved to be of considerable importance at a time when popular unrest due to food shortages was a constant risk and sometimes exploded in extreme violence. To this end, buildings were constructed according to specifications designed to preserve the wheat stored.[28] Moreover, as with the construction of the granary of Civitavecchia by Pope Benedict XIV, the *Annona* helped to strengthen the image of the pope, making visible, in the eyes of the people, the measures adopted "for the renewal and modernisation of the productive and commercial structures of the country".[29]

But, of course, in order to maintain the reserves and guarantee a constant supply, the *Annona* had to implement anti-hoarding procedures: this phenomenon was attributed to the wickedness of man rather than to any flaw in the victualling system. Investigations were carried out to identify those responsible for such frauds, and penalties were imposed on guilty parties, the severity being determined by the prevailing fear of hunger. Many proclamations (*bandi*) were issued "against hoarders of wheat, barley, legumes, and other crops, and no baron or other person shall issue proclamations or give orders intended to stop their transport to Rome": heavy penalties were imposed on those who set aside crops in quantities exceeding their personal needs. Many edicts (*editti*) were issued as well, where the names of all those who had sent the *assegne* (literally 'assignments', declarations on wheat production that had to be sworn annually by every community), together with the quantities declared, were published.[30]

However, these methods did not result in very comforting results. The massive state apparatus proved unable to fully thwart clandestine exports over time due to changes that were taking place elsewhere in Europe (in England and in the Netherlands), as well as in neighbouring countries (including Tuscany) and the special legations. Outside events increasingly undermined what was one of many systems inaugurated by the popes over the centuries, which benefited both secular and ecclesiastical potentates, but in this instance had a redistributive role inspired by rare bread-related social uprisings. Furthermore, smuggling and illegal export was sometimes committed by large merchants (who were often in close cahoots with central government), when the purchase price set by the *Annona* was too low to be profitable for them. Periodically, through the *assegne*, wheat surveys were carried out in order to know as precisely as possible the quantities of wheat harvested and sown in the country. Again, the purpose was to help guarantee an adequate supply to the city market.

The officials of the *Annona* obliged all producers to report, within a set deadline, the areas sown with wheat in view of the forthcoming harvest: the due time for declarations, published in the proclamations, ran from fifteen days to the whole month for those communities that were more than 40 miles from Rome (proclamations were usually published at the end of January). Frequent proclamations extended the terms for those who had failed to meet deadlines and wished to avoid fines and other penalties.[31] Generally, by 15 August of each year, an updated sworn declaration was issued to governors and *abbondanzieri* (the officials of the *Abbondanza*) on the quantities collected, those left from the previous year, the places where the wheat was kept, and the quantities necessary for the food needs of families and for sowing. The declarations were listed by the governors, or by other officials, in a special register, with the communities in alphabetical order, and then used for production statistics.[32]

The local private wheat trade was generally limited, and if, during favourable years, circulation was allowed from place to place within the *Distretto Annonario* (that is to say the *Districtus Urbis*), this was strictly regulated by the issuing of export or interprovincial transport licences (*tratte*) which attested the name of the seller, the quantity, and the selling price set by the victualling authorities. In 1721 Pope Innocent XIII appeared to take an innovative and more comprehensive approach to the problem of internal circulation, from province to province, than had been the case previously, when licences were approved only sporadically and in a questionable fashion. The new measure authorised to grant licences for 2 Roman *rubbia* of wheat for each *rubbio* of land cultivated with other crops, and 1 *rubbio* of wheat for each *rubbio* of land cultivated.[33]

Almost as soon as he rose to the papal throne, Benedict XIV issued the 30 March 1741 *In coena Domini* bull.[34] It reinforced ecclesiastical censures against all those who impeded the transport of crops to Rome. This pope, in the early years of his pontificate, continued the policy adopted by his predecessors through the annual enactment of rules that allowed crops to be traded at a certain time of the year, but only within the Papal States. In 1748, however, he published an act, as part of a general economic-financial reform policy, which can be considered an essential step towards establishing a definitive freedom of internal trade of victuals: the 29 June 1748 *costituzione* (literally, 'constitution') was known as *Benedicti divina Providentia Papae XIV constitutio super libero et mutuo commercio inter provincias, civitates, et loca ditionis temporalis Sanctae Sedis*, and was soon confirmed by the 8 July bull.[35] It represented a perfect osmosis between reformist thought and papal political activity, and offered an accurate analysis of the constraining apparatus of the crops trade. It was also a harsh attack against those ("subordinate officers and ministers" of the "legates, presidents, and governors of provinces") who had sabotaged the implementation of previous free trade provisions, in order to preserve those advantages that the prohibitionist system brought them.[36]

Despite the aim of juridically standardising the State, the pope practically divided it into two by adopting a different regime for the northern and southern provinces. So, while internal free trade was granted to the Legations of Bologna, Ferrara, Romagna, and Urbino, and to the Governorships of the March of Ancona and Umbria, it was denied to the Legation of Avignon, the Duchy of Benevento, the District of Rome, the Province of Sabina, the Governorships of Viterbo and Civitavecchia, and to the communities subordinated to the *Annona e Grascia* of Rome. This distinction was due to different production contexts in the two regions and to the lack, in the northern provinces, of a food consumption centre of a size comparable to that of Rome. It had been present in all previous free trade acts. Pope Clement XIII, in an edict from 11 March 1766,[37] extended full free trade rights to all territories, but they were immediately revoked due to the consequences that ensued.[38]

Those who could afford it agreed terms with farmers, securing the crops before the harvest: thus, crops hoarding impoverished the market and prompted price increases. Freedom of trade always remained subordinate to supply policy, all cities and towns being legally obliged to have sufficient foodstuffs on hand to satisfy consumption levels for at least one year. Commercial activity was largely unrestricted from the start of September to the end of May, but no crops could be taken out of provinces in June, July, or August under any circumstances, including by "our relatives, or the Roman pontiffs, our successors, and any other, even if privileged, and very privileged".[39] Food exports to foreign countries were generally forbidden, even in this act. The rare concessions that were issued could only be given by the pontiff: in the 1748 law, the details of licence requests and deadlines were minutely listed. The greatest threat to freedom of trade came from hoarders, who undermined both the agricultural sector and collective wellbeing, and took advantage of any hint of liberalism.

7.4 The *Tratte* and the Actors of the Wheat Circuits

The *tratte*, as it has stated before, were licences for exporting crops abroad or transporting them from one province of the State to another. They were granted—free of charge or against payment of a fee—with a pontifical chirograph (*chirografo*).[40] The system of these licences allowed the partial circulation of the crops harvested in years of abundance: the aim was to avoid waste of surplus produce, especially within the provinces, because the officials of the *Annona* warned that this would depress crops prices and agriculture generally. However, so structured, the apparatus allowed innumerable abuses and frauds. On the one hand, the discretionary power left to the victualling officials to grant licences created a vulnerability to corruption; on the other hand, producers could be less than truthful in declaring quantities of crops produced, thus avoiding requisitions of quantities that they could instead export illegally. The authorities came to have limited confidence in the accuracy of producers' declarations, however, so much so that the prefect of the *Annona* in concert with the chamberlain of the Apostolic Chamber often made recourse to notifications (*notificazioni*), proclamations, and edicts which obliged, in some cases, farmers and producers to repeat suspicious counts.[41] Equally scarce was the authorities' trust in merchants who, in order to obtain licences, declared large quantities of crops harvested without possessing a *rubbio* of land.[42]

Concessions of *tratte* often involved the release of quantities of crops well in excess of the sanctioned amount.[43] This could represent an additional cause of famine, as the few powerful merchants, lured by high profits from the sale of crops on foreign markets, were able to export huge quantities subtracted from the domestic supply.[44] The licences were granted on a regional basis according to the requests that were sent to the prefect of the *Annona* who, together with the particular delegated *congregazione*, selected the successful applicants.[45] For example, the 25 September 1756 bull regarded the concession of 10,000 *rubbia* at a price of 30 *baiocchi* per *rubbio* of wheat by the prefect of the *Annona*, who would decide to whom to grant licences, even free of charge, in the light of prevailing cereals production.[46] Yet another concession, this time by the secretary of State on 21 March 1761, was of 3,450 *rubbia* to the Order of Malta. On 17 August 1761, with a pontifical chirograph, licences were granted in favour of some contractors of the Apostolic Chamber and some 'privileged' individuals, for 20,000 *rubbia* of wheat. Further similar quantities were granted on 19 September 1761. On 23 September 1761, Carlo Ambrogio Lepri, a contractor of the Tolfa alunite mines, obtained a licence without paying any duty.

Table 7.1 shows the total amount in *rubbia* of the *tratte* that the central authority granted to contractors and merchants for, on the one hand, the *province annonarie*, and, on the other hand, the Legations of Ferrara, Romagna, and Urbino, and the Governorships of the March of Ancona and Umbria. It is obvious that the licences granted to the *province annonarie* were lower than to the other provinces, because of the lower produce of the firsts and of the presence of a large city like Rome. The licences granted to the *province annonarie* concerned, however, transports within the State: for the reasons stated, it was already a great privilege for them to be able to transport crops from one province to another without too many constraints. Furthermore, among the provinces exporting abroad, the March of Ancona obtained larger authorisations as the richest producing area in the country.[47]

However, it must also be kept in mind that many licences were granted free of charge and therefore not accounted for in the financial statements.

Table 7.1 Domestic *tratte* granted by the *Annona* of Rome to the *province annonarie* (1700–1797) and export *tratte* granted to the Legations of Ferrara, Romagna, and Urbino, and to the Governorships of the March of Ancona and Umbria (1710–1776)

Year	Domestic *tratte* (in Roman *rubbia*)	Export *tratte* (in Roman *rubbia*)
1700	9,700	
1701	8,800	
1702	15,500	
1703	21,500	
1704	27,900	
1705	41,100	
1706	32,000	
1707	2,600	
1708	–	
1709	10,800	
1710	11,700	29,564
1711	45,900	15,178
1712	39,400	24,474
1713	900	34,584
1714	8,900	60,211
1715	–	17,462
1716	1,100	4,340
1717	18,700	34,593
1718	14,500	31,847
1719	31,400	36,943
1720	5,000	38,514
1721	23,800	30,163
1722	13,700	28,483
1723	25,800	26,720
1724	300	27,793
1725	8,600	22,975
1726	9,100	32,685
1727	47,800	37,953
1728	10,500	25,963
1729	100	9,829
1730	20,700	37,395
1731	14,900	52,552
1732	2,700	11,654
1733	5,700	9,417
1734	22,100	44,582
1735	–	3,480

(*continued*)

Table 7.1 (continued)

Year	Domestic *tratte* (in Roman *rubbia*)	Export *tratte* (in Roman *rubbia*)
1736	21,100	66,690
1737	20,200	87,292
1738	23,700	61,620
1739	35,600	63,151
1740	8,000	–
1741	22,700	78,007
1742	–	2,440
1743	–	–
1744	–	3,375
1745	2,500	23,500
1746	33,800	29,835
1747	–	4,100
1748	9,700	28,355
1749	–	24,150
1750	–	61,529
1751	–	12,500
1752	11,000	47,430
1753	2,400	62,995
1754	21,200	102,820
1755	23,900	8,500
1756	31,200	76,700
1757	18,800	67,610
1758	4,100	117,000
1759	–	2,000
1760	11,200	52,500
1761	36,200	132,700
1762	21,700	97,675
1763	–	15,000
1764	–	–
1765	–	3,000
1766	–	1,200
1767	–	–
1768	–	3,850
1769	39,100	35,450
1770	57,100	96,350
1771	–	23,200
1772	–	59,300
1773	–	–
1774	–	–
1775	12,700	53,650

(*continued*)

Table 7.1 (continued)

Year	Domestic *tratte* (in Roman *rubbia*)	Export *tratte* (in Roman *rubbia*)
1776	53,500	108,500
1777	13,200	
1778	17,900	
1779	–	
1780	–	
1781	–	
1782	–	
1783	–	
1784	–	
1785	–	
1786	4,800	
1787	11,200	
1788	28,500	
1789	–	
1790	–	
1791	–	
1792	–	
1793	–	
1794	–	
1795	–	
1796	–	
1797	–	

Sources: ASRM, PAG, 464, 1950; CII, 2, 22

This privilege was enjoyed by the contractors of the Apostolic Chamber, the treasurers, the customs officials of Patrimonio, the *fattore* of Farfa, the States of Castro and Ronciglione, and some pious places (not to mention the anomalous concessions made at the price of huge mediations or cash gifts in favour of victualling officials). Other well-paid rights represented both the purchase and the exercise of the office of crops *rassegnatore* (literally, 'reviewer'), and very often those who held this role were members of the Roman *Curia* themselves. This is probably one of the reasons why the licence system was maintained and the attempts to liberalise the crops trade boycotted. Other exceptions included the perpetual grant, by Pope Innocent XII's 9 June 1696 chirograph, of *tratte* for no less than 300 *rubbia* to Corneto and 100 *rubbia* to Toscanella.[48]

Victualling officials themselves also occasionally enjoyed the privileges of the concession of *tratte*: for example, Gaetano Cacciari "and fellow apprentices of the galleys and pontifical ships in Civitavecchia" obtained the concession of a licence for 10,000 *rubbia* of maize, beans, and other legumes under a pontifical chirograph from 3 February 1762.[49] Of course, the authorisation was subject to the fact that the local public *Abbondanze* and bakeries had the quantity of crops necessary to satisfy the needs of their communities.[50] The letters of Tommaso Ricotti make it clear that it was he who invited the prefect of the *Annona* to grant the licences to the Marca in seasons in which a good harvest was expected and to advise farmers on export markets so that they could reap the greatest profit (on 5 August 1770, for instance, he advised his correspondent to export crops to the Kingdom of Naples, where they would be hoarded, or to Spain, which had requested supplies from Sicily).[51] Sometimes licences were granted as a reward to those producers who had sent part of their crops to Rome.[52]

Of course, in years of low yield, concessions were suspended to prevent exports, further impacting the levels of habitual consumption of the population. If in theory this system had some advantages, there was no real benefit to either farmers or the coffers of the *Annona*, let alone the wider country's economy. Farmers, in fact, rarely had an opportunity to take advantage of their licences because, under pressure from creditors or tax officials, they very often found themselves needing to sell the crops as soon as possible, and prices were lowest immediately after harvest because supplies were rapidly plentiful. Cultivation dropped because farmers did not want to sell at unsatisfactory prices or see their crops rot away while waiting for prices to rise. Neither did the Apostolic Chamber benefit hugely from selling licences, because most were granted to the contractors of the Apostolic Chamber with pre-existing deals.[53] The *tratte* system favoured, above all, the great merchants.[54]

The ban on the export of crops constituted an indirect obstacle to importation, and this did nothing to ensure availability in precarious domestic production conditions. Foreign merchants preferred to direct their attention to those markets that guaranteed freedom of export and from where they could export any unsold quantities at market prices. For this reason, the 30 April 1786 edict, issued by Pius VI, concerning customs duties, is of considerable importance.[55] Pius VI's general reform programme had the objective of gradually abolishing all fiscal burdens in the provinces of Romagna, March of Ancona, Umbria, Patrimonio, Campagna and Marittima, Lazio, and Sabina, including the Duchies of Spoleto and Urbino, and the State of Ronciglione.[56] The damage done to farmers by the constraints imposed, the spread of alarmist rumours about the harvest, the hiding of stocks, and the prohibition of exports, meant that secular and ecclesiastical potentates all took advantage of the constraints imposed by the victualling administration. They bought the licences made available annually by the governing bodies (assisted by lavish donations to the victualling officials), obtaining much greater profits from the sale of wheat abroad than were available at the *Annona*'s fixed domestic price level. They were not interested in expanding the market or increasing production, for the *status quo* allowed them to obtain maximum profits despite the constraints imposed.[57]

The division of the territory into large estates and the restrictive legislation of the wheat trade favoured, therefore, nobles and ecclesiastics to the detriment of the small owners and cultivators who had to sell at low prices immediately after harvest and were rarely in a position to capitalise on their licences. It took Pius VI's reforms to reverse this trend. He coupled international protectionism with internal liberalisation and promoted greater uniformity in the administration of cities and provinces. Notwithstanding the constraints imposed by the victualling administration, wheat prices could not completely escape market rules, and they settled at different levels than the price considered for setting the weight of bread. The business transacted in the two main sales channels, that of *Campo de' Fiori* and that of the merchants, confirms this thesis: it was impossible for the *Annona* to impose its power on any negotiation, even those involving quantitatively lower purchases than those carried out by the *Annona*. Merchants, especially the so-called *mercanti di campagna* (the merchants coming from the *Campagna Romana*, or *Agro Romano*, the plain and hills south-west of Rome), usually rented at least one estate from a single owner (or sometimes from several owners). They cultivated a part of the land, while sub-letting the remainder to a certain number of farmers: in any case, the *mercanti di campagna* were not simple farmers—given that they also carried out other activities connected to the land, activities that procured them further profits—but real agricultural entrepreneurs. Their number was small, increasing from 70 in the early eighteenth century to 138 in the early nineteenth century. They were mainly merchants and as such formed the backbone of the narrow Roman bourgeoisie.[58]

At first glance accounting records indicate that the prices of wheat traded on the city market in *Campo de' Fiori* was lower than on the merchants' circuit. This is a simplification, however. The difference depended on the specificities of the two sales channels. Larger institutions and artisans operating in cereals processing (such as bakers, who will be discussed below) could not obtain supplies from the market of *Campo de' Fiori* (the square where the officials of the *Annona* sold wheat), but had to buy wheat exclusively on the merchants' circuit. Small producers cultivating the land around Rome first fed themselves before bringing any surplus to the *Campo de' Fiori* market, where stocks were immediately taken under the control of the *Annona* officials. The buyers were mostly from the middle class and popular classes. The merchants preferred to sell from warehouses, always in the presence of an official in charge of measurements, who recorded prices, quality, quantity, identities of sellers and buyers, and origin and destination of the exchanged goods. The obligation to purchase wheat from merchants increased their bargaining power in negotiations with bakers.

On the one hand, the quantities sold at *Campo de' Fiori* reflected production levels very closely because they were based on the surplus of small farmers: the scarcer was production, the smaller was small farmers' surplus. Furthermore, the quantity placed on the market visibly diminished as the year progressed. On the other hand, merchants' sales were less conditioned by the results of the harvest as the great owners possessed means and structures capable of preserving large quantities of crops and maintaining its quality. Therefore, when production levels dropped and prices increased, merchants released stored crops to the market and maximised profits.[59] Price variability was higher in the case of the wheat sold in *Campo de' Fiori* than by merchants, due to the strict relationship between the quantity harvested and that supplied on the market. On the one hand, the obligation to entirely sell the stock helped to limit prices in *Campo de' Fiori*, especially when production levels were high. On the other hand, poor harvests meant that prices increased so much in *Campo de' Fiori* that the gap between the two channels narrowed substantially. This means that the system in force succeeded in damping down prices at times of abundance, while at times of scarcity it was powerless against the market laws.[60]

As for the bakers of Rome, the third party involved in this system, they complained that they could not profitably exercise their trade. The totality of the bakeries depended on the *Annona*. The so-called 'free bakeries' (*forni liberi*), whose existence is known through the registers of the pontifical chirographs, were very rare. This was due to the fact that they were precluded from receiving wheat from the *Annona* and, as a consequence, they did not enjoy the protection of minimum selling prices, which constituted a safety net against market drops. Regulations governing free bakeries were published by Pius VI on 16 September 1782. These bakeries could buy wheat from the *Annona* in two ways: *a rinnovo* (literally, 'by renewal', that is to say, by giving back by instalments the wheat received[61]) and *a contanti* (that is to say by cash, but only at current market prices and not at the blocked prices that the *Annona* made available to *baioccanti* bakers). Furthermore, the bread produced in free bakeries had to be sold separately from the cheaper bread of *baioccanti*, and to this aim had to be marked with distinctive signs.[62] The other bakers could be *decinanti* or *baioccanti*. The first prepared good-quality bread,[63] and the second poorer bread designed for mass consumption and sold in loaves at the price of one *baiocco* each, whence their name.[64] In Rome there were 11 bakeries managed by *decinanti* in 1754, 12 in 1764, and 15 in 1781, while the bakeries managed by *baioccanti* fell from 68 in 1754, 50 in 1781, and 45 in 1782.[65]

Although some contemporary economists expressed a positive opinion about the considerable advantages enjoyed by bakers over farmers, the trade suffered many failures during the eighteenth century, particularly the *baioccanti*: this was mainly due to the fact that they lacked strong permanent ties with large trade and laboured under constant, stifling government surveillance and control.[66] Each neighbourhood (*rione*) of Rome was assigned an *Annona* commissioner who recorded the location and number of *decinanti* and *baioccanti* bakeries therein.[67] The opening of a bakery, public or private, was authorised by pontifical chirograph and subject to the control of the prefect.[68] So-called 'privileged' (*privilegiati*) bakeries were not obliged to buy wheat from the *Annona* by cash or *a rinnovo*. In 1764 there were five such bakeries, namely those of San Giovanni, San Pietro, Santa Maria Maggiore, Santo Spirito, and *Casa Rospigliosi*, Duke of Zagarolo.[69] The possibility of opening this kind of bakeries was given to landowners producing wheat: it was a manner for encouraging this type of cultivation, together with additional facilitation, such as the possibility of keeping a part of the wheat for sowing. There were also other bakeries, called *a soccio*,[70] whose owners used to bake for "those particular people kneading the bread in their own homes".[71]

In Viterbo, the provincial capital city of the Patrimonio, there were *a soccio* bakeries as well as other bakeries, called *a diecina*.[72] They baked "for religious houses, and for particular persons and families".[73] These families provided wheat to the baker, either owner or tenant of the bakery. The baker had to mill the wheat, reduce it into flour, flatten it, and bake it before delivering at least 44 *diecine* of bread for each *rubbio* of wheat provided;[74] the profit for the baker consisted of the remaining bran (*tritello* and *semola*) and flour. The weight of the loaves produced in these bakeries should not be equal to that of the loaves produced in the public bakery (*pubblico forno venale*).[75] In Rome, there were other bakers called *vermicellari*, *ciambellonari*, and *maccheronari*, named after the particular pasta shapes they produced.[76] Near the granaries of the Baths, a shop sold flour retail 'for the benefit of the poor' (*a benefizio de' poveri*): since prices were kept low, as bakers and merchants would otherwise take advantage, individuals were limited to purchasing 50 Roman *libbre* (almost 17 kilos) of flour.[77]

With only a few exceptions (such as in case of famine), the weight of one regular loaf of *a baiocco* bread remained fixed at 8 *once*, while that of one loaf of *a diecina* bread was fixed at 10 *once*.[78] Bakers had to be licensed to prepare bread at a lower weight for use by some pious place or in some other special circumstance. Naturally, the interested bakers had to worry about keeping these loaves separate because they were not for retail sale, with severe penalties for transgressors, up to closure of business.[79] A mechanism of automatic adjustment regulated the price of bread. This was defined by Pope Paul V in 1606[80] and remained in force until the end of the eighteenth century when, with the increase in fiscal burdens for *baioccanti* bakers, "it ceased *de facto* to have legal force, although in the following years the customary values of the relationship between the two quantities [that is to say, between the selling prices of the victualling administration and the fixed weight of bread] continued to be rebalanced according to its criteria".[81] On 2 September 1800, a *motu proprio* gave notice of a new[82] system of "breadmaking to be observed permanently in places situated within 40 miles from Rome", and "price-controlled bread in proportion of the free cost of cereals" was established.[83] The price and weight varied from week to week depending on current wheat prices and once posted they had to be observed by bakers.[84]

Bakeries usually operated under contracts that were put up for public auction. Bakeries could be contracted in the various communities of the provinces of the Papal States, and in this case it was the *Sacra Congregazione del Buon Governo* that regulated the formalities. Bakeries had a monopoly over *pan venale* (literally, 'bread for sale', meaning ordinary bread). No one else, even ecclesiastics, could produce such bread or put 'foreign' (*forestiero*) bread on the market. However, bread resellers (*panecocoli*) were allowed to sell the bread they received.[85] The contractors were obliged to a three-month supply of wheat to hand.[86] Special rules were laid down in the event that a community could not contract out the bakery.[87] It was necessary to calculate the consumption of *pan venale* for the last six years, for the local council to approve the opening of an *Abbondanza* and to establish the quantity of wheat to be supplied, which, according to the rules, should not exceed one-sixth of consumption of the last six years. In addition, a board of management was to be formed for the *Abbondanza*, composed of the governor, the municipal magistracy, the officials (*abbondanzieri*) elected by the municipal council, and the deputies of the ecclesiastics, plus any designated members. The sources are very meticulous in describing the costs incurred by the bakers: using the Albano bakery, one of the most active bakeries in Rome and the District,[88] the daily entrances and exits of a *pan venale* bakery were calculated.[89]

7.5 Conclusions

Beyond closely intertwined personal and economic interests, consumer protection, and price stability were the *Annona*'s priorities. As Revel's thinking,[90] this strategy accentuated the financial pressure that the system faced in its efforts to supply a consistent stream of wheat to bakers. Balance sheets from 1713–1743 make all of this quite explicit and provide a very clear indication of how things were developing in the eighteenth century. Numerous bakers' and farmers' voices—two classes that had long suffered the negative effects of oscillating provisions—were raised against the victualling system. The quantity of food supplies was always guaranteed, but sometimes at too high a cost. The *Annona*, having to import wheat, carried a considerable financial burden, especially during times of famine: furthermore, unlike merchants, it could not redeem purchasing costs on the market, having to respect its policy of containing selling prices in favour of consumers, especially the less well off. Fig. 7.1, representing the relationship between purchase and sale prices of the wheat distributed by the *Annona*, demonstrates that there is no correlation between the two series ($r = 0.35$): an increase in purchase prices did not correspond to a proportional increase in sale prices. At the first appearance of the first difficulties and price strains, market intervention seemed an urgent necessity everywhere, and the measures implemented to control the victualling system fully demonstrated their anti-cyclical nature.

In the first place, there was a tendency to control the volume of the supply. The objective was not to increase production, because the public

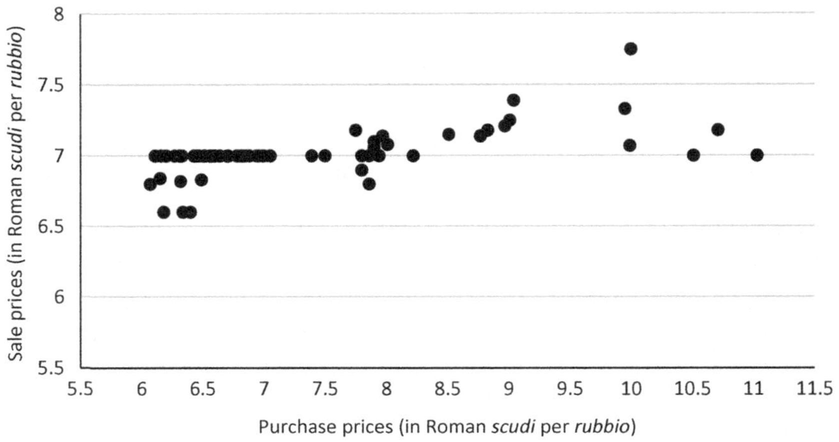

Fig. 7.1 Purchase and sale prices of the wheat distributed by the Roman *Annona* (eighteenth century). (Sources: ASR, PAG, 1963–1976, 2212–2249; BA, 460; CIIA, 22 (60); CIIAB, 110–115)

authorities were not equipped to achieve this in the short term. Instead, the aim was to increase the volume of goods available on the legal market, both locally produced and possibly imported. Furthermore, there was a tendency to control the volume of demand, both to prevent rapid depletion of reserves and to facilitate market access for the less well off. Again, attempts were made to intervene on the crucial point of these complex mechanisms, namely the price level. The increasingly strong interventionism of the eighteenth century briefly led the Roman *Annona* to control prices by officially setting them and through orders and measures that obeyed the logic of the ethical rationalisation of economic activities. When they were not sufficient, victualling authorities organised bodies, institutions, administrations, and financial supplies (as in the case of public debt) according to market economic terms, that is to say, buying wheat wherever they could do it and at any price, and then selling it at reasonable prices on the domestic market. Ultimately, the victualling authorities acted like all other economic operators, creating a monopoly market to which private operators were admitted under precise terms, terms which served the interests of the public administration. Their machinations on the supply side were often successful; on the contrary, given that demand was strongly inelastic for foodstuffs, their ambitions were harder to realise in this respect. But the two combined operations often succeeded in mitigating the most devastating effects of famine.

The irresolvability of the financial problem and the system of the so-called *latifondo* (that is to say large and extensively cultivated estates) held back any reform designed to develop the productivity of agriculture. With the 25 January 1783 *motu proprio*, Pius VI, on the basis of the land registry, imposed the observance of the obligation of cultivating a third of the land. Under the terms of the *motu proprio*, and on the basis of the knowledge of the exact extent of the Roman estates, a system of checks was organised to be carried out each March. Unfortunately, this routine did not manage to stimulate production and advance agriculture. The conditions and the privileges that determined the expansion of the large estates were not definitively cancelled by Pius VI. Nevertheless, he must be credited with perceiving the need for a new system. He attempted to contribute to reform criteria because it was not convenient for the State to intervene to support current prices. It was more appropriate to promote improved organisation of production for the market, considered its natural outlet.

The attempted reforms failed to curb the decline of the victualling system, however, and its debt spiralled. The administration did not have the technical means necessary to keep this process under control: in fact, from the arrival of the wheat in the warehouses until the receipt of payment, between two and four years passed. The scale of arrears due to suppliers pointed to both financial and administrative disorder. Furthermore, the persistent financial pressure meant that the *Annona* resorted, more and more frequently, to bank loans.[91] But public banks would no longer lend to the *Annona* before the end of the century, since its loans were never cleared. Usually, in all kinds of credit, lenders and borrowers were opposed on a very unequal basis.[92] In the agricultural sector, for example, the *Annona*, as evidenced by its budgets, had significant functions in granting loans in both cash and wheat. It had the right of pre-emption on the wheat of its debtors,[93] and during the course of the century, especially in areas of more intense cereals production, local administrations established an almost exclusive relationship with large producers, financing them alone and leaving small producers at the mercy of local usurers.[94]

Noting that the prefect of the *Annona* and provincial commissioners made loans for sowing to farmers who, instead, sold wheat speculatively, it was decided that farmers themselves could not sell wheat if they had not already cleared their debt with the *Annona* or obtained permission from the prefect or commissioner to sell a part of the wheat harvested to honour that debt. Very often it was the merchants who directly entered into agreements with farmers, securing wheat before the harvest. Thus, wheat hoarding impoverished the market and spurred price increases.[95] In particular, among the loan options, public debt was to be incurred not only to solve the financial problems of a city like Rome, but also to solve those of the State. Loans to farmers or communities for the completion of normal agricultural tasks were issued through the *monti pubblici camerali* (literally, 'public Chamber mounts'), the system of public debt created by the Apostolic Chamber. The elements that made up the *monti* were the *luoghi* (literally, 'places', meaning shares), bonds which were the minimal divisional unit with which creditors could make transactions. Loans by the *monti* were granted by papal chirographs, by which new bonds were issued, increasing the capital which had been established at the time of the creation of the *monte*.[96] The *Annona*, by the end of the sixteenth century, was able to draw on funds raised in this fashion to carry out its ever-expanding functions. Some revenue arrived indirectly through the collection of taxes on these bonds;[97] other revenue came through the erection of *monti* for a particular purpose.[98]

In the case of the communities of the Papal States, this technique was used with the consent of the central authorities so that, in some cases, the management of the issuance of bonds was delegated directly to the communities and the provinces using the work of private intermediaries or of the *Sacra Congregazione del Buon Governo* and, in any case, with the approval of the government. Moreover, since the communities, including large communities struggling under growing financial burdens and current expenses, were often forced to turn to large capitalists under 'usury' conditions, they considered access to credit through bonds (for uses as diverse as building a bridge, provisioning a bakery, or purchasing wheat for the *monti frumentari*, both for consumption and for sowing) much more convenient.[99] Interest rates were lower, and the repayment of the capital sum to the underwriters-creditors took place gradually and, depending on the availability, by drawing, albeit with a bimonthly obligation for the payment of part of the annual interest.

This public debt was an all-pontifical model that constituted a unique case in the European panorama between the sixteenth and eighteenth centuries. It represented, for Rome and the Papal States, an important support to the 'charity model' (represented by charitable institutions, financial instruments created for a particular purpose, as in the case of several *monti camerali* and *monti comunitativi*, that is to say, created for particular communities of the country or confraternities), that contributed, especially in

Rome, to maintaining peace and economic stability. The failure and the subsequent bankruptcy petition of the *Annona* in 1805, which marked the relative abandonment of the old system, represented the consequences of maintaining a system that was no longer fit for purpose and could not meet the State's need for self-transformation; however, it must be added that this was only one financial element amid the collapse of an entire model of economic policy and the diffusion of the liberal principles underlying the new capitalist economic system that was establishing itself at European level.

Notes

1. On historical training and on organisational aspects, see the specific works of Palermo (1986, pp. 79–81); (1990, 1991, 1994).
2. Among others, see Dal Pane (1932, p. 76); Palermo and Strangio (1997); Clément (1999).
3. Tilly (1984, p. 242).
4. Braudel and Spooner (1967, p. 392).
5. Gross (1990, p. 200).
6. Massimo Montanari (1993, pp. 189–190) made a periodisation of the history of cereals consumption.
7. See Schumpeter (1959 [1954], vol. I, p. 256); Palermo (1997, pp. 112–115). On the model of behaviour of cereals prices elaborated by Gregory King, see Guitton (1938); Romano (1967, p. xii); Slicher Van Bath (1972 [1963], pp. 165–166); Grigg (1980, p. 51); Wrigley (1987); Fogel (1992, pp. 255–261). On the mechanisms that determine the trend in wheat prices in relation to the structure of supply and demand, see Grenier (1996); Persson (1996). These tools support the fact that the purchase of basic necessities at any price was inevitable for the sake of survival itself, "because the fear of being without food was an essential component of the consumer behaviour of the time and pushed him to quickly exhaust the cereal goods offered in the markets", simultaneously considering also the two aspects of utility and of the costs, or tastes and obstacles, developed by Pareto (Ravallion 1997, p. 1219). Here and below, all translations of original documents and works quoted are the author's.
8. Palermo (1990, p. 22).
9. The problem of land yields in the Early Modern Age is one of the most treated and interesting issues concerning the study of cereals productivity, see Slicher Van Bath (1972 [1963], pp. 332–363). On Rome, see Nicolai (1803, vol. III); De Cupis (1911); Revel (1982); Reinhardt (1991).

10. The failed attempts at reform with Pope Lambertini, Benedict XIV, have been discussed several times; only with Pope Braschi, Pius VI, did they arouse a public debate, but once again there were different resistances, especially in the agricultural field where the pope's attention had been greater. In reality the reformism of the two most significant pontiffs cannot be defined as mercantilist or free trade, but their economic policy was characterised by a mixture of mercantilist and liberal elements which, even if delayed, demonstrate the need for the government to investigate the new trends: see Dal Pane (1957, 1959b [1954–1955]) and Piscitelli (1951), who demonstrated in their works how Pius VI had prepared his economic policy since the time of Pope Clement XIII and how his programmes were inspired by the 'economic thought' of Ferdinando Nuzzi (1702), Leone Pascoli (1733), and Ridolfino Venuti (Eschinardi 1750 [1696]).
11. ASRM, CIIA, 22.
12. ASRM, CIIA, 22. See the documents of the proceeding opened against Bischi, who had been accused of abusing his charge in completing some contracts.
13. De Cupis (1911); Canaletti Gaudenti (1947); Nicolai (1803). Jean Delumeau (1957–1959) extensively dealt with the problem of wheat in the Papal States, as well as Alberto Aubert (1986), who described the various attempts to introduce centralised systems for the supply of food during the crisis experienced by Rome under the pontificate of Paul IV. On the Roman *Annona* during the eighteenth century, see Dal Pane (1959a); Venturi (1963); (1973, pp. 987–1120). These works are dedicated, as part of a broader interest in the economic and administrative reform of the eighteenth century, especially to the legal and administrative conditions of the victualling offices.
14. Revel (1972); Strangio (1999a); Sabene (2017).
15. In this regard, see Falchi et al. (1995). Still on the role and weight of the *Annona* in regulating the Roman market, see Piola Caselli (1998, pp. 136–139).
16. In the balance sheets (ASRM, PAG, 1962–1969) the first twenty-five years of the century appear frequently with the name of a certain Guglielmotti, later replaced by Cacciari, who was in charge of purchasing cereals on behalf of the *Annona* in the port of Civitavecchia. In Corneto operated a commissioner named Ronca, replaced in 1731 by a certain Falzacappa; in Vetralla there was a certain Marini, while in Ancona, until 1770, it was Tommaso Ricotti, whose close correspondence with the prefect of the *Annona* is kept in ASRM, PAG, 1528.
17. See Monaco (1971, pp. 57–58); (1974, p. 72). 1 Roman mile (*miglio*) corresponded to approximately 1,489.48 metres (Martini 1883, p. 596). Due to the different composition of the territories, the climatic conditions,

the natural resources, and the previous historical development, the State presented a varied appearance. The internal division made the individual provinces separate and distinct from one another, even with customs barriers that hindered internal trade, with their own currency and with their own system of weights and measures, which complicated trade (see Caracciolo 1978, pp. 525–536).

18. Franco Corridore (1906, p. 23) wrote that the District of Rome in the mid-eighteenth century "stretched along the Mediterranean to the borders of Tuscany, entering in the continent for more than 60 miles". This extension underwent some changes around the second half of the following century, "when it was limited to the suburban and baronial lands of the capital city and to the district governments of Tivoli and Subiaco".
19. See Guenzi (1981, p. 153); (1982b, p. 295). This scholar also addressed the different aspects of the Bolognese victualling matter, from prices to the role of bakers, to city consumption (Guenzi 1977, 1978, 1982a).
20. With regard to the *monti frumentari* and their functions, see, among others, Checcoli (2015).
21. In ASRM there are many documents relating to the activity of these institutions; a part is kept in CBGV, 179; CIIA, 16; CIC, 171, 178; LMG, 3188–3191.
22. See Lodolini (1953, 1956); Tabacchi (2007).
23. The birth certificate of the *Congregazione*, which is usually dated to Pope Clement VIII and the year 1592, must actually be found in the most general one of modern papal administration, that is to say, in the bull *Immensa aeterni Dei*, with which Pope Sixtus V, on 22 January 1588, established the fifteen congregations for the spiritual government of the Church and for the temporal government of the Papal States. Among these, the ninth—*Pro gravaminibus sublevandis* or *Congregazione degli Sgravi* ('Congregation of Reliefs')—was one of the two branches that merged to form the *Sacra Congregazione degli Sgravi e Buon Governo*. The cardinals in charge of the dicastery were named prefects of the Congregation. The *Congregazione* was suppressed in February 1798, following the proclamation of the Roman Republic.
24. ASRM, CBGIV, 995, fos. 162–166.
25. In order to have a complete and concise idea of the papal administrative and financial organisation, see Stumpo (1985). For a vast bibliography on the Apostolic Chamber, see Del Re (1998 [1941]); Pastura Ruggiero (1984).
26. Important reflections by Palermo et al. (2018).
27. On famines and their consequences, see, among others, Ó Gráda (2009).
28. Da Gai (1994, pp. 165–166).
29. Da Gai (1994, p. 169).

30. "[C]ontro gli incettatori di grano, orzo, biade e legumi e che nessun barone, o altra persona faccia bandi, o ordini per impedirne il trasporto in Roma" (ASRM, CIIA, 2–89; CPD, 78). See also ASRM, BA, 456–460, years 1700–1801; 44, 29 November 1703 proclamation; 48, 13 August 1708 proclamation; 51, 19 May 1714 and 25 May 1716; 91, 3 July 1754; 96, 10 December 1759; 458, 10 December 1767 edict; 109, 25 July 1772 proclamation.
31. ASRM, BA, 456–460.
32. ASRM, PAG, 464.
33. *Rubbio* (plur. *rubbia*) was the name of both a unit of surface and of volume: as a unit of surface, 1 Roman *rubbio* corresponded to approximately 18,484.38 square metres; as a unit of volume, it corresponded to approximately 294.47 cubic decimetres (Martini 1883, p. 597; on Roman measures, see also Eusebio 1899).
34. AAV, BBIII, year 1741.
35. ASRM, BA, 85, 457. Interesting studies on this norm were made by Luigi Dal Pane (1965) and Franco Venturi (1983, pp. 76–79).
36. "[U]fficiali e ministri subalterni", "legati, presidi e governatori di province" (ASRM, BA, 85, 29 June 1748 constitution, fos. iv–v).
37. BCRM, BA, year 1766 (77).
38. ASRM, BA, 457.
39. "[F]amigliari nostri, o de' romani pontefici *pro tempore* nostri successori, ed altri qualsivoglia ancorché privilegiati, e privilegiatissimi" (Campilli 1783, pp. 97–98).
40. ASRM, CIIA, 16.
41. ASRM, CPD, 78.
42. ASRM, CIIA, 16. On their names and on those who were privileged, see Strangio (2004).
43. In ASRM, BA, 456–460, and PAGCB, 2287, a fairly large legislative production is preserved relative to the export and also to the free trade of cereals within the State: 24 December 1710 edict (Chamberlain Spinola); 2 April 1719 chirograph (Pope Clement XI); 11 May 1719 notification (Chamberlain Albani); 27 September 1721 chirograph (Pope Innocent XIII); 15 October 1725 constitution (Pope Benedict XIII); 10 August 1740 notification (Chamberlain Albani); 29 June 1748 constitution (Pope Benedict XIV); 16 September 1782 edict (Chamberlain Rezzonico); 22 August 1788 edict (Chamberlain Rezzonico); 9 August 1793 edict (Chamberlain Rezzonico); 24 October 1793 edict (Chamberlain Rezzonico); 16 July 1796 circular; 2 September 1800 *motu proprio* (Pope Pius VII); 10 April 1801 chirograph (Pope Pius VII); 4 November 1801 constitution (Pope Pius VII).
44. Romagna mainly supplied Ferrara and Bologna. The March of Ancona had a surplus wheat production fluctuating between 30,000 and 70,000 *rub-*

bia, to which the *Annona* of Rome often made recourse. In general, the production of the so-called *province annonarie* (literally, 'victualling provinces': Lazio in the strict sense—whose central part was the *Agro Romano*—Campagna and Marittima, Sabina, Patrimonio, see Martinat 2004, p. 121) appears to be inadequate—especially as regards Upper Sabina—as well as that of Umbria and of the Duchy of Urbino.

45. ASRM, PAGCB, 2287.
46. In the Roman monetary system of account, 1 *scudo* (plur. *scudi*) was divided into 10 *giuli* or *paoli*, and 1 *giulio* or *paolo* into 10 *baiocchi* (Balbi De Caro and Londei 1984, pp. 55, 61, 89, 127; Londei 1990, pp. 308, 311–318).
47. See Zucchini (1968).
48. ASRM, PAGCB, 2287. See also Strangio (2000), where, among the sources, a manuscript is examined with the title *Saggio di un nuovo regolamento per l'Annona di Roma* ('Essay on new regulations for the *Annona* of Rome'). In this manuscript, the 'very privileged' (*privilegiatissime*) licences, which were granted by the chamberlain without a particular chirograph of the pope, are indicated for the March of Ancona and the Duchy of Urbino, as well as the general list of the persons who enjoyed the 'privileged' (*privilegiate*) licences on the basis of contracts stipulated with the Reverend Apostolic Chamber.
49. "[E] compagni apprendisti delle galere e navi pontificie a Civitavecchia" (ASRM, PAGCB, 2287).
50. ASRM, BA, 457, 20 August 1743 edict, point 6.
51. ASRM, PAG, 1528.
52. ASRM, BA, 456–460. In a notification dated 27 August 1760 to the March of Ancona and Romagna, the prefect undertook to grant free licences for the same amount of wheat that would have led to Rome directly, establishing a purchase price of 7 *scudi* per *rubbio*—in the case of that transported to the deposits of the *Annona*—or of 6 *scudi*—in the case of that transported to the port of Civitavecchia—(ASRM, BA, 458).
53. ASRM, CIIA, 2–9, 16–39; ASRM, CIIC, 8–15.
54. See Arias (1908, pp. 11–17); Canaletti Gaudenti (1920, p. 476).
55. ASRM, BA, 460.
56. It was believed that it was necessary to maintain only three taxes, namely that on milling, that on salt, and that based on the assessment of the contributing capacity (*estimo*). In relation to this the communities had to abolish any existing tax pertaining to them on such subjects.
57. See Ciasca (1956).
58. ASRM, CSI; Girelli (2000).
59. ASRM, FMC, 17; ASRM, PAGNG, 367–408 (years 1700–1775).
60. Sabene (2017, pp. 78–81); see also Sabene (2016).

61. It was a widely used practice (ASRM, CIIAB, 110–115; see also Martinat 2004, p. 16).
62. ASRM, BA, 459, 16 September 1782 *Editto sopra la destinazione dei forni a baiocco, e dei forni liberi della città di Roma.*
63. See Campilli (1783, p. 43). As evidence of the delicate and important role that the bakers and millers played, Steven Kaplan dedicated several chapters of his work to this theme (Kaplan 1984, pp. 221–465, namely chapters vi–xii). See also de Vries (2019).
64. The *baiocco* was also a mixture coin.
65. ASRM, CIIA, 3; ASRM, BA, 459, 16 September 1782 edict. See Campilli (1783, p. 43).
66. As for the bread *a baiocco*, from the sources it appears that on average a baker of Rome prepared about 2,700 loaves, every day, for the 'people' (ASRM, CIIA, 22).
67. ASRM, CIIA, 3.
68. Benedict XIII, with a pontifical chirograph dated 10 March 1728, gave "full authority to Prince Marc'Antonio Borghese to make his own bakery for white bread, as had been the case for Cardinal Barberini, Duke Rospigliosi, the Chapter of San Giovanni in Laterano [...] for use of his house and family without selling it" ("piena facoltà al principe Marc'Antonio Borghese di fabbricare un forno suo proprio per il pane bianco, come era stato per il Cardinale Barberini, il Duca Rospigliosi, il Capitolo di San Giovanni in Laterano [...] per uso della sua casa e famiglia senza venderlo"). Its construction was completed in July 1728 (ASRM, CIIA, 2).
69. In 1781 they became four because the bakery of Santa Maria Maggiore had become *baioccante* (Campilli 1783, p. 43).
70. The owners of these bakeries earned 6 *paoli* per *rubbio* for baking bread.
71. "[Q]uelle particolari persone, che spianano il pane nelle proprie loro case" (Campilli 1783, p. 44).
72. Filippo Campilli was governor of this province from 8 July 1773 to 17 February 1781.
73. "[P]er le case religiose, e per le particolari persone, e famiglie" (Campilli 1783, p. 45). In Viterbo in 1716 there were two *a diecina* bakeries, which had the obligation to pay the community 300 *scudi*. The victualling authorities had also issued regulations concerning the purchases made by Jews, who bought bread in the bakeries indicated to them by the *Annona*. Since these were not sufficient for their needs, the order was given by the prefect of *Annona*, towards the middle of the century, to dedicate two bakeries, belonging to Christians, to the sale of bread by Jews.
74. 1 *diecina* was equal to 10 Roman *libbre*; 1 Roman *libbra* ('pound', plur. *libbre*) was divided into 12 *once* ('ounces') and corresponded to approximately 339.07 grams (Martini 1883, p. 598).

75. Campilli (1783, p. 46).
76. Between the fourteenth and sixteenth centuries, the predominant origin of the bakers was, above all, Florentine and Bavarian; subsequently, between 1559 and 1613, Roman bakers (*la Romanità*), taking note of the ever-increasing internationalisation of trades, began to take measures to protect their status (in this regard, see Schulz 1991, 1994).
77. ASRM, BA, 458.
78. These weights corresponded, respectively, to 226.05 and 282.56 grams. With the 22 March 1764 edict, it was established that the weight of one *a baiocco* loaf should be reduced to 6 *once*, while that of a *a diecina* loaf had to be reduced to 8 *once* like homemade bread, as the famine had increased the price of wheat. The same fate suffered the price of bread: 2 *baiocchi* for one *venale* loaf and 3 *baiocchi* for one *a diecina* loaf (ASRM, BA, 458, 4 April 1764 edict).
79. ASRM, BA, 456, 458. In ASRM, TCCT, 23–26, 34, 37–38, various trials are preserved against hoarders, bakers, and *tratte* fakers.
80. ASRM, BA, 10. Also in ASRM, CIIA, 1, there is a dossier relating to the *Scandaglio per regolare il prezzo dei grani che si danno a fornari fatto dal fu Virgilio Spada l'anno 1648*, by order of Pope Innocent X, where the price of bread was reported according to the weight (it could vary from 720 to 420 Roman *libbre*).
81. Reinhardt (1990, p. 114). See also Martinat (1995, pp. 327–328), where she reports the prices of *a baiocco* bread from 1605 to 1725. See also the recent Sabene (2017, pp. 77–78).
82. ASRM, BA, 460.
83. "[P]anizzazione da osservarsi stabilmente nei luoghi situati nel circondario di 40 miglia da Roma", "pane a tariffa in proporzione del libero costo dei grani" (ASRM, BA, 460, 8 October 1800 notification).
84. In ASRM, BA, 460 different notifications are kept that report the price of bread officially set in proportion to the free cost of cereals "to be observed permanently in the places located within 40 miles from Rome" ("da osservarsi stabilmente nei luoghi situati nel circondario di 40 miglia da Roma") (27 February 1800, 28 February, 21 March, 18 April, 16 May, 20 and 27 June, 15 August, 12 September, 17 October, 28 November, and 26 December 1801). They also contain the weight of different kinds of bread: the bread 'of flour'; white bread, "that is to say, solely made with flour of excellent quality, as it was made anciently" ("ossia di solo fior di farina di ottima qualità come si fabbricava anticamente"); the bread 'of a second flour', sold by weight by *decinanti* bakers; and the *pane di rifiuto* (literally, 'waste bread'), "that is to say, sold by weight, resulting from the production wastage of the aforementioned bread made by *baioccanti* bakers"

("ossia a peso risultante dai grossilli del predetto pane fabbricato dai fornai baioccanti").

85. See De Vecchis (1743, p. 163).
86. ASRM, BA, 348, 13 July and 21 September 1793 edicts.
87. De Vecchis (1743, pp. 253–271) collected the orders and the circular letters that reported the rules in case of failure to tender: they were those from 18 August 1677, 7 August 1719, 12 March 1733, and 22 September 1736.
88. ASRM CIIA, 22.
89. ASRM, CIIA, 1.
90. Revel (1972, p. 269).
91. ASUCBR, SMPCB, 618, fos. 129, 133, 145, 149, 161, 169, 173, 183, 185, 191, 199, 203, 205, 236, 240, 242, 243, 277, 286, 292, 307, 328, 333, 446, 459, 460, 480, 482.
92. See Ago (1983–1984, p. 25).
93. In this regard, all debtors and the cause of their debts were reported in the financial statements, year by year (ASRM, CIIAB, 110–115; PAG, 1962–1969).
94. See Ago (1983–1984, pp. 25–26). Usury, "it is possible to hypothesise that it represented a sector transversal to the entire market, not limited to more or less organised practices, such as those expressly forbidden in the pontifical proclamations" (d'Errico 1997, p. 477; various forms of usury are described in De Luca 1673, book V, part I, pp. 42–96).
95. Here some corrections were necessary, made obligatory with the 25 July 1772 edict, directed precisely to prevent fraud by farmers and avoid harmful dispersion of loans.
96. In fact, with the establishment or expansion of a *monte*, the 'dowry' (*dote*) was also established, that is to say, the means by which the interests of subscribers would be regularly paid.
97. Strangio (1999b). The *Annona* could count, at the time of the transaction, on the payment of one *giulio* per *luogo*. On 21 October 1616, Pope Paul V brought the contribution to two *giuli*, thanks to the transfer of one *giulio* from the remuneration of the board of the *montisti* (owners of the *luoghi*). It must be emphasised that not all the *monti* were subject to this taxation: for example, the *monti Annona Vacabile* and *Annona Ridotto* were excluded.
98. Several were the *monti* established to financially support Rome, but also other cities, such as Bologna, and the various local communities. Emblematic was the establishment of the *Monte Abbondanza delle Comunità*, erected on the occasion of three important famines for the Papal States during the eighteenth century (Strangio 2013).

99. In the Papal States and in particular in Rome (see d'Errico 1994), the creation of rents on real estate (*censi*), contracts of currency exchange (*cambi*), and interest-bearing credits required notarial deeds, with the explicit indication of the interest rate applied, the amount borrowed, the times and methods envisaged for its return. From the notarial protocols it emerges that, still at the end of the eighteenth century, they were sporadic, and established themselves as the most common form of loan during the following century.

Archival Sources

Archivio Apostolico Vaticano (AAV)
Bolle e bandi, *Serie III* (BBIII).
www.archivioapostolicovaticano.va

Archivio di Stato di Roma (ASRM)
Bandi (BA).
Camerale I, *Chirografi* (CIC).
Camerale II (CII).
Camerale II, *Annona* (CIIA).
Camerale II, *Annona*, *Bilanci* (CIIAB).
Camerale II, *Conti di entrata e di uscita della Camera (Stato generale della Camera)* (CIICC).
Congregazioni particolari deputate (CPD).
Congregazione del Sollievo, *Serie I* (CSI).
Famiglia Merolli, *Conti di entrata e di uscita* (FMC).
Luoghi di Monte, *Giustificazioni* (LMG).
Presidenza dell'Annona e Grascia (PAG).
Presidenza dell'Annona e Grascia, *Collezione di bolle*, *bandi*, *motu proprio*, *chirografi pontifici spettanti all'Annona* (PAGCB).
Presidenza dell'Annona e Grascia, *Nota dei grani introdotti in Roma* (PAGNG).
Congregazione del Buon Governo, *Serie IV* (CBGIV).
Congregazione del Buon Governo, *Serie V* (CBGV).
Tribunale criminale del Camerlengo e del Tesoriere (TCCT).
www.archiviodistatoroma.beniculturali.it

Archivio Storico UniCredit Banca di Roma (ASUCBR)
Sacro Monte di Pietà di Roma, *Chirografi e brevi pontifici* (SMPCB).
www.sie-ase.it/istituto-dettaglio.aspx?istituto=1397&persona=

Biblioteca Casanatense, Roma (BCRM)
Bandi (BA).
https://casanatense.beniculturali.it

Published Sources

Campilli, Filippo. 1783. *Racconto storico della penuria de' grani accaduta in Italia, ed in più provincie del dominio temporale della Santa Sede negli anni MDCCLXIII, e MDCCLXIV*. Roma: Stamperia Salomoni.

De Luca, Giovan Battista. 1673. *Il dottor volgare, overo Il compendio di tutta la legge civile, canonica, feudale, e municipale, nelle cose più ricevute in pratica*. Roma: Giuseppe Corvo.

De Vecchis, Andrea Pietro, ed. 1743. *Raccolta di rescritti, decreti, e lettere della S. Congregazione del Buon Governo, ed altre SS. Congregazioni, e di diverse altre cose concernenti il buon governo delle communità, e di tutto lo Stato Ecclesiastico*. Vol. II. Roma: Girolamo Mainardi.

Eschinardi, Francesco. 1750 [1696]. *Descrizione di Roma e dell'Agro romano. Fatta già ad uso della carta topografica del Cingolani*. New ed. by Ridolfino Venuti. Roma: Generoso Salomoni.

Nicolai, Nicola Maria. 1803. *Memorie, leggi, ed osservazioni sulle campagne e sull'Annona di Roma*. Roma: Stamperia Pagliarini.

Nuzzi, Ferdinando. 1702. *Discorso di monsignore Ferdinando Nuzzi chierico di Camera e prefetto dell'Annona, intorno alla coltivazione, e popolazione della Campagna di Roma*. Roma: Stamperia della Reverenda Camera Apostolica.

Pascoli, Leone. 1733. *Testamento politico d'un accademico fiorentino in cui con nuovi, e ben fondati principi si fanno vari, e diversi progetti per istabilire un ben regolato commerzio nello Stato della Chiesa, e per aumentare notabilmente le rendite della Camera. Con molti altri necessari avvertimenti, ed essenziali ricordi che in esso si lasciano pel buon governo del medesimo*. Colonia: Eredi di Cornelio d'Egmond.

References

Ago, Renata. 1983–1984. Popolo e papi. La crisi del sistema annonario. *Annali della Fondazione Lelio e Lisli Basso/Issoco* 7: 17–47.

Arias, Gino. 1908. Cause ed effetti economici delle leggi agrarie restrittive nel Settecento italiano. *Giornale degli Economisti*, 2nd series 19 (7–8/37): 11–38, 163–182.

Aubert, Alberto. 1986. La politica annonaria di Roma durante il pontificato di Paolo IV (1555–1559). *Archivio Storico Italiano* 144 (3/529): 261–288.

Balbi De Caro, Silvana, and Luigi Londei. 1984. *Moneta Pontificia (da Innocenzo XI a Gregorio XVI)*. Roma: Quasar.

Braudel, Fernand, and Frank Spooner. 1967. Prices in Europe from 1450 to 1750. In *The Cambridge economic history of Europe*, ed. by Michael Moissey Postan and Hrothgar John Habakkuk. Vol. IV: The economy of expanding Europe in the sixteenth and seventeenth centuries, ed. by Edwin Ernest Rich and Charles Henry Wilson, 374–486. Cambridge: Cambridge University Press.

Canaletti Gaudenti, Alberto. 1920. Esportazioni, censimenti agrari e requisizioni nel Settecento a Roma. *Giornale degli Economisti e Rivista di Statistica*, 3rd series 31 (11/60): 461–487.

———. 1947. *La politica agraria ed annonaria dello Stato Pontificio da Benedetto XIV a Pio VII*. Roma: Istituto di Studi Romani.

Caracciolo, Alberto. 1978. Da Sisto V a Pio IX. In *Storia d'Italia*, dir. by Giuseppe Galasso. Vol. XIV: Lo Stato pontificio da Martino V a Pio IX, by Mario Caravale and Alberto Caracciolo, 373–764. Torino: Utet.

Checcoli, Ippolita. 2015. *I monti frumentari e le forme di credito non monetarie tra Medioevo ed Età contemporanea*. Bologna: il Mulino.

Ciasca, Raffaele. 1956. Un papa riformatore e bonificatore della fine del secolo XVIII. *Economia e Storia* 3 (3): 260–280.

Clément, Alain. 1999. *Nourrir le peuple. Entre État et marché, XVIe–XIXe siècle. Contribution à l'histoire intellectuelle de l'approvisionnement alimentaire*. Paris/Montréal: l'Harmattan.

Corridore, Franco. 1906. *La popolazione dello Stato romano (1656–1901)*. Roma: Loescher.

Da Gai, Enrico. 1994. I magazzini del grano in Civitavecchia e l'annona di Roma. *Rivista Storica del Lazio* 2 (2): 157–188.

Dal Pane, Luigi. 1932. *La questione del commercio dei grani nel Settecento in Italia*. Vol. I: Parte generale-Toscana. Milano: Vita e Pensiero.

———. 1957. Discussioni e leggi annonarie in Roma nel primo quarantennio del secolo XVIII. In *Studi in onore di Armando Sapori*. Vol. II, 1185-1216. Milano: Istituto Editoriale Cisalpino.

———. 1959a. *Lo Stato pontificio e il movimento riformatore del settecento*. Milano: Giuffrè.

———. 1959b [1954–1955]. Benedetto XIV e la questione della libertà di commercio. New ed. In Dal Pane 1959a, 239–250.

———. 1965. La Congregazione economica istituita da Benedetto XIV e la libertà di commercio. *Rivista di Storia dell'Agricoltura* 5 (4): 371–418.

De Cupis, Cesare. 1911. *Le vicende dell'agricoltura e della pastorizia nell'Agro romano. L'Annona di Roma giusta memorie, consuetudini e leggi desunte da documenti anche inediti. Sommario storico*. Roma: Bertero.

Del Re, Niccolò. 1998 [1941]. *La Curia romana. Lineamenti storico-giuridici*. 4th ed. Città del Vaticano: Libreria Editrice Vaticana.

Delumeau, Jean. 1957–1959. *Vie économique et sociale de Rome dans la seconde moitié du XVIe siècle*. Paris: de Boccard.

d'Errico, Rita. 1994. Il prestito tra privati a Roma attraverso le fonti notarili e fiscali del XVIII–XIX secolo. *Roma Moderna e Contemporanea* 2 (1): 139–151.

———. 1997. Intermediazione privata e innovazione creditizia a Roma nella prima metà dell'Ottocento. In *Roma fra la Restaurazione e l'elezione di Pio IX. Amministrazione, economia, società e cultura*, ed. by Anna Lia Bonella,

Augusto Pompeo, and Manola Ida Venzo, 475–511. Roma/Freiburg/ Wien: Herder.

de Vries, Jan. 2019. *The price of bread: Regulating the market in the Dutch Republic.* Cambridge: Cambridge University Press.

Eusebio, Ludovico. 1899. *Compendio di metrologia universale (monete, pesi, misure moderne) e vocabolario metrologico (monete, pesi, misure antiche e moderne).* Torino: Utet.

Falchi, Luisa, Maria Grazia Pastura Ruggiero, and Daniela Sinisi. 1995. L'Annona di Roma nel secolo XVI. In *Gli archivi per la storia dell'alimentazione.* Vol. I, 568–589. Roma: Ministero per i Beni Culturali e Ambientali, Ufficio Centrale per i Beni Archivistici.

Fogel, Robert William. 1992. Second thoughts on the European escape from hunger: Famines, chronic malnutrition, and mortality rates. In *Nutrition and poverty*, ed. by Siddiqur Rahman Osmani, 243–286. Oxford: Clarendon Press.

Girelli, Angela Maria. 2000. Terra e affari a Roma nell'Ottocento pontificio. Mercanti di campagna e mercato dei capitali privati (1817–23). In *Studi in onore di Ciro Manca*, ed. by Donatella Strangio, 165–249. Padova: Cedam.

Grenier, Jean-Yves. 1996. *L'économie d'Ancien Régime. Un monde de l'échange et de l'incertitude.* Paris: Michel.

Grigg, David. 1980. *Population growth and agrarian change: An historical perspective.* Cambridge: Cambridge University Press.

Gross, Hanns. 1990. *Roma nel Settecento.* Roma/Bari: Laterza.

Guenzi, Alberto. 1977. Il "calmiero del formento": controllo del prezzo del pane e difesa della rendita terriera a Bologna nei secoli XVII e XVIII. *Annali della Fondazione Luigi Einaudi* 11: 143–201.

———. 1978. Un mercato regolato: pane e fornai a Bologna nell'età moderna. *Quaderni Storici* 13 (1/37): 370–397.

———. 1981. Il frumento e la città: il caso di Bologna nell'età moderna. *Quaderni Storici* 16 (1/46): 153–167.

———. 1982a. Consumi alimentari e popolazione a Bologna in età moderna. In *La demografia storica delle città italiane*, ed. by the Società Italiana di Demografia Storica, 333–344. Bologna: Clueb.

———. 1982b. Sistema annonario e controllo sociale a Bologna nei secoli XVII e XVIII. In *Città e controllo sociale in Italia tra XVIII e XIX secolo*, ed. by Ercole Sori, 293–306. Milano: Angeli.

Guitton, Henri. 1938. *Essai sur la loi de King. Études des relations entre les mouvements de l'offre et les mouvements des prix.* Paris: Sirey.

Kaplan, Steven Laurence. 1984. *Provisioning Paris: Merchants and millers in the grain and flour trade during the eighteenth century.* Ithaca/London: Cornell University Press.

Lodolini, Elio. 1953. Lo smembramento dell'Archivio della S. Congregazione del Buon Governo. *Notizie degli Archivi di Stato* 13 (1): 41–45.

———. 1956. *L'Archivio della S. Congregazione del Buon Governo (1592–1847). Inventario*. Roma: Istituto Poligrafico dello Stato.

Londei, Luigi. 1990. La monetazione pontificia e la zecca di Roma nell'età moderna (secc. XVI–XVIII). *Studi Romani* 38 (3–4): 303–318.

Martinat, Monica. 1995. Le marché des céréales à Rome au XVIIe siècle. *Histoire et Mesure* 10 (3–4): 313–338.

———. 2004. *Le juste marché. Le système annonaire romain aux XVIe et XVIIe siècles*. Rome: École Française de Rome.

Martini, Angelo. 1883. *Manuale di metrologia, ossia misure, pesi e monete in uso attualmente e anticamente presso tutti i popoli*. Torino: Loescher.

Monaco, Michele. 1971. *Lo Stato della Chiesa*. Vol. I: Dalla fine del Grande Scisma alla pace di Cateau-Cambrésis (1417–1559). Pescara: Libreria dell'Università.

———. 1974. *Lo Stato della Chiesa*. Vol. II: Dalla pace di Cateau-Cambrésis alla pace di Aquisgrana (1559–1748). Lecce: Milella.

Montanari, Massimo. 1993. *La fame e l'abbondanza. Storia dell'alimentazione in Europa*. Roma/Bari: Laterza.

Ó Gráda, Cormac. 2009. *Famine: A short history*. Princeton/Oxford: Princeton University Press.

Palermo, Luciano. 1986. Il commercio del grano in un sistema annonario: l'Italia centrale nel Tardo Medioevo. In *Mercati e consumi. Organizzazione e qualificazione del commercio in Italia dal XII al XX secolo*, ed. by the Istituto Formazione Operatori Aziendali, 79–95. Bologna: Analisi.

———. 1990. *Mercati del grano a Roma tra Medioevo e Rinascimento*. Vol. I: Il mercato distrettuale del grano in età comunale. Roma: Istituto Nazionale di Studi Romani.

———. 1991. Politica annonaria e normativa statutaria nei comuni laziali bassomedievali: la gestione dell'offerta. In *Statuti e ricerca storica*, ed. by the Comune di Ferentino, Assessorato alla Cultura, in cooperation with the Società Romana di Storia Patria, 181–208. Ferentino: Comune di Ferentino.

———. 1994. L'approvvigionamento granario della capitale. Strategie economiche e carriere curiali a Roma alla metà del Quattrocento. In *Roma Capitale (1447–1527)*, ed. by Sergio Gensini, 145–205. Pisa: Pacini/San Miniato: Comune di San Miniato.

———. 1997. *Sviluppo economico e società preindustriali. Cicli, strutture e congiunture in Europa dal medioevo alla prima età moderna*. Roma: Viella.

Palermo, Luciano, and Donatella Strangio. 1997. Politiche dell'alimentazione e carestie nello Stato della Chiesa: un modello di lungo periodo (secoli XIV–XVIII). In *Alimentazione e nutrizione. Secc. XIII–XVIII*, ed. by Simonetta Cavaciocchi, 325–338. Firenze: Le Monnier.

Palermo, Luciano, Andrea Fara, and Pere Benito i Monclús, eds. 2018. *Políticas contra el hambre y la carestía en la Europa medieval*. Lleida: Milenio.

Pastura Ruggiero, Maria Grazia. 1984. *La Reverenda Camera Apostolica e i suoi archivi (secoli XV–XVIII)*. Roma: Archivio di Stato.

Persson, Karl Gunnar. 1996. The seven lean years, elasticity traps, and intervention in grain markets in pre-industrial Europe. *The Economic History Review* 49 (4): 692–714.

Piola Caselli, Fausto. 1998. The regulation of the Roman market in the seventeenth century. In *Guilds, markets and work regulations in Italy, 16th–19th centuries*, ed. by Alberto Guenzi, Paola Massa, and Fausto Piola Caselli, 132–149. Aldershot/Brookfield/Singapore/Sydney: Ashgate.

Piscitelli, Enzo. 1951. Fabrizio Ruffo e la riforma economica dello Stato Pontificio. *Archivio della Società Romana di Storia Patria*, 3rd series 5/74 (1–4): 69–184.

Ravallion, Martin. 1997. Famines and economics. *Journal of Economic Literature* 35 (3): 1205–1242.

Reinhardt, Volker. 1990. Il prezzo del pane a Roma e la finanza pontificia dal 1563 al 1762. *Dimensioni e Problemi della Ricerca Storica* 3 (2): 109–134.

———. 1991. *Überleben in der frühneuzeitlichen Stadt. Annona und Getreideversorgung in Rom, 1563–1797*. Tübingen: Niemeyer.

Revel, Jacques. 1972. Le grain de Rome et la crise de l'Annone dans la seconde moitié du XVIIIe siècle. *Mélanges de l'École Française de Rome. Moyen Âge, Temps Modernes* 84 (1): 201–281.

———. 1982. Rendements, production et productivité agricoles: les grands domaines de la Campagne romaine, XVIIe–XVIIIe siècles. In *Prestations paysannes, dîmes, rente foncière et mouvement de la production agricole à l'époque préindustrielle*, ed. by Joseph Goy and Emmanuel Le Roy Ladurie. Vol. I, 227–236. Paris: Ehess/Paris/La Haye/New York: Mouton.

Romano, Ruggiero. 1967. Introduzione. In *I prezzi in Europa dal XIII secolo a oggi. Saggi di storia dei prezzi*, ed. by Ruggiero Romano, ix–xliv. Torino: Einaudi.

Sabene, Renata. 2016. Wheat supply, market and trade in Rome during the 18th century. In *Informal credit in the Mediterranean area (XVI–XIX centuries)*, ed. by Antonino Giuffrida, Roberto Rossi, and Gaetano Sabatini, 225–242. Palermo: New Digital Press.

———. 2017. *Lavoro e privilegio nella Città Eterna. Condizioni di vita e potere di acquisto a Roma nel Settecento*. Milano: Altravista.

Schulz, Knut. 1991. Deutsche Handwerkergruppen im Rom der Renaissance. Mitgliederstärke, Organisationsstruktur, Voraussetzungen. Eine Bestandsaufnahme. *Römische Quartalschrift für Christliche Altertumskunde und Kirchengeschichte* 86: 3–22.

———. 1994. Deutsche Handwerkergruppen in Italien, besonders in Rom (14.–16. Jahrhundert). In *Le migrazioni in Europa, secc. XIII–XVIII*, ed. by Simonetta Cavaciocchi, 567–591. Firenze: Le Monnier.

Schumpeter, Joseph Alois. 1959 [1954]. *Storia dell'analisi economica*. Italian translation. Torino: Einaudi.

Slicher Van Bath, Bernard Hendrik. 1972 [1963]. *Storia agraria dell'Europa occidentale (500–1850)*. Italian translation. Torino: Einaudi.

Strangio, Donatella. 1999a. *Crisi alimentari e politica annonaria a Roma nel Settecento.* Roma: Istituto Nazionale di Studi Romani.

———. 1999b. L'amministrazione del debito pubblico pontificio nel Settecento. *Archivio della Società Romana di Storia Patria* 122: 277–314.

———. 2000. "Il pane controllato". Un nuovo regolamento per l'Annona di Roma. *Mélanges de l'École Française de Rome. Italie et Méditerranée* 112 (2): 589–613.

———. 2004. L'approvvigionamento della città di Roma in età moderna. In *Nourrir les cités de Méditerranée. Antiquité-Temps modernes*, ed. by Brigitte Marin and Catherine Virlouvet, 125–147. Paris: Maisonneuve et Larose/Aix-en-Provence: Maison Méditerranéenne des Sciences de l'Homme/Madrid: Universidad Nacional de Educación a Distancia.

———. 2013. Public debt in the Papal States, sixteenth to eighteenth century. *Journal of Interdisciplinary History* 43 (4): 511–537.

Stumpo, Enrico. 1985. *Il capitale finanziario a Roma fra Cinque e Seicento. Contributo alla storia della fiscalità pontificia in età moderna (1570–1660).* Milano: Giuffrè.

Tabacchi, Stefano. 2007. *Il Buon Governo. Le finanze locali nello Stato della Chiesa (secoli XVI–XVIII).* Roma: Viella.

Tilly, Charles. 1984. Approvvigionamento alimentare e ordine pubblico nell'Europa moderna. In *La formazione degli Stati nazionali nell'Europa occidentale*, ed. by Charles Tilly, 227–296. Italian translation. Bologna: il Mulino.

Venturi, Franco. 1963. Elementi e tentativi di riforme nello Stato Pontificio del Settecento. *Rivista Storica Italiana* 75 (4): 778–817.

———. 1973. L'Italia fuori d'Italia. In *Storia d'Italia*, coord. by Ruggiero Romano and Corrado Vivanti. Vol. III: Dal primo Settecento all'Unità, 985–1481. Torino: Einaudi.

———. 1983. *Riforme e riformatori nell'Italia Centrale (Modena-Parma-Stato Pontificio).* Torino: Gheroni.

Wrigley, Edward Anthony. 1987. Some reflections on corn yields and prices in pre-industrial economies. In *People, cities, and wealth: The transformation of traditional society*, by Edward Anthony Wrigley, 92–130. Oxford: Blackwell.

Zucchini, Mario. 1968. Privilegi e riforme liberistiche nel Settecento. *Rivista di Storia dell'Agricoltura* 8 (2): 79–84.

Map 8.1 The Kingdom of Sicily (17[80s])

CHAPTER 8

A Two-Sided Kingdom: A Sicily of Export and Urban Wheat Supply

Ida Fazio

8.1 Introduction

The Sicilian victualling system in the Early Modern Age remained substantially unchanged, from an institutional point of view, during the entire period extending from the Spanish Viceroyalty (1516–1713) to the decline of the Old Regime. It is intriguing that the system sought to establish a mechanism that guaranteed both the subsistence of large and small cities that dotted the territory, each with its own highly distinct institutional identity, and at the same time it sought to guarantee the income of the great aristocratic landowners of large estates planted with wheat and prominent tenants interested in the international and domestic wheat market; additionally, the system had to ensure the collection of taxes and duties on trade for the Crown. These goals were sometimes in contrast, while other times they worked together synergistically, depending on the combination of several factors: the membership of the community to the feudal jurisdiction or to the royal domain; the specific location of the

I. Fazio (✉)
Università degli Studi di Palermo, Palermo, Italy
e-mail: ida.fazio@unipa.it

L. Clerici (ed.), *Italian Victualling Systems in the Early Modern Age, 16th to 18th Century*, Palgrave Studies in Economic History,
https://doi.org/10.1007/978-3-030-42064-2_8

cities, large and small, in the diversified island territory, and whether they were located in a producing or a consuming area; the political situation and local and international price trends. In this sense, Sicily is one of the cases in which it is possible to go beyond the theoretical opposition between central victualling and market-driven systems. In Sicily, public provisioning and market are two sides of the same coin, because the market was not so very regulated, nor exclusively so, as it was truly constructed and sustained by the victualling rules of the Kingdom.

8.2 The *Maestro Portulano* and the *Caricatori*: The Domestic and Foreign Market

The rules of the Sicilian victualling system created a relationship between the procurement of the *città* and *terre* (respectively, cities and territorial jurisdictions) and the Crown's need to collect duties on the *tratte*, that is to say, duties on the export licences of wheat both at home and abroad. Sicilian legislation defended as much as possible the free circulation of the wheat produced on the large landed estates, protecting both royal fiscal income and those who enjoyed income from rental of the land. The authorisation and management of exports from what since the Roman Age was considered one of the granaries of the Mediterranean were carried out by central authorities: the *Tribunale del Real Patrimonio* ('Tribunal of the Royal Estate'), with its own *Giunta* ('Board') that received data on the size of the population and on the quantities produced, and based on this data decided whether to authorise exports;[1] and the office of *maestro portulano* (literally, 'harbour master'), which, by a 1338 law,[2] had pre-eminence over the ancient institutions that since the thirteenth century[3] had jurisdiction over the ports, controlled the maritime trade, demanded taxes and duties on commercial activities, managed the docks and the royal granaries, and granted export licences.

There was thus early contact between a prematurely unified internal market[4] and the foreign market: the moment of the *apertura della tratta* (literally, the 'opening of the export licence'), that is to say, the granting of permission to export freely. The two areas of commercial circulation (domestic and foreign) came into contact, and so all prices became closely correlated; at the same time, fiscal revenues (also called *tratte*) were generated and paid to the Crown by those who had obtained export licences.[5] This operation, however, had to take into account the population's need for livelihood, and therefore the relationship between subsistence and the production of wheat. This quantitative ratio is difficult to document, except by resorting to calculations and estimates, at least until the mid-sixteenth century, when population censuses, the *riveli di anime*, began to be carried out more regularly, along with (amidst great resistance) the *riveli* that reported the production and the surface area of sown land.

The relationship between the population and wheat production is the basis for opposing interpretations of the entire Sicilian economic history from the Late Middle Ages onwards:[6] is this a story of autonomy and dynamism or of dependency and delay? According to Stephan Epstein,[7] the amount of Sicilian wheat that was exported (from which other historians deduced the dependence of the Sicilian economy on foreign demand for cereals) was in fact very limited because the local population of consumers was more than what Henri Bresc had estimated.[8] The important role of the internal market is therefore associated with the vision of 'an island for itself' and with the criticism of the paradigm of dependence. Certainly, it can be said that until 1508—the date of enactment of the *prammatica* (that is to say a royal decree) entitled *De emptionibus frumentorum*, which for the first time regulated the food supply of cities and communities in a unified manner[9]—the domestic/urban consumption needs were considered by Sicilian legislation as potential barriers to the movement of wheat directed to the internal or foreign market—and thus also to the collection of the land rent by the owners/producers and of taxes and duties by the Crown. In this period, however, the communities provided for the subsistence of the population with special rules laid down separately by municipal statutes.[10]

With the 1508 decree, the unitary rules for the public provisioning of cities were set out for the first time, made necessary by the population growth that in the sixteenth century, in Sicily and throughout Europe, drove domestic and foreign demand for wheat higher. When in the seventeenth century exports from Sicily decreased as a result of European demographic stagnation, domestic commerce increased. According to calculations by Antonino Morreale,[11] the ratio of *intra* and *extra Regnum* trade—30% versus 70% in the sixteenth century—was reversed in the seventeenth century—70% versus 30%—; it would invert back to the previous proportion in the eighteenth century. Precisely when foreign demand began to stagnate, the new foundations of feudal cities in the wheat-producing areas of Sicily (the so-called 'Sicily of wheat') were identified[12] as a ploy to uphold feudal revenues by developing a domestic market for

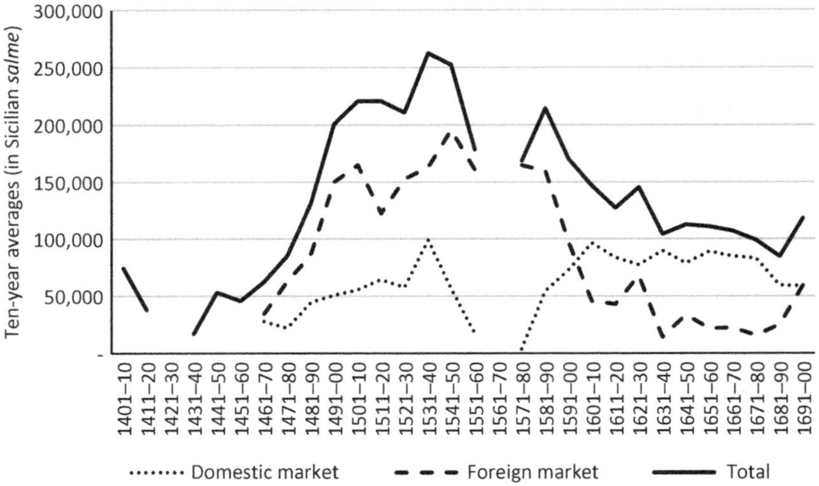

Fig. 8.1 Sicilian wheat trade on domestic and foreign markets (1401–1700). (Source: Elaboration on partial data from Morreale 2018, pp. 207–216)

the supply of new areas of settlement and to replace the declining foreign market, as it is shown in Fig. 8.1. However, these new foundations caused conflicts between old and new communities over control of the urban food supply. In fact, the newly founded feudal communities purchased areas of nearby state-owned cities whose demographic and financial strength was waning, and imposed on these areas their own taxes on the production of cereals and their own limits on exports to protect the consumption of local residents.[13] In the eighteenth century these areas, especially in the Val di Mazara area, would produce the wheat that would make Sicily a great exporter of wheat again.

The *maestro portulano* governed, through its deputies, an original system of institutions and infrastructures for the movement and distribution of wheat. This was the system of the *caricatori*, public warehouses whose role was both commercial and fiscal.[14] These were altogether unique institutions of the Kingdom of Sicily, serving both the domestic and foreign market. The *caricatori* (literally, 'loaders') were large fortified warehouses located in ports or in other guarded places, where owners deposited wheat for sale in underground deposits, the *fosse* ('pits'), paying the State for the increases in volume of the deposited wheat and after a year, a duty, too.

From these warehouses came the wheat to be sold at home and abroad, after the licences were obtained from the *maestro portulano*,[15] and the wheat could be loaded (here is the reason of the name 'loaders') onto the boats. The amounts deposited were accounted for with marketable coupons.

The *caricatori* could be under state, royal, feudal, or city jurisdiction, with varying degrees of control by the *maestro portulano*, which was responsible for defining the top-level policy of the wheat trade, which worried the viceroys,[16] and was based on the management of information on prices and crops.[17] For much of the Viceroyalty period, the *maestro portulano* continuously sought to limit the autonomy of those who ran the *caricatori*, who, at the local level, tended to manage the large amount of wheat entrusted to them like private bankers.[18] The same behaviour occurred in the warehouses managed by the victualling administration of cities.[19] The *caricatori* are interesting mainly as instituted marketplaces, where different price formation mechanisms took place and had an impact on the entire victualling system, as we will see shortly. These mechanisms interacted and produced a cumulative effect. One of these mechanisms was the meeting at the *caricatori* between the internal market and the foreign market, which had the effect of moderating spikes in prices.[20] The second was the result of the speculations—in addition to those of the *Loggia* (the market square) of Palermo[21]—made at the *caricatori* by the actors in local and international trade, with advance purchases and 'bets' on the rise or fall in prices. The third mechanism was the system of fixing the so-called *mete* (literally, 'limits') of wheat. The *mete* were officially set prices established by means of a technical and political evaluation (but taking market prices into account).

The *mete* worked in a similar way to the *voci* (literally, 'voices') in Naples,[22] in that they were used to determine the interest on transactions *da massaro a mercante* ('between farmer and merchant'), a system that pervaded the entire Sicilian wheat production system and included prepayments, refunds with interest and credit chains. The *mete* set at the *caricatori* beginning in the mid-sixteenth century would be the benchmark for the *mete* established locally in all communities, large and small, including cities. According to Maurice Aymard,[23] their institutional logic shows that the foreign market and the domestic market were substantially unified, as it is also demonstrated by the fact that all the prices were highly correlated. Also operating on this same market and controlled by no one was the viceroy, or in the eighteenth century, the king,[24] making wheat shipments to Spain and then to the Kingdom of Naples and its capital city, even in the derogation of bans on exports, in the context of a complex and conflictual political and economic relationship between these two Bourbon kingdoms.

8.3 The Urban Victualling Administrations

It is on this fundamentally unitary market that urban victualling administrations operated. They represented another of Sicily's peculiar features. The victualling administrations of large and small communities were procurement systems, but they did not limit the price of wheat, flour, bread, and other commodities such as wine, olive oil, cheese, and snow (a product purchased only by the wealthy for their refreshing drinks during the summer, which served also to preserve and cool food). Although the domestic market for individual consumers was significant, and private consumption was less residual than what Aymard maintained,[25] public procurement was very important, and it was protected also in a great wheat producer like the Kingdom of Sicily, as it was in other Italian and European cities. The wheat supply system, which was by far the most complex and fraught with detail, will now be examined. The baking of bread and the regulation of supplies and prices of other foodstuffs will then be considered.

As elsewhere in Europe, in emergencies and cases of extreme poverty, Sicily had tools like the *rabba*, a mandatory deposit of excess wheat remaining after sowing and consumption, to be sold to the poor at the *meta* price, which was lower than the market price.[26] There were also occasional extraordinary purchases made for distribution during particularly severe famines, paid for with government funds or by collections and local funds. But the typical organisation of the Sicilian victualling administration continued to be throughout the eighteenth century, with a series of modifications, that outlined by the 1508 *De emptionibus frumentorum*, whose administrative procedures were perfected under Charles III of Bourbon in 1742. It was a generalised system extending to all the communities of the Kingdom, which were obliged by law to bid every year for the contract regulating the supply of wheat intended for use in public bakeries. Cities and communities operated on the market like any other actor, without any preference or protection.

The quantities of municipal purchases differed due to several factors: the volume of production, estimated by the surveys of sown or harvested crops;[27] self-consumed quantities, which were far from negligible notwithstanding the importance of the island's market economy;[28] the volume of private purchases on which local taxes and duties were paid for milling and the *entratura*, that is to say, on being allowed to enter the city. Therefore, the Sicilian communities in the north-eastern Valdemone area—those called *dell'albero* (literally, 'the tree communities', since they did not produce wheat, but cultivated specialised crops of vines and of olive, orange, and mulberry trees, producing wine, olive oil, oranges, and silk)—were forced to make purchases regularly and in quantities greater than those purchased by the communities in the central-western area, the Val di Mazara. Indeed, it was in western Sicily where the wheat-producing communities, whose jurisdiction was most often feudal, are found. For this reason, the health of municipal finances and local taxation in these two areas were very different: the communities most dependent on public procurement, which were often under royal domain and located in the North East,[29] were disadvantaged.

There are well-known cases of some great feudal landowners, lords of towns in both production and consumption areas of the Valdemone, who established special procurement relationships to supply wheat among themselves, e.g. the Branciforte, with Leonforte and Raccuia,[30] and the Bonanno, with Canicattì and Montalbano.[31] But, in general, communities (especially the ones under royal domain) that were not protected by these privileged relationships were more exposed to price fluctuations caused by the open market and by speculation, or by local market circuits, which were more expensive because the proximity and reliability of the vendors came at a cost. Similarly, there was also a cost for the credit that vendors granted by agreeing to be paid gradually as their wheat was made into bread and sold. This occurred in all those cases where the municipality did not have what was called a *colonna* (literally, 'column') or a *peculio frumentario* ('wheat peculium'), terms which meant both the funds and revenues dedicated solely to food supply, and the public institutions which managed them. Even the *colonne*, however, were destroyed and bankrupted at the end of the eighteenth century due to the system's technical inability to counter the structural rise in wheat prices all along that century.

The way the victualling system worked in most of the communities will now be considered. We will identify the 'game rules' by which generally all the communities played, which we find more accurately and completely defined in the eighteenth century, although with some variations. Next, we will examine the procurement and redistribution systems of the major cities, Messina and Palermo, where the political implications of food riots, the institutional importance of conflicts of jurisdiction, the huge demand, and vast stores and warehouses require a distinct examination and an analysis of additional issues. In June of each year, the municipal administrators received a notice from the viceroy through the *Tribunale del Real Patrimonio*, instructing them to survey the quantities produced, to determine the need, to issue the purchase request, and to select the best offer and the various payment systems.

Until the production surveys were completed, the deadline being usually fixed on 15 August (the usual date in Sicily to settle transactions and to repay advances and loans), it was forbidden to transport wheat out of the territory of the municipality, and on the *terze parti* (one-third of this amount), the municipality could exercise a right of pre-emption, if needed. On the first Sunday after that date, the city council and its consultants established, according to the production surveys, the quantities required for the *pubblico panizzo*, that is to say, for the public production of bread (*pane*) for sale to citizens until the following August. Starting in 1767, these functions would be carried out by a special commission established for this purpose. A notice was then published to solicit offers, and a contract was stipulated with the seller whose offer was most favourable. If there were no offers, an envoy of the municipality could proceed to make direct purchases, as it was also possible if the supply purchased was consumed before the end of the year.

The payment systems, as a first option, provided for cash purchases made with the capital of the *colonne* or *peculi frumentari*. These institutions managed a fund with separate accounting and its own sources of revenue, consisting of taxes and other income. Often, however, the *colonne* were depleted or were subject to constant deficits and insolvencies due to poor administration, or to the inability to offset price increases, as we will see shortly. In the absence of a *colonna*, a mortgage could be stipulated at 7%, or the *terze parti* could be purchased (which however might not exist if there was a famine, or had been hidden by the producers), or an agreement could be reached with the seller to make delayed payments, with interest: *consignando pagando*, that is to say, with payment made at each successive delivery, or *sfacendo pagando*, that is to say, paying the price gradually as the wheat was ground and baked into bread and the bread was sold *alle piazze*, that is to say, in the market squares, by public bakers. The wheat bought by the victualling administration, in fact, was not sold directly to the public, but was made into bread and sold by bakers designated by the municipality, at a fixed price and variable weight.

A production test (*scandaglio*) carried out in the presence of the authorities determined the minimum weight the loaves should have—they always had the same price, 4 *grana*[32]—based on the full accounting of all the costs (price of wheat, transportation, taxes and duties, cost of baking the bread, interest on credit), with the aim of ensuring that the proceeds from the sale of the bread matched the costs exactly.[33] The Sicilian victualling system, therefore, let its costs weigh entirely on consumers, including fluctuations in the price of wheat, and in no way provided for price ceilings. And the price fluctuations depended not only on the market, both domestic and international, but also on the fact that all the communities were required by law to procure food in competition with each other, in the same period, between August and September–October. The prices were not only influenced by speculation: in addition, trust, economic advantages, product quality, and the willingness of sellers to grant credit produced different prices in different circuits of trade relations.

Genuine preferential circuits were created in a market which, although open, was always highly personalised and sometimes segmented into smaller circuits that were not part of those that revolved around the *caricatori*, as in the small city of Santa Lucia in Valdemone in the eighteenth century, where these phenomena have been identified clearly, and reconstructed completely for a fifty-year period.[34] But even the market circuits headed by the *caricatori* were strongly influenced by the network of relationships among the actors, by their various speculations on the wheat business and/or by their commercial status and position in the victualling institutions, as it has been suggested by case studies of brief periods in a big city like Palermo.[35] Starting with the first forms of regulation of wheat supply, those who had interests in the wheat trade were repeatedly prohibited from taking positions and roles in public procurement. Such a conflict of interest could prove costly to the public purse; paradoxically, however, if experienced players in the wheat market were also the ones procuring wheat for the city, there would also be a certain advantage for the communities.

In a system like the Sicilian one, the balance—only theoretical—between revenue and expenditure could be guaranteed only by a situation of demographic and price stability: an unrealistic and, in fact, impossible condition, because both tended towards overall long-term growth, especially in the eighteenth century. When there were several consecutive years of price increases, or of increased demand caused by population growth or insufficient production, the *colonne* were emptied and the municipal coffers were in debt. Viceroy Domenico Caracciolo, Marquis of Villamaina, a reformer, was not able to overcome this problem by liberalising the wheat market in the 1780s. The post-Restoration administrative reforms came much too late and even had to be withdrawn during certain periods of the following years because famines, though at times less severe, never ceased to afflict Sicily. In the early nineteenth century, the island had lost its lead role in the production of wheat, replaced by the immense fields of Russia and America, where the costs of renting the land did not weigh on prices.[36]

The victualling administrations of Palermo and Messina, which played a key role in the wheat trade in the eighteenth century,[37] testify to the different position in the economic and political landscape of the Kingdom of Sicily of the two largest and most populous cities of the island, in constant competition with each other for the status of capital. Abundance and speculation characterised the first, located at the summit of the wheat-producing Val di Mazara, the centre of wheat bargaining for the entire Kingdom, and surrounded by the most important *caricatori* of the northern coast; dependency and indebtedness characterised the second, a city that was at the centre of the economy and the flow of goods from Valdemone and Calabria. A city that was the reference point for the wealthy 'Sicily of silk', but which, due to the characteristics of its territory, was always short of wheat and flour to feed its inhabitants.

The population of Messina, which tripled during the sixteenth century, varied—due to political and natural disasters that periodically wiped it out—from about 60,000 inhabitants at the end of the sixteenth century, to 100,000 in the early seventeenth century, back to 60,000 after the anti-Spanish revolt, and down further to 40,000 after the 1743 plague, rising again, after 120 years, to 100,000 inhabitants at the unification of Italy. Palermo, at the end of the sixteenth century, reached 100,000 inhabitants, 143,000 in the first two decades of the seventeenth century, and after a long stagnation at around 120,000, returned to its maximum level in the second half of the eighteenth century, drawing close to 200,000 in the Italian unification years.[38] Recent calculations[39] suggested that in the sixteenth and seventeenth centuries Palermo had to purchase about 20% of its wheat requirement (contemporaries and historians today agree on calculating an annual average of one Sicilian *salma* per person[40]), while Messina purchased 40%, leaving the rest of the demand to be covered by purchases made by individuals, or by the self-consumption of landowners and farmers residing in the city. Thus, the *Amministrazione di Vettovaglie* ('Victuals Administration') in Palermo and the *Peculio Frumentario* in Messina constituted the fundamentally important branches of the respective municipal administrations and were strategic sectors of the city government. They reflected faithfully the diverse contexts existing in western and north-eastern Sicily.

Palermo was home to all the major authorities that had a say in victualling matters throughout the Kingdom: the viceroy, the *Tribunale del Real Patrimonio*, the *maestro portulano*. At the same time, as a populous city, Palermo was one of the largest poles of attraction of wheat from old and new communities in western Sicily[41] and was situated between the two largest *caricatori* on Sicily's Tyrrhenian coast, which were reference points for the wheat producers of the Val di Mazara: the *caricatori* of Castellammare and Termini, both belonging to the royal domain and under the government of the *maestro portulano*. On the wheat deposited there, the victualling administration of the city of Palermo—managed by the *pretore* ('praetor') and by the members of the city council—had the right of pre-emption, and, in the case of shortages, it could block the export of the deposited wheat. Thanks to the privileges enjoyed by the city, it was also allowed to conclude advance purchase contracts, which were usually prohibited, and could therefore benefit from lower purchase prices, then reselling the products in the city at the higher prices of the urban market.[42] In the sixteenth century, the city of Palermo could even resell wheat in excess to the royal court, as long as it was exported through the *caricatori*.[43]

For the control of such a powerful instrument, which had a major influence on two of the most crucial *caricatori* for the Kingdom's export policy, continuous clashes arose between the praetor of Palermo, the *maestro portulano*, and the viceroy, with their respective private and institutional interests, often interwoven in conflict. For example, in 1550, the praetor, who was engaged in a power struggle with the viceroy, had previously been *maestro portulano*.[44] There were also cases where the feudal lords producing wheat were simultaneously city administrators and managers of its supplies.[45] By examining the names of the holders of contracts and rights on the collection of indirect taxes and duties (*gabelle*) in Palermo at the beginning of the seventeenth century, it can be seen that much of the turnover of the supply sector passed through the hands of individuals who, sooner or later, would occupy the role of administrators.[46] They had the opportunity to manage large wheat orders, to influence prices by putting large volumes on the urban market or on the international market through the *caricatori*.

The ability of the managers of the victualling administration of Palermo to act as a major mercantile enterprise, and at the same time to have a say in the central policies of export management, led to the establishment of a new royal *caricatore* in the city itself, with the hope of arousing the interest of the city of Palermo, thereby distracting it from the *caricatori* of Termini and Castellammare. Fought over even before its establishment, in 1636 it was at the centre of a dispute over its ownership between the city and the *maestro portulano*, who, at that time, was also a major merchant of wheat and self-made man.[47] Palermo re-purchased the *caricatore* in 1651, and Viceroy Caracciolo brought it back into the royal domain in 1781 as part of his policy of centralisation and market liberalisation. The *caricatore* was finally taken over by the city council of Palermo in 1794 with the breakup of Caracciolo's reforms, including the one granting greater freedom to make bread.[48] The ability of the victualling board to play, in the name of private and public interests, a prominent role in the wheat policy-making in the Kingdom would not save it from the deficit that, in time, would ruin all Sicilian victualling administrations. The *Senato* ('Senate', the city's council), to pay in advance for the large quantities purchased by means of supply contracts (*partiti*), could benefit from a *colonna* of 200,000 Sicilian *onze*, then reduced to 100,000 *onze*; but in the mid-eighteenth century, it had been spent entirely, and to save it, 50,000 *onze* were allocated to it from the assets seized from the Jesuits after their expulsion from the Kingdom of Sicily in 1767.[49]

The victualling administration of Messina, called the *Peculio Frumentario*, was provided with a cash fund of 100,000 *scudi* only in 1591, after the great Mediterranean famine,[50] but already since the mid-fifteenth century the city had a *Deputazione Frumentaria* ('Wheat Deputation'), that is to say, a commission for the purchase of wheat elected by the city's council, which were in charge of procurement. Because the city was such an active market and because there was no hinterland where wheat was cultivated, the purchasing policy of the Crown gave Messina certain commercial privileges. The money the city offered in exchange for these privileges was procured by borrowing from wealthy members of the city's elite, who received as a guarantee the proceeds of taxes and duties imposed by the city administration. These privileges (including the monopoly on silk exports) facilitated economic activities and therefore increased the consumption and the sale of goods subject to taxes and duties that financed the victualling administration; but, at the same time, these taxes and duties made the bread sold publicly to consumers in the market squares even more expensive.

One of the privileges, established in 1479, even authorised the seizure of boats laden with wheat that passed through the Straits of Messina. This wheat was bought at a very high price, which included the military costs of assaulting the ships; therefore, citizens and the city's assets paid the high costs of those forced acquisitions, and merchants did not trust the city. In addition, the taxes imposed on wheat purchases to finance the *Peculio* encouraged smuggling; the interest on credit granted by the *Peculio* for wheat purchases increased financial liabilities, leading it towards bankruptcy. With the suppression of the 1674–1678 revolt against Spain, the assets and revenues of the city were confiscated by the royal exchequer. A special commission appointed by the king to administer the assets of the rebellious city, and later the Savoy[51] and Habsburg governments at the beginning of the eighteenth century, attempted to restore the *Peculio*. However, to increase revenue, in 1688 Viceroy Juan Francisco Pacheco, Duke of Uzeda, established the monopoly of the *Peculio* on the import and sale of wheat and flour in the city; until then, permission to import had been granted to private citizens, although it was discouraged by taxation.

This monopoly increased smuggling, producing losses in revenue for the city's treasury and victualling administration. With the arrival of Charles III of Bourbon, the *Peculio* was given back to the city and several reforms were made, aimed not only at feeding Messina, but also at improving trade. However, an experiment in liberalisation of the wheat and flour market was short-lived and lasted from 1778 to 1782. With Viceroys Domenico Caracciolo, first, and Francesco d'Aquino, Prince of Caramanico, later, a mixed system was created (in Palermo, too) in which public institutions and private citizens worked alongside each other in procuring supplies. From that time and until the definitive 1812 liberalisation, and well beyond the unification of Italy, the heirs of the creditors of the city continued to demand repayment of those debts of ancient origin,[52] perpetuating the memory of this institution until the beginning of the twentieth century.[53]

8.4 Bread and Butter: *Partiti*, *Gabelle*, *Mete*

Historians have always highlighted the many aspects and political meanings of the food riots that took place (as in all other European cities of the Old Regime) in the large and small cities of Sicily—which was a major producer of wheat—especially in the capital city. In sixteenth-century Palermo, the protest of the notary Cataldo Tarsino over the weight of bread and other basic food items reveals the conflicting factions and political interests of ruling groups of citizens;[54] the same can be said of Siracusa,[55] in 1591, the year of the great Mediterranean famine, and of the many 1647–1648 urban revolts in Palermo, Trapani, Catania, and several other Sicilian cities.[56] Food riots were always intertwined with political events; during the atypical Palermo 1773 revolt, which would overthrow Viceroy Giovanni Fogliani, who was constantly in conflict with Prime Minister Bernardo Tanucci, the wheat riots and the assaults on hoarders were part of a protest led by the masters of the craft guilds in agreement with parts of the aristocracy who exercised their patronage over them. Ten years later, Viceroy Caracciolo would reform the guilds, weakening a cornerstone of the social and institutional dynamics of Palermo.[57]

Studies on the small and medium-sized communities in the 'year of hunger' 1763–1764, more than the hardships of the famine (which in Sicily was less severe than in the rest of Italy and the Mediterranean), show the assault not only on material resources, but also on the political and institutional ones the State implemented to deal with the emergency.[58] The redistribution of food was a critical point in the interwoven matrix between the upper and lower classes, and between centre and peripheries. Artisans, guilds, bakers, guards of the victualling administration, warehouse workers, contractors, brokers (*sensali*), and merchants counted as much as municipal authorities, aristocratic landowners, holders of the highest financial offices of the Kingdom, and ministers. These interwoven relationships ran not only through the victualling administration, but through the entire system of municipal procurement of supplies and the distribution of foodstuffs other than wheat, as well as the system of indirect taxes on consumption and duties. From this perspective, it can be understood how, in Sicily, the victualling system and its practices were far-reaching and functioned as capillaries of the entire social, economic, and institutional landscape.

The three cornerstones of these dynamics were represented by the system of *partiti*, that is to say, the supply contracts for principal consumer items; by the system of *gabelle*, that is to say, indirect taxes and duties (especially municipal) on consumption and related activities, such as milling, weighing, resale, butchering; and finally, by the imposition of *mete*, the prices set by the municipal authorities to act as a benchmark in trades, and to adjust the interest rates applied to credit granted for purchases of the main food products. The purchase and resale of other food staples in Sicily—olive oil, wine, meat, cheese, or products in any way connected to these, like snow—were free and unregulated. However, the large and small cities of Sicily also concluded supply contracts, called *partiti*, for these product categories, to ensure stocks were adequate. The contractors had a special relationship with the city and its administrators, and indeed they were all part of the same network of often interchangeable roles that linked concessionaires, guarantors, *giurati* (literally, 'jurors', that is to say the members of the city's executive board), and those who had been awarded contracts related to the principal taxes on consumption and duties.[59] Those who did business with the city were sure to exercise control over each phase of the procurement chain: the purchase, reception, storage, and distribution of products, and the collection of taxes and duties.[60]

An abundant trade in commonly consumed foodstuffs and services related to their measurement and sale was essential to the health of urban finances. Income from urban taxes and duties made it possible to pay taxes to the Crown and sustain all the other expenses, from food supply to the construction and maintenance of roads, fountains, and public buildings, and the payment of personnel. The revenues were in fact composed of different annuities: among these, the most important were the *gabelle*. The city imposed these taxes and duties directly and managed them first-hand through its own employees, or sold them to concessionaires who made advanced payments against expected income; the city also paid annuities to those who had lent money to the administration. These lenders could manage the collection of *gabelle* directly and exercise decisive control on the movement of consumer products. The decisions of the city authorities regarding which food products to tax, or suspend taxes and duties on, and the relative amounts, constituted a delicate lever with which the destinies of municipal assets were guided: they had to be sustainable, to avoid stimulating contraband or depressing consumption.

During the sixteenth century, there is evidence of widespread growth of urban indirect taxes and duties in Sicily and across southern Italy,[61] in competition with those of the Crown. Their revenues were central to the interests of ecclesiastical and private institutions that had invested in the cities' public debt[62] and, at the same time, the interests of groups that included contractors, the city council, and guarantors,[63] with the risk of conflicts of interest. The problem of the administrators who had private interests in the supply of food was very clear to those who, like Viceroy Marcantonio Colonna, Prince of Tagliacozzo, wanted to limit all misappropriation.[64] Even the administrators of the city warehouses, custodians of large stocks of wheat, were constantly suspected of making private use of the wheat entrusted to them, that is to say, of selling or loaning it and replacing it with lower-quality goods.[65] The same suspicions were held against those who managed the urban warehouses where the olive oil and cheese purchased through supply contracts were kept,[66] and against the powerful administrators of the *caricatori*.[67]

To ensure the constant flow of revenue, taxes and duties were levied first and foremost on the most widely consumed product: wheat. It was taxed when it entered the cities following public or private purchases and then when it was ground into flour (a cost that weighed on the price of bread). This aspect was very onerous for consumers. The administrators understood very clearly that the imposition of indirect taxes on the sale of other less widely consumed foodstuffs—from wine, which was almost indispensable, to olive oil, cheese, lard, preserved meat and fish, fresh beef, pork, mutton, right down to snow—meant upsetting certain groups of consumers and shopkeepers. This happened also in reaction to taxes on the resale of products (*zagato*), on weighing, and on slaughtering. The fiscal exemption for the religious and the military (the latter were housed in garrisons that required large quantities of supplies, and some commercial businesses—e.g. butcheries—were dedicated exclusively to them) created an occasion for fiscal evasion and smuggling. Municipal administrations intervened on retail sales by imposing *mete* on the most common food items, which could also be subject to indirect taxes and duties.

The variable relationship between *mete* and *gabelle* was fundamental to governing the city's market. The *mete* of foodstuffs were official maximum prices set by urban authorities and were similar to the *mete* of wheat 'from farmer to merchant' that regulated loans and advance payments and seed supply in the production and marketing of wheat. The *mete* were set on foodstuffs several times a year, based on trends in market prices, to regulate sales *dal mercante alla città* ('from the merchant to the city') or *ai cittadini* ('to citizens').[68] The fact that they represented a lever for market regulation and to influence the actors involved is attested by the fact that public officials had to refrain from participating in the council meetings where the *mete* on certain foodstuffs were fixed, when they themselves were involved in commerce of the same.[69]

For consumers, in addition to the *gabelle* and the *mete*, the major concerns were about fraudulent weights and measures, and the quality of food, both that supplied by contractors and sold in the public warehouses, and that sold privately by shopkeepers and innkeepers. Bakers were naturally the first who could speculate on adulteration. They were constantly suspected of replacing the wheat and flour sent to them by the victualling administration with other products of inferior quality, of mixing them with bran and other discarded items, and of not baking the bread enough so that it weighed more.[70] For this reason, the making of bread, the sites where bread was made, and the tools and containers used were carefully controlled. Historical studies of Sicily have not yet investigated thoroughly the various aspects of food-distribution regulation, though certain legislative sources[71] provide some very useful initial indications.

The officials assigned to surveillance of the markets and shops were the *maestri di piazza* (literally, 'square masters') or *acatapani* (a term of Byzantine origin which meant 'superintendents', used in Messina and in other cities). With the help of their subordinates, they were required to check the quality of the food sold in shops and taverns. Their job was to stamp the loaves of bread from the municipal bakeries in order to certify their correct weight. For this reason they were regularly accused of managing their tasks in an arbitrary manner and even of blackmail by those who were under their control, as in the case of the conflict that broke out in Palermo between the *maestri di piazza* and the 'poor bakers' (*poveri fornai*, as they called themselves); conversely, the city authorities suspected them of conniving with the bakers they were supposed to control, and thus prohibited them from doing business with innkeepers and shopkeepers and from keeping for themselves samples of goods under their control, from accepting gratuities and gifts and even from eating in shops and taverns: all practices, therefore, that we must suppose were widespread.

From what we know about the case of Palermo, these inspectors were also connected to the political dynamics of city government,[72] as were the guilds linked to the victualling administration. These guilds had formed in Palermo during the sixteenth and seventeenth centuries, and they had had their statutes approved by the city's *Senato* under the command of the praetor. Starting in the seventeenth century, the supplies purchased by the *Senato* of Palermo were managed by these guilds: wheat had to be sold to bakers and pasta makers, meat to butchers, olive oil and cheese to shopkeepers, who would then resell them. The guilds, however, were bound by relations of patronage to the great nobles of the Kingdom who occupied key positions in the city government.[73] The Bourbon government of the eighteenth century, in the course of its attempts at political centralisation, tried to weaken them by establishing, in 1739, the *Supremo Magistrato di Commercio* ('Supreme Court of Commerce'), which was given the control over the victualling administration and over the guilds that had hitherto been exercised by the *Senato*.[74]

During the attempts of Viceroy Caracciolo to strike the various centres of power and political patronage of the feudal aristocracy in Sicily, including the presence and the protection of certain guilds in the *Senato*, Saverio Simonetti, a faithful supporter of the viceroy, succeeded in restructuring the food market square, effectively depriving the *Senato* of its power; the square was then renamed *Piazza Caracciolo* and is currently known as the *Vucciria* (literally, 'butchery').[75] Caracciolo and his successor, Caramanico, attacked the fifteen guilds dealing in foodstuffs that had remained under the control of the city's council. They, like the forty-four other guilds, were deprived of the privilege of being judged by their own judges, and they saw their statutes reformed to the point of being effectively abolished.[76] Historians gave due importance to the resurrection of guilds, by examining their political and military role in maintaining order during the Napoleonic wars, when the royal court was transferred from Naples to Palermo, and especially during the 1820 revolution, only two years before they were definitively abolished. Still to be carried out is a historical economic analysis of their role in the urban victualling administrations and the many yet unidentified practices, actors, and institutional dynamics that are currently entrusted to a small number of historical legal studies of the nineteenth century.

8.5 Conclusions

This system, which characterised the entire Old Regime period, came to an end with the economic and political changes following the Napoleonic wars and the Restoration. During the years of the Continental Blockade and the British protectorate in Sicily in the first quarter of the nineteenth century,[77] Sicilian wheat was not exported but sold to British troops for military supplies, with a consequent increase in prices, worsened by some years of scarcity. After the departure of the British, the organisation of international wheat trade totally changed. Cheaper wheat from America and Russia arrived in Europe, and foreign demand for Sicilian wheat collapsed. In 1819, in Sicily, imports and exports were liberalised, and import and export duties were equalised. The *caricatori* system was abolished, and they were considered as any other warehouse, from which it was possible to export from then on. The urban victualling system underwent similar changes, too: the 1812 Constitution, inspired by the British, abolished feudal boundaries, gave cities the freedom of choosing the system they considered the most suitable, and abolished all obligations to levy provisions and restrictions to wheat circulation.[78]

However, major political upsets, an economic crisis, and food shortages following the end of the war meant that local administrators continued with the former system for several years.[79] For the State, nevertheless, wheat had lost its central position in the commercial and fiscal organisation. New staple products aroused the interests of exporters: first sulphur, mined in the same areas where wheat was cultivated with contracting and sub-contracting agreements substantially identical to those used for wheat farming;[80] later, strong Sicilian wine, exported to France to cut local wines, and olive oil required by British textile industry as a lubricant. From the nineteenth century onwards, the entire history of agriculture, trade, and institutions in Sicily followed a completely new direction, diverging definitively from the Early Modern Age, when wheat was protagonist.

Notes

1. Brancato (1972).
2. *Pragmaticarum Regni Siciliae novissima collectio* (1637, *De officio magistri portulani*, year 1338); Blando (2003, pp. 46–60).
3. Corrao (1983); Pasciuta (2005).
4. Aymard (1976).
5. Blando (2007).
6. Petralia (1994, pp. 141–142); Verga (1980).
7. Epstein (1992).
8. Bresc (1986); Aymard (1978).
9. *Regni Siciliae pragmaticarum sanctionum* (1574, *tit.* XXIII: *De emptionibus frumentorum faciendibus pro universitatibus Regni*); Fazio (1993, pp. 19–28).
10. Genuardi (1921).
11. Morreale (2018).
12. Davies (1983).
13. Benigno (1993); Verga (1993 [1978]).

14. Blando (2008, pp. 521–526); Laudani (2008).
15. Cancila (1969).
16. di Castro (1589).
17. Blando (2007).
18. Laudani (2008).
19. Fazio (2008).
20. Fazio (1993, p. 82).
21. Caracciolo (1785); Blando (2007); Vigiano (2000); Laudani (2003, p. 426): the speculations were called, by contemporary critics, *gioco della Madonna del Cassaro* ('the Madonna del Cassaro game'), because of the nearby church of the Madonna del Cassaro.
22. Macry (1972); Ciccolella (2016).
23. Aymard (1976, 2003); *Pragmaticarum Regni Siciliae* (1800, *De meta imponenda frumentis et ordeis in oneratoriis Regni*, year 1755).
24. Laudani (2003, pp. 427–431).
25. Morreale (2018).
26. *Regni Siciliae pragmaticarum sanctionum* (1574, *tit.* XXIIII: *De frumentis rabbae*); Fazio (1990).
27. Fazio (2019).
28. Morreale (2018).
29. Fazio (1993).
30. Ligresti (1984).
31. Gallo (1989).
32. In the Sicilian monetary account system, 1 *onza* (plur. *onze*) was divided into 30 *tarì*, and 1 *tarì* into 20 *grana* (Bianchini 1971 [1841], vol. II, pp. 161–173, 294–300).
33. Fazio (1993, pp. 35–38).
34. Fazio (1993, pp. 69–103).
35. Laudani (2003); Vigiano (2008); Macrì (2010).
36. Bianchini (1971 [1841]); Fazio (1993).
37. Blando (2003, p. 215).
38. Ligresti (2002, pp. 52–53, 91–98).
39. Morreale (2018).
40. 1 Sicilian *salma* (plur. *salme*) corresponded to approximately 275.09 cubic decimetres (Martini 1883, p. 439).
41. Vigiano (2008); Macrì (2010, pp. 92–102); Fazio (2019).
42. Macrì (2007).
43. Vigiano (2008, p. 492).
44. Vigiano (2008, pp. 494–495).
45. Laudani (2003, p. 423); Fazio (2019); Vigiano (2004).
46. Macrì (2010, p. 104).
47. Vigiano (2008, p. 499).

48. Laudani (2003).
49. Bianchini (1971 [1841], vol. II, p. 226).
50. Fazio (2013–2014).
51. Fazio (1996).
52. Crispi (1880).
53. Fazio (2005).
54. Cancila (1999).
55. Gallo (1989).
56. Benigno (2011); Palermo (2004a, b, 2006, 2007, 2009).
57. Laudani (2005).
58. Blando (2005); Fazio (1993, pp. 104–116).
59. Gallo (1989, pp. 90–91).
60. Macrì (2010, p. 105).
61. Gallo (1989); Cancila (1970); Li Vecchi (1975); Caracciolo (1963).
62. Fazio (1996).
63. Gallo (1989, pp. 90–91).
64. *Capitoli del viceré Marco Antonio Colonna* (1760 [1745]).
65. Fazio (2008); Macrì (2007, pp. 50–55).
66. *Capitoli del viceré Marco Antonio Colonna* (1760 [1745], pp. 74–77).
67. Laudani (2008).
68. Gallo (1989, pp. 77–79).
69. *Capitoli del viceré Marco Antonio Colonna* (1760 [1745], p. 14).
70. Fazio (1993, pp. 161–165).
71. *Capitoli del viceré Marco Antonio Colonna* (1760 [1745]); *Il simbolo della perfezione* (1753).
72. Vigiano (2008, pp. 168–178).
73. Laudani (1999 [1998], 2000, 2003, 2005).
74. Sciuti Russi (1968).
75. Laudani (2000).
76. Pitrè (1977 [1904], pp. 118–134).
77. Crouzet (1964); Bianchini (1971 [1841], vol. II, p. 304).
78. Bianchini (1971 [1841], vol. II, pp. 282–283); Tomeucci (1957, p. 130).
79. Giuffrida (1972, pp. 223–230).
80. Barone and Torrisi (1989).

Archival Sources

Archivio di Stato di Palermo

Maestro portulano.

Real Segreteria, Incartamenti.

Real Segreteria, Materiali per frumenti.

Secrezia di Palermo.

Tribunale del Real Patrimonio, Lettere viceregie e dispacci patrimoniali.

Tribunale del Real Patrimonio, Memoriali.
Tribunale del Real Patrimonio, Mete di frumenti.
www.saassipa.beniculturali.it

Archivio Storico del Comune di Palermo
Atti del Senato.
https://siusa.archivi.beniculturali.it/cgi-bin/siusa/pagina.pl?TipoPag=cons&Chiave=11864&RicVM=ricercasemplice&RicFrmRicSemplice=palermo&RicSez=conservatori

Archivio Storico del Comune di Santa Lucia del Mela
Atti dei Giurati.
www.iccu.sbn.it/it/SBN/poli-e-biblioteche/biblioteca/SL-Biblioteca-comunale-di-Santa-Lucia-del-Mela

Archival sources recalled in this chapter and examined in the cited essays are too numerous and heterogeneous to be listed here one by one. The territorial and institutional structure of the Kingdom of Sicily in the Viceroyalty period was highly complex, and the primary sources relevant for the history of the provisioning system are to be found in a number of local archives as well as in the State Archives of Palermo (former Central Archives of the Kingdom).

The State Archives of Palermo, where the documents of the Royal Archives of the Kingdom of Sicily were all sent, conserve namely the collections: *Maestro portulano* (1,375 registers, years 1559–1823); *Real Segreteria, Incartamenti* and *Materiali per frumenti* series (91 volumes, years 1764–1819); *Tribunale del Real Patrimonio, Lettere viceregie e dispacci patrimoniali* series (4,833 registers, years 1423–1813), *Memoriali* (4,473 registers, years 1527–1808), and *Mete di frumenti* (95 registers, years 1601–1810).

At a local level, sources on the victualling system are kept mostly in the *Secrezie* (customs offices) series, and in those regarding the deliberations of the city councils (called *Senato* or *Corte Giuratoria*, according to the importance of the city). For instance, for the capital city, Palermo, see the Municipal Historical Archives, *Atti del Senato* (years 1551–1860), and the State Archives, *Secrezia di Palermo* (1,922 registers, volumes, and files, years 1397–1842); for a small city of the Valdemone area, see the Municipal Historical Archives of Santa Lucia del Mela, *Atti dei giurati* (53 volumes, years 1500–1807). In other cases, like the city of Messina, the documentation is scattered and fragmentary as a result of the destruction of the local archives due to wars and earthquakes, and so had to be gathered on the basis of diverse sources (Fazio 2005, 2013–2014).

Published Sources

Capitoli del viceré Marco Antonio Colonna dell'anno 1582 per ciò che si dee osservare dal pretore, e giurati, ed altri offiziali per gli negozi toccanti al patrimonio della città. 1760 [1745]. In *Capitoli ed ordinazioni della felice, e fedelissima città di*

Palermo, ed. by Pietro La Placa, 1–62. New. ed. Palermo: Stamperia de' Santi Apostoli/Pietro Bencivenga.

Caracciolo, Domenico. 1785. *Riflessioni su l'economia e l'estrazione de' frumenti della Sicilia fatte in occasione della carestia dell'indizione terza 1784 e 1785.* Palermo: Stamperia Reale.

Crispi, Francesco. 1880. *Ragioni del Comune di Messina contro il Demanio dello Stato e il Fondo pel Culto nella causa del Regio Campo delle Vettovaglie.* Roma: Stabilimento Tipografico Italiano.

di Castro, Scipio. 1589. Avvertimenti a Marc'Antonio Colonna quando andò viceré di Sicilia. In *Thesoro politico cioè relationi instruttioni trattati, discorsi varii d'amb.ri pertinenti alla cognitione, et intelligenza delli stati, interessi, et dipendenze de' più gran principi del mondo*, 450–483. Colonia: Accademia Italiana di Colonia/Alberto Coloresco.

Il simbolo della perfezione manifestato nel ternario delle provvidenze per il governo economico della nobile, fidelissima, ed esemplare città di Messina capitale del Regno [...] per regolamento dell'annona, patrimonio della città, e peculio frumentario di questa. 1753. Messina: Regia Stamperia/Francesco Gaipa.

Pragmaticarum Regni Siciliae. 1800. Ed. by Saverio Nicastro e Ficicchia. Vol. IV *additis.* Palermo: Salvatore Sanfilippo.

Pragmaticarum Regni Siciliae novissima collectio. 1637. Vol. II. Palermo: Decio Cirillo.

Regni Siciliae pragmaticarum sanctionum. 1574. Ed. by Raimondo Raimondetta. Vol. II. Venezia: Domenico e Giambattista Guerra.

References

Aymard, Maurice. 1976. Il commercio dei grani nella Sicilia del '500. *Archivio Storico per la Sicilia Orientale* 72: 7–40.

———. 1978. La transizione dal feudalesimo al capitalismo. In *Storia d'Italia. Annali*, coord. by Ruggiero Romano and Corrado Vivanti. Vol. I: Dal feudalesimo al capitalismo, 1158–1192. Torino: Einaudi.

———. 2003. Mercato e normative pubbliche. In *Rappresentazioni e immagini della Sicilia tra storia e storiografia*, ed. by Francesco Benigno and Claudio Torrisi, 131–147. Caltanissetta/Roma: Sciascia.

Barone, Giuseppe, and Claudio Torrisi, eds. 1989. *Economia e società nell'area dello zolfo (secoli XIX–XX).* Caltanissetta/Roma: Sciascia.

Benigno, Francesco. 1993. Assetti territoriali e ruralizzazione nella Sicilia del Seicento: note per una discussione. In *La popolazione delle campagne italiane in età moderna*, ed. by the Società Italiana di Demografia Storica, 55–72. Bologna: Clueb.

———. 2011. "Fora gabelle e malo governo". Riflessioni sulla rivolta di Palermo del 1647–48. In *Favoriti e ribelli. Stili della politica barocca*, by Francesco Benigno, 167–191. Roma: Bulzoni.

Bianchini, Lodovico. 1971 [1841]. *Storia economico-civile della Sicilia*, ed. by Francesco Brancato. Napoli: Edizioni Scientifiche Italiane.

Blando, Antonino. 2003. *Istituzioni e mercato nella Sicilia del grano*. Palermo: Puntografica.

———. 2005. La politica in tempi di scarsità: la carestia del 1764 in Sicilia. *Archivio Storico Siciliano* 31: 7–32.

———. 2007. Informazioni e buone ragioni. La politica economica del grano nella Sicilia del XVIII secolo. *Quaderni Storici*, new series 42 (1/124): 111–131.

———. 2008. I porti del grano siciliano del XVIII secolo. *Mélanges de l'École Française de Rome. Italie et Méditerranée* 120 (2): 521–540.

Brancato, Francesco. 1972. Il commercio dei grani e una proposta di riforme dei "caricatori" e della "tratta" nel Settecento in Sicilia. *Nuovi Quaderni del Meridione* 10 (38): 129–152.

Bresc, Henri. 1986. *Un monde méditerranéen: économie et société en Sicile, 1300–1450*. Rome: École Française de Rome.

Cancila, Orazio. 1969. I dazi sull'esportazione dei cereali e il commercio dei grani nel Regno di Sicilia. *Nuovi Quaderni del Meridione* 28: 408–443.

———. 1970. Le gabelle dell'università di Trapani. *Nuovi Quaderni del Meridione* 31: 255–279, 32: 403–425.

Cancila, Rossella. 1999. *Il pane e la politica. La rivolta palermitana del 1560*. Napoli: Edizioni Scientifiche Italiane.

Caracciolo, Francesco. 1963. Fisco e contribuenti in Calabria nel secolo XVI. *Nuova Rivista Storica* 47 (5–6): 504–538.

Ciccolella, Daniela. 2016. Il prezzo della patria. Stato, negozianti e regolazione dei prezzi alla voce nel Mezzogiorno nel secondo '700. *Storia Economica* 19 (2): 491–530.

Corrao, Pietro. 1983. L'ufficio di Maestro Portulano in Sicilia fra Angioini e Aragonesi. In *La società mediterranea all'epoca del Vespro*, ed. by Francesco Giunta, 419–431. Palermo: Accademia di Scienze Lettere e Arti.

Crouzet, François. 1964. Wars, blockade, and economic change in Europe, 1792–1815. *The Journal of Economic History* 24 (4): 567–588.

Davies, Timothy. 1983. Changes in the structure of the wheat trade in seventeenth-century Sicily and the building of new villages. *Journal of European Economic History* 12 (2): 371–405.

Epstein, Stephan R. 1992. *An island for itself: Economic development and social change in late medieval Sicily*. Cambridge: Cambridge University Press.

Fazio, Ida. 1990. I mercati regolati e la crisi settecentesca dei sistemi annonari italiani. *Studi Storici* 3: 655–691.

———. 1993. *La politica del grano. Annona e controllo del territorio in Sicilia nel Settecento*. Milano: Angeli.

———. 1996. Rappresentazioni di un'economia urbana. Le proposte all'amministrazione sabauda e il rilancio economico di Messina dopo la crisi di fine Seicento. *Bollettino Storico Bibliografico Subalpino* 1: 213–263.

———. 2005. *"Sterilissima di frumenti". L'annona della città di Messina in età moderna (secc. XV–XIX)*. Caltanissetta: Lussografica.

———. 2008. Magazzini, luoghi di sbarco e personale dell'annona della città di Messina in età moderna. *Mélanges de l'École Française de Rome. Italie et Méditerranée* 120 (2): 503–520.

———. 2013–2014. I Capitoli del Peculio delli scudi cento milia (1591) e la politica annonaria della città di Messina tra XVI e XVII secolo. *Archivio Storico Messinese* 94–95: 129–160.

———. 2019. Da Corleone a Palermo. L'estensione della produzione di cereali e l'approvvigionamento della capitale durante la crisi del 1646–1648. In *La* polizia de' grani. *Mercati, regole e crisi di sussistenza nelle economie di Antico Regime*, ed. by Alida Clemente and Saverio Russo, 15–35. Soveria Mannelli: Rubbettino.

Gallo, Francesca Fausta. 1989. Le gabelle e le mete dell'università di Siracusa. In *Il governo della città: patriziati e politica nella Sicilia moderna*, ed. by Domenico Ligresti. Catania: Cuecm.

Genuardi, Giuseppe. 1921. *Il Comune nel Medio Evo in Sicilia. Contributo alla storia del diritto amministrativo*. Palermo: Fiorenza.

Giuffrida, Romualdo. 1972. Aspetti dell'economia siciliana negli anni '20 del periodo preunitario. *Economia e Credito* 2: 222–243.

Laudani, Simona. 1999 [1998]. Il sistema delle arti e il governo della città: Palermo nella tarda età moderna. In *Corporazioni e gruppi professionali nell'Italia moderna*, ed. by Alberto Guenzi, Paola Massa, and Angelo Moioli, 217–240. Italian ed. Milano: Angeli.

———. 2000. Rivolte, conflitti politici e sistema annonario nella Palermo del '700. *Mélanges de l'École Française de Rome. Italie et Méditerranée* 112 (2): 669–686.

———. 2003. Pane, politica e consenso nella Palermo del '700. In *Nourrir les cités de Méditerranée. Antiquité-Temps modernes*, ed. by Brigitte Marin and Catherine Virlouvet, 419–442. Paris: Maisonneuve et Larose/Aix-en-Provence: Maison Méditerranéenne des Sciences de l'Homme/Madrid: Universidad Nacional de Educación a Distancia.

———. 2005. *"Quegli strani accadimenti". La rivolta palermitana del 1773*. Roma: Viella.

———. 2008. Dai magazzinieri ai contrascrittori: il sistema dei "caricatori" nella Sicilia d'età moderna tra mutamenti e continuità. *Mélanges de l'École Française de Rome. Italie et Méditerranée* 120 (2): 477–490.

Ligresti, Domenico. 1984. *Sicilia moderna: le città e gli uomini*. Napoli: Guida.

———. 2002. *Dinamiche demografiche nella Sicilia moderna (1505–1806)*. Milano: Angeli.

Li Vecchi, Alfredo. 1975. *Caltanissetta feudale*. Caltanissetta/Roma: Sciascia.

Macrì, Geltrude. 2007. *I conti della città: le carte dei razionali dell'università di Palermo (secoli XVI–XIX)*. Palermo: Mediterranea.

———. 2010. Il grano di Palermo fra ’500 e ’600: prerogative e reti d’interesse. *Mediterranea Ricerche Storiche* 18: 87–110.

Macry, Paolo. 1972. Ceto mercantile e azienda agricola nel Regno di Napoli: il contratto alla voce nel XVIII secolo. *Quaderni Storici* 7 (3/21): 852–909.

Martini, Angelo. 1883. *Manuale di metrologia, ossia misure, pesi e monete in uso attualmente e anticamente presso tutti i popoli*. Torino: Loescher.

Morreale, Antonino. 2018. *Capitalismo in Sicilia. Grano, zucchero e seta nei secoli XV–XVII*. Soveria Mannelli: Rubbettino.

Palermo, Daniele. 2004a. Conflitti fazionali e crisi alimentare a Trapani nel biennio 1647–48. *Mediterranea Ricerche Storiche* 1: 49–74.

———. 2004b. Tra mediazione e repressione: l’aristocrazia catanese durante la rivolta del 1647. *Mediterranea Ricerche Storiche* 2: 57–78.

———. 2006. La rivolta del 1647 a Randazzo. *Mediterranea Ricerche Storiche* 8: 485–522.

———. 2007. Le rivolte siciliane del 1647: il caso degli Stati del Principe di Paternò. *Mediterranea Ricerche Storiche* 11: 457–490.

———. 2009. *Sicilia 1647: voci, esempi, modelli di rivolta*. Palermo: Mediterranea.

Pasciuta, Beatrice. 2005. Magister Portulanus. In *Federico II. Enciclopedia fridericiana*. Vol. II, 241–242. Roma: Istituto della Enciclopedia Italiana Fondata da Giovanni Treccani.

Petralia, Giuseppe. 1994. La nuova Sicilia tardomedievale: un commento al libro di Epstein. *Revista d’Historia Medieval* 5: 137–162.

Pitrè, Giuseppe. 1977 [1904]. *La vita in Palermo cento e più anni fa*. Palermo: Il Vespro.

Sciuti Russi, Vittorio. 1968. Il Supremo Magistrato di Commercio in Sicilia. *Archivio Storico per la Sicilia Orientale* 64: 253–300.

Tomeucci, Luigi. 1957. *Appunti per una storia dell’accentramento burocratico-amministrativo borbonico in Sicilia (1816–1860)*. Messina: D’Amico.

Verga, Marcello. 1980. Mercato del grano e cerealicoltura. A proposito del feudalesimo meridionale/siciliano di M. Aymard. *Società e Storia* 3 (4/10): 877–890.

———. 1993 [1978]. *La Sicilia dei feudi. Linee di storia dell’agricoltura siciliana dalle Wüstungen alla colonizzazione interna*. New ed. In *La Sicilia dei grani. Gestione dei feudi e cultura economica fra Sei e Settecento*, by Marcello Verga, 13–58. Firenze: Olschki.

Vigiano, Valentina. 2000. I “mezzani” nella Palermo della prima metà del cinquecento: norme, pratiche, modelli aggregativi e reti fiduciarie. In *Le regole dei mestieri e delle professioni. Secoli XV–XIX*, ed. by Marco Meriggi and Alessandro Pastore, 346–364. Milano: Angeli.

———. 2004. *L’esercizio della politica: la città di Palermo nel Cinquecento*. Roma: Viella.

———. 2008. L’istituzione del Caricatore di Palermo (1547–1651). *Mélanges de l’École Française de Rome. Italie et Méditerranée* 120 (2): 491–501.

Index*

* Note: Page numbers followed by 'n' refer to notes.

L. Clerici (ed.), *Italian Victualling Systems in the Early Modern Age, 16th to 18th Century*, Palgrave Studies in Economic History,
https://doi.org/10.1007/978-3-030-42064-2

W

Z

The manufacturer's authorised representative in the EU is Springer Nature Customer Service Centre GmbH, Europaplatz 3, 69115 Heidelberg, Germany. If you have any concerns regarding our products, please contact ProductSafety@springernature.com

Printed and bound by CPI Group (UK) Ltd, Croydon, CR0 4YY

30/09/2026

02225460-0009